Christopher Melchert

Before Sufism

Islam – Thought, Culture, and Society

Volume 4

Christopher Melchert

Before Sufism

Early Islamic renunciant piety

DE GRUYTER

ISBN 978-3-11-099160-4
e-ISBN (PDF) 978-3-11-061796-2
e-ISBN (EPUB) 978-3-11-061771-9
ISSN 2628-4286

Library of Congress Control Number: 2020937392

Bibliographic information published by the Deutsche Nationalbibliothek
The Deutsche Nationalbibliothek lists this publication in the Deutsche Nationalbibliografie; detailed bibliographic data are available on the internet at http://dnb.dnb.de.

This volume is text- and page-identical with the hardback published in 2020.
Cover image: © Calligraphy by Osman Özçay. With friendly permission.
Printing and binding: CPI books GmbH, Leck

www.degruyter.com

Contents

Conventions —— VII

Chapter 1: Basic problems —— 1

Chapter 2: Physical austerities —— 20

Chapter 3: Moral austerity —— 42

Chapter 4: Supererogatory forms of required worship —— 69

Chapter 5: New devotional forms —— 92

Chapter 6: The Muslim holy man —— 108

Chapter 7: Renunciants and politics —— 125

Chapter 8: The economics of renunciation —— 140

Chapter 9: Opposition to renunciation —— 159

Chapter 10: The transition to Sufism —— 177

Works cited —— 195

Index —— 217

Conventions

There are two major systems of transliteration from Arabic to English, those of *The Encyclopaedia of Islam* followed by most specialized journals and of the Library of Congress followed by library catalogues. The *EI* standard sometimes offers a closer transcription of Arabic pronunciation (e.g., *fī l-ṭarīq* as opposed to *fī al-ṭarīq*, although *fi ṭ-ṭarīq* would be closer still) while the LOC standard more closely follows Arabic spelling (e.g., LOC *á* for *alif* in the form of *yā*ʾ as opposed to *EI ā* for every *alif*, although even LOC does not distinguish between the two forms of *alif* in *hādhā*, for example, as it is usually spelt in Arabic). The LOC standard is more internally consistent in its treatment of *tāʾ marbūṭah* (e.g., *qaḍīyah* and *quḍāh* as opposed to *qaḍiyya* and *quḍāt*) and sometimes more accurate as to the pattern (*wazn*) of the Arabic (e.g., LOC *nubūwah* and *qaḍīyah* accurately suggesting *fuʿūlah* and *faʿīlah*, respectively, as opposed to *EI nubuwwa* and *qaḍiyya* suggesting *fuʿulla* and *faʿilla*). This book therefore follows the LOC standard.

Dates will normally be provided first after the Hijri calendar, then according to the Common Era; e.g., '211/827', the year when ʿAbd al-Razzāq died. Since a Hijri year usually intersects two C.E. years, accurate conversion of Hijri year to C.E. may require a split date; e.g., '255/868–9', when al-Jāḥiẓ died, since the Hijri month specified in our sources intersects December and January in two different C.E. years. Sometimes, our sources offer more than one date of death, indicated here by a question mark; e.g., '161/777?', one reported date for the death of Sufyān al-Thawrī (Aḥmad ibn Ḥanbal), as opposed to 161/778 (Ibn Saʿd) and 162/778–9 (Khalīfah ibn Khayyāṭ), among other reported dates.[1] References to centuries will be to those of the Common Era unless expressly noted; e.g., 'the ninth century', overlapping but not exactly coinciding with 184–288 H.

Of some basic texts, there are too many commercial editions in circulation, without any standard edition to be preferred, for citation by volume and page to be appropriate. Outstandingly, the Six Books and some other major collections of hadith will be cited in this style: collector, title of book (i.e., chapter), title of section, number of hadith report. For example, 'Bukhārī, *al-shahādāt* 9, *bāb lā yashhadu ʿalá shahādat jawr*, no 2651' indicates one appearance in his *Ṣaḥīḥ* of the Prophet's saying, 'The best of you is my generation (*qarn*), then those who follow them, then those who follow them.' This is the form most likely to be traceable

---

1 Aḥmad ibn Ḥanbal, *ʿIlal* 2:365 *1:328*; Ibn Saʿd, *Ṭabaqāt* 6:258 *6:371*; Khalīfah ibn Khayyāṭ, *Ṭabaqāt*, 287; idem, *Tārīkh* 2:686.

https://doi.org/10.1515/9783110617962-001

across multiple editions. Unfortunately, the numbers of books and chapters, besides individual hadith reports, also often vary from one edition to another. I would have scholars respect the book and chapter divisions as they appear in Wensinck's concordances, commonly indicated in Arabic as those of *al-Muʿjam*.[2] (The chief competing system is that of al-Mizzī [d. 742/1341], *Tuḥfat al-ashrāf*, regrettably not yet published when Wensinck set to work.) As for numbers assigned to individual hadith reports, Muḥammad Fu'ād ʿAbd al-Bāqī scrupulously tried to make his editions compatible with Wensinck's concordances, so I advocate using his numbers for individual hadith reports in the collections of Bukhārī, Muslim, al-Tirmidhī, and Ibn Mājah.[3] Other editors' numbers have become effectively conventional for the collections of Abū Dāwūd and al-Nasāʾī, respectively those of Muḥammad Muḥyī al-Dīn ʿAbd al-Ḥamīd and Muḥammad ʿAṭāʾ Allāh al-Fūjayānī al-Amritsarī. As for al-Nasāʾī, *al-Sunan al-kubrá*, another major collection not now counted among the Six Books, its first complete and apparently most widely disseminated edition is that edited by ʿAbd al-Ghaffār al-Bundārī and Sayyid Kisrawī Ḥasan. A superior edition has appeared from Ḥasan ʿAbd al-Munʿim Shalabī, supervised by Shuʿayb al-Arnaʾūṭ, but its numbers are not widely cited; still, my references to it (abbreviated as *SK*) will be first to numbers in the Bundārī-Ḥasan edition, then in the Shalabī.

The Qur'an quoted in translation will be that of Alan Jones. In the early centuries, the Qur'an was recited according to multiple textual traditions ('readings'), differing slightly as to diacritical marks and vowels. Over time, ten traditions came to be recognized as valid for recitation in the ritual prayer. The one most widely disseminated today is that of Ḥafṣ (d. 180/796–7?) from ʿĀṣim (d. 127/745?), on which was based an influential Egyptian printing in the 1920s. In the early centuries of Islamic scholarship, there was a large literature concerning how to divide the Qur'an into verses (*ʿadad āy al-Qurʾān*). Over time, there came to be five recognized systems.[4] Again, the reading and the versification of the Egyptian printing of the 1920s are those followed by Jones and now almost all scholars.

I use a few abbreviations in the text. 'L.' stands for 'lived' (in some place), 'd.' for 'died', 'bef.' for 'before', 'cl.' for 'client' (meaning a Muslim not ancestrally Arab), 'sim.' for 'similar' or 'similarly', 'alt.' for 'alternatively', 'rec.' for 'recension

---

2 Wensinck, *Handbook* and *Concordance*.

3 For Bukhārī, ʿAbd al-Bāqī assigned numbers in Ibn Ḥajar, *Fatḥ al-bārī*, ed. Muḥibb al-Dīn al-Khaṭīb, 14 vols (Cairo: al-Maṭbaʿah al-Salafīyah, 1380/1960). For other preferred editions, see the list of Works Cited.

4 See Spitalier, *Verszählung*.

of' when a title is extant in significantly different recensions. *Fl.* is *floruit* (for someone whose death date is unknown), *r.* is *regnat* for the reign of a caliph. One acknowledgement is necessary of extraordinary support for this book: it was framed and largely written during a sabbatical year (2014–15) spent at the National Humanities Center in Research Triangle Park, North Carolina, supported by a John G. Medlin, Jr., Senior Fellowship.

Chapter 1: Basic problems

The topic

The topic of this book is early Islamic renunciant piety, which seems to have predominated before the rise of classical Sufism in the later ninth century. To state my history with utmost brevity, I might say that the renunciant piety of the eighth century was about preserving the ethos of the conquest period after the conquests were over. It became increasingly unfeasible as the military was professionalized and more and more people converted to Islam. It was one thing to call for Muslims to spend most of their nights in prayer and qur'anic recitation when the Muslims were a thin stratum at the top of society, supported by tribute from the conquered peoples. It was quite another thing to call for that when Muslims had become the majority and most of them necessarily had to work for a living. Active distrust of the life of austerity began to be respectable from about the last third of the eighth century, even as enthusiasts embraced new, more extreme forms. Following some active persecution of Sufis, a new synthetic piety crystallized around al-Junayd (d. 298/911?) in Baghdad. This was classical Sufism, still calling for austerities but not for everyone; subordinating the old fear of God to cultivating mystical communion with the Divine.

In the following chapters, I shall try to present representative examples of renunciant devotions, accounts of how they were supported materially and their stance *vis à vis* rulers, finally the rise of opposition to world-denying renunciation and the Sufi answer to that opposition. One of my theses is that it is possible to write about Islamic piety historically: to identify stages and to suggest why it moved in some directions rather than others. Scholars must reject the view, however comfortable to believers, that Sufism is a superhistorical essence manifest in the Prophet's lifetime, manifest throughout the conquest period, manifest immediately after the conquest period.

The sources

The chief problem of writing early Islamic history is that so few of our sources are contemporary. That is, to know what happened in the seventh and eighth centuries we mainly have to rely on chroniclers and others of the ninth and tenth centuries. The risk is that chroniclers of the ninth and tenth centuries were projecting backward the ideas of their own time. Sometimes, the anachronisms are obvious, as when the Companions of the Prophet are supposed to have reverently listened

https://doi.org/10.1515/9783110617962-002

to, memorized, and passed on warnings from the Prophet about errant theological views that they would never themselves hear expressed, nor any but the longest-lived of the generation after them; for example, 'Every nation has Magians (*majūs*). The Magians of this community are those who say there is no predestination (*qadar*). Whoever of them dies, do not witness his funeral. Whoever of them falls ill, do not visit him. They are the party of the Antichrist.'[1] Sometimes, it is contradictions among different versions of how something happened or what exactly was said that alert us to how little we can be sure of.

Lack of contemporary or even near-contemporary accounts from within the Islamic tradition is worsened by lack of contemporary accounts from outside it. Seventh-century Muslims did not have the sorts of institutions that generate and preserve quantities of documentation, but their neighbours were in only somewhat better condition. Seventh-century Byzantine history is also difficult to make out on account of imperial weakness. The Sasanian empire completely disappeared, and Persian letters did not revive until the later ninth century. We therefore have no Persian chronicles of the seventh and eighth centuries, either.

The authenticity of hadith remains an area of major disagreement in the academy. Briefly stated, my own position is that there are so many anachronisms and contradictions among them that attributions to the Prophet and his Companions in the seventh century are fairly certain to have originated in back projection of current ideas.[2] In descriptions of the ninth century, when most of the earliest extant literature was written, there are many fewer anachronisms but enough contradictions to require that scholars remain on their guard. Still, it seems probable that across the eighth and ninth centuries, back projection of current ideas was accomplished within a narrowing scope, ever more by the adjustment of the existing record and ever less by the outright invention of new sayings.

The *Muṣannaf*s of ʿAbd al-Razzāq and Ibn Abī Shaybah, our best sources for eighth-century debates about the law, are replete with successive topic headings 'Those who said such-and-such about this problem' and 'Those who said the opposite'; for example, 'those who discouraged talking while circumambulating the

1 Abū Dāwūd, *al-sunnah* 16, *bāb fī al-qadar*, no 4692.

2 Two surveys of the controversy, still unsurpassed, are Motzki, *Origins*, chap. 1, and Berg, *Development of exegesis*, chap. 2. Motzki himself is famous for arguing in favour of authenticity, yet he seldom pushes anything back to the seventh century, merely concluding that it is conceivable that the kernel of the hadith report in question goes back to then. See outstandingly the articles translated in Motzki with Boekhoff-van der Voort and Anthony, *Analysing Muslim traditions*, and Harald Motzki, 'Dating Muslim traditions'. See also Pavlovitch, *Formation*, and Yanagihashi, *Studies*, for recent studies prepared at the outset to accept Motzki's *isnād-cum-matn* technique but unconvinced in the end.

Ka'bah', then 'those who permitted talking while circumambulating the Ka'bah'.[3] They often quote Companions on both sides of an issue, a clear sign of back projection, representing later ideas of what these eminent authorities must have said rather than accurate recollections of what they said. And then, especially in collections of the ninth century, we get contradictory accounts of what the Prophet said—again, clearly, the product of back projection, not continuous, accurate transmission.

In the field of qur'anic commentary, lack of knowledge about the early seventh century shows up in multiple successive glosses. For example, Q. 5:51 says, 'Do not take the Jews and Christians as allies', concerning which al-Māwardī successively quotes reports that it was occasioned by the conversion of two from Judaism, 'Ubādah ibn al-Ṣāmit and 'Abd Allāh ibn Ubayy, who feared to abandon their old alliances; by Abū Lubābah ibn 'Abd al-Mundhir, who had been given to decide what to do with the Banī Qurayẓah, a Jewish clan the Muslims had just subdued (he would order the men slaughtered, the women and children enslaved); or concerning two of the Muslims of Yathrib who were wavering just before the battle of Uḥud.[4] It would be reckless to attribute any of these to continuous, accurate transmission. The upshot is that I trust eighth- and ninth-century quotations of the Prophet and his Companions to illustrate the views of eighth- and ninth-century Muslims but not to tell us what was said and thought in the seventh century.

The principal sources of this study: three genres

Our principal sources for the early history of piety are collections of short texts belonging to three traditions: *adab* (polite letters), Sufism, and hadith. The *adab* tradition aimed at forming character (corresponding to ancient *paideía*), with self-restraint an important constituent of the ideal. It was deliberately comprehensive, so that the gentleman knew something of everything. Naturally, that included something of religion. The section on sermons and renunciation (*al-mawā'iẓ wa-al-zuhd*) makes up about 1 percent of *al-'Iqd al-farīd*, for example, a monumental *adab* collection by the Andalusian Ibn 'Abd Rabbih (d. Cordova, 328/940). The *adab* tradition of renunciant literature is distinguished from the Sufi and hadith traditions by its attraction to elegant locutions (hence Ibn 'Abd Rabbih's pairing), more subtly to humour and miracles. From the ninth century

3 Ibn Abī Shaybah, *Muṣannaf* 4/1:97–8 *5:136–8*.
4 Māwardī, *Nukat* 2:46.

C.E., the *zuhd* sections of al-Jāḥiẓ (d. 255/868–9), *al-Bayān wa-al-tabyīn*, and Ibn Qutaybah (d. 276/889?), *ʿUyūn al-akhbār*, are examples of this tradition, along with the many works of Ibn Abī al-Dunyā (d. 281/894), which apparently have the most overlap with the hadith tradition.[5] For example, Ibn Qutaybah (whose section on renunciation and sermons makes up around 7 percent of *ʿUyūn al-akhbār*) reports that it is written in the Torah, by the inspiration of God,

> O Mūsá ibn ʿImrān, master of Mount Lebanon (*ṣāḥib jabal lubnān*), you are my servant and I am your God the Judge (*al-dayyān*). Do not contemn the poor man (*faqīr*) or envy the rich man for something little (*yasīr*); at my recollection be fearful (*khāshiʿan*); at the recitation of my inspiration be obedient (*ṭāʾiʿan*; give me to hear the sweetness of the Torah with a voice that is sad (*ḥazīn*).[6]

Injunctions to renounce worldly goods, fear God, be obedient, and chant with a sad voice are commonplaces of renunciant literature, but they do not usually come with rhetorical flourishes like the rhyming prose in this work of *adab*.

The Sufi literary tradition probably begins with two collections of sayings and stories from the mid-tenth century, those of Ibn al-Aʿrābī (d. 340/952?) and Jaʿfar al-Khuldī (d. 348/959), mostly lost except in quotation. Both were members of al-Junayd's circle in Baghdad at the beginning of the century. It is characterized first by a tendency to present renunciation as a precursor to Sufism (anticipating the standard view among historians today), also to project a mystical outlook onto early figures. The shorter Sufi biographical dictionary of al-Sulamī (d. Nishapur, 412/1021), for example, divides up its subjects among five generations of about twenty each. Only a minority of those in the first generation were ever called 'Sufis' in their lifetimes, and some of the earlier ones are often cited in renunciant literature.[7] The principal disadvantage of the Sufi collections is just that their main interest is in the Sufis, not their precursors, so they present less information about eighth-century piety.

---

5 As for the last, see Weipert and Weninger, 'Erhaltene Werke'. For his identification with the *adab* tradition, see Chabbi, 'Remarques', 24fn.

6 Ibn Qutaybah, *ʿUyūn* 2:266–7.

7 Al-Sulamī's greatest work, *Tārīkh al-ṣūfiyah*, is lost except for quotation and an appendix covering women, published as al-Sulamī, *Dhikr al-niswah*. Al-Sulamī declares in the introduction to *Ṭabaqāt al-ṣūfiyah* that this book covers the latter saints (*mutaʾakhkhirī al-awliyāʾ*), whereas an earlier book, apparently called *Kitāb al-Zuhd*, had covered Companions, Followers, and the Followers of the Followers (*Ṭabaqāt*, 5). Unlike *Tārīkh al-ṣūfiyah*, it is not only lost but seldom quoted by later biographers. Other works of his have been published, for which see Thibon, *L'œuvre*, part 3.

I recall no attempt to explain why Sufi authors of the 11th century and later preserved so much of the pre-Sufi, renunciant tradition despite its disagreeing with theirs. In part, presumably, the austerities and attitudes of eighth-century renunciants served to illustrate and inspire those of novices in their day. In part, presumably, it also served to justify odd behaviour of their own. For example, I have pointed to a short section that the early Sufi writer Khargūshī (d. 407/1016?) devotes to preparations for spending all night in worship.[8] First is a story of the Companion ʿImrān ibn al-Ḥuṣayn, after whose death it transpired that he had been in the habit of dressing in wool and praying all night, then changing it for cotton at daybreak. Next is a story of ʿUmar ibn ʿAbd al-ʿAzīz's having a hairshirt and iron collar in a basket, which he would pull out and wear for the second half of the night, weeping and crying out in a special chamber till daybreak, then putting them away to go out. Finally, we hear of an anonymous Khurasani who would put on his best clothes at nightfall. His wife observed that other people would put on their best clothes in the morning, before they went to their places of trade (*aswāq*). He answered, 'I am going to my place of trade' and proceeded to his place of worship (*miḥrāb*). There are many stories in other sources establishing that secret worship, uncomfortable clothing, and nighttime devotions were common features of eighth-century devotional life, although the assignment of these particular devotions to a Companion and a caliph may be doubted.[9] Khargūshī's contemporary likewise performs devotions at night, not surprising in a Sufi. (The Sufis were known, after all, for little food, little sleep, and little speech.) But he dresses well for his devotions, in exact opposition to the earlier figures in this section. (Also, what he does in his fine clothes is presumably to praise God, not to abuse himself.) The stories of the two early figures justify social nonconformity in the recent one, however different many details.

If the first disadvantage of the Sufi collections is simply that they provide much more information about the Sufi period than what went on before, the second disadvantage is that they tend to look on the renunciants of the past as they look on practitioners of renunciation in their own day; that is, as persons doing something valuable as a first stage on the Sufi path. They may report behaviour different from that of the Sufis they most admire, as in the example from Khargūshī, but they will also be tempted to give the renunciants mystical objects. Sometimes, what they quote of eighth-century figures is anachronistically mystical only by misinterpretation, as when modern students of Sufism have presumed

8 Kharkūshī, *Tahdhīb*, 469 *430*. For my long assessment of Khargūshī, see Melchert, 'Khargūshī'.
9 Abū Nuʿaym, *Ḥilyah* 6:195, relates that Riyāḥ ibn ʿAmr al-Qaysī (Basran, d. 170s/787–97?) would put a fetter on his neck at night and weep till morning.

Rābiʿah al-ʿAdawīyah (Basran, d. 185/801–2?) a mystic for emphatically proclaiming her love of God and God alone, overlooking that she never speaks of communion with God this side of the Last Judgement or of God as loving her.[10] But they also, as observed, quote some early figures as improbably anticipating later Sufi teachings, outstandingly Ibrāhīm ibn Ad'ham (d. Mesopotamia, 163/779–80?) and Dhū al-Nūn al-Miṣrī (d. Giza, 246/861?).[11] It will be objected that Sufi sources quote mystical sayings of such figures, non-Sufi sources only non-mystical, not because Sufi writers were more given to back projection than non-Sufis but because only the Sufi sources troubled to preserve mystical sayings. There is a strong risk of non-falsifiability to such claims. At least one may be systematically sceptical of a relatively late Sufi source that continually relates stories not found in any previous source, sometimes including interactions between persons known from earlier sources not to have been contemporaries.[12]

The hadith tradition is distinguished by attention to chains of transmitters (*asānīd*; sing. *isnād*). To it belong our most voluminous sources for early piety, mainly Abū Nuʿaym (d. Isfahan, 430/1038), *Ḥilyat al-awliyāʾ*, Aḥmad ibn Ḥanbal (d. Baghdad, 241/855), *al-Zuhd*, Ibn al-Mubārak (d. Hit, 181/797), *al-Zuhd*, the *zuhd* and other sections of Ibn Abī Shaybah (d. Kufa, 235/849), *al-Muṣannaf*, and Hannād ibn al-Sarī (d. Kufa, 243/857), *al-Zuhd*.[13] Abū Nuʿaym was a major collector of hadith. Most of the entries in the *Ḥilyah* begin with stories and sayings having to do with the renunciant life but conclude with hadith related by the subject of the entry. Apart from the *Ḥilyah*, two of Abū Nuʿaym's chief extant works are wholly collections of hadith: a survey of the Companions with sample hadith they transmitted and a *mustakhraj* of Muslim's *Ṣaḥīḥ*, meaning a parallel collection offering the same hadith as Muslim but by different chains of authorities.[14] (The third chief work is a biographical dictionary of Isfahani men of religion, mostly transmitters of hadith.[15])

10 See Melchert, 'Transition', 61, favourably citing Caspar, 'Râbiʿa', unfavourably some other works.

11 On Ibrāhīm ibn Ad'ham, see Gramlich, *Alte Vorbilder* 1:135–282. On Dhū al-Nūn, see now Ebstein, 'Ḏū l-Nūn', which finds most credible the notices in most of the non-Sufi biographical sources that make him out to have been a renunciant (*zāhid*; see esp. 572). I am unaware of any systematic critical survey of the sources for the biography of either one, though.

12 The outstanding example is Farīd al-Dīn ʿAṭṭār (*fl.* 12th cent.?), *Tadhkiratu 'l-awliya*.

13 For a list of over 60 early works on renunciation, including many not extant, see ʿĀmir Aḥmad Ḥaydar, introduction to Bayhaqī, *Zuhd*, 47–56.

14 Abū Nuʿaym, *Maʿrifat al-ṣaḥābah*, and idem, *al-Musnad al-mustakhraj*.

15 Abū Nuʿaym, *Geschichte Iṣbahāns*. I treat Abū Nuʿaym at greater length in 'Abū Nuʿaym's sources'.

Aḥmad ibn Ḥanbal's greatest work was the *Musnad*, a collection of almost 28,000 hadith reports from the Prophet on all topics.[16] Ibn al-Mubārak was widely quoted as a transmitter of hadith, appearing in all of the Six Books. Ibn Abī Shaybah's whole collection comprises almost 40,000 items, predominantly sayings of Followers (persons who quoted Companions but never the Prophet himself). Only Hannād ibn al-Sarī, of these five collectors, has not left us a large body of hadith on other topics than renunciation, although he is quoted in five of the Six Books and not predominantly in their sections on renunciation. All of these collections in the hadith tradition provide more sayings than any source in the traditions of *adab* and Sufism. These also include most of our earliest sources. Moreover, traditionists (collectors of hadith) seem to have been the most inclined to quote accounts of a piety that contradicted their own. Altogether, then, literature in the hadith tradition seems generally the least likely to reflect back projection from the ninth and later centuries.

Aḥmad ibn Ḥanbal, *al-Zuhd*, survives in manuscript only in an early-modern abridgement. It was redacted by Aḥmad's son ʿAbd Allāh (d. Baghdad, 290/903), and a little over a third of the extant text is made up of additions from him; that is, items he heard not from his father but from others. These additions will be identified in notes. As for items left out of the abridgement, perhaps twice as many as those included, many are quoted in another of the major hadith sources, Abū Nuʿaym's *Ḥilyat al-awliyāʾ*. These also will be identified in notes.[17]

As for Ibn al-Mubārak, *al-Zuhd*, the published version is based on three manuscripts representing two recensions, by al-Ḥusayn ibn al-Ḥasan (d. 246/860–1) and Nuʿaym ibn Ḥammād (d. 228/843?). The first three-quarters of the two recensions are very similar. The editor, Aʿẓamī, and many subsequent writers refer to the extra items in the manuscript of Nuʿaym alone as his 'additions' (*ziyādāt*), but it seems to me that this term is more appropriate to items inserted here and there (a quarter of the total) in al-Ḥusayn's recension that he received from others than Ibn al-Mubārak. These additions will be identified in notes, along with insertions from subsequent transmitters. We await a proper edition based on all the extant manuscripts, but it is my guess that our manuscript record of al-Ḥusayn's recension is incomplete, so that Nuʿaym's recension does not represent a core record from Ibn al-Mubārak to which he has liberally added items, rather represents a fuller text than what survives of al-Ḥusayn ibn al-Ḥasan's.[18]

---

16 See further Melchert, '*Musnad*'.

17 See Melchert, 'Aḥmad ibn Ḥanbal's book of renunciation', esp. 349–53.

18 See Melchert, 'Ibn al-Mubārak's *Kitāb al-Jihād*', esp. 50–8, and *idem*, 'Ibn al-Mubārak, traditionist'.

Among the hadith sources, Abū Nuʿaym's *Ḥilyat al-awliyāʾ* needs special defence. It is continually abused as a preposterous collection of faulty back projection.[19] Here is a recent example from a textbook on hadith:

> Finally, many Shiite hadiths appear in the Sunni collections that aimed merely at collecting as many hadiths as possible and made no pretension at any critical stringency. Many of these collections, such the *Hilyat al-awliyāʾ* (The Adornment of the Saints) of Abū Nuʿaym al-Isbahani (d. 430/1038), were works devoted to documenting the rich heritage of Sufism and therefore included a great deal of pro-ʿAlid material. ʿAlī was, after all, seen as the progenitor of the Sufi tradition and the beginning of most of the *isnād*s through which the Sunni Sufi orders traced their teachings to the Prophet .... These reports were generally innocuous, with no sectarian edge, and urged goodly and pious behaviour. While Ibn Bābawayh quoted the fifth imam Muhammad al-Bāqir that the Prophet had said that the best of God's slaves are those **'Who, when they seek perfection in their acts, hope for good tidings, seek forgiveness when they do wrong, are thankful to God when they give, persevere when they are tried, and forgive when they are angered,'** Abū Nuʿaym cites it through a very Sunni *isnād* in his *Hilyat al-awliyāʾ*.[20]

Brown's textbook is generally superior to all its predecessors, but we catch him here at a weak point. Not wishing to say rudely that to someone familiar with Sunni hadith collections Shiʿi collections look like a lot of rubbish, Brown seizes on an eleventh-century Sunni collection whose poor reputation makes it safe for him to suggest that it has crudely borrowed from Shiʿi sources. Had he looked more closely, though, he would have noticed that Abū Nuʿaym offers two chains of transmission for this report, the second one < Abū Muḥammad ibn Ḥayyān < Abū Yaḥyá al-Rāzī < Hannād ibn al-Sarī < Wakīʿ, both < al-Awzāʿī < ʿUrwah ibn Ruwaym al-Lakhmī (Jordanian, d. 135/752–3) < the Messenger of God. The Hannād ibn al-Sarī in the *isnād* is the author of *Kitab al-Zuhd*, and Brown would have found this report there as well had he troubled to test whether Abū Nuʿaym was making things up.[21] He might also have noticed the name Wakīʿ ibn Jarrāḥ (Kufan, d. 196/812?), whose more modest collection *al-Zuhd* includes the second half (not quoted by Brown), describing 'the worst of my community'.[22] Ibn al-Mubārak also quotes the second half from Wakīʿ's source, al-Awzāʿī.[23] Here as in many other cases it is possible to check Abū Nuʿaym against ninth-century sources; here as in many other cases his accuracy of quotation is confirmed. Abū Nuʿaym cannot

---

19 A tradition that admittedly goes back as far as Ibn al-Jawzī (d. 597/1201), who complained that it should not have included sections on the first four caliphs: *Ṣifat al-ṣafwah* 1:3.
20 Brown, *Hadith*, 140, citing Abū Nuʿaym, *Ḥilyah* 6:120.
21 Hannād ibn al-Sarī, *Zuhd* 2:363.
22 Wakīʿ, *Zuhd* 1:401–2.
23 Ibn al-Mubārak, *Zuhd*, no 758.

be more reliable than our ninth-century sources, but it is irresponsible to laugh him off. On the contrary, his quotations may fill in our knowledge of works otherwise lost to us. For example, Ibn Ḥajar describes Aḥmad's *al-Zuhd* as being three times as large as the extant version. Abū Nuʿaym's quotations of Aḥmad, just noted, confirm that the original version was indeed much larger than what survives, somewhat over 500 of them being from the extant version, over 700 evidently from the suppressed part.[24]

It is admittedly a separate question how far back we may expect that insulation against back projection to extend. How reliably do our ninth-century sources inform us of the centuries before? The principle of dissimilarity—roughly, what sounds most like later orthodoxy is most likely a back projection from that time, what is contrary to it is most likely to be a genuine relic of an earlier time—notoriously gives us a relative chronology, not an absolute. For example, the story of the Satanic Verses, some verses recognizing pagan divinities that Satan once inspired Muḥammad to dictate as part of the Qur'an, evidently goes back to before the dogma of prophetic infallibility had prevailed; however, this is not a strong argument for its going back all the way to the early seventh century.[25] My own inclination is to consider attributions to figures of the early eighth century normally reliable, at least at the level of paraphrase and with some allowance for the tendency of sayings (themselves possibly old) to float from one speaker to another. Attributions to figures of the seventh century seem more dubious. I shall continually say here 'so-and-so said', but strictly speaking this should normally be interpreted as 'so-and-so is quoted as saying'.

I would maintain that the renunciant tradition is at least as reliable as the legal. The tendency for the Prophet to call for markedly more modest austerities than renunciants of the early eighth century—austerities whose modesty is more closely in line with Sunni piety of the late eighth and early ninth centuries—has clear parallels in legal hadith. Schacht's perception that attributions to Followers are presumptively older than attributions to the Prophet would work equally well for renunciation.[26] Even when it comes to Companions, I would argue that a good measure of their power probably did depend on reputations for piety. Nomads are notoriously difficult to coerce. Presumably, the first charisma that kept them

24 See Melchert, 'Aḥmad ibn Ḥanbal's book of renunciation', 349–53.
25 See Cook, *Koran*, 128–9, also Ahmed, 'Ibn Taymiyyah and the Satanic verses'.
26 Schacht, *Origins*, 156.

 Chapter 1: Basic problems

loyal to the early caliphs was military success, but the piety of those caliphs and other leaders seems likely to have been a vital reinforcement.[27]

Where to begin?

As suggested by the review of sources, the great problem of early Islamic history is to sort out back projection from the time of our ninth-century sources. Great numbers of Arabs went from being nomads in Arabia to settled citizens in the various provinces of the empire, from North Africa to Transoxania. Their cities were peculiar: except in Syria, the early conquerors preferred to settle in garrison cities away from the existing population centres, outstandingly Kufa and Basra in Iraq, what became Old Cairo in Egypt. Presumably this isolation from the subject populations is what kept the Arabic language from disappearing like Gothic. (Arabic would also have taken over in Egypt, Syria, and Iraq because there the conquerors effectively replaced the old aristocracy, whereas in Persia and Transoxania they seem to have largely fused with the old aristocracy, gradually adopting their language.) The problems of ruling an empire of cities and permanently cultivated areas were very different from managing tribes in Arabia, so the Muslims inevitably developed new techniques. They also inevitably took over numerous administrative practices of the earlier rulers they displaced. Deliberate homogenization of administration in the formerly Byzantine and Sasanian parts of the empire, as by promulgating a uniform coinage with Arabic inscriptions, not Greek or Persian, came only some fifty years after the conquests began.[28]

The terminology of Islamic piety shows awareness of parallels in other traditions. *Asceticism* refers first to deliberate austerity as part of a life of devotion. With *renunciation*, it is a conventional translation of Arabic *zuhd*, which means more precisely *unconcern*, mainly with the world. The related active participle appears once in the Qur'an, where it is applied to the merchants who sell Yūsuf for a mean sum *zāhidīn fīh*, 'attaching no value to him' (Q. 12:20). Richard Gramlich thinks the commercial overtones worth stressing, but I doubt they were very strong to eighth- and ninth-century Muslims who used the term.[29] Al-Ṭabarī

27 More on this in chapter 7, below. See also Donner, *Narratives*, 98–103, on piety as a form of legitimization in the first Islamic century.

28 See Robinson, *'Abd al-Malik*.

29 See Gramlich, *Weltverzicht*, 43. A much-cited study is Kinberg, 'What is meant by *zuhd*', which quotes many definitions, mostly from sources of the Sufi period. It seems to me her conclusion is uselessly vague ('it becomes obvious why *zuhd* ... should be understood as a general way of conduct, or simply as ethics'; 44). She commits herself to a vague definition from the start

quotes no gloss of the word at the appropriate point in his commentary. Neither, surprisingly, does the Sufi al-Qushayrī, who mainly contrasts the small price for which the people of the caravan sold Yūsuf with the large sums bid for him in Egypt.

In the renunciant literature, *zāhid* as 'unconcerned' is continually contrasted with *rāghib*, 'desiring'. For example, Ibn ʿUmar (Medinese, d. 73/693?) heard a man asking, 'Where are the *zāhidīn fī al-dunyā* (those unconcerned with the world) and *al-rāghibīn fī al-ākhirah* (those who desire the afterworld)?' He showed him the tombs of the Prophet, Abū Bakr, and ʿUmar and said, 'You are asking about these.'[30] Bilāl ibn Saʿd (Damascene, d. 100s/719–29) said, 'It is sin enough that God should consider us to be indifferent to the world when we desire it. Your renunciant is desiring (*zāhid, rāghib*), your learnèd is ignorant (*ʿālim, jāhil*), and your worshipper is falling short (*ʿābid, muqaṣṣir*).'[31] A Shiʿi source quotes the fifth imam, Muḥammad al-Bāqir (d. Medina, 115/733?), as saying, 'The *faqīh* is the *zāhid* concerning the world, *rāghib* concerning the afterworld, holding onto the *sunnah*.'[32] ʿAwn ibn ʿAbd Allāh (Kufan, d. bef. 120/738) complained of those whose talk of the world is that of the *zāhidīn* (indifferent) while doing the work of the *rāghibīn* (desiring).[33]

I have taken to calling *zāhid*s and others who are the concern of this book 'renunciants' rather than 'ascetics' partly because the Greek word *askētēs* means literally 'athlete' and thus corresponds most closely not to *zāhid* in Arabic but to *mujtahid*.[34] In the renunciant tradition, *mujtahid* is used of someone who maintains a strenuous schedule of devotions, especially supererogatory ritual prayer (more on this in chapter 4). The Greek word corresponding most closely to Arabic *zuhd* is not *askēsis* but *apátheia*. A mystic, in the sense of someone who continu-

---

by trying to determine what it means for 'the daily life of the individual Muslim' (28) or 'the Islamic way of life' (29); that is, trying to come up with a definition to satisfy all parties.

30 Hannād, *Zuhd* 1:314–15; Aḥmad, *Zuhd*, 400 *477* (< ʿAl.); same contrast introducing a different story of Ibn Masʿūd: Abū Nuʿaym, *Ḥilyah* 1:135.

31 Aḥmad, *Zuhd*, 385 *461*. Variants (with, significantly, not *ʿābid* but *mujtahid* contrasted with the *muqaṣṣir*) *apud* Ibn al-Mubārak, *Zuhd*, nos 180, 484, Jāḥiẓ, *Bayān* 3:143, and Abū Nuʿaym, *Ḥilyah* 5:225.

32 Barqī, *Maḥāsin*, 173. *Faqīh* has the technical meaning 'jurisprudent' but means literally 'discerning', so this saying is partly one of many assertions that experts in the law urgently need to be exemplars of piety.

33 Abū Nuʿaym, *Ḥilyah* 4:262.

34 Cf. Sviri, *Perspectives*, 175, pointing out the parallel between *askēsis* and *riyāḍah*, 'exercise'. I find the latter term rare in renunciant literature, however, and doubt I have ever seen there the active participle *murtāḍ* for a practitioner.

ally seeks the experience of communion with God, may well choose to live austerely, with minimal creature comforts. For this reason, I prefer the term 'renunciation' to the previously conventional 'asceticism', except where the contrast between mystical and ascetical piety is at issue.[35]

Another word often applied to renunciants, *ʿubbād* (sing. *ʿābid*), means straightforwardly 'worshippers'. 'Worship' is *ʿibādah*, cognate with Hebrew *ʿabôdāh* ('service'), prominently applied in the legal tradition to rituals. Like *ijtihād* (in the pious tradition), it tends to connote in particular devotion to supererogatory prayer. More difficult to interpret is *nussāk* (sing. *nāsik*), also often applied to renunciants. Dictionaries state that it is a synonym of *zuhhād*, probably in its widest sense; the related noun *nusuk* is said to be a synonym of *zuhd* (likewise variants *nask*, *nisk*, and *nusk*). It is connected in the legal tradition to the pilgrimage ritual, where the *manāsik* are sites of special rituals (e.g., the Kaʿbah, the hills al-Ṣafā and al-Marwah) and, by extension, the rituals of the pilgrimage generally. However, although some renunciants were known for supererogatory pilgrimages, I have observed no special association between pilgrimage rituals and the term *nussāk*. The Hebrew cognate of *nusuk*, *nēsekh*, means a pouring out, particularly a drink offering. The Qur'an evidently uses *nusuk* for a blood sacrifice: apropos of requiring that pilgrims shave their heads, it says, 'Those of you who are sick or suffering from an injury to the head—there may be a redemption in the form of fasting or alms-giving or an *offering*' (Q. 2:196). Perhaps some idea of self-mortification (or, less probably, dedication to God) made *nussāk* equivalent to *zuhhād*. The Qur'an commentator al-Qurṭubī (d. 671/1273?) proposes that *nusuk* may have originally meant *worship*; is said by some to have originally meant *washing*, 'as if the worshipper washed off the filth of sins by worship'; and that some have said it had to do with *silver ingots*, 'as if the worshipper refined himself of the impurity of sins'.[36] These all suggest some awareness of cognates.

'Influence' and 'borrowing' have come to be rude words, as if belittling the culture that takes up styles and concepts from another. 'Cross-pollination' has been one proposed inoffensive alternative.[37] Sara Sviri has recently proposed 'continuity' as another, while I have written of 'variant development'.[38] An advantage of these two is that they will not reinforce the conception that there was

35 I also follow the example of two excellent studies of the 1990s, Karamustafa, *God's unruly friends*, and Cooperson, 'Ibn Ḥanbal and Bishr al-Ḥāfī'.
36 Qurṭubī, *Jāmiʿ* 2:384, *ad* Q. 2:196.
37 Goodman, *Jewish and Islamic philosophy: crosspollinations in the classic age*; Akasoy, Montgomery, and Pormann, eds, *Islamic crosspollinations: interactions in the medieval Middle East*.
38 Sviri, *Perspectives*, 8; *EI*³, s.v. 'Asceticism', by Melchert.

once a pristine Arabian Islam only later subjected to outside influence, also conceivably capable of being restored. Indeed, there is a restorationist project behind the late-medieval identification of certain borrowings as *isrāʾīlīyāt*.[39] Sunni Muslims have found it congenial to imagine that the Sunni Islam of the ninth century was a rediscovery of the uncontaminated Islam of the Prophet and his Companions in the seventh century. There is a similar story of how catholic Christianity was reasserted in the fourth century after two centuries of being threatened by bad ideas from outside (Judaizing, gnosticism), another of how original, law-centred Judaism was restored by the Rabbis after several centuries of being threatened by bad ideas from outside (Hellenism, Christianity). But all three stories are unlikely compared with gradual development and retrojection of later orthodoxy. (Shiʿi Muslims retrojected their own versions of orthodoxy.)

Contrary to a theory of a pristine Arabian Islam, the Qur'an itself is already heavily engaged with the biblical tradition, recounting stories of prophets so sketchily that they must have been familiar already to the Prophet's first audience, and polemicizing against Jews and Christians, although the literature of the eighth century and later denies that there were any Jews or Christians in Mecca, where the revelations began, or Christians in Medina, where the Prophet established a state. The Qur'an itself sometimes recommends consulting Jews and Christians and remarks but does not always deny charges that the Prophet depends on informants.[40] Loan words make up some of the central terms of the cult; for example, *ṣalāh* and *zakāh*, continually paired in the Qur'an as the defining duties of ritual prayer and the alms tax, whose qur'anic orthography betrays an Aramaic origin.[41] Unless we admit supernatural origins, either the Qur'an must have been generated not in faraway Mecca and Medina but the fringe of the Fertile Crescent or seventh-century Arabia must have been imbued already with the religious ideas of the larger Middle East. In the twenty-first century, the latter view has become fairly prevalent in European and North American scholarship.[42]

I have also observed that the early ascetics saw themselves as living in continuity with a longer tradition, so that, for example, a source as late as Aḥmad's *Zuhd* comprises as many stories and sayings of pre-Muḥammadan prophets as of

39 See Tottoli, 'Origin', and Calder, '*Tafsīr*', 125.

40 See Gilliot, 'Informateurs'.

41 The classic study is Jeffery, *Foreign vocabulary*.

42 The idea of development on the fringe of the Fertile Crescent is associated most strongly with Wansbrough, *Quranic studies*, and *idem*, *The sectarian milieu*. For the idea of an Arabia already imbued with religious ideas of the larger Middle East, see for example Neuwirth, Sinai, and Marx, eds, *Qur'ān in context*, and Hallaq, *Origins and evolution*, chap. 1.

Muḥammad himself.[43] The tricky question is the extent of Islamic dependence, for its pious tradition, on the Christian tradition before it. It has been proposed that earliest Islam started out as a puritanical movement meant to restore a pristine monotheism common to the Christian and Jewish traditions.[44] Several studies have sketched similarities between the early Islamic renunciant tradition and contemporary Christian monasticism.[45] For myself, Vööbus' survey of Syriac monasticism before and at the time of the Arab conquests reminds me strongly of early Islamic renunciant practice.[46] (There is admittedly one major exception, the 'visionary experience' that Vööbus identifies as a major expectation of the Syrian monks, apparently absent from the Islamic tradition until the mid-ninth century.[47] I will say only that whatever borrowing went on from one community to another, the Muslims as borrowers evidently took over what made sense to them, not everything they encountered.)

A recurrent question in modern scholarship has been the internal or external origins of Sufism. The gap between 'official Islam', the universally valid Islam of the law and jurisprudents, and Sufi Islam has sometimes seemed sufficiently wide to require separate origins.[48] The Sufi tradition portrays itself as going back to an earlier renunciant tradition, the subject of this book, most clearly in biographical dictionaries like *Ḥilyat al-awliyāʾ*. Abū Nuʿaym introduces his bio-

---

43 For two manifestations of felt continuity, see Melchert, 'Quotations of extra-qur'anic scripture', on biblical prophets, and Melchert, 'Islamic literature', on interactions with Christian monks.
44 Notably Donner, *Muhammad and the believers*. Compare Julian Baldick: 'In a way, Islam is Christianity: technically, from a Christian standpoint, it is a Christian sect, since it recognizes Jesus as the Christ; from a Muslim standpoint, it is the religion of the messiah, which the Christians have deformed' (*Mystical Islam*, 2). For monasticism as a vestige of the true religion of the messiah, see Sviri, '*Wa-rahbānīyatan*', and Pagani, 'L'invention', also Sahner, '"The monasticism of my community"'.
45 Andrae, 'Zuhd und Mönchtum'; Ogén, 'Did the term "*ṣūfī*" exist before the Sufis?'; Ofer Livne-Kafri, 'Early Muslim ascetics'; also Molé, *Mystiques musulmanes*, chap. 1.
46 E.g., 'Ephrem instructs his readers further that the grave and painful thoughts of sin, death and punishment determine all their sentiments so that only one disposition is able to conform to this spiritual atmosphere—namely sadness, mourning, grief and affliction': Vööbus, *History* 2:283. Cf., among many examples, the saying of Mālik ibn Dīnār (Basran cl., d. *ca* 130/747–8), 'A heart without sadness is like a house gone to ruin' (Ibn Abī Shaybah, *Muṣannaf* 14:49 *12:454*; Aḥmad, *Zuhd*, 320 *388*). In his discussion of what distinguished the Syriac tradition from the Hellenistic Egyptian, the similarities are almost all between the Islamic tradition and the Syriac, as in Egyptian rejection of weeping (Vööbus, *History* 1:293–8).
47 Vööbus, *History* 2:307–15.
48 'Official Islam' alludes to Waardenburg, 'Official and popular religion'. It is what the urban ulema maintain; i.e., the Qur'an and Islamic law. 'Valid Islam' is where Sufism belongs in Waardenburg's scheme, a wider or narrower category depending on who is asked.

graphies of seventh- and eighth-century figures with little rhymes that refer to Sufism, implying that these early renunciants were exemplars of Sufi values, but the stories that follow do not call them Sufis, just 'renunciants', 'worshippers', and so on, so that he actually portrays a tradition from which Sufism grew. European Islamicists have generally accepted this sequence, although more or less resisting back projection of Sufi values.[49]

If eighth-century renunciation and ninth-century Sufism are to be distinguished, it becomes a question what earlier forms renunciation developed out of. Here, too, European Islamicists have generally accepted the story of endogeny. Louis Massignon argued strenuously that the Islamic pious tradition sprang from contemplation of the Qur'an.[50] His argument is that the technical terms of Sufism overwhelmingly have qur'anic precedents. It would be surprising if the literary elaboration of Sufism were not heavily qur'anic. But the terminology of the earliest piety suggests to me mixed origins, confirming other evidence that neither the Qur'an nor even the Qur'an together with the precept and example of the Prophet were by themselves the exclusive authorities they became across the eighth and ninth centuries.

Among modern students of Sufism, the thesis of Iranian, Buddhist, or other origins has been favoured mainly by Muslims distrustful of Sufism and happy to find it an intrusion from without. For example, the editor of several important renunciant texts distinguishes what he calls 'philosophical Sufism', apparently equivalent to what I call 'classical Sufism', and the earlier form apparently equivalent to what I call 'renunciation'. 'This philosophical Sufi thought', he says, 'is alien to Islam. It goes back to the thought and schools that prevailed in the lands of the Persians and Romans. The most important sources (*maṣādir*) that influenced philosophical Sufism in a general way were the following ... .' He then lists

---

49 Standard affirmations of endogeny are Nicholson, 'Historical enquiry', esp. 305, and Massignon, *Essay*, 104–7. On opposition to Sufism among Muslims, see de Jong and Bernd Radtke, eds, *Islamic mysticism contested*, and Sirriyeh, *Sufis and anti-Sufis*. Carl Ernst continually asserts the opposite, that exogeny was the Orientalist position: *Shambhala guide*, *passim*. To my mind, this absurdly elevates R. C. Zaehner above R. A. Nicholson, Louis Massignon, Fritz Meier, and others as definers of Orientalist scholarship. Although Zaehner has had no influence that I can detect among students of Sufism (*contra* Ernst), he admittedly comes up repeatedly in theoretical surveys of mysticism for his categories of theistic, monistic, and nature mysticisms—but this contrast also has not been endorsed by later scholars. See for example King, 'Mysticism', 331–2, reviewing earlier critiques of Zaehner by Smart, Staal, and Stace.
50 Massignon, *Essai* (1922, rev. edn 1954).

 Chapter 1: Basic problems

(1) the Qur'an and hadith, (2) *kalām* (dialectical theology), (3) Platonism, (4) Indian mysticism (*al-taṣawwuf al-hindī*), (5) Christianity, and (6) the Persians.[51] The thesis of Indian and Persian origins would seem to require that the earliest signs of Islamic mysticism have been manifest early on, when Buddhism and Magianism were strongest, and in the eastern parts of the Islamic world, whereas mysticism seems to show up first in the ninth century, not the late seventh, and in Egypt and Iraq, not Khurasan or Persia. (Conversely, modern defenders of Sufism have continually been at pains to deny all extra-Islamic influence.[52])

However, the Christian background to the Islamic renunciant tradition is a major historical question that I shall largely ignore in this study, keeping to the post-conquest period. This is mainly because I do not command the sources, especially not reading Greek or Syriac. I find Julian Baldick's sketch convincing but shall not attempt to elaborate on and defend it.[53] I intend as my contribution to addressing that question little more than to present an accurate and fairly comprehensive survey of early Islamic renunciant theory and practice for comparison, as Voöbus did for the Syriac tradition of Late Antiquity.

Research covering the development of Christian and Islamic piety together has been hindered by the assignment of Eastern Christianity and Islam to different departments, by deans's impatience with prolonged language study (it is asking a lot from students also to pile years of studying Arabic on top of years spent studying Greek and Syriac, or the other way around), by the disproportion of resources devoted to each side (Byzantinists feel neglected by comparison with students of Latin Christendom, but they have been much more numerous than students of Middle Eastern history in the same period, so that they presume a great deal of preliminary work that is still to be done on the Islamic side), finally by reluctance among Arab Muslims to investigate Middle Eastern Christianity, among Arab Christians to investigate the Islamic tradition. Existing scholarship commonly compares Late Antique Christian asceticism not with contemporary Islamic renunciation but with later Sufism. The intersection of seventh- and eighth-century Syriac Christian and Islamic renunciant literatures will be investigated in time, though.[54]

---

51 Farīwā'ī, introduction to Wakī', *Zuhd* 1:130–1.

52 E.g., Fayḍī, *Ṣūfīyah*, 58–60, dismissing as absurd the suggestion of borrowing from Christianity, since the Prophet told the Muslims to be unlike Christians and Jews and since monasticism is about the rejection of property.

53 Baldick, *Mystical Islam*, chap. 1.

54 See Pietruschka, 'Apophthegmata Patrum', overemphasizing written transmission as opposed to oral, perhaps, but highly promising for a start.

To save space, I give only abbreviated references in footnotes, to be filled out from the list of works cited at the end. An embarrassingly large number of these are to articles of my own. Usually, they treat one topic or another in greater detail than I do here. As for the many passages in this book that duplicate what I have already said in articles, I can only say that I have undertaken this book largely to lay out my theses and their documentation in one convenient place.

More happily, I will name two topics I shall not separately treat here because I have satisfactorily treated them elsewhere (that is, to near the best of my ability). One is women's involvement in the renunciant movement. Women will be named in the study to come as exemplifying this or that practice, as they come up in the renunciant literature. Muslims expected to hear of saintly women. However, examining reports of women as a group, I came to the conclusion that neither in outward actions (weeping, keeping vigil at night, supererogatory prayers, and so on) nor inward attitudes were female renunciants significantly different from male.[55] There is occasionally some acknowledgment of peculiar difficulties in the way of women's participation, as when Nasīyah bint Salmān, wife to Yūsuf ibn Asbāṭ (Antiochene, *fl.* late 8th cent.), said on giving birth, 'O my Lord! You did not consider me worthy of serving you, so you have preoccupied me with this child.'[56] Progress in understanding the place of women in the Islamic renunciant movement seems likely to come not of searching out hitherto-neglected accounts by and about female renunciants but of a more sophisticated reading of the familiar extant sources, one that conceives of 'gender studies' as pertaining equally to men and women.

The other topic is renunciation among Shiʿi Muslims. The extant literature is much more voluminous on the Sunni side, and Shiʿi reworking of the past across the ninth century seems to have been even more energetic than Sunni, making it even harder to tell from it what was going on in the eighth. Still, Shiʿi imams are quoted as giving the same sorts of advice as authorities quoted in the Sunni literature. For example, Jaʿfar al-Ṣādiq (d. 148/765) is quoted as saying, 'Much laughter kills the heart.'[57] In the Sunni tradition, the Prophet said, 'Do not laugh much,

55 Melchert, 'Before *ṣūfiyyāt*'. Some further comments in Melchert, 'Transfer of knowledge'.
56 Sulamī, *Early Sufi women*, 93. This is about the only collection of renunciant sayings we have in English translation, usefully featuring parallel English and Arabic texts. I continually assign it to students. I will add that I continually find Cornell's translation questionable in detail and systematically given to projecting later Sufi conceptions (and some much later feminist ones) back into the eighth and ninth centuries.
57 Kulaynī, *Kāfī* 2:664, *al-ʿishrah, bāb al-duʿābah wa-al-ḍaḥik.*

for much laughter kills the heart.'[58] Al-Ḥasan al-Baṣrī (d. 110/728) also said, 'Much laughter kills the heart.'[59] And Sufyān al-Thawrī (d. 161/777?) said, 'Do not overeat, for it hardens the heart; suppress laughter and do not laugh much, for it kills hearts.'[60] Such sayings attributed to multiple persons are an example of how pervasive renunciant piety was in the early centuries. The only significant divergence I have uncovered concerns wool, with the Shiʿi tradition apparently hardening its position against wearing it as a badge of proper contempt for the world just as the Sunni community was embracing Sufism.[61]

Yet another topic not given special attention here is the place of apocalypticism in early Islamic piety. It is a major theme of the Qur'an that we are looking forward to the Last Judgement.[62] Hadith adds the concept of an eschaton, an imminent period when present social arrangements will be upended—when the world will be filled with justice as it is presently filled with injustice. It seems as though expecting the world to come to an end should have been especially important to starting and sustaining a movement of contempt for worldly goods. At the same time, it is widely observed, people build up sustaining institutions as apocalyptic expectations fade. Examples from the post-conquest period of Islamic history might be the issuance of words-only Arabic coinage and the elaboration of Islamic law. One might expect renunciant circles to have nurtured apocalypticism as they increasingly became differentiated from rival circles of jurisprudents; yet in fact talk of the End Times seems to be no more prevalent in collections of renunciant sayings than in general collections of hadith. Perhaps this is a measure of how far the ninth-century traditionists responsible for those general collections of hadith tried to conserve both the renunciant and juridical traditions of the century before. Anyway, although admittedly uneasy, I shall let suffice what I and others have said elsewhere about apocalypticism in the early Islamic tradition.[63]

The cultural effects of modern consumer capitalism have been enumerated as reluctance to make long-term commitments, unwillingness to put down roots,

---

58 Hannād, *Zuhd* 2:501, 553 (shortened version of same); Tirmidhī, *al-zuhd* 2, *man ittaqá al-maḥārim*, no 2305; Ibn Mājah, *al-zuhd* 19, *bāb al-ḥuzn wa-al-bukā'*, no 4193, and *al-zuhd* 24, *bāb al-waraʿ wa-al-taqwá*, no 4217; Aḥmad, *Musnad* 2:310 *13:458–459*; Abū Nuʿaym, *Ḥilyah* 1:167.

59 Abū Nuʿaym, *Ḥilyah* 2:152.

60 Abū Nuʿaym, *Ḥilyah* 7:36.

61 Melchert, 'Renunciation (*zuhd*) in the early Shiʿi tradition'.

62 'After the doctrine that God is one the doctrine of the Last Judgement may be reckoned the second great doctrine of the Qur'ān': so Watt, *Introduction*, 158.

63 See Melchert, 'Apocalypticism in Sunni hadith', esp. 267n on other studies and 272 on lack of special prominence in renunciant literature.

indifference to the heritage of the past, impatience with moral distinctions, and diminished respect for expert opinion. When the proper object of life is taken to be satisfying desires, an ascetical piety of mortifying the flesh and constantly sorrowing over sin will seem grotesque. I have not particularly tried to sell renunciant piety here. I do not say that people should read about these stern ascetics and feel ashamed of their own frivolity. But it clearly was the predominant style of piety in most of the first three centuries of Islam and has continued to attract the admiration of many Muslims to the present. The early history of the Islamic tradition will not be understood in disregard of it. And I admittedly do hope to show that it was an outlook of integrity, deserving respect.

Chapter 2: Physical austerities

The Qur'an itself, our best evidence of seventh-century Islamic piety, speaks more often and more prominently about the need to recollect one's dependence on God and to fear him than anything like theology or law. It does not lay down austerities to impose on oneself, unless perhaps the Ramadan fast, but it does continually treat '*jihād* (striving) in the way of God' as a hardship that the Arabs would rather avoid but still ought to undertake; e.g.,

> Those who were left behind
> rejoiced at sitting still behind God's messenger,
> and were averse to striving in God's way
> with their possessions and their persons.
> They said, 'Do not go out in the heat.'
> Say, 'The fire of Jahannam is hotter,
> did they but understand' (Q. 9:81, Jones transl.).

Two verses later there seems to be an appeal to honour and shame:

> If God returns to you a party of them
> and they seek permission to go out,
> say, 'You will never go forth with me.
> You will never fight an enemy with me.
> You were content to sit still on the first occasion,
> So sit with those who stay behind' (Q. 9:83).

('Go out' and 'go forth' here translate *al-khurūj*, which regularly refers to going out to fight and seems the probable source of the name Khārijī for the puritanical sect that caused so much trouble in the first three Islamic centuries.[1])

1 Crone and Zimmermann, *Epistle*, 275; admittedly *contra* a long tradition of other interpretations, as when Carol Hillenbrand refers to 'a marginal breakaway group known as the Kharijites ("the Dissenters"). Their name came from the Arabic verb *kharaja* meaning "to go out" or, by extension, "to rebel"': 'A short history of jihad', 31. In support of Crone's interpretation, she adduces among other evidences that the Khawārij applied the name to themselves. In a ninth-century work on contradictory hadith, *al-qāʿid* ('one who sits') is the term applied to their opponents, which is related to the word for "sitting" in Q. 9:81, 83, just quoted: Ibn Qutaybah, *Ta'wīl*, 4.

https://doi.org/10.1515/9783110617962-003

Poverty

Many early exemplars of piety were notable for their poverty. Wuhayb ibn al-Ward (Meccan, d. 153/771–2) said 'Nūḥ took a house of cane. He was told, "If only you took something else." He said, "For someone who will die, this is much."'[2] Al-Ḥasan al-Baṣrī (d. 110/728) said that Mūsá's lantern by night was the moon.[3] It appears to be an easier course than perfect control of one's temper in a conversation between the prophets 'Īsá (Jesus) and Yaḥyá (John the Baptist). 'Īsá said, 'Give me advice (*awṣinī*).' Yaḥyá said, 'Do not become angry.' 'Īsá said, 'I am unable.' Yaḥyá said, 'Do not acquire property (*lā taqtani mālan*).' 'Īsá said, 'As for this, maybe.'[4] Al-Ḥasan al-Baṣrī described the Prophet as sitting on the ground, putting his food on the ground, wearing rough clothing (*al-ghalīẓ*), riding an ass, putting someone behind him on his mount, and licking his hand.[5] Many stories are told of how little the Prophet Muḥammad and his dependants lived on. Al-Ḥasan al-Baṣrī, again, said, 'The table mat (*mā'idah*) of the Messenger of God ... was never taken up with food on it.'[6] 'Ā'ishah his favourite wife said, 'The family of Muḥammad ... did not, after it came to Medina, eat wheat to satiety for three days in a row until he died.'[7] The Prophet's bedding was said to consist of just a folded wrapper (*'abāyah*). When an Anṣārīyah sent him a bed roll stuffed with wool, he told 'Ā'ishah to return it.[8] 'Umar would wipe his hands on his sandals after eating, saying these were the napkins (*manādīl*) of his family.[9]

Ibn al-Zubayr (d. Mecca, 73/693) came home and saw three bed rolls (*muthul*). He said that one was for himself, one for his wife, and the third for Satan, so they threw it away.[10] Ṣafwān ibn Muḥriz (Basran, d. 74/693–4) lived in a wooden hut (*khuṣṣ*). Told to repair a trunk in the wall, he said, 'Leave it: I'll die tomorrow.'[11] Ṭāwūs (Yemeni, d. Mecca, 105/723–4?) prayed to be provided with faith and works, deprived of wealth and children.[12] Bakr ibn 'Abd Allāh (Basran, d. 106/724–5) wore a garment worth 4,000 dirhams but sat with *fuqarā'* and *masākīn*

---

2 Abū Nu'aym, *Ḥilyah* 8:157.

3 Letter to 'Umar ibn 'Abd al-'Azīz, *apud* Abū Nu'aym, *Ḥilyah* 2:137.

4 Aḥmad, *Zuhd*, 57 *75*; Abū Nu'aym, *Ḥilyah* 4:359.

5 Abū Nu'aym, *Ḥilyah* 2:153; sim., Ibn al-Mubārak, *Zuhd*, no 995 (addition < al-Ḥusayn al-Marwazī).

6 Aḥmad, *Zuhd*, 9 *14*.

7 Bukhārī, *al-riqāq* 16, *bāb faḍl al-faqr*, no 6454; Muslim, *al-zuhd wa-al-raqā'iq* 32, no 2976.

8 Aḥmad, *Zuhd*, 14 *20*.

9 Ibn Sa'd, *Ṭabaqāt* 3/1:230 *3:318*.

10 Ibn al-Mubārak, *Zuhd*, no 761.

11 Ibn Abī Shaybah, *Muṣannaf* 13:486 *12:349–50*; Aḥmad, *Zuhd*, 257 *314*.

12 Aḥmad, *Zuhd*, 376 *450*.

(the poor and destitute).[13] He said, 'I live the life of the rich, but I shall die the death of the poor (*fuqarā'*).' Accordingly, he was discovered on his death to have debts.[14] When some Basrans went to visit al-Ḥasan al-Baṣrī on his sickbed, they found 'there was nothing in the house: no bed, no carpet, no pillow, and no mat except a bed of palm fronds that he was on.'[15] Mālik ibn Dīnār (Basran, d. *ca* 130/747–8) said that love of wealth was the root of every sin, so one should do away with wealth and relax.[16] He gave away a pot because it made him fear to have it stolen.[17] He was found in a house without light or any place to put his bread.[18] The necessary equipment for the house of an *ʿālim* (learnèd man) or *qāṣṣ* (preacher), he said, was restricted to a prayer mat, a copy of the Qur'an, and a stand for his ritual ablutions.[19] Yaḥyá ibn Abī Kathīr (Basran, d. 132/749–50?) dressed well but left only 30 dirhams on his death, which was used for his shroud (that is, he had hidden his poverty).[20]

Shuʿbah ibn al-Ḥajjāj (d. Basra, 160/776?) held that a traditionist should dress cheaply. Someone had spent eight dirhams on his *qamīṣ* (gown). Shuʿbah asked why he had not rather spent four dirhams and given away the rest as alms.[21] Dāwūd al-Ṭā'ī (Kufan, d. 165/781–2?) inherited a house from his mother and moved from room to room as it fell into ruin.[22] Other stories of his inheritance stress how long he lived on only a little (for 20 years on 20 dinars from his father, 20 dinars from a freedman, 300 dirhams from his mother, &c.).[23] Shuʿayb ibn Ḥarb (d. 197/812–13), a worshipper who lived in Mecca, held that a traditionist (collector of hadith) should dress poorly and therefore proposed to cut off Abū Khaythamah's long sleeves.[24] Fatḥ al-Mawṣilī (d. 220/835) would not pray God to clothe his naked daughter so that God would see his patience.[25]

There is a tradition of disparaging construction, apparently in the first place because it bespoke confidence in long life and rootedness, not detachment from

13 Abū Nuʿaym, *Ḥilyah* 2:227; sim., Ibn Saʿd, *Ṭabaqāt* 7/1:153 *7:210*.
14 Aḥmad, *Zuhd*, 315 *382*; Abū Nuʿaym, *Ḥilyah* 2:227; sim., Ibn Saʿd, *Ṭabaqāt* 7/1:153 *7:210*.
15 Fasawī, *Maʿrifah* 2:48.
16 Abū Nuʿaym, *Ḥilyah* 2:360, 381.
17 Abū Nuʿaym, *Ḥilyah* 2:364.
18 Abū Nuʿaym, *Ḥilyah* 2:365–6, 6:189.
19 Abū Nuʿaym, *Ḥilyah* 2:373.
20 Abū Nuʿaym, *Ḥilyah* 3:67.
21 Ibn Ḥajar, *Lisān* 4:344.
22 Abū Nuʿaym, *Ḥilyah* 7:347.
23 Abū Nuʿaym, *Ḥilyah* 7:246–7, 352.
24 Al-Khaṭīb al-Baghdādī, *Tārīkh* 9:241 *10:332–3*.
25 Abū Nuʿaym, *Ḥilyah* 8:292.

the world. The Prophet is quoted as saying, 'All expenditures are in the path of God except for building, which has no good in it.'[26] Passing by Ibn ʿAmr as he was plastering a wall, the Prophet asked, 'What is this?' Ibn ʿAmr said, 'O Messenger of God, something I am repairing.' The Prophet said, 'The matter (*al-amr*) is coming to you faster than that.'[27] Abū al-Dardāʾ said, on the steps of the Damascus mosque, 'O people of Damascus, will you not listen to a brother of yours giving counsel? Those before you would gather much, build strong, and hope for the far future. Their gathering turned to fallow, their buildings to tombs, and their works to deception.'[28] In a similar spirit, Ibn ʿUmar (d. Mecca, 73/692–3?) said, 'I have not laid brick on brick or planted a date palm since the Messenger of God was taken away.'[29] Even mosque-building was suspect. The Prophet said, 'I have not commanded the construction of mosques.'[30]

Disparagement is qualified in an exchange with Ibrāhīm al-Nakhaʿī (Kufan, d. 96/714), who said, 'Every building is a curse (*wabāl*) against you.' Abū Ḥamzah, another Kufan, asked him, 'What do you think of what is necessary?' Ibrāhīm said, 'There is neither reward for that nor burden.'[31] The issue is no longer distraction from the coming Judgement but personal vanity in an exchange with Sufyān al-Thawrī (Kufan, d. 161/777?), who rebuked his companion Wakīʿ ibn al-Jarrāḥ (Kufan, d. 197/812) for looking at a new building as they passed. 'They built it only for this.'[32] He said he himself never spent a dirham on construction.[33] Aḥmad ibn Ḥanbal (d. Baghdad, 241/855) condemned the fashion of plastering the walls of one's house (as opposed to living with the bare bricks), allowing only that one plaster the floor to block dust.[34] He commented approvingly when told that the mosques of Tus were all unplastered. 'That is worldly decoration.'[35]

---

26 Tirmidhī, *ṣifat al-qiyāmah* 105, *bāb al-nafaqah kulluhā fī sabīl Allāh illā al-bināʾ*, no 2482; sim., no 2483.

27 Ibn Abī Shaybah, *Muṣannaf* 13:218 *12:153*; Hannād, *Zuhd* 1:294; Abū Dāwūd, *Sunan*, *al-adab* 156, *bāb mā jāʾa fī al-bināʾ*, no 5235; sim., no 5236; Tirmidhī, *al-zuhd* 25, *bāb mā jāʾa fī qiṣar al-amal*, no 2335; Ibn Mājah, *al-zuhd* 13, *bāb fī al-bināʾ wa-al-kharāb*, no 4160; Aḥmad, *Zuhd*, 29 *37–8*.

28 Ibn al-Mubārak, *Zuhd*, no 847 (Kufan *isnād*).

29 Ibn Saʿd, *Ṭabaqāt* 4/1:125 *4:170*.

30 Abū Dāwūd, *al-ṣalāh* 12, *bāb fī bināʾ al-masājid*, no 448; Marrūdhī, *Waraʿ*, 183 *135*.

31 Tirmidhī, *ṣifat al-qiyāmah* 39, *bāb al-bināʾ kulluh wabāl*, no 2480; sim. Prophet report in Abū Dāwūd, *al-adab* 157, *bāb fī ittikhādh al-ghuraf*, no 5237.

32 Marrūdhī, *Waraʿ*, 96 *78*. Sim. story with Yaḥyá ibn al-Mutawakkil (Medinese, d. 167/783–4) instead of Wakīʿ: Abū Nuʿaym, *Ḥilyah* 6:379–80.

33 Baghawī, *Jaʿdīyāt* 2:28.

34 Marrūdhī, *Waraʿ*, 182 *134*.

35 Marrūdhī, *Waraʿ*, 183 *135*.

Food

There are many stories of eating little. Al-Ḥasan al-Baṣrī seems to have associated hunger with humility, as in reporting that Moses was emaciated, wore wool, and walked instead of riding.[36] Al-Qāsim ibn Mukhaymirah (l. Syria, d. 100/718–19) quoted the ancient wise man (possibly a prophet) Luqmān to his son: 'My son, beware of satiety, for it betrays you by night and humiliates by day.'[37] The betrayal he refers to is probably the sleepiness it begets, interfering with nighttime devotions; its humiliation is presumably unseemly eagerness. An early Shiʿi source quotes the Prophet against eating to satiety.[38] According to an early Sunni source, he warned, 'If you fill your bellies with what is licit, you will be on the verge of filling them with what is forbidden.'[39] This saying points to *waraʿ* (scrupulosity), the principle of avoiding all that is remotely dubious so as never to stumble into something actually forbidden. ʿĀʾishah (d. 58/678?) is quoted as saying, 'The family of Muḥammad did not eat barley bread to satiety either for dinner or supper for three days in a row until he met God.'[40] She is also said to have identified it as the source of all evil in the period after the Prophet: 'The first tribulation (*balāʾ*) to come to this nation after the death of its Prophet ... was satiety (*al-shabʿ*). When people's bellies became satisfied, their bodies became fat, their hearts hard, and their desires uncontrollable.'[41] According to another Companion, 'The Prophet never ate fine bread (*khubz muraqqaq*) until he died.'[42]

As for other Companions, ʿUmar (d. 23/644) reproached ʿĀṣim ibn ʿAmr, a Hijazi Follower, for gnawing on a piece of meat. 'It is excess enough that a man should eat everything he desires.'[43] To his son ʿĀṣim, on seeing him with a piece of meat, 'It is evil enough for a man to eat everything he desires.'[44] ʿAlī refused some *fālūdhaj* (a sweet of flour and honey, the Persian name indicating a foreign delicacy), telling it he would not accustom himself to something new.[45] Samurah

36 Letter to ʿUmar ibn ʿAbd al-ʿAzīz, *apud* Abū Nuʿaym, *Ḥilyah* 2:137.
37 Abū Nuʿaym, *Ḥilyah* 6:82.
38 Barqī, *Maḥāsin*, 374.
39 Al-Muʿāfá ibn ʿImrān, *Zuhd*, 310, no 231.
40 Al-Muʿāfá ibn ʿImrān, *Zuhd*, 319, no 248; sim., Aḥmad, *Zuhd*, 30 *39* (<ʿAl.). From Abū Hurayrah in Muslim, *al-zuhd* 32, no 2976, and Tirmidhī, *abwāb al-zuhd* 38, *bāb mā jāʾa fī maʿīshat al-Nabī*, no 2358.
41 Ibn Abī al-Dunyā, *Jūʿ*, 43.
42 Bukhārī, *al-riqāq* 16, *bāb faḍl al-faqr*, no 6450.
43 Ibn al-Mubārak, *Zuhd*, no 769.
44 Al-Muʿāfá ibn ʿImrān, *Zuhd*, 324, no 260; sim., to his son ʿAbd Allāh, Aḥmad, *Zuhd*, 123 *153*.
45 Aḥmad, *Zuhd*, 131, 132–3 *164*, *165*.

ibn Jundub (Basran Companion, d. 58/677–8), told that his son had not slept the night, asked 'Is it overeating (*basham*)?' Told it was, he said, 'If he died, I would not pray over him', implying that to die of overeating was tantamount to apostasy.[46] Various estimates are quoted of Ibn 'Umar as to how long he had not eaten to satiety: four days, six months, eight years, since the death of 'Uthmān, 40 years.[47]

Al-Aswad ibn Yazīd al-Nakha'ī (d. 75/694–5?), a *mukhaḍram* (someone born in the Prophet's lifetime but who never actually saw him), fasted till he turned green and yellow, his tongue turned black from fasting in the heat, and he lost an eye from it.[48] Al-'Alā' ibn Ziyād (Basran, d. 94/712–13) ate one loaf a day, fasted till he turned green, and prayed till he dropped. He told Anas ibn Mālik and al-Ḥasan al-Baṣrī, 'I am merely an owned slave. I will not leave off any humiliation (*istikānah*) ... .'[49] 'Abd al-Raḥmān ibn Abī Nu'm (Kufan, d. bef. 100/718–19) would go 25 days without eating or drinking.[50] Ibrāhīm ibn Yazīd al-Taymī (Kufan, d. 92/710–11?) was notable for patiently enduring perpetual hunger.[51]

Al-Ḥasan al-Baṣrī said, 'A believer is properly sad morning and evening, satisfied with what satisfies a kid, mainly a handful of *tamarrud* [probably dried dates softened in milk] and a drink of water.'[52] Yazīd ibn Abān, a Basran preacher (*qāṣṣ*; d. bef. 120/737–8), made himself hungry for 60 years, besides fasting by day for 42.[53] He said to his comrades (*aṣḥāb*), 'Come, let us weep over cold water' (presumably contemplating a torment of Hell).[54] Mālik ibn Dīnār ate bread in water with salt.[55] When someone brought him yoghurt and bread, he refused it, saying, 'I have desired you for 40 years, overcoming you. Will you now overcome

---

46 Aḥmad, *Zuhd*, 199 *248*; Marrūdhī, *Wara'*, 102 *84*; sim., al-Mu'āfá ibn 'Imrān, *Zuhd*, 308, no 227.

47 Marrūdhī, *Wara'*, 100 *82*; al-Mu'āfá ibn 'Imrān, *Zuhd*, 309, no 228; Ibn al-Mubārak, *Zuhd*, no 605; Abū Dāwūd, *Zuhd*, no 302; Abū Nu'aym, *Ḥilyah* 1:300.

48 Ibn Abī Shaybah, *Muṣannaf* 13:409 *12:294*; Ibn Sa'd, *Ṭabaqāt* 6:47 *6:70–1*; Abū Nu'aym, *Ḥilyah* 2:103–4.

49 Ibn al-Mubārak, *Zuhd*, no 965; Abū Nu'aym, *Ḥilyah* 2:243.

50 Abū Nu'aym, *Ḥilyah* 5:69.

51 Ibn Ḥibbān, *Thiqāt* 4:7.

52 Aḥmad, *Zuhd*, 258 *316* (< 'Al.).

53 Abū Nu'aym, 3:50.

54 Abū Nu'aym, *Ḥilyah* 3:50; also 8:216, where followed by Prophet hadith report, 'Everyone who comes to the Resurrection will be thirsty'; sim., Ibn Qutaybah, *'Uyūn* 2:297; Ibn Abī al-Dunyā, *Jū'*, 181-2, but with first version adding 'then thirst'. Cf. 'Abd al-Wāḥid ibn Zayd, another Basran preacher of the earlier 8th cent., calling for weeping over cold water in this world, hoping it might be served them in the afterlife: Abū Nu'aym, *Ḥilyah* 6:161.

55 Abū Nu'aym, *Ḥilyah* 2:369–70.

me?'[56] This is to make control of hunger an indication of wider self-control, as moreover in a saying quoted of him: 'Whoever commands his belly commands all good works.'[57] Farqad al-Sabakhī (Basran, d. 131/748–9), recalling Samurah ibn Jundub, said, 'Satiety is the father of unbelief.'[58] Sufyān al-Thawrī met with the hero of Medinese law, Mālik (d. 179/795), who said, 'I envy a man who has a little of his provision—food for the day.' Sufyān replied, 'More enviable in my view is a man who is hungry morning and night but is satisfied with God.' Here, hunger is not a test of self-control but of trust in God, or perhaps more precisely thinking well of him. (Hadith specifically encourages thinking well of God.[59]) Sufyān is said to have had in mind a Basran of the previous generation, Muḥammad ibn Wāsiʿ (d. 123/740–1).[60] Abū Ḥamzah Muḥammad ibn Maymūn al-Sukkarī al-Marwazī (*fl.* Bagh., d. 167/783–4?) said, 'I have not eaten to satiety for 30 years except when I had a guest.'[61] Here, the virtue of suppressing one's appetite is apparently trumped by that of hospitality: one wants to feed one's guest and will not make him uncomfortable by eating only a little, oneself. Along this line, Ayyūb al-Sakhtiyānī (Basran, d. 131/749) said that if a man turns renunciant, 'let him not make his renunciation a torment to the people. It is better for a man to hide his renunciation than to practise it openly.'[62]

Sufyān al-Thawrī stayed with the Basran worshipper Ḥajjāj ibn Furāfiṣah for 13 days. 'I never saw him eat, drink, or sleep.'[63] Al-Layth ibn Saʿd (d. 175/791), rich Egyptian jurisprudent, never ate alone for 20 years, never ate meat except in illness.[64] The Basran ʿAbd al-Wāḥid ibn Zayd (d. 177/793–4?) said, 'Whoever has power over his belly has power over his religion. Whoever has power over his belly has power over good morals. Whoever has not experienced harm to his religion from his belly, that is a blind man among the worshippers.'[65] That is, he was fooling himself. 'Bishr al-Ḥāfī (d. Baghdad, 227/841?) did not eat to satiety for 50 years.[66] He also said, 'Two characters harden the heart: speaking much and

56 Ibn Abī al-Dunyā, *Jūʿ*, 55, 176-7; Abū Nuʿaym *Ḥilyah* 2:366.
57 Ibn Abī al-Dunyā, *Jūʿ*, 78.
58 Abū Nuʿaym, *Ḥilyah* 3:45.
59 E.g., Abū Dāwūd, *al-adab* 81, *bāb fī ḥusn al-ẓann*, no 4993; Tirmidhī, *al-zuhd* 51, *bāb mā jā'a fī ḥusn al-ẓann bi-Allāh*, no 2388; Aḥmad, *Musnad* 2:315, 291 13:509–10, 15:35-6.
60 Marrūdhī, *Akhbār*, 184.
61 Al-Khaṭīb al-Baghdādī, *Tārīkh* 3:268 *4:435*.
62 Abū Nuʿaym, *Ḥilyah* 3:6.
63 Ibn Ḥibbān, *Thiqāt* 6:203; Abū Nuʿaym, *Ḥilyah* 3:108.
64 Abū Nuʿaym, *Ḥilyah* 7:321.
65 Abū Nuʿaym, *Ḥilyah* 6:157.
66 Marrūdhī, *Waraʿ*, 102 *84*.

eating much.'[67] Aḥmad ibn Ḥanbal (d. 241/855) doubted whether a satiated man would find softening (*riqqah*) in his heart.[68]

Al-Layth ibn Sa'd was not alone in his vegetarianism. 'Umar (d. 23/644) said, 'Beware of meat. It has harm in it like the harm of alcohol.'[69] Al-Sha'bī (Kufan, d. 104/722–3?) said, 'I leave alone meat, although I desire it, for fear of forgetting (*nisyān*).'[70] This is probably not a theory of nutrition and the brain (or heart) but the much-attested principle that righteous living is good for the practice of hadith collection and transmission. Al-Sha'bī's own reported lament is pertinent:

> It used to be that only those pursued this knowledge in whom met two characters, reason and renunciation (*'aql, nusuk*). If one was rational but not renunciant, he was told, 'This matter is not achieved save by the renunciants, so why do you seek it?' If one was renunciant but not rational, he was told, 'This matter is not sought save by the rational, so why do you seek it?' I fear that today it is sought by those who have neither reason nor renunciation.[71]

More generally, Ibn Mas'ūd (d. Medina, 32/652–3?) reportedly said, 'I reckon that a man forgets some knowledge that he once knew on account of a sin he has committed.'[72] Al-Ḍaḥḥāk ibn Muzāḥim (Khurasani, l. Kufa, d. 106/724–5?) said, 'Nobody memorizes the Qur'an, then forgets it, save by a sin he has produced', then quoted Q. 42:30 ('Whatever misfortune may befall you is for what your hands have amassed').[73] Alternatively, it might concern forgetting to do one's duty, as in a saying from Umm al-Aswad bint Zayd al-'Adawīyah (Basran, *fl.* early 8th cent.): 'I never ate anything dubious but that I missed a prescribed prayer or one of my supererogatory night prayers (*wird min awrādī*).'[74]

Sālim ibn 'Abd Allāh (Medinese, d. 106/725) at least discouraged eating meat often, with stress again on unseemly eagerness: 'Beware of continually eating meat, for there is voracity (*ḍarāwah*) for it as there is for drink.'[75] Ziyād ibn Abī Ziyād (Medinese, d. 135/752–3), among the *abdāl*, ate no meat.[76] Al-Ḥusayn

67 Abū Nu'aym, *Ḥilyah* 8:350.
68 Marrūdhī, *al-Wara'*, 100 *82*.
69 Al-Mu'āfá ibn 'Imrān, *Zuhd*, 325–6, no 262; Abū Dāwūd, *Zuhd*, no 47.
70 Al-Mu'āfá ibn 'Imrān, *Zuhd*, 324, no 259.
71 Abū Nu'aym, *Ḥilyah* 4:223.
72 Aḥmad, *Zuhd*, 156 *195–6*; Ibn al-Mubārak, *Zuhd*, no 83.
73 Ibn al-Mubārak, *Zuhd*, no 85. So also Wakī' ibn al-Jarrāḥ (Kufan, d. 197/812) to 'Alī ibn al-Khashram, *apud* Ibn Ḥajar, *Tahdhīb* 11:129.
74 Sulamī, *Early Sufi women*, 166–7 (my translation).
75 Abū Nu'aym, *Ḥilyah* 2:194.
76 Ibn Ḥajar, *Tahdhīb* 3:368; Ibn Sa'd, *Ṭabaqāt* 5:225 *5:305*.

al-Juʿfī (d. Kufa, 203/819) never slaughtered.[77] Abū ʿAbd Allāh ʿUrwah b. Marwān al-ʿIrqī al-Ṭarābulusī (d. 210s/826–35?) was vegetarian.[78]

Some restricted their eating to undesirable food. The Prophet was quoted as saying, 'I do not care with what I repel hunger.'[79] Twelver Shiʿah are discouraged to eat hot food in the first place, probably from association of heat with Hellfire.[80] In the same spirit, early Basran jurisprudents required ritual ablutions after eating any cooked food, or, as they put it, 'anything touched by fire'.[81] In the second place, however, the dreariness of always eating cold food was probably welcomed as turning one away from worldly pleasures.[82] A Sunni source quotes Muḥammad ibn ʿAlī al-Bāqir (d. Medina, 114/732–3?) as saying, 'The Messenger of God did not die until most of his food was barley.'[83] The Medinese Follower ʿIkrimah said, 'The Prophet of God, Abū Bakr, and ʿUmar never ate refined flour (*al-mankhūl*, meaning with the husks removed) until they died.'[84] ʿUmar (d. 23/644) said, 'He used to eat barley bread. If it hurt his stomach, he would put his hand on it and say, "By God, I have nothing else for you" until he died.'[85] Al-Ḥasan al-Baṣrī said ʿUmar never ate anything save mixed with barley.[86] He also forbade refining his flour, saying it was all food.[87] Saʿīd ibn Muḥammad (Medinese, d. 160s/777–87) made his living off a small tract of salty land that yielded two dinars a year. He would go to banquets when invited but eat nothing, saying, 'I dislike to accustom my belly to good food, which would make it dissatisfied with what I normally feed it.'[88]

A major theme is fear of food from illicit sources. Abū Bakr induced vomiting on hearing he had eaten something that was supposed to have been redistributed

---

77 Dhahabī, *Tārīkh* 14 (201–210 H.): 111.

78 Dhahabī, *Tārīkh* 15 (211–220 H.): 294. Some further examples of vegetarianism (and opposition to it) cited by Goldziher, *Introduction*, 131.

79 Ibn al-Mubārak, *Zuhd*, no 572.

80 Four hadith reports *apud* Kulaynī, *Kāfī* 6:322, *al-aṭʿimah, bāb al-ṭaʿām al-ḥārr*.

81 See Katz, *Body of text*, 101–23.

82 Barqī, *Maḥāsin*, 340–1.

83 Al-Muʿāfá ibn ʿImrān, *Zuhd*, 320, no 251. Cf. *inter alia* Tirmidhī, *al-zuhd* 38, *mā jāʾa fī maʿīshat al-Nabī*, no 2360 (Basran/Medinese *isnād*): 'The Messenger of God ... would go hungry (*ṭāwiyan*) for two nights in a row while his family found no supper. Most of their bread was barley.' Also Ibn Mājah, *al-aṭʿimah* 49, *bāb khubz al-shaʿīr*, nos 3346–7. Ibn Saʿd, *Ṭabaqāt* 1/2:113–14 *1:400*; Aḥmad, *Musnad* 1:255, 373–4 *4:150–1*, *5:476*.

84 Al-Muʿāfá ibn ʿImrān, *Zuhd*, 322, no 256; sim., Abū Dāwūd, *Zuhd*, no 72.

85 Al-Muʿāfá ibn ʿImrān, *Zuhd*, 319, no 249.

86 Al-Muʿāfá ibn ʿImrān, *Zuhd*, 320, no 250.

87 Al-Muʿāfá ibn ʿImrān, *Zuhd*, 321, nos 254-5.

88 Ibn Saʿd, *Ṭabaqāt* 5:305 *5:411*.

as *zakāh* (alms).[89] ʿĀmir ibn ʿAbd Qays (*fl.* 7th cent.) would eat fat (*samn*) only from the land of the Arabs (*arḍ al-ʿarab*), since it was not known what other fat had been mixed with any from elsewhere.[90] The objection was evidently that significant parts of the conquered territories had been unjustly appropriated by individuals instead of left as tribute-paying territories for the benefit of all the Muslims. Probably for the same reason, Muḥammad ibn Sīrīn the Basran avoided food from *al-aḥwāz*, probably the edge of the city.[91] Ibn al-Mubārak (d. Hit, 181/797) ate nothing from Egypt except oil.[92] Sometimes the issue was avoiding any involvement with corrupt rulers. Yūsuf ibn Asbāṭ (Kufan, l. Antioch, d. 195/810–11) would eat only what was licit and make do with dust if he found none.[93] Bishr al-Ḥāfī refused to eat of the produce of Baghdād.[94] He had his comrades return a fish taken from Dijlat al-ʿAwrāh, which had been wrongfully taken from Umm Jaʿfar.[95] He said, 'It is not meet for a man to eat to satiety of what is licit today, for if he is satisfied with the licit, his lower self will bid him to the forbidden. How (shall we escape) from this filthiness?'[96]

However, Wakīʿ ibn al-Jarrāḥ (Kufan, d. 197/812?) despaired, saying,

> If a man swore to eat nothing but the licit, wear nothing but the licit, and walk in nothing but the licit, we would tell him, 'Take off your clothes and throw yourself in the Euphrates.' ... The purely licit we do not know today. ... The world has the status of carrion: take from it what will sustain you.[97]

Wakīʿ seems to have been right. After Bishr al-Ḥāfī, concern for eating only the licit appears to die out. It is replaced by an attenuated version, not to eat save by the gain of one's hand (on which more in chapter 8).

---

89 Marrūdhī, *Waraʿ*, 84 66; 'Umar, according to Mālik, *Muwaṭṭa'*, rec. Yaḥyá, *al-zakāh* 18, *bāb mā jā'a fī akhdh al-ṣadaqāt wa-al-tashdīd fīh*, no 721; rec. Muṣʿab, *al-zakāh* 16, *bāb mā jā'a fī akhdh al-ṣadaqāt wa-al-tashdīd fīh*, no 702.

90 Aḥmad, *Zuhd*, 220 *270*. Sim., Ibn al-Mubārak, *Zuhd*, no 866.

91 Marrūdhī, *Waraʿ*, 24 *26–7*.

92 Marrūdhī, *Waraʿ*, 86 *68*.

93 Ibn Ḥibbān, *Thiqāt* 7:638.

94 Marrūdhī, *Waraʿ*, 87 *69*.

95 Marrūdhī, *Akhbār*, 147, no 242.

96 Marrūdhī, *Waraʿ*, 7, 102 *83–4*.

97 Abū Nuʿaym, *Ḥilyah* 8:370. Similarly, Yūsuf ibn Asbāṭ said, 'If a man left the world like Abū Dharr, Salmān, and Abū al-Dardā', we would not say he was renunciant, for renunciation concerns nothing but the purely licit, whereas the purely licit is unknown today': Abū Nuʿaym, *Ḥilyah* 8:238.

Sleeping little

The prophet Sulaymān was instructed by his mother, 'Do not sleep much at night, for sleeping much at night leaves the servant poor on the Day of the Resurrection.'[98] Ibn Masʿūd said the bearer of the Qur'an (meaning one who has memorized and recites it) should be known by his night when people are sleeping (that is, he gets up to recite the Qur'an after sleeping only part of the night), his day when people are breakfasting (that is, he fasts not only during Ramadan but throughout the year), his sadness when people are joyful, and his weeping when people are laughing.[99] Abū Muslim al-Khawlānī (d. *ca* 50/670–1?) would hang up his whip in his mosque to frighten himself. If he dozed off, he would grab it and strike his thigh with it, saying 'You deserve to be beaten more than my riding animal.' When he was overcome by sleep, he would say (addressing God), 'From you, not me.'[100] Hammām ibn al-Ḥārith (Kufan, d. 65/684–5?) would not sleep except for short periods, sitting.[101] It was said of ʿAmr ibn Maymūn (Kufan, d. 74/693–4?) that when he became old, 'he drove a peg into the wall. If he became tired from long standing, he would grab hold of it or tie a cord to it and hang.'[102] Shaʿwānah (l. Ubullah, later 8th cent.) woke up her servant Kurdīyah bint ʿAmr with a kick, saying 'This is not the abode of sleep. Sleep is only in the graves.'[103] Muḥammad ibn al-Naḍr al-Ḥārithī (Kufan, d. 170s/787–97) took refuge (*ikhtafá*) with ʿAbthar Abū Zabīd for 40 days, during which time he was not seen sleeping by day or night.[104] He left off sleeping two years before his death except for taking a nap (*qaylūlah*), then left off even napping.[105] When someone told Ibn al-Mubārak that Abū Ḥanīfah (Kufan, d. 150/767) had a great reputation for worship, he said disdainfully, 'He is not deserving of that. He used to be energetic in the mornings when it came to (legal) questions. That was his way, so that he often missed napping. Then it would be evening and he was (still) energetic. One who is given to worship and vigils is exhausted in the morning.'[106]

---

98 Abū ʿUbayd, *Khuṭab*, 151–2; Ibn Mājah, *iqāmat al-ṣalāh* 174, *bāb mā jā'a fī qiyām al-layl*, no 1332.

99 Aḥmad, *Zuhd* 162 *201–2*; Ibn Abī Shaybah, *Muṣannaf* 13:24 *12:436–7*.

100 Abū Dāwūd, *Zuhd*, 253, no 503.

101 Ibn Saʿd, *Ṭabaqāt* 6:81 *6:118*.

102 Abū Nuʿaym, *Ḥilyah* 4:150.

103 Sulamī, *Early Sufi women*, 117 (my translation).

104 Aḥmad, *Zuhd*, 86 *108*.

105 Abū Nuʿaym, *Ḥilyah* 8:219 (< ʿAl., *Zuhd*).

106 ʿAbd Allāh ibn Aḥmad, *Sunnah*, *165–6* (from a section missing from the manuscript behind earlier editions).

Many slept with little or no bedding. The Prophet slept on one bed roll; alternatively, his bedding was found to be just a folded wrapper (*ʿabāyah*). An Anṣārīyah sent him a bed roll stuffed with wool, but the Prophet told ʿĀʾishah to return it.[107] His wife said that the Medinese qadi Abū Bakr ibn Muḥammad ibn ʿAmr ibn Ḥazm (d. 110/728–9?) 'did not lie on his bed by night for 40 years.'[108] ʿAṭāʾ ibn Abī Rabāḥ (Meccan, d. 114/732–3?) lived in the mosque for twenty years without having bedding laid for him.[109] Muʿādhah al-ʿAdawīyah (*fl.* early 8th cent.) did not lie on a bed from the death of Abū al-Ṣahbāʾ (Basran, *fl.* early 8th cent.) until her own.[110] Ṣafwān ibn Sulaym (Medinese, d. 132/749–50), kept his bedding (*firāsh*) rolled up for forty years and did not lie down for twenty.[111] No bedding was laid for Abū Bakr ibn ʿAyyāsh (Kufan, d. 194/809–10) for fifty years.[112]

Sometimes, sleeplessness is attributed to unease. Abū Muslim al-Khawlānī (Syrian, d. *ca* 50/670–1?) would hang up his whip in his mosque to frighten himself. If he dozed off, he would grab it and hit his thigh with it, saying 'You deserve to be beaten more than my riding animal.' When he was overcome by sleep, he would say, 'From you, not me.'[113] A woman asked ʿĀmir ibn ʿAbd Qays why others slept, not he. He said, 'My daughter, Hell (*jahannam*) will not let your father sleep.'[114] Masrūq ibn al-Ajdaʿ (Kufan, d. 63/682–3?) did not sleep on pilgrimage save in prostration on his face; that is, overcome as he performed supererogatory ritual prayers.[115] Ṭāwūs (Yemeni, d. 106/724–5?) would sometimes walk through the market on his way to the mosque. If he saw heads roasting in the market (reminding him of the torments of Hell), he could not sleep that night.[116] Qatādah (Basran, d. 117/735–6?) said, 'Piety (*birr*) has prevented sleep. They used to sleep before Islam. When Islam came, they took away, by God, from their sleep, their night and their day, their wealth and their bodies, so long as they could thereby move closer to their Lord.'[117] Muʿādhah al-ʿAdawīyah (Basran, *fl.* early 8th cent.)

---

107 Aḥmad, *Zuhd*, 14 *20*.
108 Ibn Ḥajar, *Tahdhīb* 12:39.
109 Kharkūshī, *Tahdhīb*, 470 *431*.
110 Kharkūshī, *Tahdhīb*, 470 *431*.
111 Kharkūshī, *Tahdhīb*, 470 *431*.
112 Kharkūshī, *Tahdhīb*, 470 *431*.
113 Abū Dāwūd, *Zuhd*, 253, no 503.
114 Aḥmad, *Zuhd* 337 *406*. Similarly, al-Rabīʿ ibn Khuthaym told his daughter he did not sleep like other men because he feared sins (*yakhāfu al-sayyiʾāt*), meaning the punishment due for them: Aḥmad, *Zuhd* 337 *406*.
115 Ibn al-Mubārak, *Zuhd*, no 975; Aḥmad, *Zuhd*, 348–9 *418*; Ibn Saʿd, *Ṭabaqāt* 6:52 *6:79*; Ibn Abī Shaybah, *Muṣannaf* 13:402 *12:289*.
116 Aḥmad, *Zuhd*, 375 *449*.
117 Abū Nuʿaym, *Ḥilyah* 2:338 (< Aḥmad, *Zuhd*).

would not sleep by day, fearing it would be her last, or by night, fearing it would be her last, wearing thin clothes so that the cold would keep her awake.[118] Hind ibn ʿAwf, returning from a journey, slept through the hour of his normal night vigil, hence swore never again to sleep on a bed (*firāsh*).[119] It must have been similarly to keep himself wakeful that Sulaymān al-Taymī (Basran, d. 143/760–1) kept his *firāsh* rolled up for 40 years (i.e., slept on the bare ground) and did not lie down at all for 20 years.[120] Dāwūd al-Ṭāʾī lay on the dirt floor with a brick for a pillow.[121]

A number slept only for the first part of the night. Prophet hadith recommends prayer and supplication especially at the end of the night: 'Our Lord (mighty and glorious is he) descends every night to the lowest heaven when there remains the last third of the night, saying, "Whoever prays to me, I will answer him; whoever asks of me, I will give him; whoever asks my forgiveness, I will forgive him."'[122] If one awakes at night, it is strongly encouraged to perform the minor ritual ablution and a ritual prayer. Otherwise, one will start the morning feeling ill and lazy.[123] (Alternatively, he is said to have endorsed the prophet David's habit, sleeping half the night, keeping vigil for a third, then sleeping the final sixth.[124]) Thābit al-Bunānī (Basran, d. 127/744–5?) prayed to God not to let him go back to sleep if he awoke at night.[125] Abū Isḥāq al-Sabīʿī (Kufan, d. 129/746–7?) would not go back to sleep if he awoke at night.[126] An Ismaili source quotes Jaʿfar al-Ṣādiq (d. Medina, 148/765) as saying, 'I despise that a servant should recite the Qur'an, then awaken in the night and not get up until morning is near, only then getting up and beginning to pray.'[127] A Medinese hadith report quotes the Prophet as saying, 'God have mercy on a man who gets up at night to

118 Aḥmad, *Zuhd*, 208 *257*; Hannād, *Zuhd* 1:291.
119 Ibn Abī al-Dunyā, *Muḥāsabat al-nafs*, 58.
120 Abū Nuʿaym, *Ḥilyah* 3:29.
121 Abū Nuʿaym, *Ḥilyah* 7:340.
122 Bukhārī, *al-tahajjud* 14, *bāb al-duʿā' wa-al-ṣalāh fī ākhir al-layl*, no 1145, *al-daʿawāt* 14, *bāb al-duʿā' niṣf al-layl*, no 6321, *al-tawḥīd* 35, *bāb qawl Allāh ... yurīdūna an yubaddilū kalām Allāh*, no 7494.
123 Bukhārī, *al-tahajjud* 12, *bāb ʿaqd al-shayṭān ʿalá qāfiyat al-ra's idhā lam yuṣalli bi-al-layl*, no 1142; *bad' al-khalq* 11, *ṣifat Iblīs wa-junūdih*, no 3269; Muslim, *ṣalāt al-musāfirīn* 28, *bāb mā ruwiya fīman nāma al-layl ajmaʿ ḥattá aṣbaḥ*, no 776.
124 Bukhārī, *al-tahajjud* 7, *bāb man nāma ʿinda al-saḥar*, no 1131; *aḥādīth al-anbiyā'* 38, *bāb aḥabb al-ṣalāh ilá Allāh ṣalāt Dāwūd*, no 3420; Muslim, *al-ṣiyām* 35, *bāb al-nahy ʿan ṣawm al-dahr*, no 1159.
125 Abū Nuʿaym, *Ḥilyah* 2:320 (< ʿAl., *Zuhd*).
126 Abū Nuʿaym, *Ḥilyah* 4:340 (< Aḥ., *Zuhd*).
127 Al-Qāḍī al-Nuʿmān, *Daʿāʾim al-islām* 1:213.

perform the ritual prayer and gets up his wife to perform it. If she refuses, he is to pour water in her face. God have mercy on a woman who gets up at night to perform the ritual prayer and gets up her husband to perform it. If he refuses, she is to pour water on his face.'[128]

Staying up all night could be inferred when someone did not renew his ritual purity for the dawn prayer, since sleeping is one of the occasions for it. Wahb ibn Munabbih (Yemeni, d. 113/731–2?) did not renew his ritual purity between the evening and dawn prayers for 20 years.[129] Sulaymān al-Taymī prayed the dawn and evening prayers on a single minor ritual ablution for 30-odd years. Something was wrong with one of his legs, so he stood on one leg.[130] Hushaym ibn Bashīr (Wasiti, d. Baghdad, 183/799) prayed the dawn prayer on the ablution of the previous evening for 20 years before he died.[131] 'Alī ibn Bakkār (Mopsuestian, d. 207/822–3?) prayed the dawn prayer on his ablutions of the *ʿatamah*, indicating that he slept only the first third of each night.[132]

Sex

Outright refusal of sex and marriage is exceptional but not unknown. Some pre-Muḥammadan prophets were known not to have married. Al-Ḥasan al-Baṣrī told this story of Jesus:

> 'Īsá ibn Maryam said, 'I have thrown down the world on its face and sat on its back. I have no child to die nor any house to go to ruin.' They said to him, 'Why don't you take a house?' He said, 'Build a house for me on the stream.' They said, 'It will not stand.' They said, 'Why don't you take a wife?' He said, 'What should I do with a wife who will die?'[133]

'Uthmān ibn Maẓʿūn (d. 3/624–5) is a Companion especially associated with celibacy. Sometimes, he asks the Prophet to allow him to castrate himself, the Prophet prescribing that he fast instead.[134] 'Uthmān ibn Maẓʿūn was a respected

128 Abū Dāwūd, *al-witr* 13, *bāb al-ḥaththʿalá qiyām al-layl*, no 1450.
129 Ibn Saʿd, *Ṭabaqāt* 5:396 *5:543*.
130 Ibn Saʿd, *Ṭabaqāt* 7/2:18 *7:253*.
131 Al-Khaṭīb al-Baghdādī, *Tārīkh* 14:93 *16:143*.
132 Abū Nuʿaym, *Ḥilyah* 9:318.
133 Aḥmad, *Zuhd*, 92 *117*; second half also quoted < Sufyān ibn 'Uyaynah < 'Īsá, Abū Nuʿaym, *Ḥilyah* 7:273 (< Aḥ., *Zuhd*). In the first half is an echo of Matt. 7:26, 'And every one that heareth these sayings of mine, and doeth them not, shall be likened unto a foolish man, which built his house upon the sand' (KJV).
134 Ibn al-Mubārak, *Zuhd*, nos 845, 1106; Ibn Saʿd, *Ṭabaqāt* 3/1:287–8 *3:394–5*.

early convert, among those who made the pilgrimage to Ethiopia as well as Medina. In some versions, several other renowned Companions are also named as proposing to commit themselves to celibacy, even to the point of considering castration, including ʿAlī ibn Abī Ṭālib, ʿAbd Allāh ibn ʿAmr, and Ibn Masʿūd: plainly, the proposal was taken as a sign of high piety, if mistaken.[135] The caliph ʿUmar (d. 23/644) did not marry women from desire but only to produce children. In a year of famine, he did not approach a woman till the people were relieved (perhaps to increase the effectiveness of his prayers).[136] ʿAmr ibn ʿUtbah (d. 23–35/644–56) married at the insistence of his parents, supported by the caliph ʿUthmān. However, he divorced two wives in succession after they said they would not give birth to children (from lack of sex), upon which his parents left him alone.[137]

The early Basran ʿĀmir ibn ʿAbd (al-)Qays denied being vegetarian or refusing to pray in mosques but admitted to being celibate.[138] 'I find that people live for four things: women, food, clothing, and sleep', ʿAmir said. 'As for clothing, by God, I do not care what I use of it to screen my private parts. As for women, by God, I do not care whether I see a woman or a wall. As for sleep and food, they overcome me.'[139] The early Khāriji leader Abū Bilāl Mirdās (*fl.* 55/674–5) declaimed a poem declaring his intention to avoid women until the cause was successful.[140] Sulaymān ibn Yasār (client, d. *ca* 100/718–19), one of the seven jurisprudents of Medina, was congratulated by the prophet Joseph in a dream for effortlessly resisting women's advances. 'I was aroused but you were not aroused.'[141] The Kufan traditionist al-Ḥusayn al-Juʿfī (d. 203/819) was celibate.[142] The Syrian Abū Sulaymān al-Dārānī (d. 215/830–1) said, 'Whoever wishes for children is stupid, as to both the world and the hereafter. If he wishes to eat, sleep, or have

135 See al-Ṭabarī, *Jāmiʿ al-bayān fī taʾwīl āy al-Qurʾān*, *ad* Q. 5:87. Earlier discussed by Sahner, '"The monasticism of my community is jihād"', 167–8.

136 Ibn Saʿd, *Ṭabaqāt* 3/1:227, 235 *3:315, 325*. His prayers, stressing forgiveness of sin, are described *Ṭabaqāt* 3/1:231–3 *3:329–33*.

137 Aḥmad, *Zuhd*, 354–5 *424–5* (< ʿAl., *Zuhd*).

138 Ibn Saʿd, *Ṭabaqāt* 7/1:75 *7:105*.

139 Aḥmad, *Zuhd*, 223–4 *274*; Ibn Abī Shaybah, *Muṣannaf* 13:471 *12:339–40*; Abū Nuʿaym, *Ḥilyah* 2:88, 90–1; Bayhaqī, *Zuhd*, 63–4 *27–8*. Maʿrūf al-Karkhī (d. Baghdad, 200/815–16) is also quoted as saying, 'I do not care whether I see a woman or a wall': Abū Nuʿaym, *Ḥilyah* 8:366.

140 Gaiser, Shurāt *legends*, 73.

141 Abū Nuʿaym, *Ḥilyah* 2:190–2. Q. 12:24 is commonly interpreted as meaning that he was responding lustfully to the Egyptian lady's advances when he was stopped by an apparition.

142 ʿIjlī, *Tārīkh al-thiqāt*, 120; Dhahabī, *Tārīkh* 14 (201–210 H.): 111; Ibn Ḥajar, *Tahdhīb* 2:358, last line.

sex, his pleasure will be spoilt, and if he wishes to worship, it will distract him.'[143] The traditionist Hannād ibn al-Sarī (d. 243/857), whose *Kitāb al-Zuhd* ('the book of renunciation') is much quoted here, was called *rāhib al-Kūfah* ('the monk of Kufa') for his much reciting the Qur'an, performing the ritual prayer, and weeping, also for never marrying or taking concubines.[144] In her survey of early renunciants in Andalusia, Manuela Marín found one instance of celibacy, a Saʿdūn ibn Ismāʿīl (d. 295/907–8) who would not marry or own a female slave.[145] On the other hand, the renunciant Marwān ibn ʿAbd al-Raḥmān, who came to Qayrawan from Egypt in the early ninth century, used his indifference to the usual rewards of marriage to be of service: he would marry fallen women to provide them with *iḥṣān*, the quality of being a free, married Muslim, then divorce them after they had given birth and recovered.[146]

Some figures lived conjugally for a time, then abandoned it. Wahb ibn Munabbih told this story of Moses:

> Mūsá had a sister called Maryam. She said to him, 'O Mūsá, you once married among Āl Shuʿayb, when you had nothing. Then you reached what you have reached, so marry among the kings of the children of Isrāʾīl.' He said, 'Why should I marry among the kings of the children of Isrāʾīl? By God, I have not needed women since I spoke to my Lord.'[147]

ʿUmar ibn ʿAbd al-ʿAzīz (d. 101/720) offered to free his concubines on ascending to the caliphate, since it would distract him from them.[148] Fāṭimah bint ʿAbd al-Malik doubted whether he had to wash from major ritual impurity from the time of his ascent to the caliphate to his death; that is, whether he ever again had sex.[149] Dāwūd al-Ṭāʾī said to someone who had reproached him for not marrying, 'How could I take on a second concern?'[150] But another report that he was celibate for 64 years hints that he was in this category of renouncing marriage after he had tried it for a time.[151]

More common are reports of callousness toward actual wives and children. Masrūq ibn al-Ajdaʿ kept a screen between himself and his wife.[152] Ṣilah ibn Zufar

---

143 Abū Nuʿaym, *Ḥilyah* 9:264.
144 Dhahabī, *Tārīkh* 18 (241–250 H.): 531, quoting Aḥmad ibn Salamah al-Naysābūrī.
145 Marín, 'Early development', 93–4.
146 Abū al-ʿArab, *Classes des savants*, 75.
147 ʿAbd Allāh ibn Aḥmad, *Sunnah*, 66–7 *257*, quoting his father Aḥmad.
148 Ibn al-Mubārak, *Zuhd*, no 889.
149 Ibn al-Mubārak, *Zuhd*, no 890; Ibn Saʿd, *Ṭabaqāt* 5:293 *5:397*.
150 Abū Nuʿaym, *Ḥilyah* 7:356.
151 Abū Nuʿaym, *Ḥilyah* 7:349.
152 ʿIjlī, *Tārīkh al-thiqāt*, 426.

(Kufan, d. *ca* 70/689–90) was asked whether his family had been hurt by the plague. He said, 'Its missing them is more fearful to me that its afflicting them.'[153] Ṭāwūs prayed God to be deprived of children and wealth.[154] ʿAwn ibn ʿAbd Allāh (Kufan, d. bef. 120/738), when he was near death, willed that an estate of his be sold and its price given away as alms. It was said to him, 'You give away its price as alms and leave your dependants?' He said, 'I present this to myself and pray to God for my dependants.'[155] Mālik ibn Dīnār said that one was not a *ṣiddīq* (saint) till one left his wife like a widow and lived with dogs in refuse heaps.[156] Al-Rabīʿ ibn Ṣabīḥ (Basran, d. 160/776–7) was in Ahwāz with an associate when a woman offered herself to them. He wept, explaining, 'She would not have desired two old men unless she had seen (other) old men like them.'[157] That is, he looked like a man who would lust after a strange woman, making him feel ashamed. Sufyān al-Thawrī said it was difficult for a man with dependants not to mix the licit with the illicit.[158] 'Who likes women's thighs will not prosper', he said[159]; alternatively, 'He will scarcely prosper who has dependants.'[160] Either Sufyān al-Thawrī or Ibrāhīm ibn Ad'ham (d. 163/779–80?) said, 'The needy man (*faqīr*) who marries is like a man who embarks on a ship. When he has a child, he has drowned.'[161] Somebody around the early ninth century related of the Prophet, 'The best of you in the 200s (will be) the *khafīf al-ḥādhdh*', this odd term then glossed by the Prophet as 'He who has no wife or child'.[162] Ismāʿīl ibn Rabāḥ, a prominent renunciant of Qayrawan (d. 212/827), extolled those who made widows of their wives and orphans of their children while they themselves imagined hell before them and resembled divorced women (i.e., despondent).[163]

One seldom hears from women, but Muʿādhah al-ʿAdawīyah was married to Ṣilah ibn Ashyam, who was killed with his son by Khawārij. When some women came to console her, she said, 'If you have come to congratulate me (well and

---

153 Ibn al-Mubārak, *Zuhd*, no 881.

154 Ibn Saʿd, *Ṭabaqāt* 5:393 *5:540*; Aḥmad, *Zuhd*, 375, 376 *449, 450*; al-Muʿāfá ibn ʿImrān, *Zuhd*, 192, no 25; Abū Nuʿaym, *Ḥilyah* 4:9.

155 Abū Nuʿaym, *Ḥilyah* 4:242 (< ʿAl., *Zuhd*).

156 Abū Nuʿaym, *Ḥilyah* 2:359.

157 Abū Nuʿaym, *Ḥilyah* 6:306.

158 Abū Nuʿaym, *Ḥilyah* 6:381.

159 Abū Nuʿaym, *Ḥilyah* 7:12.

160 Ibn Abī Ḥātim, *Jarḥ* 1:95.

161 Sarrāj, *Lumaʿ*, 199–200.

162 Al-Khaṭīb al-Baghdādī, *Tārīkh* 11:225 *13:74*.

163 Abū Bakr al-Mālikī, *Riyāḍ al-nufūs* 1:346.

good). Otherwise, go back.'[164] Rābi'ah bint Ismā'īl (d. Damascus, 229/843–4) proposed marriage to Aḥmad ibn Abī al-Ḥawārī (d. 230/ 844–5?), saying she had no desire but wanted to spend her (deceased) husband's wealth on him and his brethren. Aḥmad got permission from his master Abū Sulaymān al-Dārānī and married three other women besides.[165]

Clothing

Some early renunciants wore wool (Arabic *ṣūf*), which was scratchy, smelly when wet, and liable to become ragged. Scratchiness is implied by the story of Sa'īd ibn al-Musayyib (Medinese, d. 94/712–13?), who once suffered 30, 50, or 100 lashes for refusing to swear allegiance at once to both the new Umayyad caliph, 'Abd al-Malik, and his sons al-Walīd and Sulaymān as designated successors. By one account, Ibn al-Musayyib was spitefully flogged on a cold day, then had cold water thrown over him and was dressed in a woolen cloak (*jubbah*). Alternatively, he was said to have been clothed in a hair shirt (*musūḥ, tubbān min sha'r*): clearly, wool meant discomfort.[166] Discomfort is also the issue when persons are described as wearing wool under more comfortable materials. Maymūn ibn Mihrān (Mesopotamian, d. 117/735–6), on being found to be wearing wool under his garment, asked that no one be told.[167] Hārūn ibn Ri'āb (Basran, *fl.* early 8th cent.) wore wool under his clothes to hide his renunciation.[168] Both Sunni and Shi'i sources state that Ja'far al-Ṣādiq (d. Medina, 148/765) wore white wool under a silk *jubbah*.[169]

The smelliness of wool is mentioned in some hadith reports describing the Prophet and his Companions' customary dress. The Prophet himself wore a rough wool *burdah*. 'When he sweated in it, the smell of wool was found.'[170] Abū Mūsá al-Ash'arī (d. 52/672?) told his son, 'My little son, if you saw us with our Prophet ... when we were struck by the heavens [i.e. rained on], you would have found

164 Abū al-'Arab, *Miḥan*, 241.
165 Ibn 'Asākir, *Tārīkh* 69:115–16; Cornell, 'Introduction', *Early Sufi women* by al-Sulamī, 64–5.
166 Ibn Sa'd, *Ṭabaqāt* 5:93–4 *5:125–8*; Aḥmad, *Zuhd*, 383 *459*; Abū Nu'aym, *Ḥilyah* 2:168–72. For another early example of someone flogged, then dressed in wool, see van Ess, *Th.u.G.* 2:88 *2:102*.
167 Abū Nu'aym, *Ḥilyah* 4:91–2.
168 Abū Nu'aym, *Ḥilyah* 3:55.
169 Abū Nu'aym, *Ḥilyah* 3:193; sim., Kulaynī, *Kāfī* 6:450, *al-zī wa-al-tajammul, bāb lubs al-ṣūf wa-al-sha'r.*
170 Ibn Sa'd, *Ṭabaqāt* 1/2:149 *1:453.*

from us the smell of sheep from our wearing wool.'[171] Wool is a weaker fabric than cotton and linen, hence its liability to become ragged. Patches were commended as a sign of humility. 'Umar was seen throwing stones at the *jamrah* wearing a wrap patched with a piece of hide.[172] Al-Ḥasan al-Baṣrī said that 'Umar preached in a garment with twelve patches.[173] Anas ibn Mâlik (d. 92/710–11?) said, 'I saw between 'Umar's shoulders four patches of his shirt.'[174] Mu'āwiyah (d. 60/680) preached in Damascus in a patched garment (*qamīṣ marqū'*).[175] 'Umar ibn 'Abd al-'Azīz likewise addressed people in a patched *qamīṣ*.[176] Aḥmad ibn Ḥanbal (d. Baghdad, 241/855) admired someone for wearing a patched garment.[177]

Wool seems to have been the characteristic dress of the proletariat. Mālik ibn Dīnār urged the renunciant (*qāri'*) not to be impressed by vain praise but to wear a woolen gown (*dāri'ah*) and carry a shepherd's staff.[178] The later theorist al-Muḥāsibī (d. Baghdad? 243/857–8) quotes persons who recommend wool as the dress of porters and sailors.[179] Accordingly, 'Abd Allāh ibn Shaddād (d. Kufa, 81/700–1?) said, 'Whoever wears wool, holds sheep to milk them, rides an ass, and answers the invitation of a poor man or slave, nothing of conceit will be recorded against him.'[180] The Kufan 'Awn ibn 'Abd Allāh wore wool so that people would not be afraid to sit with him; that is, so as to appear properly humble.[181] Muṭarrif ibn al-Shikhkhīr wore wool and sat with poor men (*masākīn*) for the sake of humility.[182]

It was probably first as a sign of their humility that prophets were conceived of as wearing wool. Ibn Mas'ūd said, 'The prophets milked sheep, rode asses, and

---

171 Ibn Sa'd, *Ṭabaqāt*, 4/1:80 *4:108*; almost same Abū Dāwūd, *al-libās* 5, *bāb fī lubs al-ṣūf wa-al-sha'r*, no 4033; Tirmidhī, *ṣifat al-qiyāmah* 103, no 2479. Ibn Sa'd cited by Goldziher, *Introduction*, 134fn.

172 Aḥmad, *Zuhd*, 122 *151*.

173 Aḥmad, *Zuhd*, 124 *154*.

174 Ibn al-Mubārak, *Zuhd*, no 588; Ibn Abī Shaybah, *Muṣannaf* 13:264–5 *12:188*.

175 Aḥmad, *Zuhd*, 172 *215* (< 'Al.).

176 Ibn Abī Shaybah, *Muṣannaf* 13:364 *12:334*; Abū Nu'aym, *Ḥilyah* 5:297.

177 Aḥmad, *'Ilal* 1:542, 2:358 *1:199, 326*.

178 Muḥāsibī, *Masā'il*, 104.

179 Abū Nu'aym, *Ḥilyah* 2:364. All the *aḥbār* of the Israelites had walked with staffs, according to a Syrian renunciant, *apud* Abū Nu'aym, *Ḥilyah* 5:238. Ibn Qutaybah quotes a story in which someone asks an anonymous *ḥakīm* why he habitually carries a staff when he is neither old nor sick. The wise man answers, 'To remind me that I am a traveller': Ibn Qutaybah, *'Uyūn* 2:323.

180 Aḥmad, *Zuhd*, 13–14 *20*.

181 Abū Nu'aym, *Ḥilyah* 4:246.

182 Abū Nu'aym, *Ḥilyah* 2:200.

wore wool.'[183] Wahb ibn Munabbih said, 'On the day that he spoke with his Lord at the tree, Mūsá had on a woolen *jubbah* (coat), a woolen *tubbān* (long shirt), and a woolen *qalansuwah* (conical hat).'[184] Khaythamah ibn ʿAbd al-Raḥmān (Kufan, d. after 80/699) related that ʿĪsá and Yaḥyá (Jesus and John) had been cousins, the first wearing wool, the second skins.[185] Al-Zuhrī (Medinese, d. 124/741–2?) said ʿĪsá never wore anything but wool.[186] The Prophet prayed in his wives' woollen garments (*murūṭ*) worth 6 or 7 dirhams.[187]

ʿAwn ibn ʿAbd Allāh (Kufan, d. bef. 120/738) wore wool so people would not be afraid to sit with him.[188] Mālik ibn Dīnār wore wool.[189] Yazīd ibn Marthad, a Damascene Follower, went barefoot and wore wool.[190] The Medinese Ziyād ibn Abī Ziyād (d. 135/752–3), said to be among the *abdāl* by whose prayers the world was preserved, wore wool.[191] ʿAbd al-Wāḥid ibn Zayd (*fl.* early 8th cent.) sought a wife in Kufa and found a renunciant woman wearing wool.[192] The poet Kulthūm ibn ʿAmr al-ʿAttābī (*fl.* early 9th cent.) wore wool, so manifesting renunciation of the world.[193] The first individual to be called a 'Sufi' was famously a Kūfan named Abū Hāshim (d. 150/767–68?).[194]

Scrupulosity

A prominent component of early Islamic piety is scrupulosity (*waraʿ*), meaning to avoid everything remotely dubious in order never to stumble into anything clearly forbidden. As a much later Māliki jurisprudent put it, 'Scrupulosity is leaving what is harmless as a precaution (*ḥadhran*) against what is harmful.'[195]

---

183 Aḥmad, *Zuhd*, 60 *78*.
184 Ibn Abī Shaybah, *Muṣannaf* 13:495 *12:356–7*. Alt., 'a woollen *jubbah*, a woollen turban (*ʿimāmah*), and smelly sandals of asshide': ʿAbd Allāh, *Sunnah*, 67, 166–7 *76, 188*.
185 Abū Nuʿaym, *Ḥilyah* 4:117.
186 Abū ʿUbayd, *Khuṭab*, 163.
187 Aḥmad, *Zuhd*, 14 *20*.
188 Abū Nuʿaym, *Ḥilyah* 4:246.
189 Abū Nuʿaym, *Ḥilyah* 2:368, 3:47, 8:313.
190 Abū Nuʿaym, *Ḥilyah* 5:165.
191 Ibn Ḥajar, *Tahdhīb* 3:368 (among *abdāl*—more on them in chap. 6); Ibn Saʿd, *Ṭabaqāt* 5:225 *5:305* (wool).
192 Abū Nuʿaym, *Ḥilyah* 6:158.
193 Al-Khaṭīb al-Baghdādī, *Tārīkh* 12:488 *14:515–16*.
194 Nicholson, 'Historical enquiry', 305. See also Massignon, *Essay*, 104–7.
195 Qarāfī (d. 684/1285), *Dhakhīrah* 13:246.

 Chapter 2: Physical austerities

The Prophet was quoted as saying, 'An excess of knowledge is better than an excess of worship; the best of your religion is scrupulosity' (incidentally indicating controversy over the relative merits of spending time in devotions or in learning hadith).[196] 'Ā'ishah complained, 'The people have squandered the best of their religion: scrupulosity.'[197] Maymūn ibn Mihrān (Kufan, transferred to al-Raqqah, d. 117/735–6) did not use the word but evidently had precisely this idea when he said, 'What is licit will not be safe for a man until he puts between himself and the forbidden a barrier of the licit.'[198] Some such idea of a barrier is presumably behind the term *iḥtiyāṭ*, literally a surrounding but used technically by jurisprudents for taking some measure just to be on the safe side; for example, to make a blood sacrifice to atone for an unfulfilled vow to perform the pilgrimage on foot, although no sacrifice is certainly required.[199]

Scrupulosity is mostly about refraining. Number 11 of al-Nawawī's collection of forty hadith, among several others encouraging scrupulosity, is 'Leave what makes you doubt in favour of what does not make you doubt.'[200] Nu'aym ibn Ḥammād's recension of Ibn al-Mubārak, *al-Zuhd*, includes under the heading of scrupulosity a story about Muwarriq al-'Ijlī (Basran, d. after 100/718–19) that he prayed for ten years for the power of leaving what did not concern him, echoing a prophetic injunction to do just that.[201] Ḥassān ibn Abī Sinān (Basran, *fl.* earlier 8th cent.) punished himself by fasting for a year after seeing a room and asking how long ago it had been built.[202]

Sometimes, we read of renunciants who carried it to apparently grotesque extremes. Kahmas ibn al-Ḥasan (Basran, d. 149/766–7?) prayed 1,000 sets of bowings a day. 'It is said that there fell from him a dinar. He searched and found it but he did not take it up, saying, "Perhaps it is another one."'[203] A similar story is told of Sufyān al-Thawrī:

196 Hannād, *Zuhd* 2:465; sim., Wakī', *Zuhd* 2:471. Sim. attributed to Muṭarrif ibn al-Shikhkhīr (Basran, d. 95/713–14): Aḥmad, *Zuhd*, 240 *294*; Marrūdhī, *Wara'*, 73 *57*.

197 Hannād, *Zuhd* 2:467; Aḥmad, *Zuhd*, 203 *252*; Ibn Abī Shaybah, *Muṣannaf* 13:361 *12:259*.

198 Abū Nu'aym, *Ḥilyah* 4:84 (< Aḥ., *Zuhd*). Sim. attributed to Sufyān ibn 'Uyaynah: Marrūdhī, *Wara'*, 50, 135 *43, 105–6*; Abū Nu'aym, *Ḥilyah* 7:288.

199 Shāfi'ī, *Umm* 2:228 *3:658*.

200 Also attributed to Shurayḥ: Ibn al-Mubārak, *Zuhd*, no 38 < Nu'aym; 'Abd al-Razzāq, *Muṣannaf* 11:308. Also attributed to Ibn 'Umar: Aḥmad, *Zuhd*, 192 *240*.

201 Mālik, *Muwaṭṭa'*, rec. Yaḥyá, *al-jāmi'* 10, *mā jā'a fī ḥusn al-khuluq*, no 2628; rec. Abū Muṣ'ab, *al-jāmi'* 10, *mā jā'a fī ḥusn al-khuluq*, no 1883; rec. Shaybānī, *jāmi'*, *bāb faḍl al-ḥayā'*; 'Abd al-Razzāq, *Muṣannaf* 11:307–8; Wakī', *Zuhd* 2:645; Hannād, *Zuhd* 2:539; Tirmidhī, *al-zuhd* 11, nos 2317–18; Ibn Mājah, *al-fitan* 12, *bāb kaff al-lisān fī al-fitnah*, no 3976; also no 12 of Nawawī's forty.

202 Abū Nu'aym, *Ḥilyah* 3:115.

203 Dhahabī, *Siyar* 6:317.

> Sufyān al-Thawrī went to a moneychanger in Mecca to exchange with him dirhams for a dinar. He gave him a dinar, having with him another. Sufyān dropped it so he looked for it and lo, it was next to another dinar. The moneychanger said to him, 'Take your dinar.' He said, 'I do know which it is.' He said, 'Take the one that is less (*nāqiṣ*).' He said, 'Perhaps it is the one with more (*zāʾid*). So he left it and went away.[204]

The issue may have been making use of the ruler's resources when ʿUthmān ibn Zāʾidah (Kufan, *fl.* mid-8th cent.) extinguished a light that his servant had brought, saying 'We will not illuminate ourselves with their fire.'[205] But the issue was expressly just asking permission when the prominent traditionist Abū Bakr Ibn Abī ʿĀṣim al-Nabīl (d. 287/900?) lost his notebooks in Basra to the disturbance of the Zanj. He said, 'I had nothing left of my notebooks, so I rewrote from memory 50,000 hadith reports. I used to pass by a grocer's shop and write by the light of his lamp. Then I remembered that I had not asked his permission, so I went to the river and washed off what I had written, then wrote it again.'[206] Some scruples were simply impossible to keep up, such as the preference of Muḥammad ibn Sīrīn (Basran, d. 110/729) for buying with old dinars that hadn't the name of God on them.[207] One hopes that the attitude of Ḥassān ibn Abī Sinān (Basran, *fl.* mid-8th cent.) was widespread: 'Nothing I have practised seems lighter than scrupulosity (*waraʿ*). ... When something makes me uneasy (*rābanī*), I leave it.'[208]

204 Abū Nuʿaym, *Ḥilyah* 7:53.
205 Marrūdhī, *Waraʿ*, 104 *85*.
206 Dhahabī, *Tārīkh* 21 (281–290 H.): 75.
207 Marrūdhī, *Waraʿ*, 70 *54*.
208 Marrūdhī, *Waraʿ*, 69 *53*; quoted by Pitschke, *Skrupulöse Frömmigkeit*, 54.

Chapter 3: Moral austerity

The previous chapter dealt with physical austerities that early renunciants imposed on themselves. The point of physical austerity was of course moral, in the first place to reinforce perceptions of dependence on God. The Companion ʿAbd Allāh ibn Masʿūd (d. 32/652–3?) said, 'Blessèd is he whose prayer and worship of God are pure; whose heart is not distracted by what his eyes see, who is not made to forget his recollection of God by what his ears hear; who is not saddened by what someone else has been given.'[1] Abū al-Dardāʾ (d. Damascus, earlier 30s/650s?) said, 'Three things that I love but the people dislike are poverty, illness, and death.'[2] He used to say, 'O God, I take refuge with you from division of heart (*tafriqat al-qalb*).' On being asked what that was, he said, 'That there should be laid down for me in every valley wealth.'[3] Ṭalḥah ibn ʿUbayd Allāh (d. 36/656) sold an estate for 700,000 dirhams but stayed awake all night fearing for the money and so gave it away in the morning.[4] ʿAbd al-Muṭṭalib (d. 62/681–2), another Companion who lived in Syria, was told, 'You have impoverished your two sons.' He said, 'I should be ashamed before God for him to observe in my heart that I should trust on their behalf anything except him.'[5] ʿAbd Allāh ibn ʿUmar (d. 73/693?) sold an ass of his because, although useful, it slightly preoccupied his mind (*adhhaba bi-shuʿbah min qalbī*).[6] Thābit al-Bunānī (Basran, d. 120s/738–48) said, 'It was said to ʿĪsá ibn Maryam ... "O Messenger of God, if only you took an ass to ride for your needs." He said, "God honours me more than to make for me a thing by which to distract me."'[7]

The desire to devote oneself entirely to God is often put in terms of having a single *hamm* (concern). ʿĀmir ibn ʿAbd Qays (Basran, d. *ca* 55/674–5) said, 'By God, if I were able, I would certainly make my concern one.'[8] Abū Idrīs al-Khawlānī (Syrian, d. 80/699–700?) said, 'Whoever makes God his sole concern will have sufficient to concern him. Whoever finds a concern in every valley, God will

1 Ibn al-Mubārak, *Zuhd*, no 19 < Nuʿaym.
2 Ibn ʿAsākir, *Tārīkh* 47:163.
3 Ibn al-Mubārak, *Zuhd*, no 635; Abū Nuʿaym, *Ḥilyah* 1:219; 5:229.
4 Aḥmad, *Zuhd*, 145 *181*.
5 Abū Dāwūd, *Zuhd*, 212, no 412.
6 Ibn al-Mubārak, *Zuhd*, no 536; Abū Nuʿaym, *Ḥilyah* 8:148 with a camel rather than an ass.
7 Aḥmad, *Zuhd*, 55 *73*.
8 Bayhaqī, *Zuhd*, 64 *28*, no 10; parallels in Aḥmad, *Zuhd*, 222 *272* (with a comment from al-Ḥasan al-Baṣrī that he succeeded), Abū Nuʿaym, *Ḥilyah* 2:90, and elsewhere.

https://doi.org/10.1515/9783110617962-004

not care in which he perishes.'[9] A more elaborate version is attributed to the Prophet: 'Whoever makes his concerns one is concerned with the hereafter (*ma'ād*). God will give him enough as to the concern of the world. Whosever concern is dispersed among the affairs of the world, God will not care in which of them he perishes.'[10] Al-Ḥasan al-Baṣrī (d. 110/728) said, 'Son of Adam, how is your heart to be softened if your concern is elsewhere?'[11]

Sadness and fear

Morally, the early ascetics cultivated sadness and fear—sadness especially over past sins and fear of judgement to come. A Shi'i source quotes 'Alī (d. Kufa, 40/661), 'The believer is sad in the evening and sad in the morning. Nothing suits him but that (*lā yaṣluḥu lahu illā dhālik*).'[12] It was said of Yaḥyá ibn Waththāb (Kufan, d. 103/722–3), 'The wretchedness (*ka'ābah*) of the ritual prayer would mark his face for an hour after he had prayed.[13] Al-Ḥasan al-Baṣrī said, 'God is not worshipped by anything as by longstanding sadness.'[14] Asked to describe al-Ḥasan himself, someone said, 'When you saw him, it was as if he had just buried his mother. When he sat, it was as a prisoner sits who is about to have his head struck off. When he talked, he talked the talk of a man who has been condemned to the Fire.'[15] The mere sight of him would provoke 'Abd al-Wāḥid ibn Zayd (Basran, d. 177/793–4?) to weep.[16] Ja'far al-Ḍuba'ī (d. 178/794–5) said of his fellow Basran Muḥammad ibn Wāsi' (d. 123/740–1), 'I used to, if I saw hardness in my heart, look to the face of Muḥammad ibn Wāsi'. His face was like that of a woman who has lost her child.'[17]

Mālik ibn Dīnār (Basran, d. *ca* 130/747–8) has already been quoted as saying, 'A heart that does not sorrow will go to ruin as an uninhabited house goes to

---

9 Aḥmad, *Zuhd*, 380 *456*; Abū Nu'aym, *Ḥilyah* 5:123.

10 Ibn Mājah, *al-zuhd* 2, *bāb al-hamm bi-al-dunyā*, no 4106; with preface from Ibn Mas'ūd, idem, *al-muqaddimah* 23, *bāb al-intifā' bi-al-'ilm wa-al-'amal bih*, no 257; Ibn Abī Shaybah, *Muṣannaf* 13:221 *12:155–6*; Abū Nu'aym, *Ḥilyah* 2:105.

11 Aḥmad, *Zuhd*, 259 *317*.

12 Iskāfī, *Tamḥīṣ*, 44, no 55. Sim. attrib'd to al-Ḥasan al-Baṣrī, Aḥmad, *Zuhd*, 258 *316*, and Ibn al-Mubārak, *Zuhd*, no 989.

13 Ibn Abī Shaybah, *Muṣannaf* 13:545 *12:393*.

14 Ibn al-Mubārak, *Zuhd*, no 126.

15 Aḥmad, *Jāmi'* 1:65–6; sim., Jāḥiẓ, *Bayān* 3:171.

16 Abū Nu'aym, *Ḥilyah* 6:160–1.

17 Abū Nu'aym, *Ḥilyah* 2:347, 6:288.

ruin.'[18] On hearing Q. 59:21, 'Had We sent this Recitation down on a mountain, you would have seen it humbled and split asunder through fear of God', he wept and said, 'I swear to you, no servant believes in this Qur'an without having his heart split.'[19] To him is also attributed an instrumental interpretation of sadness: 'Insofar as you are sad over this world, care for the Afterworld will be driven from your heart, while insofar as you are sad over the Afterworld, care for this world will go out of your heart.'[20] Muḥammad ibn Sūqah (d. 140s/758–67) would meet with his fellow Kufan Ḍirār ibn Murrah (d. 132/749–50) on Fridays for them to weep together.[21]

There are even more stories of fear. Prophets exemplify it (and so how much should ordinary Muslims be afraid). Mūsá said to God, 'My Lord, which of your worshippers most fears you (*akhshá lak*)?' God said to Mūsá, 'The one who knows me best (*aʿlamuhum bī*).'[22] Among the prayers of Maryam umm ʿĪsá was 'O God, fill my heart with fear of you and cover my face with shame before you.'[23] Kaʿb (d. 23–35/644–56), a *mukhaḍram* (one who was alive in the time of the Prophet but did not see him) said, 'If a man had to his credit the work of 70 prophets, he would still fear not to escape the evil of Resurrection Day.'[24] Extreme fear of the Last Judgement is attributed to a number of early figures; for example, the famous jurisprudent and qur'anic commentator Ibn Masʿūd would have preferred not to be raised after death.[25] How much more, implicitly, should ordinary Muslims fear it. Al-Ḥasan al-Baṣrī explains the believer's fear:

> The believer does not begin the day anything but fearful (*khāʾifan*). ... He does not end the day anything but fearful, even if he has done well. This is because he is between two fears: between a sin that has passed, concerning which he does not know what God will do, and a term that remains, in which he does not know what ruinations will befall him.[26]

---

18 Ibn Abī Shaybah, *Muṣannaf* 14:49 *12:454*; Aḥmad, *Zuhd*, 320 *388* (< ʿAl.); Abū Nuʿaym, *Ḥilyah* 6:287.
19 Aḥmad, *Zuhd*, 318 *386*.
20 Aḥmad, *Zuhd*, 319 *387*.
21 Abū Nuʿaym, *Ḥilyah* 5:4 (< ʿAl., *Zuhd*).
22 Ibn al-Mubārak, *Zuhd*, no 223; sim., no 533. Similarly, Abū al-Khalīl (Ṭalq ibn Ḥabīb, Basran, d. after 90/708–9) commented on Q. 35:28, 'The one of them most knowledgeable of him is he who most fears him (*ashadd khashyatan lah*)': Ibn Abī Shaybah, *Muṣannaf* 13:491 *12:353*.
23 Khuttalī, *Maḥabbah*, 88.
24 Ibn al-Mubārak, *Zuhd*, no 159.
25 Wakīʿ, *Zuhd* 1:396; Aḥmad, *Zuhd*, 156 *195*; Ibn Abī Shaybah, *Muṣannaf* 13:292 *12:209*; sim., Aḥmad, *Zuhd*, 161 *200*. For further examples, see Melchert, 'Exaggerated fear', 200–4.
26 Abū Nuʿaym, *Ḥilyah* 2:158; sim., Aḥmad, *Zuhd*, 279 *340*; sim. attrib'd to Prophet without *isnād*, Ibn al-Mubārak, *Zuhd*, no 304.

Complementarily, Ziyād al-Numayrī (Basran, *fl.* 1st half 8th cent.) saw no need for longstanding sadness and pallor if only one knew one's term (which of course no one did).[27]

Extreme fear of the Last Judgement is attributed to a number of early figures. ʻĪsá ibn Maryam would cry out on mention of Last Judgement before Him.[28] By another report, 'When ʻĪsá ibn Maryam mentioned the Hour, his mouth filled up with lowing (*malaʾa khuwāran*).'[29] Ibn Masʻūd fell down when he passed some people working a forge (reminding him of Hell).[30] ʻAṭāʾ al-Salīmī (Basran, *fl.* 1st half 8th cent.) fell unconscious when he saw a neighbour woman lighting the oven.[31] Ibn Wahb (Egyptian, d. 197/813) heard *Kitāb Ahwāl al-qiyāmah* ('the book of the terrors of the Resurrection') read aloud, fainted, and died three days later.[32]

There was no certainty, according to the early Sunnis, that all Muslims would be saved in the end.[33] ʻĀmir ibn ʻAbd Qays wept not for desire of the world or fear of death but from uncertainty whether he was going to Paradise or Hell.[34] Abū Hurayrah (d. 58/677–8) wept in his death illness not over the world but uncertainty whether he would be taken by Paradise or Hell.[35] Abū Maysarah (Kufan, d. 63/682–3) took to his bed and said, 'Would that my mother had never borne me.' His wife said, 'Abū Maysarah: God has done well by you, having guided you to Islam.' He said, 'Yes, but God has made it clear to us that we are bound for the Fire, without making clear to us that we are going out of it', with allusion to Q. 19:71, 'There is none of you but he is going to it.'[36] Ibrāhīm al-Nakhaʻī (Kufan, d.

---

27 Abū Nuʻaym, *Ḥilyah* 6:267.

28 Ibn al-Mubārak, *Zuhd*, no 229; Aḥmad, *Zuhd*, 57–8 *75*; Ibn Abī Shaybah *Muṣannaf* 13:198 *12:137–8*.

29 Abū ʻUbayd, *Khuṭab*, 162, no 86.

30 Ibn Abī Shaybah, *Muṣannaf* 13:514 *12:371*.

31 Abū Nuʻaym, *Ḥilyah* 6:218 (< ʻAl., *Zuhd*).

32 Abū Nuʻaym, *Ḥilyah* 8:324.

33 For example, Creed V of six attributed to Aḥmad ibn Ḥanbal begins, 'Whoever meets God with a sin for which he should go to the Fire, penitent for it or determined, God may make him repent. Whoever meets him having suffered the penalty for that sin in the world, it is his atonement (*kaffārah*)—so the hadith report came from the Messenger of God. ... Whoever meets him determined, impenitent for his sins that merit punishment, his affair is God's, whether he wishes to punish him or forgive him, so long as he has died in Islam and the *sunnah*': Ibn Abī Yaʻlá, *Ṭabaqāt al-ḥanābilah* 1:311 *2:339–40*.

34 Abū Nuʻaym, *Ḥilyah* 2:88; Gramlich, *Weltverzicht*, 90.

35 Ibn al-Mubārak, *Zuhd*, no 154 < Nuʻaym; Aḥmad, *Zuhd*, 153 *192* (< ʻAl. < Ibn al-Mubārak); sim., Aḥmad, *Zuhd*, 178 *223*; Ibn Saʻd, *Ṭabaqāt* 4/2:62–3 *4:339*; Abū Nuʻaym *Ḥilyah* 1:383.

36 Ibn al-Mubārak, *Zuhd*, no 312; Ibn Abī Shaybah, *Muṣannaf* 13:413 *12:296*; Aḥmad, *Zuhd*, 363 *435* (< ʻAl.); Abū Nu'aym, *Ḥilyah* 4:141.

96/714), on being found weeping, explained that he was uncertain whether the angel of death would announce he was heading for Paradise or the Fire.[37] On someone's asking al-Ḥasan al-Baṣrī 'How are you?' he said, 'O evil condition—what is the condition of someone who morning and evening awaits death without knowing what God will do with him?'[38]

Morally, the early ascetics cultivated sadness and fear—sadness especially over past sins and fear of judgement to come. The Prophet said, 'The Fire has been forbidden (to touch) an eye that has filled with tears or wept from fear of God and the Fire has been forbidden (to touch) an eye that has stayed awake on the path of God.'[39] Abū al-Dardā' said, 'If you knew what you will meet after death, you would never relish either eating or drinking. You would never go into a house to seek shade but rather go out to the high places beating your breasts, weeping over yourselves.'[40] Abū Dharr (d. 32/652–3) said, 'If you knew what I know, you would not take pleasure in your wives and couches but go out to the heights to supplicate and weep.'[41] In a widely-attested hadith report, the Prophet himself says, 'If you knew what I know, you would laugh little and weep much.'[42] In one version, he states exactly what has made him suggest weeping:

> O people, I am your prayer leader, so do not go ahead of me in either inclination or prostration, in either standing or in leaving. I see you behind me and before me. By him in whose hand is Muḥammad's soul, if you saw what I have seen, you would laugh little and weep much.' They said, 'O Messenger of God, what have you seen?' He said, 'I have seen Paradise and Hell.'[43]

Fear of Hell is most often associated with sleeplessness but also with weeping. The prophet Dāwūd (David) was reproached for his much weeping but said,

---

37 Ibn al-Mubārak, *Zuhd*, no 437; Aḥmad, *Zuhd* 364 *437*; Abū Nu'aym, *Ḥilyah* 4:224. Sim., Ibn Abī Shaybah, *Muṣannaf* 13:551 *12:397.*

38 Aḥmad, *Zuhd*, 262 *321* (< 'Al.); many parallels from others.

39 Aḥmad, *Musnad* 4:134–5 28:445–8; Dārimī, *Musnad*, 574; Tirmidhī, *faḍā'il al-jihād* 12, *bāb mā jā'a fī faḍl al-ḥars fī sabīl Allāh*, no 1639.

40 Abū Dāwūd, *Zuhd*, 122.

41 Wakī', *Zuhd* 1:261–2; Ibn Abī Shaybah, *Muṣannaf* 13:312 *12:223*; Hannād, *Zuhd* 1:269; Abū Nu'aym, *Ḥilyah* 1:164, 2:236.

42 E.g., Bukhārī, *al-kusūf* 2, *bāb al-ṣadaqah fī al-kusūf*, no 1044, *tafsīr sūrat al-mā'idah* 12, no 4621, *al-nikāḥ* 107, *bāb al-ghayrah*, no 5221, *al-riqāq* 28, *bāb qawl al-nabī law ta'lamūna mā a'lamu la-ḍaḥiktum qalīlan*, nos 6485–6, *al-aymān wa-al-nudhūr* 3, *bāb kayfa kānat yamīn al-nabī*, no 6637.

43 Muslim, *al-ṣalāh* 25, *bāb al-nahy 'an sabq al-imām bi-rukū' aw sujūd*, no 426.

'Leave me to weep before the day of weeping; before the burning of bones and the blazing of beards ... .'[44]

The Companion ʿAbd Allāh ibn Rawāḥah al-Anṣārī (d. 8/629) wept on being called out to *jihād*. He explained, 'By God, I have not wept from fear of death ... but rather I have wept on account of God's saying, "There is none of you but he is going to it [Q. 19:71]." I am sure I am going to it, but I do not know whether I shall escape or not.'[45] The Companion Abū Mūsá al-Ashʿarī (d. 50/670–1?) said, 'O people, weep. If you do not weep, pretend to weep. The people of the Fire are weeping tears till they are cut off, then they weep blood such that if a boat were sent among them, it would float.'[46] Al-Ḥasan al-Baṣrī, commenting on Q. 25:63, 'The servants of the Merciful are those who walk on the earth in humility', said that the believers weep from fear of the Fire.[47] Yazīd ibn Marthad (Syrian, *fl.* early 8th cent.) wept at God's threat, commenting that he would be right to weep continually even had he threatened only to lock him in the bath.[48] Abū ʿImrān al-Jawnī (Basran, d. 128/745–6?) said, 'We were in the mosque when a shaykh stood by us and said, "By God, O people of the mosque, God will certainly complete by you either the number of the people of Paradise or the number of the people of the Fire", which made us weep.'[49] Saʿīd ibn ʿAbd al-ʿAzīz (Damascene, d. 168/784–5?), who always wept at prayer, explained that Hell was always then prepresented to him.[50] ʿAbd al-Wāḥid ibn Zayd (Basran, d. 177/793–4?) similarly explained that he wept from fear of the Fire.[51]

Some other reasons for weeping are mentioned. On hearing someone's qur'anic recitation and prayer, Abū Bakr commented, 'How good are those who have mourned for themselves before the Day of the Resurrection.'[52] Hadith also is mentioned as an occasion for weeping. Ayyūb al-Sakhtiyānī (Basran, d. 131/749?) wept on hearing Prophet hadith[53]; also on relating hadith, it is said, but pretending it was rather just a cold.[54] His contemporary Hishām ibn Ḥassān (Basran, d.

---

44 Aḥmad, *Zuhd*, 69 *88*; Abū Nuʿaym, *Ḥilyah* 6:80 (< ʿAl., *Zuhd*).

45 Ibn al-Mubārak, *Zuhd*, nos 309–10; Abū Nuʿaym, *Ḥilyah* 1:118–19. Without any express connection with *jihād*: Hannād, *Zuhd* 1:163; Ibn Abī Shaybah, *Muṣannaf* 13:357 *12:257*.

46 Ibn Saʿd, *Ṭabaqāt* 4/1:81 *4:110*; Aḥmad., *Zuhd*, 199 *247*.

47 Ibn al-Mubārak, *Zuhd*, no 397; sim., shorter, no 531.

48 Ibn al-Mubārak, *Zuhd*, no 481; Aḥmad, *Zuhd*, 382 *458*; Abū Nuʿaym, *Ḥilyah* 5:164.

49 Aḥmad, *Zuhd*, 313 *380* (< ʿAl.).

50 Abū Nuʿaym, *Ḥilyah* 8:274.

51 Abū Nuʿaym, *Ḥilyah* 6:160–1.

52 Ibn al-Mubārak, *Zuhd*, no 96; Aḥmad, *Zuhd*, 204 *253*.

53 Abū Nuʿaym, *Ḥilyah* 3:4; Ismāʿīl ibn Isḥāq, *Juzʾ*, 39.

54 Aḥmad, *ʿIlal* 1:405 *1:155*.

148/765–6?) is also said to have wept as he related hadith.[55] Ibn al-Mubārak is described as bellowing like a slaughtered bull or cow as he read from his *Kitāb al-Riqāq* ('the book of sayings to soften the heart').[56]

Various motives are attached to this weeping. Ziyād ibn Ḥudayr (Kufan, *fl.* 7th cent.) told someone to recite to him, so he recited Q. 94:1–3, 'Have we not sliced open your breast and put away from you your burden, which was destroying your back?' 'He said, "O son of the mother of Ziyād, was the back of the Messenger of God ... destroyed?" whereupon he began to weep like a boy.'[57] Pity seems to be the predominant emotion here. On telling some stories of *wariʿīn*, persons especially careful not to do anything remotely dubious, Aḥmad ibn Ḥanbal exclaimed, 'I beg God not to hate us. Where are we by comparison with them?'[58] Here the frightening comparison is between the virtue of earlier paragons and the unworthiness of men in the present.

I have come across one report by which longing for Paradise could equally induce weeping: Zādhān (Kufan, d. 82/701–2) said, 'We have heard that whoever weeps from fear of the Fire, God will give him refuge from it, and whoever weeps from longing for Paradise, God will make him dwell in it.'[59] Shaʿwānah, a preacher and qur'anic reciter of Ubullah (near Basra; *fl.* later 8th cent.) said, 'An eye that has been parted from its beloved and longs to meet him without weeping is no good.'[60] But the former quotation is from an *adab* work, the latter from a Sufi, and I fear they reflect not actual eighth-century renunciant feeling but much later genre expectations, *adab* prizing balance, Sufism communion with divinity. From a hadith source, I have come across a quotation of the Prophet indicating that weeping was to have an educative effect on the worshipper: 'O God,' he prayed, 'provide me with pouring eyes that weep and shed tears to cure me of fearing you before tears turn to blood and molars hot coals.'[61]

---

55 Abū Nuʿaym, *Ḥilyah* 6:273.
56 Al-Khaṭīb al-Baghdādī, *Tārīkh* 10:167 *11:406*.
57 Abū Nuʿaym, *Ḥilyah* 4:197 (< ʿAl., *Zuhd*).
58 Ibn al-Jawzī, *Manāqib Aḥmad*, 276–7 *369*.
59 Ibn Abī al-Dunyā, *Riqqah*, 20–1.
60 Sulamī, *Early Sufi women*, 106–7 (my translation).
61 Aḥmad, *Zuhd*, 10 *15*; Ibn al-Mubārak, *Zuhd*, no 480.

Withdrawal

Some preferred at least short-term withdrawal from society. The Muʿtazilah (lit., 'withdrawers') were probably distinguished at first by their renunciant piety rather than a peculiar theology,[62] and they were by no means the only ones who practised withdrawal. The term could be used non-technically, as when Ibn Saʿd reports that Ziyād ibn Abī Ziyād (Medinese, d. 135/752–3) 'was a withdrawer (*muʿtazil*), staying by himself to recollect God.'[63] ʿUmar (d. 23/644) said, 'Take your share of withdrawal (*ʿuzlah*).'[64] 'In withdrawal', he explained, 'there is rest from the disturbances of evil.'[65] (The Qur'an reports God approved when the Seven Sleepers of Ephesus resolved to withdraw from the polytheists [Q. 18:16], although not that pious Muslims should withdraw.) ʿAmr ibn ʿUtbah (Kufan, d. dur. caliphate of ʿUthmān, 23–35/644–56) would ride out to the cemetery at night, address the people in the tombs, then return for the dawn prayer.[66] Abū Muslim al-Khawlānī (Syrian, d. 60/680 or after) never sat with people, having once done so and found them speaking of worldly matters.[67] Al-Rabīʿ ibn Khuthaym (Kufan, d. 63/682–3?) said, 'Learn jurisprudence, then withdraw (*tafaqqah thumma iʿtazil*).'[68] He would go out by night to the cemetery and address the people of the graves.[69] 'In the past,' said ʿAbd Allāh ibn ʿAmr (d. 77/696–7?), 'when a man met a man, it was if he were meeting his brother by the same father and mother. As for today, when a man of you meets a man, it is as if he were meeting an enemy.'[70]

Ziyād ibn Ḥudayr (Kufan, *fl.* later 7th cent.) said, 'I wish I were in a garden (*ḥayr*) fenced off with iron, having what I need, not speaking to the people nor they speaking to me until I meet God.'[71] Saʿīd ibn al-Musayyib (Medinese, d. 93/711–12?) said, 'You must practise withdrawal, for it is worship (*ʿibādah*).'[72] Muṭarrif ibn al-Shikhkhīr (Basran, d. 95/713–14) called for learning law, then worshipping, then withdrawing.[73] Makḥūl al-Shāmī (d. 110s/729–38) said, 'If there is

---

62 See Sarah Stroumsa, 'The beginnings of the Muʿtazilah'.

63 Ibn Saʿd, *Ṭabaqāt* 5:225 *5:305*.

64 Wakīʿ, *Zuhd* 2:517; Ibn al-Mubārak, *Zuhd*, no 11 < Nuʿaym.

65 Aḥmad, *Zuhd*, 119 *149*, reading *khilāl* for printed *khilālī*; however, a letter from Sufyān al-Thawrī says, 'In withdrawal is rest from evil associates (*khulaṭā' al-sū'*)': Marrūdhī, *Akhbār*, 185.

66 Ibn al-Mubārak, *Zuhd*, no 29; Aḥmad, *Zuhd*, 353 *423* (< 'Al.); Abū Nuʿaym, *Ḥilyah* 4:158.

67 Abū Nuʿaym, *Ḥilyah* 2:123.

68 Aḥmad, *Zuhd*, 85 *108* (< 'Al.), also 334 *403*.

69 Aḥmad, *Zuhd*, 333 *401–2* (< 'Al.).

70 Ibn al-Mubārak, *Zuhd*, no 361.

71 Aḥmad, *Zuhd*, 370 *442*; Abū Nuʿaym, *Ḥilyah* 4:197.

72 Abū Dāwūd, *Zuhd*, ed. Ḥusayn, 221, no 432; sim., Marrūdhī, *Akhbār*, 185.

73 Aḥmad, *Zuhd*, 240 *294* (< 'Al.).

virtue in the assembly (*jamāʿah*), there is safety in withdrawal.'[74] Mālik ibn Dīnār said that the saints (*abrār*) had used to enjoin one to three things: imprisoning the tongue (i.e., not to speak), often asking forgiveness, and withdrawal.[75] Sufyān al-Thawrī (Kufan, d. 161/777?) said, 'It used to be that when people met, they benefitted from one another. As for today, that is gone, so that deliverance is found in leaving them, we believe.'[76] He complained that meeting some of the brethren would render him inattentive (*ghāfil*) for a month.[77] Shaqīq al-Balkhī (d. 194/809–10) said, 'Keep company with people as you do with fire: take benefit from it but beware lest it burn you.'[78]

Sometimes one's house is the favoured resort. Abū al-Dardāʾ is quoted as saying, 'What a good cell for a man is his house. There he preserves his tongue and sight.'[79] Sufyān al-Thawrī said of the Yemeni Ṭāwūs that he was asked why he sat in his house. He said, 'The injustice (*ḥayf*) of the rulers (*aʾimmah*) and the corruption (*fasād*) of the people.'[80] The Companion ʿUthmān ibn Abī al-ʿĀṣ (d. Basra, *ca* 50/670–1) said, 'If not for Friday and the assembly (group prayer), I would build a chamber in the uppermost part of my house and not leave until I go out to my grave.'[81] Ṣafwān ibn Muḥriz (Basran, d. 74/693–4?) had a basement (*sarab*) from which he did not go out save for the ritual prayer.[82] He was also said to have had a *sarab* for weeping.[83] Al-Ḥasan al-Baṣrī said, 'The believers' cells are their houses.'[84] A Shiʿi source quotes Jaʿfar al-Ṣādiq (d. 148/765): 'Bowing in the mosque is the monasticism (*rahbānīyah*) of the Arabs. The believer's session is his mosque and his cell is his house.'[85]

---

74 Abū Nuʿaym, *Ḥilyah* 5:181. A more cautious variant is 'If there is no good in sitting with people and mixing with them, then withdrawal is safer': Abū Khaythamah, *ʿIlm*, no 44.
75 Abū Nuʿaym, *Ḥilyah* 2:377.
76 Marrūdhī, *Akhbār*, 185; Abū Nuʿaym, *Ḥilyah* 6:376.
77 Abū Nuʿaym, *Ḥilyah* 7:53.
78 Abū Nuʿaym, *Ḥilyah* 8:77.
79 Ibn Abī Shaybah, *Muṣannaf* 13:309–10 *12:221*; Aḥmad, *Zuhd*, 135 *168*; Ibn al-Mubārak, *Zuhd*, no 14 < Nuʿaym.
80 Abū Nuʿaym, *Ḥilyah* 4:4.
81 Aḥmad, *Zuhd*, 151 *190*.
82 Ibn Saʿd, *Ṭabaqāt* 7/1:107 *7:147*.
83 Ibn Saʿd, *Ṭabaqāt* 7/1:107 *7:147*.
84 Ibn Abī Shaybah, *Muṣannaf* 13:528 *12:380*.
85 Kulaynī, *Kāfī* 2:662, *al-ʿishrah, bāb al-ittikāʾ wa-al-iḥtibāʾ*.

ʿAṭāʾ al-Salīmī stayed in bed for 40 years.[86] Sufyān al-Thawrī said, 'Stick to your cells at the end of time, your cells being your houses.'[87] He associated sociability with corruption: 'If all the neighbours praise a man, he is an evil one.' Asked to explain, he said, 'He sees them acting sinfully but does not correct them (*lā yughayyiruhum*), meeting them cheerfully.'[88] But public rebuke of evildoers was also subject to corruption:

> Formerly, the best people, who were honoured and looked up to in religion, were those who stood up to those [i.e. rulers], commanding and forbidding them. There were others who stuck to their houses, not having that in them. They were not exalted or remembered. With us, it has come to the point where the worst of people stand up to those and command and forbid them, while those who stick to their houses and do not go to them are the best of people.[89]

Dāwūd al-Ṭāʾī went to the mosque by an indirect route to avoid mixing with people, hurried away from the Friday prayer to avoid meeting people, and stayed at home except during prayer times.[90] 'He sat in his house for as long as twenty years before he died.'[91]

Sometimes, rather, the mosque is favoured. The prophet ʿĪsá said, 'Make your houses (temporary) resting places (*manāzil*), taking mosques as your dwellings (*buyūt*).'[92] This seems to commend avoidance of normal family life in favour of living in the mosque. Transferring to the mosque for part or all of Ramaḍān (*iʿtikāf*) is a devotional form described in all handbooks of Islamic law and widely practised to the present. Muṭarrif ibn Shikhkhīr preferred the company of his brethren, since they prayed for him, to meeting his family, since they just said 'O father', 'O father'.[93] But the mosque might fill up with hypocrites. When al-Shaʿbī (Kufan, d. 104/722–3?) came upon Ḥammād ibn Abī Sulaymān and his disciples making noise in the mosque (discussing jurisprudence, no doubt), he said, 'By God, they have made me despise this mosque. Until they leave it, I shall despise it more than the garbage heap by my house.'[94]

---

86 Abū Nuʿaym, *Ḥilyah* 6:217.
87 Abū Nuʿaym, *Ḥilyah* 7:70.
88 Abū Nuʿaym, *Ḥilyah* 7:35.
89 Marrūdhī, *Akhbār*, 185; Abū Nuʿaym, *Ḥilyah* 7:79, sim. 6:376.
90 Abū Nuʿaym, *Ḥilyah* 7:342–4.
91 Ibn Saʿd, *Ṭabaqāt* 6:255 *6:367*.
92 Abū ʿUbayd, *Khuṭab*, 156–7.
93 Aḥmad, *Zuhd*, 242 *296*.
94 Ibn Saʿd, *Ṭabaqāt* 6:175 *6:251*; another version, al-Muʿāfá ibn ʿImrān, *Zuhd*, 213, no 49.

Renunciation had to continually interfere with normal social intercourse. Sufyān al-Thawrī's contempt for the man whom all the neighbours praise suggests how disruptive renunciants could be. 'It used to be that when people met,' he said, 'they benefitted from one another. As for today, that is gone, so that deliverance is found in leaving them, as we see.'[95] In an introductory survey of Islam, I once asked whether anyone would volunteer to live for a day by the principle of leaving what does not concern one.[96] Next week, the man who volunteered said it had turned out to be very difficult: an old friend of his and his wife's happened to visit them that day, and it was a trial to suppress idle curiosity about common friends. I thought this was a good example of how living the pious life must interfere with normal socializing.

The renunciant tradition strongly commends self-reliance. More will be said in chapter 8 about how renunciants were supported, but the implications for removing renunciants from normal society require notice here. The Prophet said, 'Who will guarantee me he will not ask the people for anything for me to guarantee him Paradise?' Thawbān, his client, said, 'I', so he never asked anyone for anything.[97] Sālim ibn ʿAbd Allāh (d. 106/725), one of the seven jurisprudents of Medina, went to the market himself to buy his necessities. 'Ask no one but God', he said.[98] An anonymous Kufan of the 2nd/8th century 'readied himself for death for thirty years. He said, "The people have nothing of mine and I have nothing of anyone else's. I do not wish to talk to anyone nor that anyone talk to me except recollecting God (be he exalted)." He took refuge in the mountains and cemeteries.'[99] Yūsuf ibn Asbāṭ (l. Antioch, d. 195/810–11) said, 'I have heard that God (be he exalted) spoke to Ibrāhīm (peace be upon him) by inspiration, "Do you know why I have chosen you for a friend? Because you give to people but take nothing from anyone."'[100]

---

95 Marrūdhī, *Akhbār*, 185; Abū Nuʿaym, *Ḥilyah* 6:376.

96 For the principle—'A comely part of a man's Islam is his leaving what does not concern him'—, see Mālik, *Muwaṭṭaʾ*, rec. Yaḥyá, *al-jāmiʿ* 10, *mā jāʾa fī ḥusn a.l-khuluq*, no 2628; rec. Abū Muṣʿab, *al-jāmiʿ* 10, *mā jāʾa fī ḥusn al-khuluq*, no 1883; rec. Shaybānī, *jāmiʿ*, *bāb faḍl al-ḥayāʾ*; ʿAbd al-Razzāq, *Muṣannaf* 11:307–8; Wakīʿ, *Zuhd* 2:645; Hannād, *Zuhd* 2:539; Tirmidhī, *al-zuhd* 11, nos 2317–18; Ibn Mājah, *al-fitan* 12, *bāb kaff al-lisān fī al-fitnah*, no 3976.

97 ʿAbd al-Razzāq, *Muṣannaf* 11:91, Basran/Kufan *isnād* but Maʿmar adds without an *isnād* that ʿĀʾishah said he would not even pick up his whip if it dropped from his hand; Abū Dāwūd, *zakāh* 27, *bāb karāhiyat al-masʾalah*, no 1643, Basran *isnād*; Wakīʿ, *Zuhd* 1:370–1, Medinese *isnād*, similarly adding that he would not even ask someone to pick up his whip if it dropped from his hand as he was riding.

98 Abū Nuʿaym, *Ḥilyah* 2:194.

99 Ibn al-Jawzī, *Ṣifah* 3:111.

100 Abū Nuʿaym, *Ḥilyah* 8:242.

The renunciant tradition was of two minds, though, about withdrawal, sometimes preferring that one mix. ʿAbd Allāh ibn Masʿūd went to some Kufans who had withdrawn and established themselves somewhere near (i.e., out in the desert) to worship. 'What induced you to do what you have done?' he asked. They said, 'We wished to go away from the crowd (*ghumār al-nās*).' Ibn Masʿūd said, 'If the people did what you have done, who would fight the enemy? I will not go away till you return.'[101] There were to be no Muslim Desert Fathers. Ibn ʿUmar said, 'I go out to the market when I have no need save to salute and be saluted.'[102]

Somebody asked Muḥammad ibn al-Ḥanafīyah (Medinese, d. 81/700) about withdrawing from politics, going through the world, worshipping God till he should meet him. He said, 'Do not do it, for that is the monkish (*ruhbānī*) innovation.'[103] Somebody told Wahb ibn Munabbih (Yemeni, d. 114/732?) of the worshippers of the Children of Israel and their wandering. He said, 'God have mercy on whoever mixes with the people, is scrupulous, and has patience with their annoyances. That is better, in my view.'[104] ʿAwn ibn ʿAbd Allāh (Kufan, d. bef. 120/738) said, 'The believer is sociable (*muʾālif*). There is no good in one who does not keep company nor can be kept company.'[105] Inasmuch as the renunciant movement went back to the habits of a conquering élite, it was probably predisposed to putting a high value on social solidarity, even as it recoiled from majority habits. We read of encounters with monks in the wilderness but almost never Muslims, at least before the ninth century: renunciation remained an affair of the cities, like politics, jurisprudence, and other features of the Islamic community. Also, it prized constant struggle with the world over the serenity that might come of avoiding temptation, as by withdrawing to the desert.

Restricted speech

Others, if not avoiding society, at least restricted their speech. The Prophet said, 'Shame and taciturnity (*ḥayāʾ*, *ʿī*) are two branches of faith; obscenity and eloquence (*badhāʾ*, *bayān*) are two branches of hypocrisy.'[106] The Companion Ibn

101 Ibn al-Mubārak, *Zuhd*, no 1104 (< al-Ḥu.).
102 Ibn Saʿd, *Ṭabaqāt* 4/1:114 *4:155–6*.
103 Ibn Saʿd, *Ṭabaqāt* 5:70 *5:96*.
104 Aḥmad, *Zuhd*, 372 *445*; sim. recommendation against withdrawal, Ibn al-Mubārak, *Zuhd*, no 955.
105 Abū Nuʿaym, *Ḥilyah* 4:254.
106 Tirmidhī, *abwāb al-birr wa-al-ṣilah* 80, no 2027; first half in Ibn Abī Shaybah, *Muṣannaf* 11:44 *10:314*.

Mas'ūd said, 'By God, if a man speaks a frivolous word (*kalimah fī al-rafāhiyah*) for his companions to laugh at, his downfall will be greater than between heaven and earth.'[107] Ibn 'Umar 'never cursed a servant except one whom he then set free.' Alternatively, if he wanted to curse his servant, he said *allāhumma il'a* without completing it (that is, without saying *il'anh*, 'curse him').[108] When two men of the Mashriq (probably meaning Iraq) came and pleased people by their eloquent preaching, he quoted the Prophet: 'Some of eloquence (*bayān*) is sorcery.'[109] Abū al-Jawzā' al-Rab'ī (Basran, d. 83/702–3) never cursed anything and never ate anything that had been cursed. He paid his servant a dirham or two each month not to curse the food if he was injured by the heat of the oven.[110] Muslim ibn Yasār (Basran, l. Mecca, d. 100/718–19?) said, 'It is not meet for the saint (*ṣiddīq*) to curse much (*an yakūna la''ānan*). If I ever curse anything, I do not leave it in my house.'[111]

Al-Rabī' ibn Khuthaym said,

> There is no good in speech save in nine: *lā ilāha illā Allāh* ('there is no god but God'), *subḥāna Allāh* (roughly 'I magnify God'), *Allāhu akbar* ('God is greater'), *al-ḥamdu lillāh* ('praise be to God'), asking for good, taking refuge from evil, commanding the good, forbidding evil, and reciting the Qur'an.[112]

Sa'īd ibn Ḥayyān (Kufan, *fl.* early 8th cent.) said, 'I never heard al-Rabī' ibn Khuthaym mention a thing of the world save that one day he asked, "How many mosques do Taym have?"'[113] Abū Wā'il (Kufan, d. *ca* 99/717–18) was never observed to ask anyone 'How are you this evening?' or 'How are you this morning?'[114] This would have been idle curiosity. 'Aṭā' ibn Abī Rabāḥ said,

> O nephew, those who were before you disliked excessive talk (*fuḍūl al-kalām*). They considered excessive all but the Book of God (be he exalted) to recite, to command the good or forbid the bad, or that you say something concerning your need in your life from which there is no escape. Do you deny this? 'Generous, recording' (Q. 82:11), 'When the two Receivers receive him, one sitting on the right, one sitting on the left' (Q. 50:17)—would not

---

107 Ibn al-Mubārak, *Zuhd*, no 993 (< al-Ḥu.); Hannād, *Zuhd* 2:552–3.
108 Abū Nu'aym, *Ḥilyah* 1:307.
109 Mālik, Muwaṭṭa', rec. Yaḥyá, *al-jāmi'* 73, *bāb mā yukrahu min al-kalām*, no 2820.
110 Ibn Sa'd, *Ṭabaqāt* 7/1:162 *7:223*.
111 Abū Nu'aym, *Ḥilyah* 2:293.
112 Ibn Abī Shaybah, *Muṣannaf* 14:16 *12:430*; another list of nine from Ibn Sa'd, *Ṭabaqāt* 6:132 *6:190*.
113 Ibn Sa'd, *Ṭabaqāt* 6:127 *6:183*.
114 Abū Nu'aym, *Ḥilyah* 4:105 (< Aḥ., *Zuhd*).

> one of you be ashamed if the scroll that he had dictated in the prime of his life should have to do with neither his religion nor his material life?[115]

ʿAbd Allāh ibn Zakarīyāʾ (Syrian, d. 119/717) worked twenty years to control his tongue, putting rocks in his mouth to learn silence.[116] He would not mention persons in his session.[117] Shufayy ibn Mātiʿ al-Aṣbaḥī (d. 125/743 or earlier) said, 'Who speaks much sins much.'[118] A Bakkār ibn Muḥammad said of ʿAbd Allāh ibn ʿAwn (Basran, d. 151/768?), 'I never saw Ibn ʿAwn insulting anyone—not a slave or a slave-girl, a sheep or a fowl, or anything. I never saw anyone with better control of his tongue.'[119] Someone else said, 'I followed Ibn ʿAwn for a long time, until he died. ... I never saw him swear truly or falsely until death separated us.'[120] Muḥammad ibn al-Naḍr al-Ḥārithī (Kufan, d. 170s/787–97) said only three things on his way to ʿAbadan, one of them to tell someone to perform his ritual prayer well.[121] Muḥammad ibn Yūsuf al-Iṣbahānī (d. *ca* 200/815–16) spoke only once between Baghdad and Damascus.[122] Bishr al-Ḥāfī (d. Baghdad, 227/841) said, 'Two characters harden the heart: speaking much and eating much.'[123] Musāwir al-Maghribī (*fl.* first half, 9th cent.?) met a monk (*rāhib*) who had not spoken in forty years.[124] Qays ibn al-Sakan (*fl.* first half, 9th cent.?) considered his tongue a wild animal that he feared to release.[125]

Often, the stress is on speaking softly. ʿUmar, on hearing a man in the mosque, said, 'Do you know where you are?'[126] Ibn ʿUmar said, 'O people, you are not praying to someone absent or deaf.'[127] Qays ibn ʿUbād (Basran, d. after 80/699)

---

115 Abū Nuʿaym, *Ḥilyah* 3:315.
116 Abū Nuʿaym, *Ḥilyah* 5:149, 152.
117 Abū Nuʿaym, *Ḥilyah* 5:149.
118 Ibn al-Mubārak, *Zuhd*, no 842; Abū Nuʿaym, *Ḥilyah* 5:167.
119 Ibn Saʿd, *Ṭabaqāt* 7/2:25 *7:263*.
120 Ibn Saʿd, *Ṭabaqāt* 7/2:26 *7:263*.
121 Abū Nuʿaym, *Ḥilyah* 8:218. Alternatively, he said nothing on his way to ʿAbadan, gesturing to his son when he needed something: Abū Nuʿaym, *Ḥilyah* 8:219.
122 Abū Nuʿaym, *Ḥilyah* 8:229.
123 Abū Nuʿaym, *Ḥilyah* 8:350. Sim. attributed to Sufyān al-Thawrī, Abū Nuʿaym, *Ḥilyah* 7:36; see also Ibn al-Mubārak, *Zuhd*, no 269.
124 Abū Nuʿaym, *Ḥilyah* 10:162.
125 Abū Nuʿaym, *Ḥilyah* 10:140.
126 Ibn al-Mubārak, *Zuhd*, no 405.
127 Wakīʿ, *Zuhd* 2:619; Ibn Abī Shaybah, *Muṣannaf* 2:488, 10:376 *3:552–3*, *10:143–4*. Also attributed to the Prophet, as by Ibn al-Mubārak, *Zuhd*, no 1121 (< al-Ḥu.); Wakīʿ, *Zuhd* 2:617; Ibn Abī Shaybah, *Muṣannaf* 10:376 *10:143*; Bukhārī, *al-jihād* 131, *bāb mā yukrahu min rafʿ al-ṣawt*, no 2992, *al-daʿawāt* 50, *bāb al-duʿāʾ idhā ʿalā ʿaqabah*, no 6384, *al-daʿawāt* 67, *bāb qawl lā ḥawl*

recalled, 'The Companions of the Messenger of God used to dislike raising the voice at funerals, in fighting, and in recollection.'[128] Mujāhid (Meccan, d. 103/721–2?) 'heard a man raising his voice in supplication (*du'ā'*) and so threw rocks at him.'[129] Abū Qilābah (Basran, d. 104/722–3?), on hearing a preacher (*qāṣṣ*) raise his voice at a funeral, said, 'If they magnified death by silence (it would be better).'[130] Al-Ḥasan al-Baṣrī's saying has been quoted already: 'They used to exert themselves in prayer (*du'ā'*) but you would not hear anything but mumbling (*hams*).'[131] Praying and reciting in a loud voice was naturally associated with praying and reciting for show. Al-'Alā' ibn Ziyād (Basran, d. 94/712–13) told this story:

> A man used to perform his work hypocritically, gathering up his garments and raising his voice when he recited. It came to the point that he was insulted and cursed by everyone he approached. Then God gave him some provision and after that he lowered his voice and made his ritual prayer something between himself and his lord (mighty and glorious is he). Then everyone he met wished him well and invoked God's mercy on him.[132]

As often with accusations of hypocrisy, to be sure, the line of thought is confused: the man evidently made a better impression in the world when he followed the approved course of keeping his devotions quiet.

There are many injunctions to restrict speech especially in the mosque; for example, from Sa'īd ibn al-Musayyib: 'Whoever sits in the mosque sits with God, so how much he should not say anything but good.'[133] 'Umar repeatedly discouraged a man to preach (*yaquṣṣ*), although requested to. 'I fear for you that you will raise yourself, then God will put you down.'[134] Another Kufan Follower said, 'I never heard al-Rabī' ibn Khuthaym mention a thing of the world save that one day he asked, "How many mosques do Taym have?"'[135] Ibrāhīm al-Nakha'ī was

---

wa-lā qūwah illā bi-Allāh, no 6409, *al-qadar* 7, *bāb lā ḥawl wa-lā qūwah illā bi-Allāh*, no 6610, *al-tawḥīd* 9, *bāb wa-kāna Allāh samī'an baṣīran*, no 7386.

128 Wakī', *Zuhd* 2:462; Ibn Abī Shaybah, *Muṣannaf* 10:530 *10:257* (recollection only); Ibn al-Mubārak, *Zuhd*, no 247; Abū Nu'aym, *Ḥilyah* 9:58. Sa'īd ibn Jubayr (Kufan, d. 95/714?) was recalled as disliking the voice to be raised at funerals, in reciting the Qur'an, and in fighting: Wakī', *Zuhd* 2:463.

129 Wakī', *Zuhd* 2:616; Ibn Abī Shaybah, *Muṣannaf* 2:488, 10:377 *3:552*, *10:144*.

130 Wakī', *Zuhd* 2:461; Aḥmad, *Zuhd*, 303 *368*; Abū Nu'aym, *Ḥilyah* 2:285.

131 Wakī', *Zuhd* 2:616; Ibn Abī Shaybah, *Muṣannaf* 2:488, 10:377 *3:553*, *10:144*; longer version from Ibn al-Mubārak, *Zuhd*, no 140.

132 Aḥmad, *Zuhd*, 254 *255*.

133 Ibn al-Mubārak, *Zuhd*, no 416.

134 Aḥmad, *Zuhd*, 122 *152*.

135 Ibn Sa'd, *Ṭabaqāt* 6:127 *6:183*; sim., 6:133 *6:191*; Ibn al-Mubārak, *Zuhd*, no 24 < Nu'aym; sim., Hannād, *Zuhd* 2:537–8.

said not to have spoken unless asked a question; that is, concerning law and hadith.[136] Ibn Muḥayrīz (Syrian, d. 99/717–18 or later) was for restricting talk in the mosque to that of one praying, one recollecting, or asking or giving the truth.[137] Al-Ḥasan al-Baṣrī said, 'I have met many who, if the man sits with the group and they think he has a speech impediment (*bihi ʿī*) when he doesn't, then he is a Muslim *faqīh*' (a man with discernment, used nontechnically).[138] The Egyptian Shufayy ibn Māti' al-Aṣbaḥī (d. 125/743 or earlier) said, 'Who speaks much sins much.'[139] Al-Rabīʿ ibn Abī Rāshid (Kufan, *fl.* earlier 8th cent.) would loosen his *ḥubwah* (a strap around his bent legs to aid long sitting), put on his sandals, and leave the session when someone took to gossip (*takallama bi-kalām al-nās*).[140] It was said that 'Sufyān al-Thawrī would (say) no more to anyone, even if he had been away for years, than "How are you?"'[141]

Poetry was controversial. The Qur'an is cool toward it (see especially 26: 221–7), and some Prophet hadith is fiercely hostile; for example, 'It would be better for one of you for his interior to be filled with pus than for it to be filled with poetry.'[142] The companion Muʿādh ibn Jabal (d. Damascus, 18/40) said,

> Mosques should be free of five things: that the *ḥudūd* (scriptural punishments) should be carried out there, that the wounded should be treated there, that poetry should be declaimed there (*an yunṭaqa fīhā bi-al-ashʿār*), that someone should chant there for strayed animals, and that they should be taken for markets.[143]

A man asked Ibn al-Mubārak (d. 181/797) about poetry. Ibn al-Mubārak told him, 'Do not say it.' He said, 'But you say it.' Ibn al-Mubārak said, 'Have you been commanded to follow me in my faults (*masāwiʾī*)?'[144]

136 Aḥmad, *ʿIlal* 3:490 *2:280* (< ʿAl.); Abū Nuʿaym, *Ḥilyah* 4:226.
137 Ibn Abī Shaybah, *Muṣannaf* 13:576–7 *12:414–15*; Abū Nuʿaym, *Ḥilyah* 5:143.
138 Wakīʿ, *Zuhd* 1:307, 2:593; Aḥmad, *Zuhd*, 261 *320*; Abū Khaythamah, *ʿIlm*, no 20.
139 Ibn al-Mubārak, *Zuhd*, no 842.
140 Abū Nuʿaym, *Ḥilyah* 5:77.
141 Abū al-Qāsim al-Baghawī, *Jaʿdīyāt* 2:37.
142 Bukhārī, *al-adab*, *bāb mā yukrahu an yakūna al-ghālib ʿalá al-insān al-shiʿr*, nos 6154–5; Muslim, *al-shiʿr*, nos 2257–8; Abū Dāwūd, *al-adab* 87, *bāb mā jāʾa fī al-shiʿr*, no 5009; Tirmidhī, *al-adab* 71, *bāb mā jāʾa la-an yamtaliʾa jawf aḥadikum qayḥan*, nos 2851–2; Ibn Mājah, *al-adab* 42, *bāb mā kuriha min al-shiʿr*, nos 3759–60. See also G. H. A. Juynboll, *Encyclopedia*, 118, with attribution to al-Awzāʿī (Syrian, d. 157/773–4?). Same attributed to the Prophet but also to ʿAbd Allāh ibn Masʿūd, ʿUthmān, Abū Hurayrah, ʿUmar, and Masrūq, Ibn Abī Shaybah, *Muṣannaf* 8:719–21 8:512–14.
143 Ibn al-Mubārak, *Zuhd*, no 413.
144 Marrūdhī, *Akhbār*, 167, no 286; sim., no 287.

To the contrary, collections of renunciant sayings usually include some poetry, also some express defences of it. ʿAsʿas ibn Salāmah (Basran, *fl.* 7th cent.) recited some to his companions, who at first said 'What are you doing with poetry?' but afterwards wept as no one had seen them weep before.[145] Saʿīd ibn al-Musayyib said of someone who deprecated poetry that he was following the austerity (*nusk*) of the *ʿajam* (non-Arabs, especially Persians).[146] Al-Shaʿbī said, 'Abū Bakr was a poet. ʿUmar was a poet. ʿAlī declaimed poetry, and was the most given of them to poetry.'[147] The littérateur Abū ʿUbayd softened the Prophet hadith about pus as applying to one who is pre-occupied from spending time with the Qur'an and hadith. 'If the Qur'an prevails with him, then in our view this one's insides are not filled with poetry.'[148] Aḥmad ibn Ḥanbal approved of a similar comment by al-Naḍr ibn Shumayl (Khurasani, d. 204/819–20) on the same hadith report: 'Our insides have not filled up with poetry: in them are the Qur'an, *ʿilm* (hadith), and recollection (*dhikr*). This is for those Arabs who can do nothing well except poetry.' Isḥāq ibn Rāhūyah warmly agreed.[149]

Against laughter

It may be that nothing cut off early Muslim renunciants from normal society more than their hostility to laughter. Al-Khaḍir instructed Moses, 'Avoid disputatiousness, do not walk without a need, do not laugh except in wonder, stick to your house, and weep over your sin.'[150] ('Wonder' here translates *ʿajab*. In hadith literature, it is often used sarcastically, of amazing effrontery. Here, I take it, the intention is to rule out mockery.) ʿĪsá reproached his disciples for two characters, 'laughter for other than wonder and awakening without having stayed up.'[151] A Companion reminisced of sitting with the prophet Muḥammad, 'They would chat with one another, taking up the matter of the *jāhilīyah* (the period before Islam). They would laugh while he would smile.'[152] Several reports stress that the

145 Ibn al-Mubārak, *Zuhd*, no 232.
146 ʿAbd al-Malik ibn Ḥabīb, *Tārīkh*, 161.
147 Aḥmad, *ʿIlal* 2:244 *1:280*.
148 Abū ʿUbayd, *Gharīb al-ḥadīth* 1:36–7.
149 Kawsaj, *Masāʾil* 2:530.
150 Aḥmad, *Zuhd*, 61 *79*.
151 Ibn Abī Shaybah, *Muṣannaf* 13:197 *12:137*.
152 Muslim, *al-masājid* 52, *bāb faḍl al-julūs fī al-muṣallāh baʿda al-ṣubḥ*, no 670; *al-faḍāʾil* 17, *bāb tabassumuhu wa-ḥusn ʿishratih*, no 2322. Sim., Tirmidhī, *al-istiʾdhān* 104, *bāb mā jāʾa fī inshād al-shiʿr*, no 2850. See Juynboll, *Encyclopedia*, 566.

Prophet's laughter was just smiling.[153] Or it is said that the Prophet was not seen laughing after the descent of Q. 53:59–60 ('And do you then marvel at this discourse, And do you laugh, and do you not weep?').[154] 'Much laughter kills the heart', he warned.[155]

Muʿādh ibn Jabal (d. Syria, 18/639–40) said, 'Three things expose one to abhorrence: laughter without wonder, sleep without staying up, and eating without hunger.'[156] Ibn Masʿūd said, 'I am amazed by one who laughs behind whom is the Fire and one who hopes (*muʾammil*) behind whom is death.'[157] Similarly, ʿAbd Allāh ibn Thaʿlabah (d. 89/707–8?) said, 'You laugh when your shroud may have come out of the fuller's.'[158] ʿAlī (d. Medina, 40/661) advocated impassiveness: 'Suppress anger, laugh little—let not minds spit it out (*lā tamujjahu al-qulūb*).'[159] ʿAlī Zayn al-ʿĀbidīn (d. 93/711–12?) apparently saw in laughter a cause of forgetting: 'Whoever laughs a laugh has spat out a piece of knowledge.'[160] The Kufan brothers al-Rabīʿ and Ribʿī ibnā Ḥirāsh (*fl.* later 7th cent.) would not show their teeth laughing till they knew whether they were bound for heaven or hell. They finally smiled and laughed as their corpses were being washed.[161] Their Basran contemporary Ghazwān ibn Ghazwān resolved that God should not see him laugh till he knew which realm was his.[162] He did not laugh for 40 years.[163] He said, 'The believer's laughter is only inattention on his part.'[164] Asked why he would not laugh, he said '*Hah hah*—what should I do with this?'[165]

---

153 Tirmidhī, *al-manāqib* 22, *bāb fī bashāshat al-nabī*, no 3642; *al-manāqib* 24, *fī ṣifat al-nabī*, no 3645.

154 Hannād, *Zuhd* 1:271; Ibn Abī Shaybah, *Muṣannaf* 13:234 *12:165*.

155 Abū ʿUbayd, *Khuṭab*, 196; Bukhārī, *Adab*, 253; Ibn Mājah, *al-zuhd* 19, *bāb al-ḥuzn wa-al-bukāʾ*, no 4193. At end of longer speech, Ibn Mājah, *al-zuhd* 24, *bāb al-waraʿ wa-al-taqwá*, no 4217; Hannād, *Zuhd* 2:501, 553. Sim. attributed to al-Ḥasan al-Baṣrī: Ibn Saʿd, *Ṭabaqāt* 7/1:124 *7:170*. Sim. attributed to Sufyān al-Thawrī: Abū Nuʿaym, *Ḥilyah* 7:36.

156 Aḥmad, *Zuhd*, 183 *228*.

157 Ibn al-Mubārak, *Zuhd*, no 323 < Nuʿaym.

158 Ibn Qutaybah, *ʿUyūn al-akhbār* 2:359; Ibn Abī al-Dunyā, *Qiṣar al-amal*, 74; Abū Nuʿaym, *Ḥilyah* 6:245.

159 Ibn Abī Shaybah, *Muṣannaf* 13:284 *12:202*.

160 Aḥmad, *Zuhd*, 166 *208* (< ʿAl.)

161 Samʿānī, *Ansāb* 3:311.

162 Aḥmad, *Zuhd*, 206 *255*.

163 Ibn Saʿd, *Ṭabaqāt* 7/1:158 *7:217*.

164 Aḥmad, *Zuhd*, 279 *340*.

165 Aḥmad, *Zuhd*, 206 *256*.

Bakr ibn ʿAbd Allāh (Basran, d. 106/724–5) said, 'Who sins laughing will enter hell weeping.'[166] Al-Ḥasan al-Baṣrī did not laugh for thirty years or joke for forty.[167] 'How can we laugh when we do not know whether God will accept our works?'[168] He told the story,

> One man said to his brother, 'Brother, have you heard that you are going to the Fire [allusion to Q. 19:71]?' He said, 'Yes.' He said, 'Have you heard that you are going out of it?' He said, 'No.' He said, 'So what is there to laugh about?' The man was not seen laughing until he died.[169]

According to Shahr ibn Ḥawshab (Syrian, d. 111/729–30), Adam did not laugh for 100 years after one son killed the other.[170] Ṭalḥah ibn Muṣarrif (Kufan, d. 112/730–1 or after) swore not to laugh till he crossed *al-sirāṭ* ('the path', alluding to Q. 1:6–7, evidently interpreted as the path into Paradise).[171] ʿAṭāʾ al-Salīmī did not laugh or look up to heaven for 40 years.[172] Hishām al-Dastuwāʾī (Basran, d. 154/770–1) said, 'It is amazing that a knowledgeable man should be able to laugh.'[173] Al-Awzāʿī (d. 157/773–4?) the Syrian jurisprudent said, 'We used to laugh and joke. But now that our example is being followed (*idhā ṣirnā yuqtadá binā*), I don't think we may even smile.'[174] Someone said of him, 'I never saw al-Awzāʿī laughing out loud, turning to look at anything, or weeping. When he took up recollection of the hereafter and the like, I would say to myself, "Is there anyone in the session who is not weeping in his heart?" But that was not seen on him.'[175] Impassiveness seems again the predominant value.

Sufyān al-Thawrī said, 'It used to be said, "Beware of overeating (*biṭnah*), for it hardens hearts; keep back knowledge (*ikẓimū al-ʿilm*); and do not laugh much, for hearts spit it out (*tamujjuh*)."'[176] He rebuked a qadi for laughing, with the effect

166 Abū Nuʿaym, *Ḥilyah* 2:229, 6:185 (< ʿAl., *Zuhd*).
167 Abū Nuʿaym, *Ḥilyah* 8:239–40.
168 Abū Nuʿaym, *Ḥilyah* 2:134.
169 Ibn al-Mubārak, *Zuhd*, no 311; another version, Ibn Abī Shaybah, *Muṣannaf* 13:500 *12:360*.
170 Abū Nuʿaym, *Ḥilyah* 6:63.
171 Abū Nuʿaym, *Ḥilyah* 5:15.
172 Abū Nuʿaym, *Ḥilyah* 6:221.
173 Abū Nuʿaym, *Ḥilyah* 6:279, perhaps < lost § of Ibn al-Mubārak, *Zuhd*, recension of Nuʿaym.
174 Abū Nuʿaym, *Ḥilyah* 6:143.
175 Ibn Abī Ḥātim, *Jarḥ* 1:217.
176 Ibn al-Mubārak, *Zuhd*, no 269. Alternatively, 'Do not overeat, for it hardens the heart, suppress laughter, and do not laugh much, for it kills hearts': Abū Nuʿaym, *Ḥilyah* 7:36. The main point of holding back knowledge would have been to avoid conceitedness, but there are also expressions of concern not to spread it among persons not ready for it. For example, Ibn Masʿūd

seen on his face till he died.[177] ʿAwn ibn Muʿammar (*fl.* mid-8th cent.) related from al-Khiḍr the advice not to walk without purpose, laugh without wonder, or try to make sinners ashamed of their sin.[178] Wuhayb ibn al-Ward (Meccan, *fl.* mid-8th cent.) resolved not to laugh till dying.[179] He wondered that someone knowledgeable could laugh, knowing of the terrors of the Resurrection.[180] Ḥammād ibn Salamah (Basran, d. 167/783–4) was never seen laughing.[181]

ʿAbd al-Raḥmān ibn Abī al-Zinād (Medinese cl., d. Baghdad, 174/790–1) had someone reciting to him who did not observe the case endings (*yalḥan*). Those who were about laughed. After the man left, though, Ibn Abī al-Zinād said, 'Are you not ashamed of this?'[182] ʿAbd Allāh ibn Thaʿlabah (Basran, *fl.* later 8th cent.) said, 'How can you laugh when you do not know whether your grave clothes have not already left the fuller (*qaṣṣār*)?'[183] Al-Fuḍayl ibn ʿIyāḍ (d. Mecca, 187/803) said, 'In you are two traits that come of ignorance: laughter without wonder and getting up in the morning without having stayed up late into the night (*sahr*).'[184] Abū ʿAlī al-Rāzī said, 'I associated with al-Fuḍayl for 30 years and never saw him laugh or smile, save the day when his son ʿAlī died. I asked him about that, so he told me, "God loved this affair, so I have loved it."'[185] Yūsuf ibn Asbāṭ (l. Antioch, d. 195/810–11) did not laugh for 30 years or jest (*yamzaḥu*) for 40.[186] Ismāʿīl ibn ʿUlayyah (Kufan cl., d. Baghdad, 193/809) was not seen to laugh for 14 years or smile for seven.[187] The grandson of Yaḥyá ibn Saʿīd al-Qaṭṭān (Basran, d. 198/813) said, 'Abū Saʿīd did not use to joke or laugh save smiling. I do not know that I ever saw him laugh out loud (*qahqaha*).'[188] ʿAbd al-Raḥmān ibn Mahdī (d. Basra, 198/814) refused to relate hadith for two months after someone in his session laughed.[189] Al-Ḥusayn ibn ʿAlī al-Juʿfī (Kufan cl., d. 203/818–19?) was never seen

said, 'A man may relate some hadith so that there hears it someone whose reason the understanding of that hadith does not reach, so that it is a trial for him' (ʿAbd al-Razzāq, *Muṣannaf* 11:286).

177 Abū Nuʿaym, *Ḥilyah* 7:51.
178 Aḥmad, *ʿIlal* 2:373 *1:333*.
179 Abū Nuʿaym, *Ḥilyah* 8:141, 152.
180 Abū Nuʿaym, *Ḥilyah* 8:141.
181 Abū Nuʿaym, *Ḥilyah* 6:250.
182 Ibn Saʿd, *Ṭabaqāt* 5:308 *5:416*.
183 Abū Nuʿaym, *Ḥilyah* 6:246.
184 Sulamī, *Ṭabaqāt*, 11.
185 Abū Nuʿaym, *Ḥilyah* 8:100.
186 Abū Nuʿaym, *Ḥilyah* 8:240.
187 Al-Khaṭīb al-Baghdādī, *Tārīkh* 6:235 *7:205*.
188 Ibn Abī Ḥātim, *Jarḥ* 1:250.
189 Abū Nuʿaym, *Ḥilyah* 9:6.

laughing or smiling.[190] ʿUbayd Allāh ibn Mūsá al-ʿAbsī (Kufan Shiʿi, d. 213/828–9) was never seen raising his head or laughing.[191]

There was some resistance. Widely reported hadith said that the Prophet would laugh till his molars showed, although this was also often glossed as a peculiar way of smiling.[192] Ibn ʿUmar was asked, 'Did the Prophet's companions use to laugh?' He said, 'Yes, the faith in their hearts being greater than the mountains.'[193] The suggestion is that it was safe for them to indulge in laughter, although doubtfully for anyone in the decadent age to follow. The Kufan al-Shaʿbī joked in his house. When questioned, he said, '*Qurrā*' inside, *qurrā*' outside—we'd die of gloominess.'[194] He evidently felt that the importance of setting a good example need govern only public behaviour. Someone said, 'When we went to Muḥammad (ibn Sīrīn, d. 110/729), we laughed as long as we liked; when we went to al-Ḥasan, we wept as much as we liked.'[195] Wahb ibn Munabbih heard it was better to laugh and admit one's sin than to weep and be a hypocrite.[196] A very few traditionists and renunciants were notable for lightheartedness. ʿAbd Allāh ibn Abī Zakarīyāʾ (Syrian worshipper, d. 119/737) 'was among the most cheerful people and the greatest as to smiling.'[197] Abū Nuʿaym al-Faḍl ibn Dukayn (major Kufan traditionist, d. 219/834?) was given to joking.[198]

Sticking to what is important

Because the point of austerity was mainly moral, early ascetics are often associated with measures to conceal their austerities from public view. It has already been mentioned how some wore wool underneath more respectable fabrics so as to suffer from scratchiness unseen. Nighttime devotions have been mentioned already, with stress on their implication for lack of sleep. The main reason for nighttime devotions was to perform them out of people's sight so that one was sure they were directed at God, not acquiring a popular reputation for piety. The

190 Ibn Ḥajar, *Tahdhīb* 2:358.
191 ʿIjlī, *Tārīkh al-thiqāt*, 319.
192 The hadith literature concerning laughter is surveyed by Ammann, *Vorbild und Vernunft*, chap. 3.
193 ʿAbd al-Razzāq, *Muṣannaf* 11:327, 451.
194 Abū Nuʿaym, *Ḥilyah* 4:324.
195 ʿAbd al-Malik ibn Ḥabīb, *Tārīkh*, 169.
196 Abū Nuʿaym, *Ḥilyah* 4:28.
197 Abū Nuʿaym, *Ḥilyah* 5:150–1.
198 Yaḥyá ibn Maʿīn, *apud* Ibn Ḥajar, *Tahdhīb* 8:276.

Prophet said, 'The one who (recites) the Qur'an openly is like the one who (gives) alms openly, while the one who (recites) the Qur'an secretly is like the one who (gives) alms secretly.'[199] Ibn Mas'ūd said, 'Ritual prayer at night is worth more than by daytime as secret almsgiving is worth more than public.'[200]

Others anyway sought to avoid notice. 'Amr ibn 'Utbah (Kufan *mukhaḍram*, d. dur. caliphate of 'Uthmān, 23–35/644–56) insisted on serving his comrades and so minded their animals. When they found him shaded by his own cloud, he asked them to keep it secret.[201] Here the point is not to keep secret his devotions but God's honouring him by a miracle. Sa'd ibn Abī Waqqāṣ (d. 55/674–5?), one of the ten Companions promised Paradise, would pray quickly in public but at length at home, explaining, 'We are imams who are followed.'[202] That is, it would not do equally for people to remark his not praying in the mosque and to remark his performing strenuous supererogatory prayers. (More will be said about supererogatory prayers in the next chapter.) 'Abd Allāh ibn 'Amr (d. 77/696–7?) would close the door and weep till his eyes secreted a white substance (*ramaṣat 'aynāh*).[203] Not even his wife knew how he had recited the Qur'an till he was on his deathbed.[204] 'Alī ibn al-Ḥusayn Zayn al-'Ābidīn (d. 93/711–12?) gave food to the poor in secret, which was missed on his death.[205] Ibrāhīm al-Nakha'ī would hide the Qur'an when someone came to his house.[206] 'If a servant hides his worship as he hides his immorality (*fujūr*),' he said, 'God will make that apparent on him.'[207]

No one in the army prayed more than Ibn Muḥayrīz in public till he became famous for it, whereupon he cut back.[208] He said, 'If you can know without being known, ask without being asked, and walk without anyone's walking after you, do so.'[209] Muwarriq al-'Ijlī (Basran, d. after 100/718–19) said, 'I do not wish to be known for obeying him by anyone else.'[210] Al-Ḥasan al-Baṣrī said, 'What you do

199 Aḥmad, *Musnad* 4:151 *28:598* (Homsi *isnād*); sim., 4:201 *29:332–3*.
200 Ibn Abī Shaybah, *Muṣannaf* 13:298 *12:212–13*; Ibn al-Mubārak, *Zuhd*, no 23. Also attributed to the Prophet: Ibn al-Mubārak, *Zuhd*, no 25 (< Ibn Ṣā'id).
201 Aḥmad, *Zuhd*, 353, 354 *423, 424* (both < 'Al.).
202 Ibn al-Mubārak, *Zuhd*, no 1468.
203 Abū Nu'aym, *Ḥilyah* 1:290 (< Aḥ., *Zuhd*).
204 Abū Nu'aym, *Ḥilyah* 4:115 (< 'Al., *Zuhd*).
205 Aḥmad, *Zuhd*, 166 *208–9* (< 'Al.).
206 Wakī', *Zuhd* 2:592; Ibn al-Mubārak, *Zuhd*, nos 1100–1; Aḥmad, *Zuhd*, 365 *437*; Abū Nu'aym, *Ḥilyah* 4:220.
207 Ibn Abī Shaybah, *Muṣannaf* 13:550 *12:396*.
208 Abū Nu'aym, *Ḥilyah* 5:141, < lost § of Aḥmad, *Zuhd* (< 'Al.).
209 Ibn Qutaybah, *'Uyūn* 2:358.
210 Ibn Abī al-Dunyā, *Tawāḍu'*, 113.

is closer to you (*awlâ bik*) than what you say, and what you do secretly than what you do publicly.'[211] Muḥammad ibn Wāsiʿ quoted the wise man Luqmān to his son: 'Beware of God and do not show the people that you fear God in order that they honour you for that while your heart is reprobate.'[212] Hilāl ibn Yisāf (Kufan cl., *fl.* early 8th cent.) quoted the prophet ʿĪsá: 'When one of you is fasting, let him anoint his beard and wipe his lips so that (when) he goes out to the people, they say he is not fasting.'[213] Hārūn ibn Riʾāb al-Asadī (Basran, *fl.* early 8th cent.) was commended for keeping secret his renunciation, as in wearing wool under another garment.[214] ʿAbd al-Wāḥid ibn Zayd (Kufan, *fl.* early 8th cent.), Maymūn ibn Mihrān (Mesopotamian, d. 117/735–736), and in the next generation later Jaʿfar al-Ṣādiq (Medinese, d. 148/765) also wore wool under other clothes to hide their renunciation.[215] Someone recollected of Dāwūd al-Ṭāʾī (Kufan, d. 165/781–2?), 'He did not resemble the renunicants (*qurrāʾ*). He had on a long black *qalansuwah* such as traders wear.'[216] (But Dāwūd was also known for unkempt hair, telling someone that he was preoccupied from combing his beard.[217])

Some renunciants even advocated public carelessness to avoid acquiring a reputation for scrupulosity. The Damascene Bilāl ibn Saʿd (d. 86–96/705–15?) knew persons who were busy by day and laughed with one another but were monks by night.[218] Ibn Sīrīn is said to have laughed by day but wept all night.[219] Al-Ḥasan al-Baṣrī said that some would not remove a nuisance from the way (the usual reference is to dung) for fear of repute (*shuhrah*).[220] In somewhat the same spirit, Ibn ʿUmar is said to have told his son, on seeing him in an ugly, mean garment, 'Do not wear this, for it is the garment of repute (*shuhrah*).'[221] Al-Aʿmash (Kufan, d. 148/765–6?) would have stayed up after the evening prayer if not for repute (*shuhrah*).[222] Wuhayb

---

211 Aḥmad, *Zuhd*, 282 *343*.

212 Aḥmad, *Zuhd*, 49, 105 *64 130*; Abū ʿUbayd, *Khuṭab*, 178–9; Ibn al-Mubārak, *Zuhd*, no 192.

213 Aḥmad, *Zuhd*, 57 *74*; cf. Matt. 6:17–18, 'But thou, when thou fastest, anoint thine head, and wash thy face; That thou appear not unto men to fast, but unto thy Father which is in secret: and thy Father, which seeth in secret, shall reward thee openly.'

214 Abū Nuʿaym, *Ḥilyah* 3:55.

215 ʿAbd al-Wāḥid ibn Zayd, Abū Nuʿaym, *Ḥilyah* 6:232; Maymūn ibn Mihrān, Abū Nuʿaym, *Ḥilyah* 4:91–2; Jaʿfar al-Ṣādiq, Abū Nuʿaym, *Ḥilyah* 3:193.

216 Ibn Saʿd, *Ṭabaqāt* 6:255 *6:367*.

217 Abū Nuʿaym, *Ḥilyah* 7:339.

218 Ibn al-Mubārak, *Zuhd*, no 144.

219 Aḥmad, *Zuhd*, 307 *374* (< ʿAl.); Abū Nuʿaym, *Ḥilyah* 2:263, 272, 274.

220 Ibn al-Mubārak, *Zuhd*, no 138.

221 According to Sulaymān al-Shaybānī (Kufan, d. *ca* 140/757–8): Ibn Abī al-Dunyā, *Tawāḍuʿ*, 128–9.

222 Aḥmad, *ʿIlal* 1:233 *1:101*.

al-Makkī (d. 153/771–2) recommended such works (i.e., ritual prayers) without excess as would not make anyone suspect that one did more than the required, with only commanding the good (*al-amr bi-al-maʿrūf*) to be public.[223]

Some calls for secrecy have to do especially with scholarship, which normally took place in the mosque, hence in public view. Al-Ḥārith ibn Qays (Kufan *mukhaḍram*, d. *ca* 40/661) would get up and leave if two men met with him.[224] The Companion Faḍālah ibn ʿUbayd (d. 53/672–3?), qadi for Damascus under Muʿāwiyah, said, 'If you are able to learn without being known, to hear without speaking, do so.'[225] ʿAbd al-Raḥmān ibn Yazīd said to ʿAlqamah (Medinese, d. bef. 86/705), 'Won't you got to the mosque for people to sit with you and for you to give opinions?' ʿAlqamah said, 'I dislike that anyone walk behind me and that it be said, "This is ʿAlqamah."'[226] Abū al-ʿĀliyah (Basran, d. 90/709) said he had learnt writing and the Qur'an without his wife's knowing it, ink never being seen on his clothing.[227] He would get up if more than four sat by him.[228] Sufyān al-Thawrī said, 'I have never seen renunciation of anything less than in leadership (*riyāsah*). You will see a man renounce money, clothing, and food, but when he is challenged as to leadership, he defends and attacks.'[229]

Frivolity was severely disapproved of. The Prophet said, 'Woe betide whoever speaks a lie in order to make people laugh. Woe betide him, woe!'[230] Ibn Masʿūd said, 'If I mocked a dog, I should fear to become a dog.'[231] When his daughter asked him if she might go out to play, al-Rabīʿ ibn Khuthaym refused to have it written of him that he had commanded his daughter to play.[232] Al-Musayyab ibn Rāfiʿ (blind Kufan, d. 105/723–4) said, 'I despise a man I see unoccupied, involved in the work neither of the afterlife nor of this world.'[233]

---

223 Abū Nuʿaym, *Ḥilyah* 8:152–3.
224 Ibn Abī Shaybah, *Muṣannaf* 13:420 *12:301.*
225 Bukhārī, *al-Tārīkh al-kabīr* 3:238.
226 Al-Muʿāfá ibn ʿImrān, 210, no 44.
227 Abū Nuʿaym, *Ḥilyah* 2:217.
228 Abū Nuʿaym, *Ḥilyah* 2:218.
229 Marrūdhī, *Waraʿ*, 96 *77–8.*
230 Ibn al-Mubārak, *Zuhd*, no 733; Tirmidhī, *al-zuhd* 10, *bāb fīman takallama bi-kalimah yuḍḥiku bihā al-nās*, no 2315.
231 Ibn al-Mubārak, *Zuhd*, no 741.
232 Ibn al-Mubārak, *Zuhd*, no 374; Ibn Saʿd, *Ṭabaqāt* 6:131 *6:188*; Ibn Abī Shaybah, *Muṣannaf* 14:14–15 *12:429*; Marrūdhī, *Waraʿ*, 74 *58.*
233 Aḥmad, *Zuhd*, 159 *199*. Also attributed to Ibn Masʿūd: Ibn al-Mubārak, *Zuhd*, no 741; Wakīʿ, *Zuhd* 2:652.

Chess and backgammon are condemned. The Prophet said that a chess player was accursed, a spectator like an eater of pork.[234] According to an early Shiʿi source, ʿAlī struck backgammon-players with his whip, denounced various games, and ended with saying, 'Chess is like backgammon.'[235] According to Sunni sources, he suggested that being intent on chess pieces was like bowing to idols and forbade saluting chess players, implying that they were apostates; similarly Ibrāhīm al-Nakhaʿī.[236] Muḥammad ibn Kaʿb (Medinese, also l. Kufa, d. 120/737–8?), on being asked about a chess player, said. 'The least that will be on the Day of the Resurrection is that he is reviewed along with the people of frivolity (*ahl al-bāṭil*).'[237] ʿAbd al-Raḥmān ibn Khālid (governor of Egypt, d. 127/744–5) heard a voice from heaven announce, 'God forgives the people of the earth except for the possessors of kings. One of them says, "I have killed him, by God" when he has not killed him; when he has not died, by God.'[238] (English 'checkmate' is from Perso-Arabic *shāhak māt*, 'Your king has died.')

Jaʿfar al-Ṣādiq (d. Medina, 148/765), asked what was *maysir* (condemned by the Qur'an along with wine, Q. 2:219, 5:90–1), said it was chess (along with backgammon, in a variant).[239] Concerning Q. 22:30, he said the *awthān* to be avoided (usually interpreted as 'idols') meant chess, while *zūr* (usually 'falsehood') meant singing.[240] As for the schools of law, Mālik (d. Medina, 179/795) disliked all that was played by way of backgammon and 14 (a board game, for Ibn ʿUmar once found a family member playing it and so broke it over his head[241]). 'He disliked chess and said, "It is more distracting and worse (*hiya alhá wa-asharr*)."' However, he did permit saluting a group of players.[242] (It appears that opposition to chess was especially a Kufan position, the early Basran tradition being more relaxed.) Al-Shaybānī (d. Ranbuyah, 189/804–5) said that chess was disliked along with backgammon and 14.[243] Aḥmad ibn Ḥanbal (d. Baghdad, 241/855) said that

234 Marrūdhī, *Wara*ʿ, 92 *73*; sim., 97 *79*.
235 Zayd ibn ʿAlī, *Corpus iuris*, 296, no 1000.
236 Marrūdhī, *Wara*ʿ, 92 *74*; Ḥarb al-Kirmānī, *Masāʾil*, 338.
237 Ḥarb al-Kirmānī, *Masāʾil*, 338.
238 Ḥarb al-Kirmānī, *Masāʾil*, 337. Sim. attributed to Prophet: Ḥarb, *loc. cit.*; Ibn Ḥibbān, *Majrūḥīn* 2:297. Sim. attributed to ʿAbd al-Malik ibn ʿUmayr (Kufan, d. 136/754): Marrūdhī, *Wara*ʿ, 93 *75*.
239 Kulaynī, *Kāfī* 6:435–6, *al-ashribah, bāb al-nard wa-al-shaṭranj*.
240 Kulaynī, *Kāfī* 6:435, *al-ashribah, bāb al-nard wa-al-shaṭranj*.
241 Marrūdhī, *Wara*ʿ, 93 *75*.
242 Ibn Abī Zayd, *Jāmi*ʿ, 263–4.
243 Shaybānī, *al-Jāmiʿ al-ṣaghīr*, in margin of Abū Yūsuf, *Kharāj*, 111.

a chess player was reportedly accursed, a spectator like an eater of pork.[244] It was good to upset a chess board if they would not listen to counsel.[245]

Chess also had its defenders, of course. Al-Shāfiʿī (d. 204/820) thought it lighter than backgammon.[246] Al-Māwardī lists five Companions and six Followers reported to have played chess.[247] He concludes that Mālik outright forbade testimony from chessplayers, Abū Ḥanīfah considered it so discouraged as to be forbidden, but that al-Shāfiʿī held that it just depended on how one played.[248]

Good works: the impractical dimension

Concomitant with concern for attention to God was a certain indifference to good works in the world. Good works are not unknown in the renunciant tradition. Uways al-Qaranī (d. 37/657) 'would give alms with his clothing till he sat naked, not finding enough to come to the Friday assembly.'[249] Muwarriq al-ʿIjlī (Basran, d. after 100/718–19) said, 'If not for the poor, I would not expose myself to trade.'[250] That is, although he would have preferred to be free to practise his devotions all the time, he would continue to trade for the sake of giving alms. ʿĀmir ibn ʿAbd Allāh (Medinese, d. 121/738–9) often gave away 10,000 dirhams in a day.[251] Ḥassān ibn Abī Sinān (Basran, *fl.* mid-8th cent.) once had his partner weigh out 200 dirhams for a beggar woman he feared might otherwise turn to prostitution.[252] At that, stress would be laid on the benefit of almsgiving to the giver rather than worldly benefit to anyone else. Al-Ḥasan al-Baṣrī praised the one who, on coming to his evening meal, says, 'I will not put all of this in my belly: let me give some of it to God', and so gives some away in alms, even though the one giving alms is more needy than the one receiving.[253]

To the contrary, however, there are many parallels to the comment of Kaʿb al-Aḥbār (Yemeni, d. Homs, 32/652–3?), 'By him in whose hand is my soul, I should prefer to weep from fear of God until my tears flow down my cheeks to

244 Marrūdhī, *Waraʿ*, 92 *73*.
245 Abū Dāwūd, *Masāʾil*, 278–9.
246 Shāfiʿī, *Umm* 6:213 *7:515*.
247 Māwardī, *Ḥāwī* 21:192–3 (*k. al-shahādāt al-thānī*).
248 Māwardī, *Ḥāwī* 21:194.
249 Aḥmad, *Zuhd*, 346 *415* (< ʿAl.).
250 Aḥmad, *Zuhd*, 314 *381*. Sim. attributed to Ḥassān ibn Abī Sinān: Abū Nuʿaym, *Ḥilyah* 3:115–16.
251 Abū Nuʿaym, *Ḥilyah* 3:166.
252 Abū Nuʿaym, *Ḥilyah* 3:116.
253 Abū Nuʿaym, *Ḥilyah* 2:134.

giving in alms a mountain of gold.'[254] Abū Hurayrah (d. 58/677–8?) said that saying ten times 'There is no god but God alone, without a partner; the kingdom is his; to him be praise, he having power over everything' was worth freeing a slave.[255] The Kufan Abū 'Ubaydah ibn 'Abd Allāh ibn Mas'ūd (d. after 80/699–700) held that there was less reward for standing in the road, giving a dinar to everyone who came, than for standing there saying *Allāhu akbar*.[256] More will be said about fighting the holy war (*jihād*) in chapter 7 on politics, but it seems appropriate to quote Sufyān al-Thawrī here that it was better to recite the Qur'an than to go raiding on the frontier.[257]

254 Abū Nu'aym, *Ḥilyah* 5:366 (< 'Al., *Zuhd*).
255 'Abd al-Razzāq, *Muṣannaf* 11:293; Muslim, *al-dhikr wa-al-du'ā'* 10, *bāb faḍl al-tahlīl*, no 2693, freeing four sons of Ishmael; also attributed to Ibn Mas'ūd, Ibn Abī Shaybah, *Muṣannaf* 10:310 *10:96*.
256 Aḥmad, *Zuhd*, 393 *470*; sim. attributed to Abū al-Dardā' at 137 *170*.
257 Abū Nu'aym, *Ḥilyah* 7:65.

Chapter 4: Supererogatory forms of required worship

Reflecting typologies popular in the 1960s, Marshall Hodgson sketches

> the *paradigm-tracing* component in personal piety, when ultimacy is sought in enduring cosmic patterns, in recurrent *nature* (including social nature). ... For instance, as the worshipper faces Mecca in the mosque and bows, he sets himself symbolically in the right relation to God—submission; and to the other Muslims—all facing the same way; and so ever again restores some cosmic harmony to his life. (Some writers speak as if this were religion par excellence.)[1]

When the Muslims were a minority, as everywhere in the first two centuries, some places till much later, distinguishing their community from others must have been equally important. At any rate, the renunciants were intensively interested in manifesting their submission to God. Of the five chief Islamic rituals (ritual purity, prayer, the alms tax, the Ramadan fast, and pilgrimage to Mecca), prayer suited them best, perhaps because it was the least individualistic, the most egalitarian. But renunciants took them all as occasions to do more than they were required to.

Principal devotional practices: ritual purity and ritual prayer

Muslims make themselves ritually pure in order to perform further actions, most prominently the required ritual prayer. There are two forms of ritual ablutions, the minor (*wuḍū'*) and the major (*ghusl*). The former is the familiar activity of washing the arms to the elbows, then parts of the head, then the feet, whereas the latter requires that the whole body be covered with water. Ritual impurity is not communicable from person to person, so whether or not one is ritually pure has no effect on social activity.[2] A separate concern is to remove various pollutants, such as urine on the clothing one will pray in and the saliva of a dog that has licked the plate one will eat from.

Occasionally, the renunciant literature remarks someone who restored his ritual purity more often than just before performing the ritual prayer, touching a

1 Hodgson, *Venture* 1:363, naming Mircea Eliade and Clifford Geertz in a note.
2 Surveys include Gauvain, 'Ritual rewards', 331–42, and Freidenreich, 'Holiness and impurity', esp. 13–14. See also Maghen 'Much ado about *wuḍū'*', Katz, *Body of text*, and Reinhart, 'Impurity/No Danger'.

https://doi.org/10.1515/9783110617962-005

Qur'an, or some other religious work. The Companion Ibn ʿUmar (d. 73/693?) was said to have always sat in a state of ritual purity, extending readiness to pray to readiness to discuss religion.[3] Al-Ḥasan al-Baṣrī (d. 110/728) asserted that former generations had maintained constant ritual purity, not merely renewing it in time for the next ritual prayer. He probably had in mind the coming of the Last Judgement, or at least their death hours, which they wanted to encounter in a state of purity.[4] A recent convert named Yassá who had become a good Muslim said, 'God told Moses by inspiration, "If death comes to you when you are not in a state of ritual purity, do not blame anyone but yourself."'[5] Al-Ḥasan is also quoted as saying, 'They used to prefer to recollect God in a state of ritual purity', referring to the repetition of pious phrases.[6] This is exactly opposed by what Kaʿb al-Aḥbār (d. Homs, 32/652–3?) related of how the prophet Moses asked God whether to recollect him even in a state of major ritual impurity or in the latrine. God told him, 'Recollect me in every condition.'[7]

There is clear hadith on the effectiveness of ritual ablution at washing away sin. Marion Katz cites this hadith report:

> The Prophet said: When someone stands to perform *wuḍūʾ* and washes his hands, the sins flow out of his hands; when he washes out his mouth, the sins flow out of his mouth; when he blows water out of his nose, the sins flow out of his nose, and so on until he washes his feet.[8]

Renunciants occasionally called for ritual ablutions to cancel out foul speech. Ibrāhīm al-Nakhaʿī (Kufan, d. 96/714) called for ritual ablutions after someone had disparaged another man in his absence (constituting *ghībah*).[9] Hannād ibn al-Sarī mentions a Meccan Follower who called for ritual ablutions after some fellows had indulged in insulting an effeminate.[10] There is also some suggestion in hadith

3 Ibn al-Mubārak, *Zuhd*, no 291.
4 Ibn al-Mubārak, *Zuhd*, no 293.
5 Abū ʿUbayd, *Khuṭab*, 130–1.
6 Aḥmad, *Zuhd*, 258 *315*.
7 Abū ʿUbayd, *Khuṭab*, 128–9; sim., Aḥmad, *Zuhd*, 68 *86*.
8 Katz, 'The study of Islamic ritual', 118, citing ʿAbd al-Razzāq, *Muṣannaf* 1:50–1; Mālik, *al-Muwaṭṭaʾ*, rec. Yaḥyá, *al-ṣalāh* 14, *jāmiʿ al-wuḍūʾ*, no 66; rec. Abū Muṣʿab, *al-ʿamal fī al-wuḍūʾ* 6, *jāmiʿ al-wuḍūʾ*, no 74. Cf. Juynboll, *Encyclopedia*, 356, considering this form of words an invention of Mālik's.
9 Ibn Abī Shaybah, *al-Muṣannaf* 1:134–5 *1:246*; Hannād, *Zuhd* 2:571; Abū Nuʿaym, *Ḥilyah* 4:227 (< Aḥ., *Zuhd*).
10 Hannād, *Zuhd* 2:571.

of the value of ritual ablutions before supplication (*duʿāʾ*). G. H. A. Juynboll attributes this hadith report to Shuʿbah (Basran cl., d. 160/777?):

> The prophet ordered a man from the Anṣār to utter the following words when going to bed: 'O God, I have surrendered myself to You, I have turned my face towards You, I have entrusted my affairs to You, I ask You to protect my back, out of desire (sc. for Your reward) and in awe (sc. of Your punishment); there is no refuge or security from You except with You; I believe in Your Book which you have revealed and in Your Messenger whom You have sent; if he dies, he dies in (the profession of) the true religion (*fiṭra*).'[11]

The last words ('if he dies') should actually be the Prophet's comment, not part of the recommended prayer. Juynboll goes on to assert that there are many elaborations by others than Shuʿbah. In many of these alternative versions, the Prophet starts by telling the man, 'perform the minor ritual ablution as for the ritual prayer' or refers to his 'going to bed, being in a state of ritual purity', before giving him the words to pronounce. Some of these alternative versions go through figures of the renunciant tradition, notably Ibn al-Mubārak (d.181/797) and al-Fuḍayl ibn ʿIyāḍ (d. 187/803).[12] However, they do not appear in specialized collections of renunciant sayings, such as *al-Zuhd* by Ibn al-Mubārak himself.

The specialized literature of renunciation on the whole shows remarkably little interest in ritual ablutions. One can easily conceive of renunciant moralists' denouncing persons who think they may do as they please, then escape all consequences in the Afterlife by washing themselves. Abū al-ʿĀliyah (Basran, d. 90/709?) said of Q. 2:222 ('God loves those who repent, and He loves those who keep themselves clean'), 'This is not those who purify themselves by water but those who are purified of sins.'[13] Later, I shall review renunciant comments suggesting distrust of the pilgrimage ritual, similar to comments Marion Katz has uncovered from later jurisprudents.[14] Never actually having seen an expression of disdain for ritual ablutions in the renunciant literature, I would guess first that renunciants associated ritual ablutions so strongly with preparing for the ritual prayer that they seemed to have no independent significance.

More speculatively, I would observe that anthropological accounts of ritual purity correlate them with concern to reinforce social hierarchy.[15] The Islamic

---

11 Juynboll, *Encyclopedia*, 493. I prefer the translation, 'I hereby surrender myself to you, turn my face towards you', and so on, interpreting the past tense in its performative sense (*inshāʾ*).
12 E.g., Bukhārī, *al-wuḍūʾ* 75, *bāb faḍl man bāta ʿalá al-wuḍūʾ*, no 247; Aḥmad, *Musnad* 4:292–3 30:550–1.
13 Abū Nuʿaym, *Ḥilyah* 2:222.
14 Katz, 'The ḥajj and the study of Islamic ritual', 105–6, 129.
15 See esp. Katz, *Body of text*, also Douglas, *Purity and danger*, and *Natural symbols*.

rules, compared especially with Jewish and Zoroastrian, have seemed relatively lenient, perhaps maintaining a minimal version of a general Near Eastern purity code.[16] They were elaborated especially in the early eighth century, when an ongoing process of Islamization made out emphatically that Islam was a separate religion, distinct from Christianity and Judaism, also as a new hierarchy developed among the Muslims on the basis of office and landholding. The renunciant movement was not particularly opposed to Islamization, but renunciant literature did preserve more acknowledgements of interaction with non-Muslim renunciants and especially taking inspiration from pre-Muḥammadan prophets and their scriptures than other bodies of Islamic literature.[17] The renunciants were also skeptical of hierarchy among the Muslims. Possibly, then, exaggerated concern with ritual purity may have looked to them like a sign of conceit, which they much preferred to avoid.

As for ritual prayer, it is a strict requirement of Islamic law. Five times a day, adult Muslims are required go through a series of set gestures and phrases, in a state of ritual purity, at set times. As for the times, they are sounded out by muezzins in all Muslim-majority countries (and some schools require anyone about to pray by himself to sound the call as well). They occur at sunset, in the evening about an hour later, at the crack of dawn, just after high noon, and halfway between noon and sunset, when a stick's shadow is equal to its length. At the moments of sunset, sunrise, and the very zenith, it is forbidden to pray, lest someone think that the Muslim is worshipping the sun; likewise certain places are forbidden, such as a refuse heap, a slaughterhouse, a cemetery, a bath, a thoroughfare, a place where camels are stood, and the top of the Kaʿbah. A Twelver Shiʿi variant mentions ten places, including most of the same.[18] There is more reward for performing a prayer in the mosque than elsewhere (at least for men), at the beginning of the prescribed time than later in it, during the prescribed time than after it, but no punishment except for skipping a prayer altogether, unless one has a prescribed excuse, as during one's menstrual period. It is meritorious to perform additional prayers (with one, the *witr* prayer, almost required by the Ḥanafi school).

Unsurprisingly, it was a regular feature of pious living to perform ritual prayers. Saʿīd ibn al-Musayyib (d. Medina, 94/712–13?) did not miss prayer in the

---

16 Calder, *Studies*, 210–12; also Katz, *Body of text*, 3–11.

17 See Melchert, 'Quotations of extra-Qur'anic scripture', and 'The Islamic literature on encounters between Muslim renunciants and Christian monks', and Khoury, 'Quelques réflexions sur les citations de la Bible'.

18 Melchert, 'When not to recite the Qur'an', 141.

mosque for 40 years;[19] alternatively, he heard the prayer from inside the mosque for 30 years.[20] He did not see their napes for 20 years (i.e., he got there early and prayed from the front row).[21] An Ismaili source mentions that ʿAlī ibn al-Ḥusayn Zayn al-ʿĀbidīn (d. 95/714) would pray 1,000 supererogatory cycles a day.[22] The Kufan jurisprudent and qur'anic reciter al-Aʿmash (d. 148/765?) 'kept up prayer in the assembly and in the first row. ... He would come touching the wall till he could stand in the front row.'[23] ʿAlī ibn ʿAbd Allāh ibn al-ʿAbbās (Medinese, d. 118/736–7) is said to have prayed over 1,000 prostrations a day.[24] Bilāl ibn Saʿd (Basran, d. *ca* 120/737–8), a Syrian worshipper and preacher, prayed 1,000 cycles a day.[25] ʿUmayr ibn Hāniʾ (Damascene, d. 127/144–5?) would pray 1,000 prostrations a day and say *subḥāna 'Llāh* 100,000 times.[26] Bishr ibn al-Mufaḍḍal (Basran, d. 187/802–3?) would pray 400 cycles a day and fast alternate days.[27] (Fasting alternate days might be more trying than a continuous fast, for it would not allow one's mind and body to become accustomed to either schedule.) A Shiʿi source recounts that a Ṣafwān ibn Yaḥyá (Kufan, *fl.* early 9th cent.) prayed 500 cycles a day, fasted three months of the year, and paid *zakāh* three times a year, since he and two others had agreed that if one died, the others would pray his prayers, and if two died, the third would pray all their prayers.[28] A similar pact is reported of the earlier Kufan jurisprudent al-Ḥasan ibn Ṣāliḥ ibn Ḥayy (d. 167/783–4?), his brother ʿAlī (d. 151/768–9?), and their mother. At first, they would recite the Qur'an nightly in shifts; then the two brothers in shifts after their mother died; finally al-Ḥasan alone after his brother died.[29]

The prescribed gestures of the ritual prayer begin with the sacralization (*taḥrīm*), accomplished by standing, raising the hands, and saying *Allāhu akbar*. Outstandingly pious persons would prolong some of them to the point of injuring themselves. Masrūq ibn al-Ajdaʿ (Kufan, d. 63/682–3?) prayed till his feet swelled

---

19 Aḥmad, *Zuhd*, 383 *458*; Abū Nuʿaym, *Ḥilyah* 2:162–3.
20 Aḥmad, *Zuhd*, 383 *459*.
21 Aḥmad, *Zuhd*, 383 *458*; Abū Nuʿaym, *Ḥilyah* 2:163.
22 Al-Qāḍī al-Nuʿmān, *Daʿāʾim al-islām* 1:211.
23 Abū al-Qāsim al-Baghawī, *Jaʿdīyāt* 1:242; Abū Nuʿaym, *Ḥilyah* 5:50.
24 Abū Dāwūd, *Zuhd*, 231, nos 451–2; Abū Nuʿaym, *Ḥilyah* 6:91.
25 Abū Zurʿah al-Dimashqī, *apud* Ibn Ḥajar, *Tahdhīb* 1:503.
26 Tirmidhī, *al-daʿawāt* 26, *bāb mā jāʾa fī al-duʿāʾ idhā intabaha min al-layl*, no 3415.
27 Fasawī, *Maʿrifah* 3:497.
28 Ṭūsī, *Fihrist*, 83.
29 ʿIjlī, *Tārīkh al-thiqāt*, 114, 347. Alī's son al-Hasan (d. 50/670–1?) would at any rate stay up the first part of the night, his brother al-Ḥusayn (d. 61/680) the second: Aḥmad., *Zuhd*, 170–1 *213* (< ʿAl.). Abū Hurayrah (d. 58/677–8?) would stay up nights in shifts with his wife and son, each getting up for a third of the night: Aḥmad, *Zuhd*, 177 *221*; Abū Dāwūd, *Zuhd*, 158.

up.[30] Another report mentions his swollen thighs, which provoked his wife to sit behind him and weep for pity.[31] Abū Maysarah (ʿAmr ibn Shuraḥbīl, Kufan, d. 63/682–3?) evidently prolonged his kneeling, so that 'his knees were like those of a camel from much ritual prayer.'[32]

A minor injury, visible on many Muslims today, is a callus on the forehead from touching it to the ground. It is apparently mentioned in the Qur'an: 'You see them bowing and prostrating themselves, seeking bounty and approval from God. Their mark (*sīmā*) is on their faces from the effect of prostration (*min athar al-sujūd*)' (Q. 48:29). Ibn Saʿd remarks it of several early figures: the Yemeni Follower Ṭāwūs (d. 106/725?), the Homsi Khālid ibn Maʿdān, (d. 108/726–7?), and the Damascene Ḥakīm ibn ʿUmayr (*fl.* early 2nd/8th cent.).[33] Murrah ibn Sharāḥīl of the 500 or 1,000 daily bowings was remembered also for marks on his forehead, palms, knees, and feet.[34] It is commended in hadith: in the middle of a long hadith report on the Last Judgement, when nearly all the Muslims will be put into Hell for a time, the Prophet says, 'God will command the angels to put out anyone who worshipped God, so they will put them out. They will know them by the traces of prostration, God having forbidden to the Fire that it eat the trace of prostration.'[35] Alternatively, perhaps, present benefit is promised: according to the Meccan preacher (*qāṣṣ*) ʿUbayd ibn ʿUmayr (d. bef. 70/689–90), 'The angels continue to pray over the servant so long as the trace of worship is on his face.'[36]

There is also admittedly disapproval of performing prayers to the point of leaving marks. Ibn Abī Shaybah (Kufan, d. 235/849) has successive sections on those who approved and disapproved of letting one's face be marked by prostration. The prominent Kufan Follower Abū Isḥāq al-Sabīʿī (d. 129/746–7?) said, 'I saw the companions of ʿAlī and ʿAbd Allāh (ibn Masʿūd). Prostration had marked their foreheads and noses.'[37] He quotes al-Ḥasan al-Baṣrī, 'I saw what went next to the earth on ʿĀmir ibn ʿAbd Qays something like the callus of a camel.'[38] On the

30 ʿIjlī, *Tārīkh al-thiqāt*, 426.
31 Ibn al-Mubārak, *Zuhd*, no 95; Aḥmad, *Zuhd*, 350 *420* (< ʿAl.); Ibn Abī Shaybah, *Muṣannaf* 13:407 *12:292*; Wakīʿ, *Zuhd* 1:387–8.
32 Ibn Ḥibbān, *Thiqāt* 5:168.
33 Ibn Saʿd, *Ṭabaqāt* 5:393, 7/2:160, 162 *5:539*, *7:452*, *455*.
34 Aḥmad, *Zuhd*, 348 *418*.
35 E.g., Bukhārī, *al-adhān* 129, *bāb faḍl al-sujūd*, no 806; ibid., *al-riqāq* 52, *bāb ṣirāṭ jisr jahannum*, no 6573; ibid., *al-tawḥīd* 24, *bāb qawl Allāh wujūh yawmaʾidhin nāḍirah*, no 7435; Muslim, *al-īmān* 81, *bāb maʿrifat ṭarīq al-ruʾyah*, no 182 (Medinese *isnād*).
36 Abū Nuʿaym, *Ḥilyah* 3:272 (Basran *isnād*).
37 Ibn Abī Shaybah, *Muṣannaf* 1:308 *2:191–2*.
38 Ibn Abī Shaybah, *Muṣannaf* 1:308–9 *2:192*.

other hand, he quotes through a Homsi *isnād* (chain of transmitters) a famous Companion's deprecation: when Abū al-Dardā' (d. early 30s/650s?) saw a woman whose eyes were like a sheep's callus, he said, 'If this were not between your eyes, that would be better.'[39] Through a mixed Kufan/Mesopotamian *isnād*, a man is apparently found guilty of deliberately trying to make himself look pious: 'Maymūnah was asked, "What do you think of so-and-so who carves out his forehead on the earth, wanting to effect on it the mark of prostration?" She said, "Leave him alone. Perhaps it will go through."'[40] Then, by more Kufan *isnād*s, it is simply discouraged. Sulaym ibn Aswad al-Muḥāribī (d. 83/702–3?) says, 'I was sitting by Ibn 'Umar. He saw a man whose face was scarred by prostration. He said, "A man's face is his image (*ṣūrah*), so let none of you disfigure his image."'[41] The Kufan al-Sha'bī (d. 104/722–3?) is said to have disliked the mark on the face.[42] A Kufan complains to the Meccan qur'anic commentator Mujāhid (d. 104/722–3?) of a mark between his eyes. Mujāhid tells him, 'When you prostrate yourself, make it short (*tajāfa*).'[43] A Māliki source, characteristically hostile to demonstrative devotions, reports that the Companion Sa'd ibn Abī Waqqāṣ (d. 55/674–5?) saw a man who had a *sajdah* between his eyes. He said, 'How long ago did you convert?' The man said, 'Since such-and-such.' Sa'd said, 'I converted since such-and-such, but do you see anything between my eyes?'[44]

An unmoving posture in prayer was highly prized. Ibn Mas'ūd, when he undertook prayer, was like a garment thrown down.[45] A saying attributed to 'Alī (d. 40/661) relates an unmoving posture to humility: '*Khushū'* is in the heart: that you soften your side (*an tulayyina kanfak*) to a Muslim man (treat him kindly) and that you not turn aside in the ritual prayer.'[46] Al-Rabī' ibn Khuthaym (Kufan, d. 63/682–3?) in prostration was like a garment thrown down on which the sparrows would alight.[47] The anticaliph 'Abd Allāh ibn al-Zubayr (73/692) would prostrate himself till the birds landed on his back, thinking him the base of a wall.[48] He was

---

39 Ibn Abī Shaybah, *Muṣannaf* 1:308 *2:191*.
40 Ibn Abī Shaybah, *Muṣannaf* 1:308 *2:191*. Maymūnah bint al-Ḥārith was one of the Prophet's wives.
41 Ibn Abī Shaybah, *Muṣannaf* 1:308 *2:190–1*.
42 Ibn Abī Shaybah, *Muṣannaf* 1:308 *2:191*.
43 Ibn Abī Shaybah, *Muṣannaf* 1:308 *2:191*.
44 Ibn Abī Zayd, *Nawādir* 1:540; al-Bājī, *Sunan al-ṣāliḥīn* 1:285. For a similar story with Ibn 'Umar rather than Sa'd, see Ibn Sa'd, *Ṭabaqāt* 4/1:119 *4:162* (Kufan/Medinese *isnād*).
45 Ibn al-Mubārak, *Zuhd*, no 119; Aḥmad, *Zuhd*, 158 *197*.
46 Wakī', *Zuhd* 2:599; sim., as a gloss on Q. 23:2, Ibn al-Mubārak, *Zuhd*, no 1148.
47 Aḥmad, *Zuhd*, 341 *410*.
48 Aḥmad, *Zuhd*, 200 *249*; Ibn Abī al-Dunyā, *Tahajjud*, 484; Abū Nu'aym, *Ḥilyah* 1:335.

likened to a tent post when he stood for prayer.[49] Birds would land on the back of the Kufan Follower ʿAnbas ibn ʿUqbah al-Taymī (*fl.* 1st/7th cent.), in prostration, he was so still[50]; likewise, it was said, Ibrāhīm al-Taymī (Kufan, d. 92/710–11)[51] and Abū Wā'il Shaqīq ibn Salamah (Kufan, d. *ca* 99/717–18).[52] The last was notable for never turning in prayer or on the way.[53] Zādhān (Kufan, d. 82/701–2) prayed like a tree trunk.[54] Someone said of Saʿīd ibn Jubayr, 'I never saw him pray except as if he were a peg (*watad*).'[55] Muslim ibn Yasār (Basran, d. 100/718–19 or after) stood like a tent post in prayer, not shifting his weight to right or left.[56] Praying, he looked like a garment thrown down, nothing of him moving.[57] Ḥabīb ibn Abī Thābit (Kufan, d. 119/737) looked dead when prostrating himself, he stayed so long.[58] Of Manṣūr ibn al-Muʿtamir (Kufan, d. 132/750?), 'A girl said to her father, "Father: the pillar that was in Manṣūr's house—what happened to it?" He said, "My little girl, that was Manṣūr, praying by night. He has died."'[59] The Basran Salām ibn Abī Muṭīʿ (d. 164/780–1?), looked like something thrown down when he prayed without moving.[60]

My guess is that stillness in prayer was valued first as a sign of intense mental concentration, so that God was better honoured. This is clearly illustrated by Muslim ibn Yasār's self-reproach when someone praised him for turning so little in the ritual prayer: 'How do you know where my heart is?'[61] Resistance to distractions was likewise valued. Al-Rabīʿ ibn Khuthaym did not stop praying at night as his horse worth 30,000 dirhams was being stolen.[62] Ibn al-Zubayr did not move even when a stone took away part of his garment (from a catapult at the siege of Mecca).[63] The unmoving Muslim ibn Yasār also did not notice a fire next

49 Ibn Abī Shaybah, *Muṣannaf* 13:388 *12:279*.
50 Ibn Saʿd, *Ṭabaqāt* 6:144 *6:208*; Ibn Abī Shaybah, *Muṣannaf* 14:47 *12:445*; Aḥmad, *Zuhd*, 359 *429*.
51 Aḥmad, *Zuhd* 362–3 *434* (< ʿAl.); Abū Nuʿaym, *Ḥilyah* 4:212.
52 Aḥmad, *Zuhd* 357 *427* (< Aḥ.).
53 Ibn Saʿd, *Ṭabaqāt* 6:67 *6:99*.
54 Abū Nuʿaym, *Ḥilyah* 4:199.
55 Ibn Saʿd, *Ṭabaqāt* 6:186 *6:266*.
56 Ibn Saʿd, *Ṭabaqāt* 7/1:135 *7:186*; Abū Nuʿaym, *Ḥilyah* 2:293.
57 Ibn al-Mubārak, *Zuhd*, no 218 < Nuʿaym; Abū Nuʿaym, *Ḥilyah* 2:291.
58 Abū Nuʿaym, *Ḥilyah* 5:61.
59 ʿIjlī, *Tārīkh al-thiqāt*, 441.
60 Abū Nuʿaym, *Ḥilyah* 6:188 (< ʿAl., *Zuhd*).
61 Aḥmad, *Zuhd*, 251 *307*.
62 Ibn Abī Shaybah, *Muṣannaf* 13:399 *12:287*.
63 Abū Dāwūd, *Zuhd*, 201–2, no 388; Aḥmad, *Zuhd*, 200 *249*, also 145, 187 *181*, *233* (< ʿAl.).

to him as he stood in his house praying.[64] They were quiet when he came home but talked and laughed when he prayed (knowing he would not then notice them).[65] Indifference to the rich and powerful of the world is indicated by this story of the Yemeni Ṭāwūs (d. Mecca, 106/724–5?):

> Ṭāwūs was praying on a cold, cloudy morning. Muḥammad ibn Yūsuf, brother to al-Ḥajjāj ibn Yūsuf [governor of Iraq], passed with Ayyūb as he was prostrating himself in his procession. He ordered a wide scarf (*sāj*) and a high *ṭaylasān*. He threw them on him but he did not raise his head until he had finished his business. When he had saluted, he looked and the scarf was on him. He shook, not looking at it, and went on to his house.[66]

Dāwūd al-Ṭā'ī (Kufan, d. 165/781–2?) continued to pray despite the falling of a balcony near him.[67] Impassiveness also seems to be the issue when not turning the head is named as a principal feature of the Prophet's own deportment: 'The Prophet would not laugh, only smile. He would not turn to the side except with his whole body.'[68] To the contrary, however, agitation could also be admired if it proceeded from the fear of God. For example, ʿAbd Allāh ibn Wāqid (Medinese, d. 119/737) reported, 'I saw Ibn ʿUmar standing up to perform the ritual prayer. If you saw him, you thought him *muqlawlin*', using a somewhat obscure word meaning untranquil, not resting in place.[69]

Supererogatory ritual prayer was often carried on in secret. The Prophet said, 'The servant does not approach God (be he exalted) by means of anything better than a secret prostration (*sujūd khafī*).'[70] Kaʿb al-Aḥbār (d. bef. 23/644) said, 'The angels look from the heavens at those who pray at night in their houses as you look up at the stars of the heavens.'[71]

ʿAbd al-Raḥmān ibn Abī Laylá (Kufan, d. 86/705) would perform ritual prayers, but if someone came in, he would go to his mat and lean on it.[72] Al-Ḥasan al-Baṣrī praised those who could pray in their houses without their guests' detecting it.[73] Abū al-ʿAlā' (Basran, d. 111/729–30?) had heard that God always considered a prayer performed out of sight as being for him. He says, 'This one prays such

64 Ibn Saʿd, *Ṭabaqāt* 7/1:135 *7:186*; Aḥmad, *Zuhd*, 252 *308*; Abū Nuʿaym, *Ḥilyah* 2:290.
65 Aḥmad, *Zuhd*, 252 *308*.
66 Aḥmad, *Zuhd*, 376 *450*; Abū Nuʿaym, *Ḥilyah* 4:4.
67 Abū Nuʿaym, *Ḥilyah* 7:358.
68 Ibn al-Mubārak, *Zuhd*, no 146.
69 Wakīʿ, *Zuhd* 1:390–1.
70 Ibn al-Mubārak, *Zuhd*, no 154.
71 Abū Nuʿaym, *Ḥilyah* 6:43.
72 Ibn Abī Shaybah, *Muṣannaf* 13:426 *12:306*.
73 Ibn al-Mubārak, *Zuhd*, no 140; Aḥmad, *Zuhd*, 262 *320–1*.

that no one sees him and he shows off to no one.'[74] Ḥassān ibn Abī Sinān would keep the accounts in his shop visible lest someone notice his praying.[75] At home, he would play with his wife, then when she was asleep get up to perform supererogatory prayers.[76]

The tradition is of two minds about public prayer in the mosque. On the one hand, there were certainly many encouragements to pray there. The Prophet said, 'Group prayer is 25 times better than someone's prayer by himself.'[77] On the other hand, to perform supererogatory prayers in the mosque risked one's gaining a reputation for piety; that is, it risked being done for the sake of appearances. Abū Umāmah (probably the Companion Iyās ibn Thaʿlabah) actually kicked someone for praying long and weeping, saying this should be done at home.[78] ʿAbd al-Raḥmān ibn al-Aswad (Kufan, d. 199/814–15) would pray the required prayers in the mosque, then spend all day performing supererogatory prayers at home.[79] Al-Rabīʿ ibn Khuthaym was only once seen praying a supererogatory prayer in the neighbourhood mosque.[80] Dāwūd al-Ṭāʾī opposed praying any supererogatory prayers in the mosque.[81]

A word often associated with prayer in the renunciant literature is *ijtihād*, meaning literally 'exertion'. The term is most famous, of course, in the context of Islamic law, where it refers to the jurisprudent's exertion at examining the evidence in order to discover God's will. An absolute *mujtahid* (one who exerts himself) goes back to the Qur'an and hadith, a qualified *mujtahid* refines and ramifies the existing rules of his school of law. In the renunciant literature, *ijtihād* sometimes seems to mean any sort of exertion; for example, when the Companion Ibn Masʿūd is quoted as saying, 'Whoever exerts himself (*ijtahada*) for the sake of the world harms (his prospects in) the afterlife, while whoever exerts himself for the sake of the afterlife harms (his prospects in) the world.'[82] But most often it is associated with strenuous devotional routines. ʿAmr ibn ʿUtbah ibn Farqad (Kufan, d. Tustar, 22–35/644–56) is said to have been one of the *mujtahidīn* in worship. The story is then told of his reciting a little Qur'an, weeping, then reciting more,

---

74 Ibn al-Mubārak, *Zuhd*, no 203.
75 Abū Nuʿaym, *Ḥilyah* 3:115.
76 Abū Nuʿaym, *Ḥilyah* 3:117 (< Aḥ., *Zuhd*).
77 Bukhārī, *al-adhān* 31, *bāb faḍl al-ṣalāh fī al-jamāʿah*, no 648; ibid., *al-tafsīr*, *ad* Q. 17:78, no 4717; Muslim, *al-masājid* 42, *bāb faḍl ṣalāt al-jamāʿah*, no 649.
78 Aḥmad, *Zuhd*, 176 *219* (< ʿAl.); sim., Ibn al-Mubārak, *Zuhd*, no 156.
79 Aḥmad, *Zuhd*, 360 *431*.
80 Ibn al-Mubārak, *Zuhd*, no 59 < Nuʿaym; Aḥmad, *Zuhd*, 336–7 *405*.
81 Abū Nuʿaym, *Ḥilyah* 7:345.
82 Hannād, *Zuhd* 2:353.

weeping, and so on through the length of the night.[83] It is said that ʿAbd al-Raḥmān ibn al-Aswad would pray 700 bowings a day. Someone said, 'They used to say he was the least of the people of his house in *ijtihād*. I have heard that he became bone and skin.'[84] Al-Ḥasan al-Baṣrī said, 'They used to exert themselves (*yajtahidūna*) in supplication, but you would hear nothing but whispering.'[85] Abū Bakr ibn ʿAbd Allāh ibn Abī Maryam (Syrian, d. 156/772–3) was said to be among the worshipping *mujtahidīn*. He would not take off his gown for his wife to delouse it, being occupied day and night by ritual prayer.[86] Jaʿfar al-Ṣādiq (d. Medina, 148/765?) said, 'Be bidders of the people by other means than your tongues. Let them see from you scrupulosity (*waraʿ*), athleticism (*ijtihād*), ritual prayer, and goodness. That is bidding.'[87] (Here, by the way, is encouragement of public devotions.) Ibn Abī Dhiʾb (Medinese, d. Kufa, 159/775–6, 'used to pray the whole night and exert himself (*yajtahidu*) in worship. If he had been told that the Resurrection would come tomorrow, he could not have increased his *ijtihād*.'[88] The section in which Muslim (d. Nishapur, 261/875) put hadith reports about the Prophet's conducting ritual prayer till his feet were swollen was later given the title *ikthār al-aʿmāl wa-al-ijtihād fī al-ʿibādah*, 'performing much work and exertion in worship'.[89]

This brings up *ʿamal*, literally 'work', another word often associated with worship. Sometimes, of course, the Arabic word is as general as 'to do' in English. In an Islamic context, however, it commonly refers specifically to ritual worship. The word is familiar from Paul's opposition of faith and works; for example, 'Where is boasting then? It is excluded. By what law? of works (*tōn érgōn*)? Nay: but by the law of faith' (Rom. 3:27). The works Paul mentions expressly are not good deeds such as feeding the poor but ritual works such as circumcision and observing days that separated Jews from non-Jews. One sometimes encounters confusion on this point; for example, when a Sufi specialist interprets a letter from the Andalusian Sufi Ibn al-ʿArīf (d. Marrakech, 536/1141):

> Later ..., he relates the following anecdote: 'At the age of twenty-six I asked a man who was well versed in the Qur'an, the *Muwaṭṭa'* [of Mālik ibn Anas] and travel [for the sake of learning]: "How is it with those who have cut short their knowledge?" "Exertion (*ijtihād*) and

83 Ibn Saʿd, *Ṭabaqāt* 6:143–4 *6:206–7.*
84 Aḥmad, *Zuhd*, 360 *430.*
85 Ibn Abī Shaybah, *Muṣannaf* 10:377 *10:144*; Wakīʿ, *Zuhd* 2:616.
86 Ibn Saʿd, *Ṭabaqāt* 7/2:170 *7:467.*
87 Kulaynī, *Kāfī* 2:78, *al-īmān wa-al-kufr, bāb al-waraʿ.*
88 Ibn Saʿd, *Qism*, 413.
89 Muslim, *ṣifāt al-munāfiqīn* 18, *bāb ikthār al-aʿmāl wa-al-ijtihād fī al-ʿibādah*, nos 2819–20.

> effort (*'amal*) have conquered them," he replied, "thereby lessening for them knowledge (*'ilm*) and inquiry (*baḥth*)."' This statement seems to indicate that Ibn al-'Arīf doubted Ibn Qasī's ability in the very fields that would have legitimated his self-proclaimed status as the Seal of Authority.[90]

He need not have worried: *ijtihād* and *'amal* refer specifically to ritual worship, here, while *'ilm* and *baḥth* refer specifically to hadith and jurisprudence. These people have not fallen short from being worn out in the course of their studies. Rather, having have given themselves over to worship, they now have less regard for exoteric knowledge.

Occasionally, one comes across explanations of what the ritual prayer was supposed to be about. Yaḥyá ibn Ja'dah (Kufan Follower) said, 'When one prostrates oneself (alternative version: puts his forehead to the ground), one makes himself innocent of all conceit.'[91] Sufyān al-Thawrī said that one intends converse with one's lord.[92] 'Abd Allāh ibn Lahī'ah, a prominent Egyptian jurisprudent (d. 174/790–1), quotes someone as saying that God likes the slave who likes to meet God and that the slave is closest to God when he falls down in prostration.[93] Prostration is just the part of the prayer where jurisprudents were most inclined to call for supplication (*du'ā'*), whereas they tended to restrict qur'anic recitation to the times when the worshipper is standing.[94]

Supplication (*du'ā'*)

Supplication (*du'ā'*) is called for at certain points within the ritual prayer. The opening chapter of the Qur'an, the Fātiḥah, repeated multiple times at every ritual prayer, is itself a prayer to God, likewise the two short chapters at the end (Q. 113–14, *al-Mu'awwidhatayn*) frequently repeated in the ritual prayer. Other formulaic non-qur'anic prayers are said at different points; for example, *subḥāna rabbi al-'aẓīm* at the bowing and the *tashahhud* prayer at the end of each set of bowings. The Ḥanafi writer al-Ṣadr al-Shahīd ibn Māzah (d. Samarqand, 536/1141) may be taken as a typical representative of the classical schools:

> The one supplicating does not pray with whatever prayer occurs to him (*bi-mā yaḥḍuruhu min al-du'ā'*), rather it is meet for him to supplicate in his ritual prayer with a memorized

90 Cornell, *Realm of the saint*, 22.
91 Ibn Abī Shaybah, *Muṣannaf* 13:434–5 *12:312*.
92 Abū Nu'aym, *Ḥilyah* 7:60.
93 Ibn al-Mubārak, *Zuhd*, no 279.
94 See Melchert, 'When not to recite the Qur'an', 143–7.

> prayer, for he will fear that there cross his tongue something resembling people's speech by which he corrupts his prayer. As for when he is not in the ritual prayer, it is meet for him to supplicate with what occurs to him and not to recite a prayer from memory (*lā yastaẓhira al-du'ā'*), for memorizing prayer takes away softness of heart.[95]

Be that as it may, hadith collections offer very many model prayers from the Prophet; for example, 'He who says a hundred times a day, "There is no god but God, the One who has no sharer; to him belongs the kingdom and the praise; he is powerful over all things," will receive the reward of someone who manumits ten slaves.'[96] A Twelver Shi'i collection states that the Messenger of God would say (among other prayers) 'I ask forgiveness of God (*astaghfiru 'Llāh*)' 70 times a day and 'I repent to God (*atūbu ilá 'Llāh*)' 70 times a day.[97]

Sometimes, we read of particular gestures accompanying supplication. A Prophet hadith report says, 'If you ask God (for something), ask him with the palms of your hands; do not ask him with their backs.'[98] Salmān al-Fārisī (d. 34/654–5) said, 'God (be he exalted) is ashamed that a servant should extend his hands to him and ask for goodness in them and he push them away disappointed (*khā'-ibayn*).'[99] A Shi'i source quotes instructions from al-Ḥusayn ibn 'Alī (d. 61/680):

> Mention of a desire [at this he showed the insides of his palms to heaven]; thus is fear (*rahbah*) [at this he put the backs of his hands to heaven]; thus is beseeching (*taḍarru'*) [at this he moved his fingers right and left]; thus is chastity (*tabattul*) [at this he raised his fingers once and put them down once]; thus is supplication (*ibtihāl*) [at this he extended his hand before his face to the *qiblah*]. One does not supplicate until a tear flows.[100]

Ibn 'Abbās (d. Ṭā'if, 68/687–8) said, 'Sincerity (*ikhlāṣ*) is like this [he pointed with his finger], supplication (*du'ā'*) is so [he pointed with the palms of his hands], and bidding God to decide (*istikhārah*) is so [he raised his hands so that their backs were near his face].'[101] Shahr ibn Ḥawshab (Syrian, d. 112/730–1) spread his hands toward his face when asking some good (*mas'alah*), reversed them when

95 Ibn Māzah, *Muḥīṭ* 6:40.
96 E.g., Bukhārī, *bad' al-khalq* 11, *bāb ṣifat Iblīs wa-junūdih*, no 3293; *al-da'awāt* 64, *bāb faḍl al-tahlīl*, no 6403.
97 Kulaynī, *Kāfī* 2:505, *al-du'ā'*, *bāb al-istighfār*. Cf. *inter alia* Bukhārī, *al-da'awāt* 3, *bāb istighfār al-nabī*, no 6307: 'By God, I ask forgiveness of God and repent to him more than 70 times a day.'
98 Ibn Abī Shaybah, *Muṣannaf* 10:286 10:78; Ibn Mājah, *iqāmat al-ṣalāh wa-al-sunnah fīhā* 119, *bāb man rafa'a yadayhi fī al-du'ā' wa-masaḥa bihimā wajhah*, no 1181.
99 Aḥmad, *Zuhd*, 151 *189*, through Sulaymān al-Taymī (Basran, d. 143/760–1); also attributed to the Prophet, for which see 'Abd al-Razzāq, *Muṣannaf* 2:251.
100 Kulaynī, *Kāfī* 2:480, *al-du'ā'*, *bāb al-raghbah wa-al-rahbah*.
101 Ibn Abī Shaybah, *Muṣannaf* 10:287 *10:79*.

taking refuge from some evil (*taʿawwudh*).[102] Al-Ḥasan al-Baṣrī looked to heaven during the ritual prayer and prayed standing, but many others are cited against looking up, among other things holding that it was the practice of the Jews to look up.[103] It seems that the hands were thought to pick up blessings from being extended toward God in prayer.[104] By one report, the Prophet would always wipe his face with his hands after raising them to pray.[105] Aḥmad ibn Ḥanbal said, 'It is related of al-Ḥasan that he used to wipe his face with his hands in the course of his supplication (*duʿāʾ*) when he prayed.' He himself hoped there was no harm in it.[106] However, although Aḥmad is reported to have once used a rosary (*sabbāḥah*) as he and another man prayed. When they finished, the other man wiped his face with his hand but Aḥmad did not.[107]

A gesture that attracted particular attention was to pray with pointed finger. This is a required part of the ritual prayer during the *tashahhud* (with some disagreement as to whether the finger should be moved), where association with the words *illā 'Llāh* suggest that it is an affirmation of monotheism. It is also often mentioned in connection with supplication (that is, outside the ritual prayer). The Prophet told Saʿd to supplicate with just one finger.[108] Abū Hurayrah (d. 58/677–8?) forbade someone to supplicate with two fingers, telling him to pray with just one, the right.[109] ʿĀʾishah (d. 58/678?) corrected a woman who was supplicating with her two forefingers raised.[110] ʿAbd Allāh ibn al-Zubayr said, 'You make

102 Ibn Abī Shaybah, *Muṣannaf* 10:286–7 *10:79*.
103 Ibn Abī Shaybah, *Muṣannaf* 10:384 *10:150*. Cf. eight items in the previous section, 10:383–4 *10:149–50*.
104 ʿAbd al-Razzāq, *Muṣannaf* 2:253.
105 Tirmidhī, *al-daʿawāt* 11, *bāb mā jāʾa fī rafʿ al-aydī ʿinda al-duʿāʾ*, no 3386. It is commanded by the Prophet according to Abū Dāwūd, *al-witr* 23, *bāb al-duʿāʾ*, no 1485; also Ibn Mājah, *iftitāḥ al-ṣalawāt* 119, *bāb man rafaʿa yadayhi fī al-duʿāʾ wa-masaḥa bihimā wajhah*, no 1181, repeated *al-duʿāʾ* 13, *bāb rafʿal-yadayn fī al-duʿāʾ*, no 3866 (Medinese isnād). Rejected by Mālik according to Ibn Bashīr, *al-Majmūʿah*, *apud* Ibn Abī Zayd, *Nawādir* 1:530.
106 ʿAbd Allāh ibn Aḥmad, *Masāʾil*, 91, 95.
107 Ibn Hāniʾ, *Masāʾil* 2:183. There is perhaps better-attested hadith by which the Prophet continually spat on his hands, recited the last three chapters of the Qur'an over them, then rubbed them on his head and body before going to bed: among other places, Bukhārī, *faḍāʾil al-Qurʾān* 14, *bāb faḍl al-muʿawwidhāt*, no 5017; *al-ṭibb* 39, *al-nafth fī al-ruqyah*, no 5748; *al-daʿawāt* 12, *bāb al-taʿawwudh wa-al-qirāʾah ʿinda al-manām*, no 6319. The mechanism is presumably similar, that the spittle picks up blessing from the Qur'an, which is then communicated to the body by rubbing. However, I have not come across reports of renunciants' spitting on and reciting the Qur'an over their hands after this pattern.
108 Ibn Abī Shaybah, *Muṣannaf* 10:381 *10:147*.
109 Ibn Abī Shaybah, *Muṣannaf* 10:382 *10:148*.
110 ʿAbd al-Razzāq, *Muṣannaf* 2:249.

the best supplication thus' and pointed with his finger.[111] Ibn ʿUmar forbade ʿAbd Allāh ibn Dīnār (Medinese cl., d. 127/744–5) to raise one finger from each hand as he supplicated.[112] Muḥammad ibn Sīrīn (Basran, d. 110/729) said, 'It used to be that if they saw a man supplicating (*yadʿū*) with his fingers, they would strike one of them, saying "He is only one god (*innamā huwa ilāh wāḥid*)."'[113] Of course, this is stronger evidence of what he or someone of the next generation quoting him wished to see done in his own time than of what had actually gone on in the seventh century. When Ibn Sīrīn's contemporary Muḥammad ibn Wāsiʿ (Basran, d. 120/737–8?) was praying alone in the mosque with his fingers raised, Qutaybah ibn Muslim (governor of Khurasan *ca* 85–96/704–15) was moved to say, 'I prefer that one's fingers to thirty thousand horses.'[114] The point of the story is the governor's reliance on the renunciant's powerful intercession. The incidental detail that he was raising two fingers, not one, is therefore all the stronger evidence that well-regarded eighth-century Muslims were still using that form.

Group supplication must have been common. A standard form seems to have been for one to pray and another to say *āmīn*. ʿIkrimah (Meccan cl., d. Medina, 106/724–5?) commented on Q. 10:89, 'Your prayer (*daʿwah*) has been answered', 'Mūsá would pray and Hārūn would say *āmīn*.'[115] ʿĀmir ibn ʿAbd Qays (Basran, d. *ca* 55/674–5) was sent to Syria for interceding for a non-Muslim subject. When his comrades saw him off, he said, 'I shall pray, so you say *āmīn*.' Then he prayed that the one who had slandered him and put him out of his metropolis should enjoy much wealth and children, good health, and long life.[116] Ḥassān ibn ʿAṭīyah (Damascene, d. 120s/738–48) met a monk (*rāhib*). The monk began to pray for him while Ḥassān would say *āmīn*. Others said, 'Abū Bakr, do you say *āmīn* to his prayer?' He said, 'I hope God will answer it for my sake (*fīya*), not answer it for his sake (*fī nafsih*).'[117] The story indicates that it was not normal (at least by the mid-eighth century) for Christian and Muslim to pray together but also, incidentally, that it was normal for one to pray, the other to say *āmīn*.

Group supplication by Muslims also was controversial. Abū ʿUthmān al-Nahdī (Iraqi, d. 95/713–14?) said,

111 Ibn Abī Shaybah, *Muṣannaf* 10:382 *10:148*.

112 Mālik, *Muwaṭṭaʾ*, rec. Yaḥyá, *al-ṣalāh* 138, *bāb al-ʿamal fī al-duʿāʾ*, no 577; rec. Abū Muṣʿab, *al-ṣalāh* 98, *bāb al-ʿamal fī alduʿāʾ*, no 626.

113 Ibn Abī Shaybah, *Muṣannaf* 10:382 *10:149*.

114 Abū Nuʿaym, *Ḥilyah* 2:353.

115 ʿAbd al-Razzāq, *Tafsīr* 1:261.

116 Abū Nuʿaym, *Ḥilyah* 2:91.

117 Abū Nuʿaym, *Ḥilyah* 6:73.

> A governor wrote to ʿUmar ibn al-Khaṭṭāb saying that there was a group here who met to pray for the Muslims and the commander (of the faithful). ʿUmar wrote to him saying, ʻCome, and bring them with you.' So he came. ʿUmar said to the doorman, ʻPrepare me a whip.' When they came in to ʿUmar, he advanced on their leader to strike him with the whip. He said, ʻO Commander of the Faithful, we are not the ones you have in mind. They are a group who come from the East.'[118]

It was acceptable for some groups to pray but not for others (Khawārij?). An Abū Saʿīd, cl. to Abū Usīd, recounts how ʿUmar himself once participated in group supplication:

> ʿUmar, when he had prayed, would put the people out of the mosque. Then he turned to us. When he saw his comrades (*aṣḥāb*), he put down his whip and sat. He said, ʻPray' and they prayed. They took to praying and praying until the prayer ended up with me, so I prayed although I was a slave (*mamlūk*). I saw him pray and weep as a woman weeps who has lost her child. I said to myself, ʻThis is the one they say is rough (*ghalīẓ*).'[119]

Here, members of the circle evidently take turns saying prayers. Rituals in which participants are ranged in a circle seem more egalitarian than those in which participants are arranged in ranks. For a ritual prayer, a slave would not lead but pray behind a free man, reaffirming social hierarchy, but in the prayer circle, a slave would participate equally. (There is some inequality in the mosque circle as measured by proximity to the leader, if there is one. Meanwhile, the ritual prayer becomes circular around the Kaʿbah, where we expect the heightened egalitarianism of the liminal state.) Another story of ʿUmar expressly mentions the sorts of repeated phrases that would be repeated:

> ʿUmar joined a circle in the mosque after prayer, on being told, ʻWe have sat to recollect God.' He bade each speak in turn, something like *Allāhumma 'ghfir lanā* (ʻO God forgive us'), *Allāhumma 'rḥamnā* (ʻO God have mercy on us'). No one in the group wept more or harder than he.[120]

A report from Jaʿfar al-Ṣādiq likewise apparently assumes praying in turn, probably repeating set phrases:

> There is no group of 40 men who meet and pray to God (mighty and glorious is he) concerning a matter save that God will answer them. If they are not forty, then four will not pray to God ten times (mighty and glorious is he) save that God will answer them. If they are not

---

118 Ibn Abī Shaybah, *Muṣannaf* 8:746 *8:531* (Kufan/Basran *isnād*).
119 Ibn Abī Shaybah, *Muṣannaf* 14:6 *12:423*.
120 Ibn Saʿd, *Ṭabaqāt* 3/1:211 *3:294*.

four, then one will not pray to God forty times save that God the mighty and all-powerful will answer him.[121]

ʿUmar's son ʿAbd Allāh ibn ʿUmar is said to have passed by a preacher (*qāṣṣ*) as they were raising their hands. He said, 'God cut off these hands. Woe betide you. God (be he exalted) is nearer than what you are lifting up. He is nearer to one of you than your jugular.'[122] The point here seems to be disapproval of popular preaching, apparently as distinguished by the participants' praying as a group, presumably speaking in unison. Speaking in unison is sometimes mentioned explicitly. The Companion ʿAbd Allāh ibn Masʿūd (d. Medina, 32/652–3?) reproached someone for sitting in the mosque and having his circle repeat *Allāhu akbar*, *subḥāna 'Llāh*, and so on, for a set number of times.[123]

Almsgiving, fasting, and pilgrimage

Next on the list of the five pillars of Islam is either the alms tax (*zakāh*) or the Ramadan fast.[124] The word *zakāh* sometimes refers specifically to the fortieth part of one's property over a minimum amount that Muslims are required to yield up for redistribution, sometimes vestigially to any almsgiving. There are stories of meritorious almsgiving above and beyond the required *zakāh*. Zayn al-ʿĀbidīn's back was found to be blackened from carrying sacks of food at night for the poor (*fuqarā'* and *masākīn* in alternative versions) of Medina.[125] He had done this at night to avoid being seen. Like some others, he was concerned not to act superior to the recipients of his generosity, kissing a beggar before giving.[126] Al-Ḥasan al-Baṣrī distributed his military pension (*ʿaṭā'*) amongst other families until reminded by a son that he had dependants of his own to support as well.[127] The African Saḥnūn (d. 240/854), who had a great reputation for abstemious living as well as expertise in Māliki jurisprudence, made 500 dinars a year from his olive groves yet he would always end the year in debt from giving away such alms.[128]

121 Kulaynī, *Kāfī* 2:487, *al-duʿā'*, *bāb al-ijtimāʿ*.
122 Abū Nuʿaym, *Ḥilyah* 1:311–12, with allusion to Q. 50:16.
123 Aḥmad, *Zuhd*, 358 *428–9* (< ʿAl.); Abū Nuʿaym, *Ḥilyah* 4:381.
124 E.g., Bukhārī, *al-īmān* 2, *bāb duʿā'ukum īmānukum*, no 8, where the alms tax comes first, as opposed to ibid., *al-tafsīr*, *ad* Q. 7:30, no 4514, where the fast comes first.
125 Abū Nuʿaym, *Ḥilyah* 3:136.
126 Abū Nuʿaym, *Ḥilyah* 3:137.
127 Hannād, *Zuhd* 1:338; Aḥmad, *Zuhd*, 277–8 *338*.
128 Al-Qāḍī ʿIyāḍ, *Tartīb al-madārik* 4:81.

Perhaps relatively few stories are told of renunciant almsgiving because of the tendency for almsgivers to attract attention and feel superior. Secret almsgiving is encouraged by the Qur'an itself: 'If you make public your alms-giving, that is excellent; but if you conceal it and give it to the poor, that is better for you' (Q. 2:271). Abū al-ʿĀliyah said, 'When you give alms with your right hand, cover it with your left.'[129] Perhaps more importantly, it was not thought meet for renunciants to depend on alms. The Prophet said, 'By him in whose hand is my soul, that one of you should take a cord and carry firewood on his back is better than that a man should come to him whom God has given of his bounty for him to ask, whether he gives him or refuses him.'[130] (More on this to come in chapter 8 on the economics of renunciation.)

There are rather more stories of strenuous régimes of voluntary fasting, mainly not eating or drinking by daylight. Some persons extended the fast to almost all days in addition to the required month of Ramadan. Mālik ibn ʿAbd Allāh al-Khathʿamī (Palestinian, d. *ca* 60/679–80 or later) fasted for 60 years.[131] ʿAbd Allāh ibn al-Zubayr fasted on all but three days every month, also not removing the garment from his back for 40 years.[132] His younger brother ʿUrwah ibn al-Zubayr (Medinese, d. 94/712–13?) fasted during the last 30 or 40 years of his life except for feast days.[133] Al-Aswad ibn Yazīd al-Nakhaʿī (Kufan, d. 75/694–5?) lost one of his eyes from fasting.[134] Al-Zuhrī fasted perpetually (*al-dahr*).[135] An anonymous neighbour woman to ʿUtbah al-Ghulām (Basran, d. bef. 153/770) fasted perpetually.[136] Ibrāhīm ibn Ismāʿīl ibn Abī Ḥabībah (Medinese, d. 165/781–2) prayed continually and fasted for 60 years.[137] Abū Bakr ibn ʿAyyāsh (Kufan, d. 193/809?) fasted for 70 years.[138] Wakīʿ ibn al-Jarrāḥ (d. Kufa, 197/812) fasted perpetually.[139]

---

129 Wakīʿ, *Zuhd* 2:513–14.

130 E.g., Mālik, *Muwaṭṭa'*, rec. Yaḥyá, *al-jāmiʿ* 85, *bāb mā jā'a fī al-taʿaffuf ʿan al-mas'alah*, no 2853, rec. Abū Muṣʿab, *al-jāmiʿ* 77, *bāb mā jā'a fī al-taʿaffuf ʿan al-mas'alah*, no 2110; Bukhārī, *al-zakāh* 50, *bāb al-istiʿfāf ʿan al-mas'alah*, no 1472, *k. al-buyūʿ* 15, *bāb kasb al-rajul*, no 2074, *al-musāqāh* 13, *bāb bayʿ al-ḥaṭab wa-al-kala'*, nos 2373–4.

131 Aḥmad, *Zuhd*, 228–9 *279* (< ʿAl.).

132 Ibn Abī Shaybah, *Muṣannaf* 13:573–4 *12:413*.

133 Ibn Saʿd, *Ṭabaqāt* 5:134 *5:180*; Aḥmad, *Zuhd*, 371 *445*.

134 Ibn Abī Shaybah, *Muṣannaf* 13:409 *12:294*. The Prophet warns that staying up all night may damage the eyesight: Bukhārī, *al-ṣawm* 59, *ṣawm Dāwūd*, no 1979.

135 Abū Nuʿaym, *Ḥilyah* 3:169.

136 Abū Nuʿaym, *Ḥilyah* 6:238.

137 Ibn Saʿd, *Ṭabaqāt* 5:305 *5:412*.

138 Ibn Ḥibbān, *al-Thiqāt* 7:669–70.

139 Al-Khaṭīb al-Baghdādī, *Tārīkh* 13^2:500–1, 503 15:652–3, 655.

Fasting on alternate days has been mentioned already. It is sometimes recommended in Prophet hadith as the fast of the prophet Dāwūd.[140] Ibrāhīm al-Nakhaʿī fasted alternate days.[141] Muḥammad ibn Sīrīn fasted alternate days.[142] Abū Jaʿfar (d. Medina, 130/747–8?), one of the Ten Readers of the Qur'an, fasted alternate days (*ṣawm Dāwūd*), saying that was to train himself (*li-urawwiḍa bihi nafsī*) for the worship of God.[143] Sulaymān al-Taymī (Basran, d. 143/760–1) fasted alternate days and stayed up nights for 40 years.[144] It is also said that he fasted perpetually (*yaṣūmu al-dahr*) for 20 years.[145] Ḥanbali sources mention admiringly that Mālik ibn Anas (Medinese, d. 179/795) fasted on alternate days for 60 years and prayed 800 prostrations a day.[146] Bishr ibn al-Mufaḍḍal (Basran, d. 187/802–3?) would perform 400 prayers a day and fast on alternate days.[147]

Sometimes, particular days to fast are specified. Hadith encourages fasting the traditional Jewish fast days of Mondays and Thursdays, among others, perhaps because the Prophet was born on one of them and began to hear the Qur'an on the other or because the servants' works are reviewed on these days.[148] Al-Ḥasan al-Baṣrī fasted on the days of whiteness (the day of the full moon and the two days preceding), the four sacred months, and every Monday and Thursday (*kāna yaṣūmu min al-sanah ayyām al-bīḍ wa-al-ashhur al-ḥurum wa-al-ithnayn wa-al-khamīs*).[149] Makḥūl al-Shāmī (d. 110s/729–38) fasted on Monday and Thursday.[150] Abū Isḥāq al-Sabīʿī (Kufan, d. 129/746–7?) went to a régime of fasting only on Monday and Thursday of every month and all of the sacred months when he weakened in

140 E.g., Bukhārī, *al-tahajjud* 7, *bāb man nāma ʿinda al-saḥar*, no 1131; *al-ṣawm* 59, *ṣawm Dāwūd*, nos 1979–80; *istiʾdhān* 38, *bāb man ulqiya lahu wisādah*, no. 6277; Ibn Saʿd, *Ṭabaqāt* 4/2:219 4:262–3.

141 Ibn Saʿd, *Ṭabaqāt* 6:192 *6:276*; Abū Nuʿaym, *Ḥilyah* 4:224.

142 ʿAbd al-Razzāq, *Muṣannaf* 2:571; Aḥmad, *Zuhd*, 307 *373*.

143 Ibn al-Jazarī, *Ghāyat al-nihāyah* 2:383, ll. 17–19.

144 Abū Nuʿaym, *Ḥilyah* 3:28.

145 Abū Nuʿaym, *Ḥilyah* 3:29.

146 Ibn Abī Yaʿlá, *Ṭabaqāt* 1:63 *1:150–1*. Māliki sources are a little more reticent; e.g., al-Qāḍī ʿIyāḍ quotes reports that he seldom prayed the morning prayer on other than the ablution of the previous evening's (i.e., had not slept all night) and performed more devotions in secret than publicly: *Tartīb al-madārik* 2:51.

147 Fasawī, *Maʿrifah* 3:497.

148 E.g., Abū Dāwūd, *al-ṣawm* 54, *bāb fī ṣawm al-dahr*, no 2426; *al-ṣawm* 60, *bāb fī ṣawm al-ithnayn wa-al-khamīs*, no 2436; Tirmidhī, *al-ṣawm* 44, *bāb mā jāʾa fī ṣawm yawm al-ithnayn wa-al-khamīs*, nos 745, 747.

149 Aḥmad, *Zuhd*, 269 *329* (< ʿAl.).

150 Abū Nuʿaym, *Ḥilyah* 5:180.

his old age.[151] Aḥmad ibn Ḥanbal (d. 241/855) fasted on Monday, Thursday, and the days of whiteness, then constantly (*admana al-ṣawm*) after returning from Samarra about four years before his death, indicating acceptance of perpetual fasting in traditionalist circles into the ninth century.[152] A Twelver Shiʿi source has the Prophet instruct ʿAlī to fast on three days in the month: 'Thursday at the beginning of it, Wednesday in the middle of it, and Thursday at the end of it.'[153]

Fasting especially lent itself to secrecy. Muḥammad ibn Wāsiʿ (Basran, d. 123/740–1) fasted perpetually but hid it.[154] Abū al-Tayyāḥ (Basran, d. 128/745–6) said that people used to anoint themselves and put on their best clothes when fasting (recalling Matt. 6:17–18, 'But thou, when thou fastest, anoint thine head, and wash thy face; That thou appear not unto men to fast, but unto thy Father which is in secret'); also that a man would practise strenuous devotions (*yataqarraʾu*) for 20 years without his neighbours' knowing.[155] Dāwūd ibn Abī Hind (Basran, d. 140/757–8?) fasted for 40 years without his family's knowing.[156] According to one *ḥadīth qudsī*, God says, 'Every work of the son of Adam is for him except for fasting, which is for me.'[157]

As renunciants often prayed and fasted more than they were required to, so, again unsurprisingly, they often made frequent pilgrimages. The Companion ʿAbd Allāh ibn ʿUmar freed a thousand slaves and made 50-odd pilgrimages.[158] ʿAmr ibn Maymūn (Kufan, d. 74/693–4?) made 60 between the lesser and greater.[159] Al-Aswad ibn Yazīd al-Nakhaʿī made 80.[160] He would not pray the funeral prayer over a rich man who had failed to make the pilgrimage, implying that he had apostatized.[161] Saʿīd ibn al-Musayyib made 40.[162] Saʿīd ibn Jubayr (Kufan, d. 95/714?) made the greater and lesser pilgrimages yearly;[163] alternatively, two

151 Abū Nuʿaym, *Ḥilyah* 4:239.
152 Dhahabī, *Siyar* 11:223.
153 Kulaynī, *Kāfī* 8:79, *waṣīyat al-nabī*.
154 Abū Nuʿaym, *Ḥilyah* 2:352 (< Aḥ., *Zuhd*).
155 Abū Nuʿaym, *Ḥilyah* 6:290.
156 Abū Nuʿaym, *Ḥilyah* 3:94.
157 E.g., Bukhārī, *al-ṣawm* 9, *bāb hal yaqūlu innī ṣāʾim*, no 1904; *al-libās* 78, *bāb mā yudhkaru fī al-misk*, no 5927.
158 ʿAbd al-Malik ibn Ḥabīb, *Tārīkh*, 160.
159 Ibn Abī Shaybah, *Muṣannaf* 13:424 *12:304*; Abū Nuʿaym, *Ḥilyah* 2:103.
160 Ibn Saʿd, *Ṭabaqāt* 6:47 *6:71*; Abū Nuʿaym, *Ḥilyah* 2:103. He made the pilgrimage annually according to ʿIjlī, *Tārīkh al-thiqāt*, 68.
161 Ibn Saʿd, *Ṭabaqāt* 6:48 *6:72–3*.
162 Aḥmad, *Zuhd*, 384 *460* (< ʿAl.); Abū Nuʿaym, *Ḥilyah* 2:164.
163 Abū Nuʿaym, *Ḥilyah* 4:275.

lesser and one greater every year.[164] Muḥammad ibn al-Munkadir (Medinese, d. 130/747–8?) made the pilgrimage even though indebted, saying it would help pay his debt.[165] Ayyūb al-Sakhtiyānī (Basran, d. 131/749?) made 40 pilgrimages.[166] Muḥammad ibn Sūqah (Kufan, d. 140s/758–67) entered Mecca 80 times on either the greater or lesser pilgrimage.[167] Hammām ibn Nāfiʿ (Yemeni, *fl.* earlier 2nd/8th cent.) made over 60 pilgrimages.[168]

Renunciants also sometimes performed the pilgrimage in notable ways. The Companion Tamīm al-Dārī (d. 40/660–1?) made the pilgrimage trotting.[169] When Masrūq ibn al-Ajdaʿ made the pilgrimage, he did not sleep save in prostration (*sājidan*); that is, overcome as he performed supererogatory prayers.[170] Mujāhid (Meccan cl., d. 103/721–2?) related that '100,000 Israelites would make the pilgrimage. When they got to the border markers of the sacred zone (*anṣāb al-ḥaram*), they would take off their sandals, then enter the sacred zone barefoot.'[171] Presumably, this was an echo of God's command to Moses to take off his sandals on account of being in 'the holy valley' (Q. 20:12, in turn, of course, echoing Ex. 3:5).[172] The Imami Aḥmad ibn Hilāl al-ʿAbartānī (*fl.* early 3rd/9th cent.) made 54 pilgrimages, of which 20 were on foot. (The imam denounced him as a deceiving Sufi [*ṣūfī mutaṣanniʿ*].)[173] Aḥmad ibn Ḥanbal's five pilgrimages are counted separately, those he performed on foot and those he performed riding.[174] Naṣr al-Ṣāmit (Baghdadi, d. 230s/845–55), made 40 pilgrimages without speaking.[175] Aḥmad ibn al-Muʿadhdhal (Basran, d. *ca* 240/854–5) would not shade himself while making the pilgrimage.[176]

However, the renunciant tradition sometimes shows unease with regard to the pilgrimage. Perhaps this is because it was necessarily so public a devotion,

---

164 Aḥmad, *Zuhd*, 370 *443* (< ʿAl.).
165 Abū Nuʿaym, *Ḥilyah* 3:149.
166 Abū Nuʿaym, *Ḥilyah* 3:5.
167 Abū Nuʿaym, *Ḥilyah* 5:6.
168 Bukhārī, *al-Tārīkh al-kabīr* 8:237.
169 Aḥmad *Zuhd*, 199–200 *248* (< ʿAl.)
170 Ibn al-Mubārak, *Zuhd*, no 975; Ibn Saʿd, *Ṭabaqāt* 6:52 *6:79*; Ibn Abī Shaybah, *Muṣannaf* 13:402 *12:289*; Aḥmad, *Zuhd* 349 *419*; Abū Nuʿaym, *Ḥilyah* 2:95.
171 Abū Nuʿaym, *Ḥilyah* 3:298.
172 More on barefootedness before the ninth century in Jarrar, 'Bišr al-Ḥāfī und die Barfüßigkeit', 205–19.
173 Kashshī, *Rijāl*, 449–50.
174 Two of the five on foot, according to Khallāl, *Ḥathth*, 138; three according to Ibn Abī Ḥātim, *Jarḥ* 1:304, and Abū Nuʿaym, *Ḥilyah* 9:175.
175 Abū Nuʿaym, *Ḥilyah* 10:320.
176 Al-Qāḍī ʿIyāḍ, *Tartīb* 4:8–9.

impossible to perform out of sight and therefore bound to impress people. Al-Ḥallāj was famously put to death in 309/922 for denying that the pilgrimage was obligatory, but he was anticipated by various figures of the eighth century who at least went so far as to say that other works were equally valuable. ʿUqbah ibn ʿAbd al-Ghāfir (Basran, d. 83/702–3) said an evening prayer in the assembly was worth a greater pilgrimage, a dawn prayer in the assembly like a lesser pilgrimage.[177] Jābir ibn Zayd (Basran, d. 103/721–2) said, 'Better a dirham to an orphan or a poor man than one pilgrimage after another.'[178] Al-Ḥasan al-Baṣrī said, 'An acceptable pilgrimage (*al-ḥajj al-mabrūr*) is that one returns renunciant and wishing for the Afterlife.'[179] He also said it was better to help a fellow Muslim than to practise *iʿtikāf* (living in the mosque) for a year.[180] Thawr ibn Yazīd (Homsi Qadari, d. 150/767–8?) related a hadith report whereby going to the mosque purely to teach and learn will have the reward of one who completes his pilgrimage.[181] Sufyān al-Thawrī asserted that putting off a black *qalansuwah* (a hat; the point would have been to repudiate the ʿAbbāsids, whose dynastic colour was black) was equal to a pilgrimage.[182] Ibrāhīm ibn Ad'ham (d. 162/778–9?), responding to someone's suggestion that they go to Medina for the last ten days of Ramadan for the sake of catching *laylat al-qadr* (when angels and the Spirit descend, from Q. 97), said, 'Stay here and work well, and every night will be *laylat al-qadr* for you.'[183] Bishr al-Ḥāfī (Baghdadi, d. 227/841) said that alms (*ṣadaqah*) was better than the greater and lesser pilgrimages, also the holy war, inasmuch as alms were paid in secret.[184]

Perhaps more subtly, the pilgrimage also made them uncomfortable because it was so tied to a particular time and place, whereas their ascetic outlook tended to insist on the equality of times and places. Aḥmad ibn Ḥarb (Khurasani, d. 234/849?) was famous for his renunciation, as by not sleeping nights.[185] His metaphorical interpretation of the pilgrimage is quoted by Ibn al-Jawzī:

> The stages (*manāzil*) are four, of which three are figurative (*majāz*) and the fourth true (*ḥaqīqah*): our life in this world, our stay in the grave, our resurrection and rising up at the

177 Abū Nuʿaym, *Ḥilyah* 2:261.
178 Abū Nuʿaym, *Ḥilyah* 3:89–90.
179 Bukhārī, *al-Tārīkh al-kabīr* 3:238.
180 Ibn al-Mubārak, *Zuhd*, no 747.
181 Abū Nuʿaym, *Ḥilyah* 6:97.
182 Abū Nuʿaym, *Ḥilyah* 7:50.
183 Abū Nuʿaym, *Ḥilyah* 7:378.
184 Abū Nuʿaym, *Ḥilyah* 8:339.
185 See Dhahabī, *Siyar* 11:32–5, mainly based on al-Ḥākim al-Naysābūrī, *Tārīkh Naysābūr*.

> Resurrection, and our going to Eternity, for which we were created. Our living in the world is like supper to the pilgrim, who dares not relax or undo the burdens of his animals because he will leave again soon. Our stay in the grave is like one of the stages of the pilgrimage, when they put down their burdens and relax for a day and a night, then take off. Our arising in the muster is like their coming to Mecca, fulfilling their vows and cropping their hair, then splitting up, as at the Resurrection the people split up to go to either Paradise or the Fire.[186]

He does not state that one need not literally perform these rites, but such might be inferred, especially since he concludes that three of the four stages identified are metaphorical, only the last true, which must mean that the chief virtue of the pilgrimage ritual is pointing to the truth of the final disposition to Heaven or Hell.

186 Ibn al-Jawzī, *Muntaẓam* 11:210–11, s.a. 234.

Chapter 5: New devotional forms

The previous chapter described how early Muslim renunciants performed duties of all Muslims, such as performing the ritual prayer and going on pilgrimage to Mecca. They also developed special devotional forms, most notably *dhikr*, 'recollection'. Later, the Sufis further developed *dhikr*, to the point that it has sometimes been described as an entirely Sufi institution.

Qur'anic recitation

Dhikr is commonly translated as 'recollection' and 'mention'. The first form of *dhikr* is reciting the Qur'an. If the Qur'an has one message, it is to be mindful and not forgot one's dependence on God. *Dhikr* is applied to the Qur'an itself; for example, 'We have indeed sent down the Reminder' (15:9) and 'It is nothing but a reminder for all beings' (38:87). The believers are enjoined to recollect God; for example, 'And mention God (*udhkur rabbak*) when you forget' (18:24) and 'Make mention of your Lord morning and evening And part of the night' (76:25–6). The Companion Abū Mūsá al-Ashʿarī (d. 52/672?) was especially notable for Qur'an recitation. "ʿUmar ibn al-Khaṭṭāb would often say to Abū Mūsá al-Ashʿarī, "Remind us of our Lord (*dhakkirnā rabbanā*)", whereupon Abū Mūsá would recite to him. He had a comely voice for the Qur'an.'[1] This is to identify *dhikr* with qur'anic recitation. Sufyān al-Thawrī (Kufan, d. 161/777?) said, 'The best *dhikr* is reciting the Qur'an in the course of the ritual prayer, then reciting the Qur'an other than in prayer, then fasting, then *dhikr*' (the last evidently referring to repeated phrases).[2]

There are many stories of renunciants who recited much. The anti-caliph ʿAbd Allāh ibn al-Zubayr (d. 73/693) recited Q. 2–5 in one bowing before raising his head.[3] Ṭalq ibn Ḥabīb (Basran, d. after 90/708–9) would begin reciting at prayer, standing straight, not making his first bow till he had got to Q. 29 (over halfway through).[4] Yazīd ibn ʿAbd Allāh ibn al-Shikhkhīr (Basran, d. 101/719–20?) would recite from the written copy till he was overcome.[5] Someone said of Manṣūr ibn Zādhān (Wasiti, d. 129/746–7), 'I prayed next to Manṣūr ibn Zādhān

1 Ibn Saʿd, *Ṭabaqāt* 4/1:81 *4:109*; sim., 4/1:80 *4:109* (Mesopotamian *isnād*).
2 Abū Nuʿaym, *Ḥilyah* 7:67.
3 Abū Dāwūd, *Zuhd*, 201, no 287.
4 Abū Nuʿaym, *Ḥilyah* 3:64.
5 Ibn Abī Shaybah, *Muṣannaf* 14:42 *12:449*.

https://doi.org/10.1515/9783110617962-006

between the sunset and evening prayers. He recited the Qur'an, reaching by the second (bowing) al-Naḥl' (i.e., he recited Q. 1–16, almost a third of the whole).[6] Muḥammad ibn Juḥādah (Kufan, d. 131/748–9) said that they used to prefer to complete the recitation of the Qur'an in the course of the two bowings after the evening prayer, if at night, or the two bowings (of the *witr* prayer) before the dawn prayer if by day.[7] ʿAṭāʾ al-Khurāsānī (l. Damascus, d. 135/750–1) advocated reciting the entire Qur'an in the course of prayer.[8]

It was controversial whether to recite the Qur'an in all postures. Tamīm al-Dārī (d. Damascus? 40/660–1?) recited the Qur'an standing, inclining, and prostrating himself.[9] A Kufan renunciant, ʿAwn ibn ʿAbd Allāh ibn ʿUtbah (d. 110s/ 729–37), rebuked Nāfiʿ, a famous Medinese reciter (d. 169/785–6?), for reciting the Qur'an while sitting.[10] There was presumably some idea that positions connoting humility (bowing and prostration) were most appropriate to supplication, whereas standing up was most appropriate to reciting the word of God.[11]

It was less controversial to weep on hearing the Qur'an. Early renunciants interpreted the Qur'an as enjoining such sadness and fear. The Qur'an itself describes people as falling down and weeping in response to it: 'They fall on their chins weeping, and it increases them in humility' (Q. 17:109) and 'When the signs of the Merciful are recited to them, they fall down, prostrating themselves and weeping' (Q. 19:58). The Prophet wept on hearing Q. 4:41 ('How will it be when We bring a witness from each community and We bring you as a witness against these?').[12] He sobbed on hearing Q. 73:12 ('With Us are fetters and the hot fire').[13] 'I am reciting to you a chapter,' he told some Companions, 'so whoever weeps has Paradise.' He recited it but not one wept. Then he repeated it a second and a third time. Finally, he said, 'Weep, and if you do not weep, pretend to weep.'[14] Noah

6 Abū Nuʿaym, *Ḥilyah* 3:58.
7 Ibn al-Mubārak, *Zuhd*, no 811.
8 Abū Nuʿaym, *Ḥilyah* 5:200.
9 Aḥmad, *Zuhd*, 199–200 *248*.
10 Ibn al-Jazarī, *Ghāyah* 2:333, ll. 7–13.
11 See further Melchert, 'When not to recite the Qur'an', 143–6, 149–51.
12 Ibn al-Mubārak, *Zuhd*, no 110; Bukhārī, *tafsīr*, ad Q. 4:41, no 4582; *faḍāʾil al-Q. 32, bāb man aḥabba an yastamiʿa al-Qurʾān min ghayrih*, no 5049; *faḍāʾil al-Q. 33, bāb qawl al-muqriʾ lil-qāriʾ ḥasbuk*, no 5050; *faḍāʾil al-Q.* 35, *bāb al-bukāʾ ʿinda qirāʾat al-Qurʾān*, nos 5055–6.
13 Aḥmad, *Zuhd*, 27 *36*.
14 Abū ʿUbayd, *Faḍāʾil al-Qurʾān*, 135. Other attributions to the Prophet *apud* Ibn Mājah, *al-zuhd* 19, *bāb al-ḥuzn wa-al-bukāʾ*, no 4196; Hannād, *Zuhd* 1:270; *Aḥmad*, Zuhd, 27 *36*. Sim. attribution to Abū Bakr the first caliph *apud* Ibn al-Mubārak, *Zuhd*, no 131; Wakīʿ, *Zuhd* 1:254; Aḥmad, *Zuhd*, 108 *135*; Ibn Abī Shaybah, *Muṣannaf*, *al-zuhd* 92, *mā qālū fī al-bukāʾ*, 12:424. Sim. attributed to Abū Mūsá al-Ashʿarī (d. 50/570–1?), *apud* Aḥmad, *Zuhd*, 199 *247*; Abū Nuʿaym, *Ḥilyah* 1:261. Sim.

wept for 300 years when Q. 11:46 ('Do not ask me for that of which you have no knowledge. I admonish you not to be one of the ignorant') was revealed in his reproach.[15]

It was reported of Abū Bakr the first caliph (d. 13/34), 'He was a man given to much weeping. He could not control his eyes when he recited the Qur'an.'[16] The next caliph 'Umar is said to have recited Q. 19:58 and prostrated himself, then said, 'This is prostration, so where is the weeping?'[17] Al-Rabīʿ ibn Khuthaym (d. 61/680–1?) wept all night over Q. 45:21, 'Or do those who commit evil deeds reckon that We shall make them as those who believe and do righteous deeds ...?'[18] Ibn 'Umar (d. 73/693–4?) recited Q. 83:1–6 (ending with 'The day when men will stand before the Lord of all beings'), then wept till he fell down and was unable to recite any further.[19] Zurārah ibn Awfá (d. 93/711–12), sometime qadi for Basra, fell unconscious as he led the prayer and reached the words 'When there is a blast on the trumpet' (Q. 74:8).[20] Asad ibn Muhallab (Kufan, *fl.* earlier 8th cent.) cried out and died on hearing the Qur'an recited to him, fulfilling a prediction from Sufyān al-Thawrī that nothing else would kill him.[21] Three centuries later, the littérateur al-Thaʿlabī (d. 427/1035–6) collected stories of persons (about twenty in all; in one case *jinn*) who died on hearing the Qur'an recited or on contemplating it.[22] Thābit al-Bunānī (Basran, d. 127/744–5?) was said to have left no pillar in the mosque where he had not recited the whole Qur'an and wept.[23] Ghazālī (d. 505/1111) presents ten rules for outward deportment in reciting the Qur'an, including as number six that one weep.[24] It is good form even today for the eyes to well up on reciting the Qur'an or hearing it recited. Some commentators are uneasy with the idea that this has to do with sadness. Whatever brings

---

attributed to ʿAbd Allāh ibn ʿAmr (d. 63/683?) *apud* Ibn Abī Shaybah, *Muṣannaf*, 14:7–8 *12:425*; sim., Abū Nuʿaym, *Ḥilyah* 8:193. Sim. attributed to Jaʿfar al-Ṣādiq (d. 148/765) *apud* Kulaynī, *Kāfī* 2:483, *k. al-duʿā'*, *bāb al-raghbah wa-al-rahbah*.

15 Aḥmad, *Zuhd*, 50 *66*.

16 E.g., Bukhārī, *al-ṣalāh* 86, *bāb al-masjid yakūnu fī al-ṭarīq*, no 476, *al-kafālah* 4, *bāb jiwār Abī Bakr*, no 2297, *manāqib al-anṣār* 45, *bāb hijrat al-nabī*, no 3905. The first of these hadith reports is remarked by Chittick, 'Weeping', 133.

17 Ṭabarī, *Jāmiʿ al-bayān*, *ad* Q. 19:58. Similar attribution to Ṣafīyah bint Ḥuyayy (d. 40s/661–70?), wife to the Prophet, *apud* Abū Nuʿaym, *Ḥilyah* 2:55.

18 Aḥmad, *Zuhd*, 329 *397*.

19 Hannād, *Zuhd* 1:201 < Wakīʿ, likewise Aḥmad, *Zuhd*, 192 *240*; Abū Nuʿaym *Ḥilyah* 1:305.

20 Aḥmad, *Zuhd*, *247* 302.

21 ʿIjlī, *Tārīkh al-thiqāt*, 63.

22 Thaʿlabī, *Vom Koran Getöteten*. A little more in Melchert, 'Locating Hell', 119–20.

23 Abū al-Qāsim al-Baghawī, *Jaʿdīyāt* 1:398; Abū Nuʿaym, *Ḥilyah* 2:321 (< ʿAl., *Zuhd*).

24 Ghazālī, *Iḥyā' ʿulūm al-dīn* 8, *ādāb tilāwat al-Qur'ān* 2, *fī ẓāhir ādāb al-tilāwah*.

on tears today (I readily concede that tears may reflect more than sadness), it seems clear from quotations of lines that particularly affected eighth-century renunciants that tears were expected as a sign of distress over the prospect of judgement.[25]

There are many reports of staying up nights, usually with some indication that the time would be spent on ritual prayer, recitation of the Qur'an, or both. Reciting the Qur'an at night is sometimes commended in Prophet hadith; for example,

> Fasting and the Qur'an will intercede for the servant on the Day of the Resurrection. Fasting will say, 'O my lord, I forbade him food and desires by day, so make me an intercessor for him.' The Qur'an will say, 'I forbade him sleep by night, so make me an intercessor for him.' They will be made intercessors.[26]

'There are three eyes that will never be burnt by the fire: an eye that has wept from fear of God, an eye that has stayed awake at night with the Book of God, and an eye that has kept watch on the path of God.'[27] The Prophet spent a whole night repeating a verse to himself.[28] 'Abd Allāh ibn Mas'ūd (d. 32/652–3?) said, 'The superiority of ritual prayer by night to ritual prayer by day is like the superiority of almsgiving in secret to almsgiving in public', connecting night vigils to the recurrent renunciant concern that rituals be performed for the sake of serving God, not to impress creatures.[29] By one report, Ibn Mas'ūd recited the Qur'an every three days, seldom making use of daylight.[30] Al-Rabī' ibn Khuthaym recited one verse all night, bowing and prostrating himself.[31] 'Abd al-Wāḥid ibn Zayd (Basran, *fl.* early 8th cent.) was rebuked in a dream for sleeping rather than reciting his *juz'* (thirtieth part of the Qur'an).[32]

Ayyūb al-Sakhtiyānī (Basran, d. 131/749?) would stay up all night but there is contradictory testimony as to whether he recited the Qur'an in a loud voice

---

25 More in Melchert, 'Exaggerated fear', 289–90.

26 Aḥmad, *Musnad* 2:174 *11:199–200*; sim., Abū Nu'aym, *Ḥilyah* 8:161.

27 Ibn al-Mubārak, *Jihād*, no 188. More widely reported is a version that mentions only two eyes, the weeping and the watching; e.g., Tirmidhī, *faḍā'il al-jihād, bāb mā jā'a fī faḍl al-ḥars fī sabīl Allāh*, no 1639, Aḥmad, *Musnad* 4:134 *28:445–8*, Dārimī, *Musnad*, 574.

28 Ibn al-Mubārak, *Zuhd*, no 104.

29 Ibn Abī al-Dunyā, *Tahajjud*, 118, 297–8; 'Abd al-Razzāq, *Muṣannaf* 3:47; Ibn Abī Shaybah, *Muṣannaf* 2:271 *3:194*; also Ibn al-Mubārak, *Zuhd*, no 25, in which it is Ibn Mas'ūd's quotation of the Prophet.

30 Ibn Abī Shaybah, *Muṣannaf*, 2:501 *3:575*.

31 Ibn Abī Shaybah, *Muṣannaf* 13:396 *12:285*; Aḥmad, *Zuhd*, 336 *405*.

32 Abū Nu'aym, *Ḥilyah* 6:162.

throughout or only at the end (lest people notice that he was staying up all night).[33] Al-Aʿmash (Kufan, d. 148/765?) said, 'Our comrades (*aṣḥāb*) like to finish reciting it at the beginning of day or night.'[34]

It was controversial whether one should recite the whole Qur'an in a single day. According to a Prophet hadith report, 'He has not understood (*lam yafqah*) who has recited the Qur'an in less than three.'[35] 'Ā'ishah (d. 57/676–7?), on hearing of persons who recited the Qur'an two or three times a night, protested their lack of deliberation: 'They have recited without reciting. The Messenger of God ... used to stay up a whole night and recite just *al-Baqarah*, *Āl 'Imrān*, and *al-Nisā'* [i.e., Q. 2–4, about a seventh of the whole Qur'an], not passing a verse in which there was good news without praying to God in aspiration, nor passing a fearful verse without praying to God for deliverance.'[36] Muʿādh ibn Jabal (d. 17/638–9?) disliked that the Qur'an be recited in less than three.[37] Ibn Masʿūd considered that whoever recited the Qur'an in less than three was just babbling, although unnamed Kufans approved of it in that time, according to al-Shāfiʿī.[38] Ibn Abī Shaybah quotes him as saying, 'Recite the Qur'an in seven. Do not recite it in three.'[39] A man came to Ibn 'Umar (d. 73/693?) and said, 'I have recited the Qur'an in a night (or a set of bowings).' Ibn 'Umar said, 'Did you do them? Had God willed, he might have sent it down in one lot (*jumlah*). He separated it to give every chapter its share of bowing and prostration.'[40] Jaʿfar al-Ṣādiq (d. 148/765) permitted it every three days in Ramadan, according to a Shiʿi source, but disliked generally that it be recited in less than a month.[41]

Some renunciants favoured prolonged meditation on a few verses. Muḥammad ibn Kaʿb al-Quraẓī (Kufan, d. 120/737–8?) preferred repeating two chapters, 99 and 101, to hurrying through the whole Qur'an in a night.[42] The important thing for him was to be attentive: 'One listens to the Qur'an with the heart there,

33 Abū Nuʿaym, *Ḥilyah* 3:7–8.

34 Abū Nuʿaym, *Ḥilyah* 4:227.

35 Basran *isnāds*: see Abū Dāwūd, *shahr Ramaḍān* 8, *bāb fī kam yuqra'u al-Qur'ān*, nos 1390, 1394; Tirmidhī, *al-qirā'āt* 11, nos 2946, 2949; Nasā'ī, *SK*, no 8067 *8013*; Ibn Abī Shaybah, *Muṣannaf* 2:500–1 *3:575*; Juynboll, *Encyclopedia*, 444 (attributing it in this form to the Basran Qatādah, d. 117/735–6?).

36 Ibn al-Mubārak, *Zuhd*, no 1196.

37 Ibn Abī Shaybah, *Muṣannaf* 2:501 *3:576*.

38 Ibn Abī Shaybah, *Muṣanna* 2:500 *3:575*; Shāfiʿī, *Umm* 7:175 *8:502*.

39 Ibn Abī Shaybah, *Muṣannaf* 2:502 *3:578*.

40 Abū 'Ubayd, *Faḍā'il al-Qur'ān*, 174.

41 Kulaynī, *Kāfī* 2:617–19, *faḍl al-Qur'ān*.

42 Ibn al-Mubārak, *Zuhd*, no 287; Wakīʿ, *Zuhd* 2:479; Abū Nuʿaym, *Ḥilyah* 3:214.

not in another place.'[43] Thābit al-Bunānī (Basran, d. 127/744–5?) would recite Q. 18:37 ('Are you ungrateful to Him who created you from dust and then from seed?'), wailing and repeating it all night in the course of ritual prayer.[44] Sulaymān al-Taymī (Basran, d. 143/760–1) repeated one verse all night long.[45] 'Amr ibn 'Ubayd (Basran, d. 144/761–2) would stay up all night in one prostration, repeating one verse.[46] Maryam al-Baṣrīyah (*fl.* late 8th cent.) stood up at the beginning of the night, recited Q. 42:19 ('God is kind to His servants. He gives sustenance to those whom He wishes. He is the Strong and the Mighty'), and did not go beyond it till dawn.[47]

Despite contrary hadith, there are many reports of reciting the Qur'an in two days or one, even more than once a day. Al-Aswad ibn Yazīd (Kufan, d. 75/694–5?), would recite the Qur'an in two days during Ramadan, otherwise six.[48] Sa'īd ibn Jubayr (Kufan, d. 95/714?) would recite the Qur'an in two days;[49] alternatively, twice a day since the killing of al-Ḥusayn except when travelling or ill.[50] He recited the whole Qur'an in the course of one set of ritual bowings (*rak'ah*), praying inside the Ka'bah.[51] The prominent Kufan traditionist Mis'ar ibn Kidām (d. 155/771–2?) recited half the Qur'an nightly in his *wird* prayer.[52] The Basran traditionist 'Abd al-Raḥmān ibn Mahdī (d. 198/814) likewise recited half the Qur'an nightly in his *wird*.[53] Sufyān al-Thawrī defended it: 'There is no harm in reciting the Qur'an in a night if you have understood it (*idhā fahimta ḥurūfah*).'[54]

As for daily recitation, the caliph 'Uthmān (d. 35/56) would recite the Qur'an in one set of ritual bowings by night.[55] Tamīm al-Dārī (d. 40/660–1) likewise recited the whole Qur'an in one set.[56] 'Alqamah ibn Qays (Kufan, d. 62/681–2?)

---

43 Abū Nu'aym, *Ḥilyah* 3:216.
44 Ibn Sa'd, *Ṭabaqāt* 7/2:4 *7:233*.
45 Abū Nu'aym, *Ḥilyah* 3:29.
46 Jāḥiẓ, *apud* Ibn al-Murtaḍá, *Klassen*, 36.
47 Sulamī, *Early Sufi women*, 84–5.
48 Ibn Abī Shaybah, *Muṣannaf* 2:500 *3:576*.
49 Ibn Sa'd, *Ṭabaqāt* 6:180–1 *6:259*; Aḥmad, *Zuhd*, 370 *443*.
50 Ibn Sa'd, *Ṭabaqāt* 6:181 *6:259–60*; Ibn Abī Shaybah, *Muṣannaf* 2:503 *3:579*.
51 Ibn Sa'd, *Ṭabaqāt* 6:181 *6:259*; Aḥmad, *Zuhd*, 370 *443* (< 'Al.); Ibn Abī Shaybah, *Muṣannaf* 2:503 *3:579*; Tirmidhī, *faḍā'il al-Qur'ān* 13, no 2946.
52 Abū Nu'aym, *Ḥilyah* 7:216.
53 Al-Khaṭīb al-Baghdādī, *Tārīkh* 10:247 *11:522*.
54 'Abd al-Razzāq, *Muṣannaf* 3:355.
55 'Abd al-Razzāq, *Muṣannaf* 3:354; Ibn Sa'd, *Ṭabaqāt* 3:53 *3:75–6*; Aḥmad, *Zuhd*, 127 *158*; Abū Nu'aym, *Ḥilyah* 1:57; Ibn Abī Shaybah, *Muṣannaf* 2:503 *3:579*; Tirmidhī, *faḍā'il al-Qur'ān* 13, no 2946.
56 Ibn Abī Shaybah, *Muṣannaf* 2:502 *3:578*.

would recite the Qur'an in a night.'[57] Murrah ibn Sharāḥīl (Kufan, d. 76/695–6) recited the Qur'an daily and so was safe from the trial (*fitnah*) of Ibn al-Zubayr; that is, I take it, he had no time to participate in the Second Civil War.[58] 'Alī ibn 'Abd Allāh al-Azdī (Yemeni, *fl.* late 7th cent.) would recite the Qur'an nightly during Ramadan.[59] Al-Zuhrī (d. 125/742–3?) recited the Qur'an before breaking his fast on 21, 23, 25, 27, and 29 Ramadan.[60] Thābit al-Bunānī (Basran, d. 127/744–5?) recited the Qur'an daily and fasted perpetually,[61] likewise the Medinese qadi Sa'd ibn Ibrāhīm (d. 127/744–5?).[62] Manṣūr ibn Zādhān (Wasiti, d. 129/746–7?), reputed for his austerity and devotion to religion (*min al-mutaqashshifīn wa-al-mutajarridīn li-dīn*), recited the Qur'an daily between the first prayer (here I take it the dawn prayer) and mid-afternoon.[63] The routine of al-Ḥasan ibn Ṣāliḥ ibn Ḥayy with his mother and brother has been mentioned already. Aḥmad ibn Ḥanbal (d. 241/855) would recite the Qur'an twice weekly, once by day and once by night. He once recited the whole Qur'an while praying in Mecca.[64] A thorough search of the sources would presumably turn up more examples as well as later.

Pious phrases

Dhikr most often refers to repeating phrases. The Prophet said, 'The best recollection (*dhikr*) is *lā ilāha illa 'Llāh*. The best supplication (*du'ā'*) is *al-ḥamdu lillāh*.'[65] As often, *dhikr* here plainly refers to a locution, not a mental process (as *du'ā'* shades off into repeated phrases, not necessarily express asking). For example, al-Ḥasan al-Baṣrī reported that the Prophet, on being asked what was the best work, said, 'That you die on the day that you die with your tongue moist from the

57 Ibn Abī Shaybah, *Muṣannaf* 2:503, 526 *3:579, 618–19* (on recitation of the entire Qur'an while circumambulating the Ka'bah, indicating integration with the pilgrimage ritual as well as the prayer), 13:410 *12:295*.

58 Abū Nu'aym, *Ḥilyah* 4:162–3 < Ibn al-Mubārak but not < Ḥusayn al-Marwazī and not in *al-Zuhd*.

59 Al-Sam'ānī, *al-Ansāb* 1:177, s.n. 'Bāriqī'; Ibn Ḥajar, *Tahdhīb* 7:359.

60 Abū Nu'aym, *Ḥilyah* 3:170.

61 Aḥmad, *'Ilal* 1:486 *1:181*.

62 Ibn Sa'd, *al-Ṭabaqāt al-kubrá: al-qism al-mutammim*, 204–5.

63 Ibn Ḥibbān, *Thiqāt* 7:474–5.

64 Ibn Abī Ya'lá, *Ṭabaqāt* 1:9 *1:20*.

65 Tirmidhī, *al-da'awāt* 9, *bāb mā jā'a anna da'wat al-muslim mustajābah*, no 3383; Ibn Mājah, *al-adab* 55, *bāb faḍl al-ḥāmidīn*, no 3800; Nasā'ī, *SK*, no 10667 10599.

recollection of God.'[66] Abū al-Dardā' (d. 32/652–3?) said that better than freeing 100 slaves is 'that your tongue remain moist from the recollection of God', plainly referring to continual speech.[67] Ibn Mas'ūd said almost the same: better than freeing 100 slaves is 'to stick to one's faith night and day and to keep one's tongue moist with recollecting God.'[68] Abū Idrīs (Yemeni, *fl.* early 8th cent.?) used to say, 'God, make my sight weeping (*'abar*), my silence meditation (*tafakkur*), and my pronunciation recollection (*dhikr*).'[69]

Fairly strenuous routines are envisioned; for example, the Prophet said,

> Whoever says a hundred times a day "There is no god but God, without a sharer; his is the kingdom; to him be praise; he has power over everything" has (to his credit) the equivalent of (setting free) ten slaves; is credited with a hundred good deeds and has a hundred bad deeds effaced; and is protected from Satan for the rest of the day until night. No one does better except him who says more.[70]

Hadith collections offer many examples of things the Prophet continually repeated; for example, from various Companions, 'The Prophet ... used to say, when he went to bed, "O God, by your name I live and by your name I die." When he awoke, he said, "Praise be to God who has given us life after giving us death, to him belonging the Day of Resurrection."'[71]

Accordingly, various renunciants are remembered as continually repeating pious phrases aloud. Abū Muslim al-Khawlānī (d. *ca* 60/679–80?) would retreat to his house after the evening prayer and say the *takbīr* (i.e., *Allāhu akbar*) and *dhikr* aloud. When his wife approached the house and heard, she would answer his *takbīr*. When he went inside, he would say, 'O Umm Muslim, may you start on

---

66 Ibn al-Mubārak, *Zuhd*, no 1141 (< al-Ḥu.); sim., no 935; sim., Tirmidhī, *al-da'awāt* 4, *mā jā'a fī faḍl al-dhikr*, no 3375 (Homsi *isnād*).

67 Ibn Abī Shaybah, *Muṣannaf* 13:458 *12:329*; Aḥmad, *Zuhd*, 136 *170* (Kufan *isnād*). Alternatively, 'That I should say 100 times *subḥāna 'Llāh* is preferable to me to giving 100 dinars in alms to the poor': Ibn Abī Shaybah, *Muṣannaf* 10:294 *10:84* (Basran *isnād*).

68 Ibn al-Mubārak, *Zuhd*, no 959.

69 Ibn Abī Shaybah, *Muṣannaf* 13:546 *12:393–4*.

70 Mālik, *Muwaṭṭa'*, rec. Yaḥyá, *al-ṣalāh* 136, *mā jā'a fī dhikr Allāh*, no 560, rec. Abū Muṣ'ab, *al-ṣalāh* 75, *bāb faḍl al-du'ā'*, no 520; Bukhārī, *bad' al-khalq* 11, *ṣifat Iblīs wa-junūdih*, no 3293; *al-da'awāt* 64, *bāb faḍl al-tahlīl*, no 6403; Muslim, *al-dhikr wa-al-du'ā'* 10, *bāb faḍl al-tahlīl*, no 2691; Tirmidhī, *al-da'awāt* 61, no 3773; Ibn Mājah, *al-adab* 54, *bāb faḍl lā ilāha illā Allāh*, no 3798; *SK*, no 9857 *9769*.

71 Bukhārī, *al-da'awāt* 7, *bāb mā yaqūlu idhā nāma*, no 6312, *al-da'awāt* 8, *bāb waḍ' al-yad al-yumná taḥta al-khadd al-yumná*, no 6314, *al-da'awāt* 16, *bāb mā yaqūlu idhā aṣbaḥa*, nos 6324–5, *al-tawḥīd* 13, *bāb al-su'āl bi-asmā' Allāh*, nos 7394–5; Muslim, *al-dhikr wa-al-du'ā'* 17, *bāb mā yaqūlu 'inda al-nawm*, no 2711.

your journey (*shadda raḥluki*), for there is no one to make you cross the bridge of Jahannam.'[72] Sa'īd ibn al-Musayyib (Medinese, d. 94/712–13?) often said in his session *allāhumma sallim sallim* ('O God, save, save').[73] Muḥammad ibn Sīrīn (Basran, d. 110/729) was seen entering the market at midday, saying *Allāhu akbar*, *subḥāna 'Llāh*, and some unspecified recollection (*yadhkuru Allāh*). On being asked 'At this hour?', he said, 'It is the hour of heedlessness (*ghaflah*).'[74]

Unsurprisingly, given preference for devotions out of public sight, the house is often the site of recollecting, as for Abū Muslim al-Khawlānī. Abū Hurayrah said, 'The people of Heaven see the houses of the people of recollection lit up as the stars are lit up for the people of Earth.'[75] 'Abd al-Raḥmān ibn Sābiṭ (Medinese, d. 118/736–7) said, 'Illuminate your houses with the recollection of God, giving them a share of your prayer.'[76] Here, recollection is integrated with the ritual prayer. Khulayd al-'Aṣarī (Basran, *fl.* early 8th cent.) would practise recollecting God all night, then pray the dawn prayer, then go home and repeat *subḥāna 'Llāh*, *lā ilāha illā 'Llāh*, and *Allāhu akbar* till his eyes overcame him or it was time for the noon prayer.[77] Sleeping time could be put to use at home: Khālid ibn Ma'dān (Homsi, d. 103/721–2?) said, 'There is no slave who puts his temple to the bed as he recollects God (be he exalted) but that he will be recorded as one who recollects (*dhākir*) when he awakes, whenever he awakes.'[78]

Also unsurprisingly, though, the place for recollecting God is often the mosque. 'Amr ibn Maymūn al-Awdī (Kufan, d. 74/693–4?) would recollect God whenever he entered the mosque.[79] Ḥassān ibn 'Aṭīyah (Basran client, transferred to Beirut, d. 120s/738–48) would perform the afternoon prayer, then practise recollection of God in a corner of the mosque till sunset.[80]

There are also numerous reports of group sessions devoted to recollection. The Prophet said, 'There does not meet a group (*qawm*) to recollect God but that the angels surround them, mercy covers them, perfect peace (*al-sakīnah*) descends on them, and God recollects them among those with him.'[81] It is a good

72 Abū Dāwūd, *Zuhd*, 254, no 504.
73 Ibn Sa'd, *Ṭabaqāt* 5:100 *5:136*; Ibn Abī Shaybah, *Muṣannaf* 13:533 *12:384*. Sufyān al-Thawrī said, 'I have heard that one of the Prophet's prayers was *sallim sallim*': Ibn al-Mubārak, *Zuhd*, no 386.
74 Aḥmad, *Zuhd*, 307 *373*.
75 Ibn Abī Shaybah, *Muṣannaf* 13:456 *12:384*.
76 Ibn Abī Shaybah, *Muṣannaf* 13:456 *12:384*.
77 Aḥmad, *Zuhd*, 237 *290–1*.
78 Ibn al-Mubārak, *Zuhd*, no 927.
79 Abū Nu'aym, *Ḥilyah* 4:148–9 (< Aḥ., *Zuhd*).
80 Ibn 'Asākir, *Tārīkh* 12:441.
81 Aḥmad, *Musnad* 3:94 *18:389–90* (Kufan *isnād*).

guess that the group is to recollect aloud, but God is probably also, here, to be thought of as speaking, as expressly in another report:

> The Messenger of God ... came out on a circle of his Companions. He said, 'What has made you sit?' They said, 'We have sat to recollect God and to praise him for leading us to Islam and how he has thereby obliged us.' He said, 'By God, did nothing make you sit but that?' They said, 'By God, nothing made us sit but that.' He said, 'I did not ask you to swear from suspicion of you, but Jibrīl came to me and told me that God (mighty and glorious is he) is boasting of you to the angels.'[82]

Mosques are especially the place for group recitation. The Prophet said,

> The Lord (mighty and glorious is he) will say on the Day of the Resurrection, 'Today, the people of the harvest (*ahl al-jamʿ*) will be distinguished from the people of the vineyard (*ahl al-karam*).' It will be asked, 'Who are the people of the vineyard?' He will say, 'Sessions of recollection in the mosques.'[83]

Mosques are places to pause and listen to praises, anticipating the pleasures of Paradise: '"When you pass by the pastures of Paradise, graze." They asked, "And what are the pastures of Paradise?" He said, "Circles of recollection."'[84] In another version, the Prophet names specific locutions to repeat there:

> 'When you pass the pastures of Paradise, graze.' Abū Hurayrah: 'What are the pastures of Paradise?' He said, 'The mosques.' Abū Hurayrah: 'And what is grazing, O Messenger of God?' He said, '*Subḥāna 'Llāh*, *al-ḥamdu lillāh*, *lā ilāha illā 'Llāh*, and *Allāhu akbar*.'[85]

Muʿādh ibn Jabal (d. 18/639–40?) said to another Companion, 'Sit by us for us to say "Amen" for a while (*ijlis binā nuʾamminu sāʿah*)', presumably indicating alternation between someone's offering praises and the group's vocal affirmation. The quotation is followed by a gloss, 'meaning to recollect God'.[86] But there are other reports suggesting that worshippers would say 'Amen'. For example, Muṭarrif ibn al-Shikhkhīr (Basran, d. 95/713–14) prayed while his companions said *āmīn*; similarly, Mālik ibn Dīnar asked someone to say *āmīn* after his prayer.[87] (And of course all Muslims say *āmīn* after the recitation of Q. 1, the *Fātiḥah*.)

---

82 Muslim, *al-dhikr wa-al-duʿāʾ* 11, no 2701.
83 Aḥmad, *Musnad* 3:68 *18:195* (Egyptian *isnād*).
84 Tirmidhī, *al-daʿawāt* 87, no 3110; Aḥmad, *Musnad* 3:76 *18:249–50* (Basran *isnād*).
85 Tirmidhī, *al-daʿawāt* 87, no 3009 (Kufan/Meccan *isnād*).
86 Ibn Abī Shaybah, *Muṣannaf* 13:347 *12:249* (Kufan *isnād*); by another *isnād*, Abū Nuʿaym, *Ḥilyah* 1:235.
87 Abū Nuʿaym, *Ḥilyah* 2:206–7 (Muṭarrif), 370 (Mālik).

ʿUmar ibn al-Khaṭṭāb (d. 23/644) said to his comrades, 'Let us go increase in faith', and so they would recollect God (*yadhkurūna Allāh*).[88] ʿUmar (d. 23/44) joined a circle in mosque after prayer, on being told, 'We have sat to recollect God.' He bade each one to speak in turn, something like *Allāhumma 'ghfir lanā, Allāhumma 'rḥamnā* (O God, forgive us; O God, have mercy on us'). He wept more than anyone but broke up the session himself.[89] (There is obviously some overlap here with group supplication, discussed in the previous chapter.) Khulayd al-ʿAṣarī said the adornment of mosques were men who help one another to recollect God.[90] ʿAwn ibn ʿAbd Allāh (Kufan, d. bef. 120/738) recalled meeting with Umm al-Dardāʾ (d. 81/700–1) to recollect God before her.[91] (Implicitly, recollection aloud was to be a single-sex activity.) He said, 'Sessions of recollection are the cure of hearts.'[92] Thābit al-Bunānī (Basran, d. 127/744–5?) said they used to recollect God with his comrades for a tenth of each day.[93] On his deathbed, he prayed God not to let him die when he was no longer capable of praying as he was accustomed, fasting as he was accustomed, and recollecting God to his companions as he was accustomed, whereupon he died.[94]

There is some discussion of silent as opposed to audible recollection. ʿĀʾishah (d. 57/676–7) said, 'The subdued recollection (*al-dhikr al-khafī*) that the guardian angels do not write down is worth 70 times as much as other recollection.'[95] If not even the guardian angels can hear it, it is probably silent. Saʿīd ibn al-Musayyib said, 'We were sitting with Saʿd ibn Mālik [Companion, d. 64/683–4?] when he fell silent for a bit. Then he said, "By this silence I have hit on something like the flood of the Nile and the Tigris." We said, "What have you hit on?" He said, "*Subḥāna 'Llāh, al-ḥamdu lillāh, lā ilāha illā 'Llāh*, and *Allāhu akbar*."'[96] Masrūq (Kufan, d. 63/682–3?) said, 'So long as a man's heart is recollecting God, he is in the ritual prayer, even if he is in the market.'[97] The same is attributed to Abū ʿUbaydah (the son of Ibn Masʿūd, Kufan, d. after 80/699–700) but in one version

88 Ḥarb al-Kirmānī, *Masāʾil*, 370.
89 Ibn Saʿd, *Ṭabaqāt* 3/1:211 *3:294*.
90 Aḥmad, *Zuhd*, 237 *291* (< ʿAl.); this version and another *apud* Abū Nuʿaym, *Ḥilyah* 2:233 (< Aḥ., *Zuhd*).
91 Abū Nuʿaym, *Ḥilyah* 4:241.
92 Abū Nuʿaym, *Ḥilyah* 4:241.
93 Abū Nuʿaym, *Ḥilyah* 2:323.
94 Abū Nuʿaym, *Ḥilyah* 2:320.
95 Ibn Abī Shaybah, *Muṣannaf* 10:376 *10:143*.
96 Ibn Abī Shaybah, *Muṣannaf* 13:455 *12:326*.
97 Ibn Abī Shaybah, *Muṣannaf* 13:458 *12:329*; Aḥmad, *Zuhd*, 348–9 *418*.

with the addition, 'If he moves his lips, it is better.'[98] Muḥammad ibn Sīrīn's audible recollection in the market has been mentioned already. Abū Muslim al-Khawlānī (Syrian. d. early 60s/680s) was notable for raising his voice to say *Allāhu akbar* and said, 'Recollect God until the ignorant think you mad.'[99] Unison praises seem to be implied by the report that Mujāhid (Meccan cl., d. 104/722–3?), 'when he saw a group supplicating (*yadʿūna*), having raised their voices, would throw stones at them and interpret to them, "Do not be loud in your prayer, nor hushed in it"'; that is, extending Q. 17:110 on the ritual prayer (*ṣalāh*) to informal supplication.[100]

Qays ibn al-ʿUbād (Basran, d. 82/701 or after) said, 'The Companions of the Messenger of God ... used to dislike raising the voice at funerals, in fighting, and in recollection.'[101] There is good and bad of both spoken and silent recollection, according to a Shiʿi report from the Prophet condemning chess: 'Whoever speaks [during a chess game], his speech is other than the recollection of God, rather he is being frivolous (*lāghī*). As for whoever is silent, his silence is for other than the recollection of God, rather he is neglectful (*sāhī*).'[102] Silent recollection is preferable to audible in the view of those who prize unostentatiousness. Mālik (d. 179/795) said, 'Saʿīd ibn Abī Hind, Nāfiʿ the client of Ibn ʿUmar, and Mūsá ibn Maysarah used to sit until the sun rose, then disperse. They would not talk to one another from preoccupation with the recollection of God.'[103]

Probably, majority opinion favours a subdued voice. The Prophet said, 'The best recollection is the subdued, the best provision what suffices (*khayr al-dhikr al-khafī wa-khayr al-rizq mā yakfī*).'[104] This probably covers the many reports of a mumbling or humming sound. Someone said of Ibn Masʿūd, 'When the eyes had rested (*hadaʾat al-ʿuyūn*; i.e., after a nap), he got up. I heard from him a humming like that of bees.'[105] There is the saying of Abū al-Aḥwaṣ (Kufan, d. late 7th cent.)

---

98 Ibn Abī Shaybah, *Muṣannaf* 10:305 *10:93*; also 13:458 *12:329*; Aḥmad, *Zuhd*, 381 *457*; Abū Nuʿaym, *Ḥilyah* 4:204.

99 Aḥmad, *Zuhd*, 382 *458*. The Prophet himself is quoted as saying, 'Recollect God so much that the hypocrites think you do it to be seen': Ibn al-Mubārak, *Zuhd*, no 1022; Aḥmad, *Zuhd*, 108 *134* (< 'Al.).

100 Sufyān al-Thawrī, *Tafsīr*, 175, among half a dozen instances of applying this verse to *duʿāʾ*.

101 Wakīʿ, *Zuhd* 2:462; Ibn Abī Shaybah, *Muṣannaf* 10:530 *10:257*; Ibn al-Mubārak, *Zuhd*, no 247 (with *al-Qurʾān* in place of *al-dhikr*).

102 Kulaynī, *Kāfī* 6:437, *al-ashribah, bāb al-nard wa-al-shaṭranj*.

103 Ibn Abī Zayd, *Jāmiʿ*, 163–4.

104 Wakīʿ, *Zuhd* 1:242, 2:616; Ibn Abī Shaybah, *Muṣannaf*, 10:375–6, 13:240 *10:143*, *12:170*; Aḥmad, *Zuhd* 10 *16*; Aḥmad, *Musnad* 1:172, 180 *3:76*, *131–2*.

105 Wakīʿ, *Zuhd* 1:391; Aḥmad, *Zuhd*, 156 *195*; Ibn al-Mubārak, *Zuhd*, no 97.

of, apparently, the army that conquered Egypt: 'If a man went through the camp and heard from its people a humming like that of bees, then how could those (the enemy) feel safe so long as these (the Muslims busy with recollection) feared?'[106] (The angels' recollection around God's throne also was likened to the humming of bees.[107]) The two senses of speaking aloud and silent attentiveness come together in various sayings contrasting those who recollect with those who are heedless. For example, ʿAwn ibn ʿAbd Allāh (Kufan, d. bef. 120/738) said, 'The *dhākir* (recollecting) among the *ghāfilīn* (heedless) is like the *muqātil* (fighter) separating himself from the *fārrīn* (retreaters).'[108]

It would later be held that purely mental recollection was the earlier form, spoken being a later development. For example, the qur'anic commentator al-Qurṭubī (d. 671/1273?) says,

> The original meaning of *dhikr* is attentiveness (*al-tanabbuh*) by the heart to the thing attended to and being aware of it (*al-tayaqquẓ lahu*). Recollection by the tongue is called *dhikr* because it is an indication of mental recollection (*al-dhikr al-qalbī*). However, as the application of *dhikr* to mention by the tongue has increased, it has become the first thing one understands by it.[109]

But it seems much more likely that spoken recollection actually preceded purely mental, as reading aloud historically preceded reading silently. Indeed, Islamic law is suspicious of silent affirmations; for example, most schools hold that the parts of the ritual prayer not to be said aloud are not left to mental activity alone but spoken softly, so that only the one praying hears.

Silent recollection shades off into *fikr*, *tafakkur*, and *iʿtibār*, different sorts of contemplation. As for *fikr* ('thought'), the pious caliph ʿUmar ibn ʿAbd al-ʿAzīz (*r.* 99–101/717–20) said, 'The recollection of God is good speech, while contemplation (*fikrah*) of God's blessings is the best worship.'[110] ʿUtbah al-Ghulām (Basran, d. bef. 153/770) would divide his nights between *fikr* and weeping, presumably having contemplated things that suggested his unworthiness.[111] Sufyān al-Thawrī

---

106 So I take it—*mā bāl hā'ulā' ya'manūn mā kāna ulā'ika yakhāfūn*: Wakīʿ, *Zuhd* 1:389; Aḥmad, *Zuhd*, 348 *418*; Ibn Abī Shaybah, *Muṣannaf* 13:420 *12:301*; Ibn al-Mubārak, *Zuhd*, no 98; Abū ʿUbayd, *Faḍā'il al-Qur'ān*, ed. ʿAṭīyah, 128.

107 Aḥmad, *Zuhd*, 244 *298* (< ʿAl.); sim., Abū Nuʿaym, *Ḥilyah* 6:4–5.

108 Ibn al-Mubārak, *Zuhd*, no 357; Ibn Abī Shaybah, *Muṣannaf* 13:428 *12:307*; Abū Nuʿaym, *Ḥilyah* 4:241 (< Aḥ., *Zuhd*). Sim., Kulaynī, *Kāfī* 2:502, *al-duʿā'*, *bāb dhikr Allāh … fī al-ghāfilīn*; Barqī, *Maḥāsin*, 32.

109 Qurṭubī, *Jāmiʿ* 2:166, *ad* Q. 2:152.

110 Abū Nuʿaym, *Ḥilyah* 5:314.

111 Abū Nuʿaym, *Ḥilyah* 6:235.

was thrown down unconscious by *fikr* on looking up at the sky after praying two sets of bowings by the Kaʿbah.[112]

Tafakkur is spoken of most highly. Abū al-Dardāʾ said, ‘*Tafakkur* for an hour is better than staying up the night.’[113] Al-Ḥasan al-Baṣrī said the same.[114] From a Shiʿi tradition comes an explanation: Jaʿfar al-Ṣādiq (d. Medina, 148/765), asked whether *tafakkur* for an hour was better than staying up all night, said, ‘Yes. The Messenger of God ... said that *tafakkur* for an hour is better than staying up all night. One passes by a ruined house and says, “Where are those who built you? Where are those who lived in you? What is wrong with you, that you do not speak?”’[115] As looking for edifying examples in the world, it is naturally close to *iʿtibār*, ‘taking warning’. Umm al-Dardāʾ said of her husband Abū al-Dardāʾ that his best work was *tafakkur* and *iʿtibār*.[116] Of course, there are many examples of taking phenomena as warnings not using these technical terms. For example, ʿAbd Allāh ibn ʿAmr (d. 77/696–7?), on hearing the sound of a fire, said, ‘I, too.’ Asked about it, he said, ‘By him in whose hand is my soul, it is taking refuge from the greatest fire, lest it be returned to it.’[117]

One especially prominent object of contemplation is death (although the term used is usually *dhikr* rather than *tafakkur*). The Prophet, on hearing his Companions praising someone, asked, ‘How is his recollection of death?’ They said, ‘He is not like that.’ The Prophet said, ‘Then he is not as you say.’[118] Asked who was the best of people, the Prophet said, ‘The one who most recollects death and is the readiest for it.’[119] He said, ‘Often recollect the sharp sword of pleasures: death.’[120]

An anonymous *rāhib* quoted by Wahb ibn Munabbih (Yemeni, d. 114/732?), on being asked of his recollection of death, said, ‘I do not lift a foot nor lay down

---

112 Abū al-Shaykh, *ʿAẓamah* 1:316–17.
113 Abū Dāwūd, *Zuhd*, 121, no 209.
114 Ibn Abī Shaybah, *Muṣannaf* 13:507 *12:365*; Abū Nuʿaym, *Ḥilyah* 6:271.
115 Barqī, *Maḥāsin*, 23; Kulaynī, *Kāfī* 2:54–5, *al-īmān wa-al-kufr, bāb al-tafakkur.*
116 Ibn al-Mubārak, *Zuhd*, no 286; Aḥmad, *Zuhd* 135 *168*; Abū Nuʿaym, *Ḥilyah* 4:253.
117 Abū Nuʿaym, *Ḥilyah* 1:289 < lost § of Aḥmad, *Zuhd* (< ʿAl.).
118 Aḥmad, *Zuhd* 17 *24*.
119 Al-Qāḍī al-Nuʿmān, *Daʿāʾim* 1:224; sim., Abū Nuʿaym, *Ḥilyah* 1:313.
120 Ibn al-Mubārak, *Zuhd*, nos 145–6 < Nuʿaym; Aḥmad, *Zuhd*, 17 *23*; Tirmidhī, *al-zuhd* 4, *bāb mā jāʾa fī dhikr al-mawt*, no 2307; al-Nasāʾī, *Mujtabá*, *al-janāʾiz* 3, *kathrat dhikr al-mawt*, no 1824; Ibn Mājah, *al-zuhd* 31, *bāb dhikr al-mawt wa-al-istiʿdād lah*, no 4258.

a foot without thinking that I have died.'[121] Abū al-Dardā' said, 'Consider yourselves among the dead.'[122] Al-Rabī' ibn Khuthaym said, 'Often recollect this death whose like you have never before tasted.'[123] He said of himself, 'If recollection of death departed from my heart for a moment (*sā'atan*), it would be corrupted.'[124] Yazīd ibn Sharīk (Kufan, d. 65–86/685–705) or his son Ibrāhīm (d. 92/710–11) was unable to have sex with his wife from his recollecting death.[125] Al-Ḥasan al-Baṣrī warned, 'O son of Adam, tread the earth with your foot, for it will soon be your grave. You have been going to destruction since you fell from your mother's belly.'[126] Hishām al-Dastuwā'ī (Basran, d. 153/770?) would toss and turn in bed if lamplight did not reach him. He explained to his wife, 'When I miss the lamp, I recollect the darkness of the tomb.'[127] This was apparently undeliberate recollection but still praiseworthy.

Some explanations are offered. Al-'Alā' ibn Ziyād (Basran, d. 94/712–13) advised imagining oneself on the point of death, which would conduce to acting in obedience to God.[128] 'Umar ibn 'Abd al-'Azīz said, 'Recollect death often, for if you are straitened in life, it will relax it for you, whereas if you are relaxed in life, it will straiten it for you.'[129] (However, it was also reported, 'When he recollected death, he shook like a bird and wept until the tears flowed onto his beard.'[130]) Muḥammad al-Bāqir (d. Medina, 115/733) said, 'Recollect death often, for no man recollects death often without renouncing the world.'[131] Shumayṭ ibn 'Ajlān (Basran, *fl.* early 8th cent.) said, 'Whoever puts up death before his eyes will not care about the narrowness or wideness of the world.'[132]

---

121 Aḥmad, *Zuhd*, 97 *122*. *Rāhib*, literally 'fearer', by extension 'monk'—the latter is presumably what Wahb has in mind. For examples of *rāhib* applied to Muslim renunciants, see Melchert, 'Islamic literature', 137–8, also Massignon, *Essay*, 99, 104, and Ṣādir, *Ruhbān*.

122 Ibn al-Mubārak, *Zuhd*, no. 1155 (< al-Ḥu.); Aḥmad, *Zuhd*, 134–5 *168*; Hannād, *Zuhd* 1:290.

123 Ibn Abī Shaybah, *Muṣannaf* 14:17 *12:431*; Abū Nu'aym, *Ḥilyah* 2:114.

124 Ibn al-Mubārak, *Zuhd*. no 266; Abū Nu'aym, *Ḥilyah* 2:116. Sim. attributed to Sa'īd ibn Jubayr (Kufan, d. 95/713–14): Aḥmad, *Zuhd*, 371 *444*. Sim. attributed to al-Rabī' ibn Abī Rāshid (Kufan, *fl.* early 8th cent.): Ibn al-Mubārak, *Zuhd*, no 266; Ibn Abī Shaybah, *Muṣannaf* 13:561 *12:405*; Abū Nu'aym, *Ḥilyah* 5:75–6; Aḥmad, *Zuhd*, 394 *472*.

125 Abū Nu'aym, *Ḥilyah* 4:210.

126 Ibn al-Mubārak, *Zuhd*, no 852; Jāḥiẓ, *Bayān* 3:133; Abū Nu'aym, *Ḥilyah* 2:155; sim., Ibn Abī Shaybah, *Muṣannaf* 14:55 *12:459*.

127 Ibn Sa'd, *Ṭabaqāt* 7/2:39 *7:279*.

128 Aḥmad, *Zuhd*, 255 *312*.

129 Abū Nu'aym, *Ḥilyah* 5:264–5.

130 Abū Nu'aym, *Ḥilyah* 5:316.

131 Al-Qāḍī al-Nu'mān, *Da'ā'im al-islām* 1:224.

132 Abū Nu'aym, *Ḥilyah* 3:129.

Later forms

Some devotional forms have apparently been associated with the early renunciants by mistake. *Samāʿ*, literally 'hearing' but meaning here music as an aid to meditation, has been proposed as a practice of pre-classical Sufis opposed by the general religious movement.[133] It certainly became a prominent Sufi practice, despite discouragement of music in Islamic law, but actually seems to have been rare in the eighth century. 'In fact,' says Jean During, 'apart from Qur'ānic psalmody, the tradition of musical audition for spiritual purposes is not attested before the middle of the ninth century.'[134] This is probably an overstatement. Poems encouraging renunciation of the world, *zuhdīyāt*, were an established genre by the mid-eighth century and presumably were performed to music the same as other poetry.[135] Ibn al-Jawzī reports indignantly that Saʿd ibn ʿAbd Allāh, a Damascene worshipper of the early eighth century, bought a slave girl who sang *qaṣāʾid* (presumably *zuhdīyāt*) to the *fuqarāʾ*, while the Kūfan ʿAwn ibn ʿAbd Allāh (d. before 120/737–8) had a slave girl preach and sing after he had finished his own sermon.[136] Still, it cannot be said that musical performances were a prominent innovative ritual practice of the eighth-century renunciants.

From the mid-ninth century, there is a curious story by which Aḥmad ibn Ḥanbal's son Ṣāliḥ invited one Ibn al-Khabbāzah to sing renunciant poems, one night. By one account, he thought it was safe because his father had gone to bed, then heard a noise on the roof, went up to investigate, and, in his words, 'I saw my father on the roof, listening with his train under his armpit, prancing about on the roof as if he were dancing.' According to other versions, he came and went listening from behind a door, and was seen to sway left and right. Ibn al-Jawzī, who relates the series of stories, does not deny them, although he protests that this at least did not involve profane singing and suggests that the detail of dancing in addition to listening was a later, tendentious interpolation.[137] This is possible, but the stories in question seem to have appeared in Ḥanbali literature no later than the early tenth century and establish that listening to renunciant poems set to music was not the practice of a few aberrant Sufis in the century before.

---

133 *EI*², s.v. 'taṣawwuf', by B. Radtke.

134 During, 'Musique', 159. Sim., Gribetz, '*Samāʿ*', 44; Massignon, *Essay*, 106.

135 See Hamori, 'Ascetic poetry'.

136 Ibn al-Jawzī, *Talbīs*, 316–17; *Devil's delusion, Islamic culture* 19 (1945): 281. Abū Nuʿaym does not mention preaching but does describe a slave girl of ʿAwn's named Bishrah who recited the Qur'an to tones so sorrowfully that ʿAwn's associates all threw off their turbans and wept: *Ḥilyah* 4:264. On music and reciting the Qur'an by tones, see Melchert, 'Controversy'.

137 Ibn al-Jawzī, *Talbīs*, 317–18; *Devil's delusion, Islamic culture* 19 (1945): 282–3.

Chapter 6: The Muslim holy man

My chapter title comes of course from Peter Brown's widely hailed, seminal article on the holy man in Late Antiquity.[1] That article has provoked much new research from students of spirituality in Late Antiquity and the early Byzantine period. I mostly leave it aside here.[2] Second is the issue of intercession. It turns out that this is much easier to document for Christian holy men than political intervention, and likewise for Muslim holy men. Third is the Muslim holy man as a worker of miracles. They are not a prominent part of the Islamic record, but they are there. In all respects, I hope to show, it is possible to demonstrate substantial continuity between patterns of spirituality in Late Antiquity and among early Muslims, as Brown suggested, if not just the patterns that Brown made out. If one avoids projecting backwards the familiar, more differentiated social rôles of the ninth century and later, one can see that holiness was both widely diffused and contested in the early Islamic centuries.

Holy man as arbitrator

Peter Brown's description of the holy man in Late Antiquity has been widely hailed as presaging the holy man of the early Islamic period. The social rôle of Brown's holy man as arbitrator roughly fits the prophet Muḥammad composing quarrels among the clans of Yathrib, although it seems to anticipate Gellner's early-modern saints of the Atlas more closely than eighth-century Muslim renunciants of Syria and Iraq.[3] It turns out there are important Christian precedents as well for Muslim renunciants as military leaders.[4] There may be echoes of the pre-Islamic tradition of political intervention by holy men in the institution of *al-amr bi-al-maʿrūf wa-al-nahy ʿan al-munkar*, commanding right and forbidding wrong. Historically, it has normally covered two related activities: rebuke of misbehaving rulers and private correction of misbehaviour where the ruler has failed to

1 Brown, 'Rise and function of the holy man'.

2 See notably Howard-Johnson and Howard, eds, *The cult of saints*, and two surveys by Brown himself, 'The saint as exemplar' and 'The rise and function ... 1971–1997'.

3 See Gellner, *Saints of the Atlas*. For the life of the Prophet, see Cook, *Muhammad*, also Watt, *Muhammad at Mecca* and *Muhammad at Medina*, and Ibn Hishām, *Sīrah*.

4 See notably Gaddis, *There is no crime for those who have Christ*, and Walker, *The legend of Mar Qardagh*. The rhetoric of violence in the Christian and Islamic traditions is scrutinized by Sizgorich, *Violence and belief*.

https://doi.org/10.1515/9783110617962-007

enforce the law. (The phrase occurs several times in the Qur'an but its meaning there, to judge by the context, is rather different from what it came to mean in practice.[5]) Brown mentions first late-antique philosophers, then bishops and hermits who would act as disinterested advisers, even critics, to rulers.[6] Michael Cook has studied the problem more thoroughly than anyone else and finds the closest theoretical precedent for *al-amr bi-al-maʿrūf* in the Rabbinic tradition.[7] The renunciant without social attachments, with nothing in the world to lose, was best qualified to rebuke the ruler. There is certainly a tradition of Muslim holy men whipped by rulers for reproaching them or otherwise resisting; for example, Abū al-Sawwār al-ʿAdawī (Basran, *fl.* 7th cent.), whose example comforted Aḥmad ibn Ḥanbal, Saʿīd ibn al-Musayyib (Medinese, d. 93/711–12?) for refusing to swear oaths of allegiance both to the reigning caliph and his designated successor, and Wahb ibn Munabbih (d. 114/732?), beaten to death by the Umayyads' governor of Yemen.[8] In the ninth century, renunciants expressly called Sufis were often associated with commanding right and forbidding wrong.[9] This is a sort of arbitration by holy men.

The institution of *iftāʾ*, answering juridical questions, is also a sort of arbitration, either between Muslims in the case of civil disputes or between Muslims and God. The Medinese Muḥammad ibn al-Munkadir (d. 130/747–8?) is quoted as saying, 'The jurisprudent comes between God and his servants.'[10] The classical model is that the layman submits a written question to the *muftī*, a certified expert in Islamic law after one or another school; the *muftī* goes over the sources in his mind (mainly Qur'an and Sunnah, the latter comprising mainly the teaching and precedent of the Prophet; with time, increasingly the opinions of earlier jurisprudents in the *muftī*'s own school); then the *muftī* hands the paper with the question back to the layman with his answer written on it.[11] The layman is probably free to submit the same question to another *muftī* and, in case of contradictory opinions, is free to follow any. (There are some questions where God has chosen to reveal his will so clearly that there is no disagreement, but more normally the evidence of God's will bears more than one plausible interpretation, and God will punish

5 See Cook, *Commanding right and forbidding wrong*, 13–17, for *al-amr bi-al-maʿrūf* in the Qur'an.
6 Brown, *Power and persuasion*, 4.
7 Cook, *Commanding right*, 569–79, for pre-Islamic precedents.
8 Abū Nuʿaym, *Ḥilyah* 2:250 (Abū al-Sawwār), 170–2 (Saʿīd); Ibn Ḥajar, *Tahdhīb* 11:168 (Wahb).
9 See further chapter 10, below.
10 Ibn Abī Khaythamah, *Tārīkh* 2:260; Abū al-Qāsim al-Baghawī, *Jaʿdīyāt* 1:493; Abū Nuʿaym, *Ḥilyah* 3:153.
11 For a description of medieval practice, see Jackson, 'The second education of the *muftī*'; for traditional practice directly observed in modern Yemen, Messick, 'The mufti, the text and the world'.

no one for making a mistake so long as all have done their best to infer his will in the prescribed fashion.[12]) A Shāfiʿi jurisprudent of the late classical period, Taqī al-Dīn al-Subkī (d. Damascus, 756/1355?), describes *iftāʾ* as the application of universals to particular events.[13] Alongside Sufism, it was the principal means by which ordinary Muslims were connected with divinity.

In the classical procedure, of course, the *muftī* is like a Jewish rabbi, characterized by superior learning but not necessarily, and certainly not in coming up with juridical opinions, immediate, charismatic insight—that is the province of the Sufi. Before the classical period, however, the *muftī* often appears to have been not only a mediator but specifically a holy man. A great many of the earliest jurisprudents also appear in our biographical dictionaries of holy men. For example, all of the Seven Jurisprudents of Medina have entries in *Ḥilyat al-awliyāʾ*.[14] Joseph Schacht proposed that the authoritative opinions of eighth-century jurisprudents were gradually reframed as the authoritative opinions of Companions and only last as the authoritative hadith of the Prophet himself.[15] In other words, jurisprudents themselves were earlier on more frankly the originators of Islamic law, not merely interpreters of what the Prophet had said and done. Schacht's scheme is roughly confirmed by two massive collections of opinions, the *Muṣannafs* of ʿAbd al-Razzāq (Yemeni, d. 211/827) and Abū Bakr Ibn Abī Shaybah (d. Kufa, 235/849), published only after Schacht wrote.[16] These present overwhelmingly (over 80%) not reports of what the Prophet said and did, such as fill the Six Books (the roughly canonical Sunni collections of hadith, all from the later ninth century or early tenth), but what the Companions and later Muslims said and did.

12 A *muftī* will normally assert that his school's answer is most probably the correct rule but seldom that it is certainly correct and the other schools' answers certainly wrong. See, among other studies, Weiss, *The spirit of Islamic law*, chap. 5; Chaumont, 'Tout chercheur qualifié dit-il juste?'; and Calder, 'Ikhtilâf and ijmâʿ'.

13 Subkī, *Fatāwá* 1:213; *apud* Calder, *Islamic jurisprudence*, 121.

14 Abū Nuʿaym, *Ḥilyah* 2:176–98.

15 Schacht, *Origins*, esp. 156.

16 On the *Muṣannaf* of ʿAbd al-Razzāq, see further Motzki, *Origins*. Motzki argues against Schacht that much of the material in the *Muṣannaf* must go back to its ultimate purported sources, including the Companions of the Prophet if not the Prophet himself, and was not simply projected back onto them by later generations. Motzki does not dispute the essential point here: that in the eighth century, the opinions of Companions and later Muslims were much more important in determining the law (by comparison with the sayings and actions of the Prophet) than in the Classical period. On dependence on Companions and later Muslims in the *Muṣannaf* of Ibn Abī Shaybah, see Lucas, 'Where are the legal *ḥadīth*?'

In particular, I would stress how our most primitive presentations of the law often cite not just the dicta but the practice of early jurisprudents. For example, several jurisprudents report that al-Ḥasan al-Baṣrī (d. 110/728) concluded the ritual prayer in public by saluting once rather than twice, as became normal.[17] The authority of such men as teachers of the law and as examples of righteous living were closely connected. For example, Ibn Abī al-Zinād (d. Baghdad, 174/790–1) is quoted as saying, 'The people of Medina disliked to take concubines until there arose among them the leading renunciants ʿAlī ibn al-Ḥusayn ibn ʿAlī ibn Abī Ṭālib and al-Qāsim ibn Musālim ibn ʿAbd Allāh. They exceeded the people of Medina in knowledge, piety, worship, and scrupulosity, so from then on, the people wanted concubines.'[18] ('Worship', here, means especially their engaging in supererogatory ritual prayer.) To conclude, then, it appears that, although arbitration between social classes is difficult to discern in the record of early Muslim renunciants (of course, inasmuch as the Muslims constituted the aristocracy), they were busy with other sorts of arbitration and mediation.

Intercession

Peter Brown's holy man of Late Antiquity is strongly associated with intercession—for Brown, in 1971, especially between officials and subjects, but subsequent research has shown that intercessory prayer was also crucial to the authority of Christian religious leaders.[19] Intercessory prayer is recognized by the Qur'an, albeit with the qualification that it takes place by God's permission and alongside many warnings for unbelievers not to count on it.[20] Many hadith reports describe how many Muslims, henceforth known as the Jahannamīyūn, will be condemned to the Fire at the Last Judgement, which they enter till they are burnt to

17 Ibn Abī Shaybah, *Muṣannaf* 1:300–1 *2:177–9*. On learning the law by observing the Rabbi's behaviour, presumably a precedent for the early Islamic phenomenon, see for example Gerhardsson, *Memory and manuscript*, esp. 185–7, and Neusner, 'Judaism'.

18 Ibn Ḥajar, *Tahdhīb* 3:437. There is evidently a parallel here in Late Antique bishops, insofar as an ascetic lifestyle was a foundation and justification of their power, for which see Nürnberg, *Askese als sozialer Impuls*, and Sterk, *Renouncing the world*.

19 See Rapp, '"For next to God, you are my salvation"' and *Holy bishops in Late Antiquity*, esp. chap. 3.

20 The survey in *EQ*, s.v. 'Intercession', by Hoffman, is mainly concerned with intercession as presented in hadith, contrary to the announced editorial policy of this encyclopaedia, betraying unease with the apparent harshness of the Qur'an. Cf. Bowker, 'Intercession in the Qur'an', esp. 69–75.

coals, then will be delivered and sent to Paradise by the Prophet's intercession.[21] Other hadith reports name the angels, prophets, and generality of believers as interceding at the Last Judgement.[22] Intercession is also allowed to believers in the world now; for example, the Prophet is quoted as saying, 'There is no one dead who is prayed over by an *ummah* of the Muslims who reach 100, all of them interceding for him, but that they will be made intercessors for him.'[23] Some inanimate things also will be allowed to intercede; for example, fasting and the Qur'an, which on the Day of Resurrection will ask for the power to intercede for having denied the servant food and desires and sleep (indicating recitation by night).[24]

Moreover, although less often, one certainly does find in the Islamic sources the particular idea that the order and prosperity of the world depend on the prayers of holy men. The Syrian worshipper ʿAbd Allāh ibn Abī Zakarīyāʾ (d. 119/737) is quoted as saying, 'No community will be tormented so long as in it are fifteen men who ask God for forgiveness 25 times a day.'[25] Many other numbers are proposed. Sometimes, just one or two apparently suffice. Someone said of the Baghdadi Sarī al-Saqaṭī (d. 253/867?), 'Aḥmad ibn Ḥanbal was here and Bishr ibn al-Ḥārith was here. We hoped that God would preserve us on account of them. Then they died while Sarī remained, so I hope that God will preserve me on account of Sarī.'[26] Abū Nuʿaym quotes the Prophet through al-Awzāʿī as saying,

> The choice of my community are 500 in every generation. The *abdāl* (lit. 'substitutes') are forty. The 500 are never lacking, nor the forty. Whenever one man dies, God fills his place from among the 500 (*abdala Allāh ... min al-khamsimi'ah makānah*).[27]

21 E.g., Bukhārī, *al-riqāq* 51, *bāb ṣifat al-jannah wa-al-nār*, nos 6559, 6566, *al-tawḥīd* 25, *bāb mā jāʾa fī qawl Allāh inna raḥmat Allāh qarīb min al-muḥsinīn*, no 7450; Abū Dāwūd, *al-sunnah* 20, *bāb fī al-shafāʿah*, no 4740; Tirmidhī, *abwāb ṣifat jahannam* 10, no 2600; Ibn Mājah, *al-zuhd* 37, *bāb dhikr al-shafāʿah*, no 4315; Ibn al-Mubārak, *Zuhd*, no 1267 (Basran *isnād*, < al-Ḥu.). See also Juynboll, *Encyclopedia*, 665–6.

22 E.g., Bukhārī, *al-tawḥīd* 24, Q. 75:22–3, no 7439; Aḥmad, *Musnad* 3:94 *18:394–6*; Hannād ibn al-Sarī, *Zuhd* 1:153.

23 Muslim, *al-janāʾiz* 18, *bāb man ṣallá ʿalayhi mi'ah*, no 947 (Basran *isnād*); sim., Ibn Mājah, *mā jāʾa fī al-janāʾiz* 19, *bāb mā jāʾa fīman ṣallá ʿalayhi jamāʿah min al-muslimīn*, no 1488 (Kufan *isnād*). Other reports reduce the required number to forty; e.g., Muslim, *al-janāʾiz* 18, *bāb man ṣallá ʿalayhi mi'ah*, no 948, Abū Dāwūd, *al-janāʾiz* 41, no 3170; Ibn Mājah, *mā jāʾa fī al-janāʾiz* 19, *bāb mā jāʾa fīman ṣallá ʿalayhi jamāʿah min al-muslimīn*, no 1489; and Aḥmad, *Musnad* 1:277–8, 6:334 *4:307–8*, *44:417–18*.

24 Aḥmad, *Musnad* 2:174 *11:199–200*.

25 Abū Nuʿaym, *Ḥilyah* 5:149.

26 Al-Khaṭīb al-Baghdādī, *Tārīkh* 9:191–2 *10:266*, evidently quoting from the early Sufi biographer Jaʿfar al-Khuldī.

27 Abū Nuʿaym, *Ḥilyah* 1:8.

Through Sufyān al-Thawrī, he quotes the Prophet as describing 300 hearts as being like Adam's, 40 like Moses', seven like Abraham's, five like Gabriel's, three like Michael's, and one like Israfel's. When the one dies, God substitutes for him one of the three, when one of the three, of the five, and so on up to the 300, to be replaced from the general. By their means, God deals out life and death, causes rain and germination, and turns away tribulation. Ibn Masʿūd (d. 32/652–3?) was asked how he might cause life and death through them. He answered,

> 'They ask God to increase the nations and so they increase; they imprecate tyrants, and so they are divided; they beg and so the earth sprouts for them; and they pray, and so all sorts of tribulation are repulsed by their means.'[28]

From this feature of being continually replaced come the terms *abdāl* and *budalāʾ*, literally 'substitutes'.[29] Another word Abū Nuʿaym proposes for this spiritual élite is *subbāq*, meaning 'those who precede', especially who lead in a race. On their account come victory and rain.[30] He relates a hadith report (related earlier by Aḥmad ibn Ḥanbal) that praises the *sābiqūn*, while the most self-possessed or rational persons (*aʿqal al-nās*) are those whose concern is *al-musābaqah ilá rabbihim*, racing to their Lord.[31] Although he does not mention what happens on the Earth because of them, Aḥmad ibn Ḥanbal moreover relates numerous hadith reports about the *awliyāʾ*, *muḥābbūn*, *mutaḥābbūn*, *mutabādhilūn fī Allāh*, *mutaṣādiqūn*, and *mutawāṣilūn* who, although not themselves either prophets or martyrs, will be envied by the prophets and martyrs on the Last Day.[32]

The *abdāl* were for long treated only as a feature of Sufism, as in *The Encyclopaedia of Islam*.[33] Writing for *The Encyclopaedia Iranica*, Jacqueline Chabbi cast her net more widely and discovered earlier treatments outside the literature of Sufism.[34] For this, she is to be congratulated. She connects the idea with extremist Shiʿism because it arises early on in an essay by Jāḥiẓ against the Shīʿah.

---

28 Abū Nuʿaym, *Ḥilyah* 1:9.

29 Sing. *badal* and *badīl*, respectively. The singular forms are rarely encountered, but see for example al-Khaṭīb, *Tārīkh* 11:305 *13:195* ('a *badal* among the *abdāl*').

30 Abū Nuʿaym, *Ḥilyah* 1:8.

31 Abū Nuʿaym, *Ḥilyah* 1:26 (*sābiqūn*), 17 (*aʿqal al-nās*); cf. Aḥmad ibn Ḥanbal, *Musnad* 6:67, 69 *40:440–1, 462*. The form *sābiqūn* appears in the Qur'an, sometimes apparently designating a spiritual élite; e.g., at Q. 56:10, 'Those who win the race, who win the race' (Jones translation).

32 See Wensinck, &al., *Concordance*, s.v. *yaghbiṭūn*.

33 *EI*[2], s.v. '*abdāl*', by Goldziher and Kissling.

34 *EIr*, s.v. '*abdāl*', by Chabbi. Other discussions, still overly restricted to the Sufi tradition, are Bernd Radtke and John O'Kane, introduction to al-Ḥakīm al-Tirmidhī, *Concept*, 109–10, and

However, despite her questioning common wisdom, she makes certain assumptions that I would not. It is interesting to see Muʿtazilism described as conservative—in some respects, it probably was, as Kevin Reinhart has argued apropos of the question of responsibility before the coming of revelation.[35] Chabbi thinks the concept of *abdāl* must have come in from Shiʿi and ultimately Christian sources. Ofer Livne-Kafri has also proposed Christian origins, without much evidence.[36] There seems to be a yet closer parallel in the Jewish tradition, although it needs demonstration that it goes back to before Islam.[37] But one is now willing to see in Shiʿism, too, traits of a primitive Islam minimized by later Sunnism; for example, this focus on charismatic individuals.[38] If Crone and Hinds are right, this was the mainstream conception of prophet and caliphs in the first century of Islam. Consider how the Umayyad caliphs had spokesmen describe them: that they showed clearly 'the paths of guidance', brought rain, constituted 'a firm rope for mankind', and so forth.[39] The whole question of foreign origins changes significance dramatically if we suppose that Islamic institutions did not normally appear fully formed in Arabia, like Athene from the head of Zeus, but developed in the conquered territories in dialectic with and substantially in continuity with their traditions. The idea of *abdāl* may originally be non-Islamic, then, but equally so the idea of the *fatwá*. Differentiation over time tended to dissociate charisma from Sunni jurisprudents, concentrating it in Sufi masters. But I hope that my preliminary trawl through traditionalist, Sunni sources will show that it was fully as well represented there as elsewhere, and had no need to enter the Ḥanbali tradition from outside.

Sviri, *Understanding*, 218–22; likewise, *Encyclopaedia Islamica*, s.v. '*abdāl*', by La-Shay', which also pays some attention to hadith but stresses later sources as to both hadith and Sufi ideas.

35 Reinhart, *Before revelation*.

36 Livne-Kafri, 'Early Muslim ascetics'.

37 'According to a tradition that goes back to Talmudic times there are, in every generation, thirty-six righteous men who are the found in the world. If the anonymity, which is part of their very nature, were broken, they would be nothing': so Scholem, *On the Kabbalah*, 6. Reviewed at greater length but with no judgement as to who was borrowing from whom by Fenton, 'La hiérarchie des saints'.

38 See Amir-Moezzi, *Spirituality of Shiʿi Islam*, esp. chap. 3. Admittedly, Amir-Moezzi's stress is on the imam as the object of devotion and means of revelation, not maintenance of the cosmic order. My own more cursory reading of the early Shiʿi sources confirms this stress on the imams' knowledge, not their power of answered prayer, which tends to weaken the alleged link between Shiʿism and the theory of *abdāl*.

39 Crone and Hinds, *God's caliph*, chap. 3. See further Jamil, 'Caliph and quṭb'.

The *abdāl* are normally associated with Syria. Aḥmad's *Musnad* includes the story that ʿAlī was asked to curse the Syrians but refused because the Prophet had said,

> The *abdāl* will be in Syria. They are forty men. Whenever a man dies, God installs a substitute in his place. By means of them, rain is caused to fall and victory over their enemies is accomplished. Torment is averted from the people of Syria by means of them.[40]

Ibn ʿAsākir relates many hadith reports concerning the *abdāl* near the beginning of *Tārīkh Dimashq*.[41]

The Syrian connection is exclusively stressed in a welcome article by Rana Mikati, who proposes that the term *abdāl* originated there at the time of the First Civil War.

> I argue that the concept originated in hadith circles as part of a tradition with a specific purported historical context, the showdown between the Syrians and Iraqis at the Battle of Ṣiffīn (37/657). The gradual loss of this context went hand-in-hand with the emergence of the mystical saintly *abdāl*. Second, the emergence of the *abdāl* of the Sufis marked their insertion into a saintly hierarchy and their mutation away from the *abdāl* of the hadith.[42]

That is, the *abdāl* were originally Syrian turncoats who supported ʿAlī. Later versions shifted the name to intercessors thanks to whom harm was averted, rain fell, and so on. The association of *abdāl* with militancy, not holiness, is illustrated by Ibn al-Mubārak's including ʿAlī's description of them in *Kitāb al-Jihād* but not *al-Zuhd*, although in both works he also offers similar reports of intercessors not named *abdāl*.[43]

However, *abdāl* could be imagined in other places, as well. Abū Nuʿaym quotes this account:

---

40 ʿAbd al-Razzāq, *Muṣannaf* 11:249; Aḥmad, *Musnad* 1:112 *2:231*. Similarly, Ibn al-Mubārak, *Jihād*, no 192; two versions *apud* Fasawī, *Maʿrifah* 2:305.

41 Ibn ʿAsākir, *Tārīkh* 1:289–304.

42 Mikati, 'On the identity of the Syrian *abdāl*', 22.

43 E.g., he quotes the Prophet as saying, 'There will not cease to be in my community seven who do not supplicate God (mighty and glorious is he) for anything but that they are answered. By their means you are given victory and rain' (Ibn al-Mubārak, *Jihād*, no 95). See notably this quotation of Khālid ibn Maʿdān (Homsi, d. 103/721–2?): 'God said, "The most beloved of my servants are those who love me (*al-mutaḥābbūn bi-ḥubbī*), whose hearts are hung in the mosques, who ask forgiveness in the evenings. Those are they whom, if I wish to punish the people of the Earth, I remember and so avert my punishment for their sakes"' (Ibn al-Mubārak, *Zuhd*, no 412; Abū Nuʿaym, *Ḥilyah* 5:212).

> I saw the Prophet ... in a dream. I said, 'O Messenger of God, where are the *abdāl* in your community?' He said with his hand 'In the direction of Syria.' I said, 'O Messenger of God, is there not one of them in Iraq?' He said, 'Yes: Muḥammad ibn Wāsiʿ, Ḥassān ibn Abī Sinān, and Mālik ibn Dīnār.'[44]

Of one Maʿdān (*fl.* mid-8th cent.), Ibn al-Mubārak himself is quoted as saying, 'If there if any of the *abdāl* in Khurasan, it is Maʿdān.'[45] An Abū Ḥafṣ ʿUmar ibn ʿAbd Allāh al-Fattāl of Qayrawan (*fl.* late 8th cent.), who never laughed, slept lying down, or ate fat, was reputedly among the *abdāl*.[46] The Nishapuran traditionist Yaḥyá ibn Yaḥyá (d. 226/839?) was certain the local renunciant Aḥmad ibn Ḥarb (d. 234/949) was among them.[47] Aḥmad ibn Ḥanbal himself identified as *abdāl* the Baghdadi renunciants Maʿrūf al-Karkhī (d. 200/815–16?), Bishr al-Ḥāfī (d. 227/841), and Ibrāhīm ibn Hāniʾ (d. 265/878).[48] Even Ibn ʿAsākir relates hadith reports locating some outside Syria: twenty-two of the *budalāʾ* are in Syria, eighteen in Iraq, or sixty *abdāl* in Syria, ten in other territories.[49] G. H. A. Juynboll recently published a list of 45 traditionists (collectors of hadith) also identified as *abdāl*, of whom over twice as many were from Iraq as Syria and Palestine (17 as opposed to eight), although there is at least one from every major region of the eighth- and ninth-century Islamic world except the West.[50]

This report of three Basran *abdāl* identified in a dream is fairly typical in additional respects. For one, the *abdāl* are usually identified retrospectively. They almost never declare themselves.[51] For another, it must be admitted, the sources are fairly casual about someone's being among the *abdāl*. Our early biographer Ibn Saʿd (d. 230/845) does not mention that any of these three (or, so far as I have noticed, anyone at all, in Syria or outside it) was among the *abdāl*.[52] In the entry

---

44 Abū Nuʿaym, *Ḥilyah* 3:114; variant (alternative chain of transmission; *budalāʾ* instead of *abdāl*) at Aḥmad, *Zuhd*, 324 *392*.

45 ʿAbd Allāh ibn Aḥmad, *Sunnah*, 72 *272*.

46 Abū Bakr al-Mālikī, *Riyāḍ* 1:197–8.

47 Al-Khaṭīb al-Baghdādī, *Tārīkh* 4:118 *5:191–2*.

48 Ibn Abī Yaʿlá, *Ṭabaqāt al-ḥanābilah* 1:382 *2:478* (Maʿrūf); al-Khaṭīb al-Baghdādī, *Tārīkh* 7:72–3 *7:552* (Bishr), 6:205 *7:162* (Ibn Hāniʾ).

49 Ibn ʿAsākir, *Tārīkh* 1:291, 300.

50 Juynboll, *Encyclopedia*, 731–2.

51 Exceptionally, seven Syrian renunciants, praying for one by whom came rain, identify themselves as *abdāl*: Abū Nuʿaym, *Ḥilyah* 10:319.

52 Ibn Saʿd, *Ṭabaqāt* 7/2:10–11 *7:241–3*. But Ibn Saʿd is generally uneasy about the renunciant tradition, as observed by Massignon, *Essay*, 97, 136fn.

on Muḥammad ibn Wāsiʿ (d. 123/740–1?), Abū Nuʿaym offers an abbreviated version of the same report, according to which the Prophet named only him.[53] Perhaps Abū Nuʿaym was mindful of reports that Muḥammad ibn Wāsiʿ had been superior to Mālik ibn Dīnār.[54]

The *abdāl* were not necessarily aware of being *abdāl* at all. For example, Abū Bakr Maḥmūd al-Iṣbahānī (d. 284/897–8) appeared after his death to someone in a dream and informed him that he had been one of the *abdāl* without knowing it.[55] Naturally, there was wide disagreement over what might distinguish them. ʿAṭāʾ al-Khurāsānī (d. 135/752–3) is quoted as warning that one should say the *abdāl* are forty *persons*, not *men*, for there might be women among them.[56] Sometimes, their characters are those of the ideal Muslim traditionist or jurisprudent. For example, the Medinese jurisprudent Abū al-Zinād (d. 130/748?) is quoted as saying,

> When prophecy left, they having been the tent pegs (*awtād*) of the world, God put in their place forty men of the *ummah* of Muḥammad ... called *abdāl*. If one dies, God always puts another in his place to succeed him. They are the tent pegs of the Earth. Thirty have hearts as certain as Abraham's. They are not distinct from other people by their praying much, fasting much, comeliness of austerity, or comeliness of adornment, but by true scrupulosity, good intention, soundness of heart, hoping to satisfy God by much patience and mild hearts .... They do not curse anything, hurt anyone, lord it over anyone beneath them, contemn anyone, or envy anyone above them. They do not practise extreme austerities or self-mortification.[57]

Sometimes, one of these characters is singled out as distinguishing one of the *abdāl*. In a dream, the Prophet confirmed that the Kufan traditionist Wakīʿ ibn al-Jarrāḥ (d. 197/812) was one of them, for he had never struck anything with his hand.[58]

The *abdāl* are also sometimes distinguished by items not on Abū al-Zinād's list. After relating the dream in which the Prophet identifies the Basran Ḥassān ibn Abī Sinān (*fl.* early 8th cent.) as one of the *abdāl*, he relates that a man was told by the Prophet in another dream that if Ḥassān prayed that a mountain turn, it would turn.[59] When someone had the temerity to berate Mālik ibn Dīnār in his

---

53 Abū Nuʿaym, *Ḥilyah* 2:348. Sim., Aḥmad ibn Ḥanbal, *Zuhd*, 324 *392.*
54 Abū Nuʿaym, *Ḥilyah* 2:349, 354.
55 Abū al-Shaykh, *Ṭabaqāt* 3:392.
56 Ibn ʿAsākir, *Tārīkh* 1:299.
57 Ibn ʿAsākir, *Tārīkh* 1:304.
58 Abū Nuʿaym, *Ḥilyah* 8:371.
59 Abū Nuʿaym, *Ḥilyah* 3:114–15.

circle over a commercial transaction, Mālik prayed, 'O God, if this one has distracted us from recollecting you, relieve us of him however you will', whereupon the man fell down dead.[60] Some of the reputed *abdāl*, far from being harmless, engaged in warfare on the frontier, such as Muḥammad ibn Wāsiʿ.[61] Abū al-Zinād's reported disregard of supererogatory austerities is not a uniform feature of the tradition. For example, we are told that Ḥassān ibn Abī Sinān merely played with his wife every night, then got up to pray when he thought she was asleep.[62]

The concept of *abdāl* has seemed to fit oddly with Sunni Islam (except for later Sufism), so that most previous treatments have speculated on its external origin. What I propose is to see holy individuals with intercessory powers (whether called *abdāl* or not) as a normal phenomenon of early Islam. The Shiʿi idea of the charismatic imam was once characteristic of all parties: what was disputed in the early centuries was how to identify the correct imam, not the necessity of loyalty to him.[63] It was part of widespread concern among Muslims with arbitration and mediation, in large measure continuous with such concern among their Christian and Jewish predecessors and contemporaries.

Miracles

I address miracles partly because of their peculiar prominence in the secondary literature. As argued above, they seem to have been less definitive of the holy man of Late Antiquity than Peter Brown originally made out. Still, they do seem to constitute a point of discontinuity, inasmuch as the Islamic tradition seems to be more reserved about them than the Christian before. In the Islamic tradition, miracles are a sign that someone is in the favour of God, but the saint characteristically regards them with reserve, as a temptation to self-importance.[64] The

---

60 Ibn Abī al-Dunyā, *Mujābū al-daʿwah*, 55–6 *119*.
61 Abū Nuʿaym, *Ḥilyah* 3:352–3.
62 Abū Nuʿaym, *Ḥilyah* 3:117.
63 On early Shiʿi ideas of the imamate, see Amir-Moezzi, *Spirituality*, esp. chap. 3 on *walāyah*. I have also found Haider, *Shīʿī Islam*, helpful as to the theological issues dividing Sunnis and Shiʿis, also different Shiʿi sects. Like Amir-Moezzi, Haider is inconsistently attentive to change over time. The religious necessity of knowing and being loyal to the correct imam is developed by Crone, *Medieval Islamic political thought*, pt. 1.
64 See Gril, 'Miracle', and Geoffroy, 'Attitudes contrastées'.

argument here will be that they are certainly present in the earliest Islamic tradition but to concede that the Islamic tradition extends the earlier tradition in a different direction.[65]

To the Prophet himself are ascribed numerous miracles. The Qur'an is closest in style to the Book of Psalms, tending to refer to known stories rather than retelling them itself and not narrating the life of the Prophet. As for miracles in particular, it does mention a number in association with earlier figures, mostly biblical prophets, but repulses the reported demand of Muḥammad's own adversaries for a miracle to prove that he himself is a prophet.[66] According to the exegetical tradition, however, it does refer to some miracles of his, most notably his ascent to heaven.[67] Ibn Hishām's recension of Ibn Isḥāq's biography mentions the Prophet's ascent to heaven, his foretelling the conquest of Medina, being warned by some mutton that it was poisoned, and causing the death of ʿĀmir ibn al-Ṭufayl by imprecation (to name examples in order of chronology, not significance to the tradition). Ibn Saʿd mentions many more, devoting substantial chapters to signs marking out the Prophet before actual revelations began, such as being saluted by rocks and trees, and the even more signs marking him out after the beginning of revelation, such as releasing ablution water from his fingers.[68] Many such stories also appear in very orthodox hadith collections, such as that of al-Bukhārī (d. 256/870).[69] However, it must be admitted that these are few and incidental compared with the miracle stories related in the Gospels.

As for miracles among pious early Muslims, there are many stories of correct dream interpretation, dreaming being identified by hadith as a minor species of prophecy.[70] For example, Sufyān al-Thawrī correctly interpreted a dream as telling that al-Awzāʿī had died.[71] His Meccan contemporary Wuhayb ibn al-Ward (presumably in his youth) correctly interpreted a dream as foretelling the accession of the

---

65 Two overviews not mainly concerned with the early period are Gramlich, *Die Wunder der Freunde Gottes*, and Jihad, *Le livre des prodiges*.

66 Watt, *Introduction*, 125, citing Q. 6:37, 13:7, and 21:5.

67 See Gril, 'Fondements scriptuaires'. On the heavenly ascent, see Colby, *Narrating Muḥammad's night journey*, Gilliot, 'Coran 17', and van Ess, 'Le *miʿrāǧ* et la vision de Dieu', all with further references to earlier studies. See also Gruber and Colby, eds, *The Prophet's ascension*.

68 Ibn Hishām, *Sīrah* 1:216–17 = Guillaume, *Life*, 105; Ibn Saʿd, *Ṭabaqāt* 1/1:112–26 *1:170–90*. See also now Koertner, '*Dalāʾil al-nubuwwa*'.

69 Bukhārī, notably 61 instances at *al-manāqib* 25, *bāb ʿalāmāt al-nubūwah fī al-islām*, nos 3571–634.

70 On dreams and dream interpretation in the Islamic tradition, see Moin, 'Partisan dreams', with further references; also Green, 'Religious and cultural roles'. For the dream as a forty-sixth part of prophecy, see for example Muslim, *al-ruʾyā*, no 2263.

71 Aḥmad, *ʿIlal* 3:232 *2:171*.

pious caliph ʿUmar ibn ʿAbd al-ʿAzīz (*r.* 99–101/717–20).[72] Other forms of precognition are also not rare. The famous traditionist Abū Hurayrah (d. late 60s/680s) was able to predict who would be the caliph A.H. 200 (A.D. 815–16).[73] On being told that a monk who had correctly predicted his accession was now predicting his death by poison, ʿUmar ibn ʿAbd al-ʿAzīz commented that he himself, if he wished, could tell them the exact time when it would happen.[74]

Multiple stories associate miracles with the performance of ritual duties. Al-ʿAlāʾ ibn al-Ḥaḍramī (d. 14/635–6?) prayed for ablution water, which appeared for himself and his comrades but no one else.[75] ʿAmr ibn ʿUtbah (d. 23–35/644–56) was protected by a lion as he prayed.[76] Kurz ibn Wabarah (*fl.* early 8th cent.) was protected by a special cloud as he prayed in the middle of a hot day (but asked a witness to keep it secret).[77] The Basran ʿAbd al-Wāḥid ibn Zayd (*fl.* early 8th cent.) was paralysed by a stroke except when it was time for the minor ritual ablution.[78]

Occasionally, disdain for holy men was miraculously punished. The Syrian Abū Muslim al-Khawlānī (d. 60–4/680–3) made a woman go blind, then prayed for restoration on her repentance.[79] A man's hand withered on poking the Basran worshipper Sulaymān al-Taymī (d. 143/760–1).[80] Probably in the same category, from the Islamic point of view, are miracles in the course of prosecuting the holy war. For example, Abū Muʿāwiyah al-Aswad (d. 190s/806–16?) nullified catapults in a fortress under siege.[81] It is rare but not unheard of for miracles to be associated with orthodoxy and heresy. For example, a dog told Sufyān al-Thawrī it bit only those who had insulted Abū Bakr and ʿUmar; that is, extreme Shiʿah.[82] And

72 Abū Nuʿaym, *Ḥilyah* 8:146.
73 Aḥmad, *ʿIlal* 1:223 *1:99*.
74 Aḥmad, *Zuhd*, 297 *361*.
75 Aḥmad, *Zuhd*, 169–70 *212–13* (< ʿAl.). Sim., with the Kufan Zubayd ibn al-Ḥārith (d. 122/739–40 or after) and his comrades instead of al-ʿAlāʾ and his, Abū Nuʿaym, *Ḥilyah* 5:30.
76 Aḥmad, *Zuhd*, 353 *423*.
77 Abū Nuʿaym, *Ḥilyah* 5:80–1. ʿAmr ibn ʿUtbah is more often associated with a special cloud to shade him, although not in association with ritual prayer; e.g., Ibn al-Mubārak, *Jihād*, no 210; *Zuhd*, no 869; Aḥmad, *Zuhd*, 353 *423*. A cloud over one's head was said to be a regular honour for Israelites who reached a certain rank (Abū Nuʿaym, *Ḥilyah* 2:226 < ʿAl., *Zuhd*). It was also a sign marking out the prophet Muḥammad as a boy: Ibn Hishām, *Sīrah* 1:166 = Guillaume, *Life*, 80; Ibn Saʿd, *Ṭabaqāt* 1/1:98–9 *1:152, 154*.
78 Abū Nuʿaym, *Ḥilyah* 6:155.
79 Abū Nuʿaym, *Ḥilyah* 2:130 (his wife, for complaining), 5:121 (a woman who insulted him).
80 Aḥmad, *Zuhd*, 382–3 *458*; Ibn Abī al-Dunyā, *Mujābū al-daʿwah*, 55–6 *119*; Abū Nuʿaym, *Ḥilyah* 3:31.
81 Abū Nuʿaym, *Ḥilyah* 8:271.
82 Abū Nuʿaym, *Ḥilyah* 7:74.

there are other forms of miracle. Abū Muslim al-Khawlānī walked on water and was thrown into a fire but not harmed, among other miracles.[83] These all have parallels among Christian saints of Late Antiquity.

However, the most common sorts of miracles among the Christian holy men of Late Antiquity are said to have been healing from illness, relief of famine, and the restoration of social order.[84] These are all fairly uncommon in the Islamic record. I have remarked a few stories of miraculous cures. Kurz ibn Wabarah, again, cured the Kufan judge Ibn Shubrumah.[85] Aḥmad ibn Ḥanbal cured a woman who had been crippled for twenty years.[86] But then the famous hadith critic Abū Ḥātim al-Rāzī (d. 277/890) was said to know the greatest name of God, any prayer in which would necessarily be answered. When his son became ill, he resisted praying for him, saying that prayers in the greatest name were reserved for otherworldly matters. At last, however, as his son's condition worsened, he prayed for him to be cured. It happened as he had prayed, but then he was told in a dream that because he had prayed in the name for something worldly, his son would never have offspring. Indeed, although his son (who also became a famous hadith critic) was married for 70 years, he never had offspring.[87] Perhaps the paucity of reported miraculous cures is related to Islamic theodicy, which generally holds that worldly afflictions, coming by God's decree, are not to flee from or lament but rather for the Muslims to patiently endure as a sign of their faith, even as they anticipate and sometimes speed unbelievers to the torments of Hellfire.[88] Ibn Masʿūd's unconcern is exemplary: 'I do not care, when I return to my family, in what condition I find them, whether in prosperity or distress. Nor have I ever started the day in any condition such that I wished I were in some other.'[89]

Apart from general claims about the *abdāl*'s and others' bringing rain, famine relief seems to be even less common in the Islamic tradition of miracles than healing from illness. The prominent traditionist Muḥammad ibn al-Munkadir (d. 130/747–8?) saw a Persian in Medina whose prayer for rain was answered but who wanted to remain unknown.[90] More usual is to read of food miraculously provided for individuals. Zādhān of Kufa (d. 82/701–2) was provided with bread

83 Ibn Abī al-Dunyā, *Mujābū al-daʿwah*, 46 *103–4*; Abū Nuʿaym, *Ḥilyah* 2:129, 5:120.
84 Rapp, *Holy bishops*, 6.
85 Abū Nuʿaym, *Ḥilyah* 5:80.
86 Abū Nuʿaym, *Ḥilyah* 9:186–7.
87 Khalīlī, *Irshād*, 229.
88 See Conrad, 'Medicine and martyrdom'.
89 Ibn al-Mubārak, *Zuhd*, no 125 < Nuʿaym.
90 Abū Nuʿaym, *Ḥilyah* 3:152.

on praying, 'My Lord, I am hungry.'[91] The Basran Ṣilah (*fl.* early 8th cent.) refused some illicit food, whereupon fresh dates appeared out of season.[92] Food appeared for Muḥammad ibn al-Munkadir while he was on Byzantine territory with his comrades.[93] Dates appeared for the Basran 'Utbah al-Ghulām (d. bef. 153/770) when he prayed.[94] 'Abd Allāh ibn Sa'īd, probably a Syrian (*fl.* early 9th cent.?), was normally supported by an aunt. On going three days without, he asked God whether his provision had been stopped, whereupon food appeared in the corner of the mosque but also a voice that said 'O you of little patience', which made him refuse to taste it.[95] One story combines famine relief with the appearance of food to an individual: the Basran Ḥabīb al-Fārisī (*fl.* early 8th cent.) bought grain to relieve famine, then paid it back miraculously from sacks he had put under his bed empty before praying.[96] This was obviously famine relief on a very small scale.

Continuity and discontinuity

I have proposed that the tradition of ordering the good and prohibiting evil is a sort of arbitration by holy men. The particular form of arbitration identified by Peter Brown in his first, seminal article on the holy man was his acting as advocate, protector, and intercessor with the authorities on behalf of villagers. His authority to act was based on his miracle-working. It is unsurprising that we have no parallel to this special concern with the rural population in the early Islamic tradition, for Islam was slow to move to the countryside and our early Muslim holy men are practically all urbanites, although they occasionally make excursions into the country. Prophetic hadith and many renunciant sayings advocate social withdrawal, but over and over this means withdrawal to one's house, not the countryside or desert. Al-Ḥasan al-Baṣrī said not only, as observed before, 'The believers' cells are their houses', but specifically lamented, 'You used to meet the Muslims only in their mosques or their cells, meaning their houses.'[97] Here is plainly a conscious contrast to the practice of Christian monks. The example of Ibn Mas'ūd and some persons who had withdrawn from Kufa to worship

91 Abū Nu'aym, *Ḥilyah* 4:199.
92 Abū Nu'aym, *Ḥilyah* 2:239.
93 Abū Nu'aym, *Ḥilyah* 3:151.
94 Abū Nu'aym, *Ḥilyah* 6:237.
95 Abū Nu'aym, *Ḥilyah* 8:335.
96 Abū Nu'aym, *Ḥilyah* 6:150.
97 Ibn al-Mubārak, *Zuhd*, no 15 < Nu'aym.

nearby has been mentioned before. His rebuke makes the holy war an obstacle to rural retreat. The requirement of ritual prayer in the assembly also comes up as a hindrance to withdrawal, as when Saʿīd ibn al-Musayyib, refusing advice to hide from the caliph on refusing to swear allegiance to both him and his chosen successor, said, 'When I am called to prosperity (*al-falāḥ*), shall I refuse to come?'[98]

On the other hand, Chase Robinson seems to have gone too far in opposing the Prophet and the early caliphs as charismatic holy warriors to other sorts of holy men coming only much later. In Robinson's view, Khawārij waging war and extremist Shiʿah demanding a charismatic ruler represent the primitive forms of Islam, whereas Sufi holy men were a later development, emerging in the later ninth century just as the caliphs lost their claims to charisma and the Sunni ulema consolidated their nomocratic Islam. On this model, we cannot expect any early Muslim figures similar to Brown's holy men, for Islamic militarism was contrary to both Christian and Jewish traditions of what constituted holiness.[99] Robinson seems to jump too quickly, though, from the late seventh century to the late ninth. Khāriji activism looked old-fashioned already in 695, says Robinson, yet the decisive defeat by the ulema of caliphal pretensions did not come until the mid-ninth century and Sufism is not granted to appear until later still.[100] Besides underestimating the acceptability of military prowess in the Jewish and Christian traditions, this is to ignore the many holy men and women not famous for military prowess who come between the Prophet and the classical Sufis. It also exaggerates the importance of miracle-making in the character of a holy man.

I should deal with other apparent discontinuities. It is very often objected that a major and necessary character of the Christian holy man was celibacy, not found among Muslims. As developed in chapter 2, there was some celibacy among Muslim holy men (and women), but it must be conceded that celibacy always distinguished only a minority, while the hadith tradition strongly encourages marriage and procreation. It is possible to contend on this evidence that Muslims had only an attenuated conception of holiness, but of course this runs the risk of sectarianism, like defining *mysticism* such that it cannot be applied outside orthodox Christianity. The restricted place of celibacy in the Islamic tradition of holiness may suggest a conception of the whole Islamic community as a holy one. Such a conception could not survive the transition from the Muslims' being a small stratum at the top of society to a large part of society, even the majority.

98 Ibn al-Mubārak, *Zuhd*, no 2 < Nuʿaym.
99 Robinson, 'Prophecy and holy men', 249–52.
100 On the old-fashioned appearance of a Khāriji rebellion, Robinson, 'Prophecy and holy men', 255; defeat of the caliphs, 256; appearance of Sufism, 259–60.

The urban character of early Islam, related to the Muslims' military requirements as a small ruling minority, probably accounts for our knowing of no early Islamic literature of travel to holy sites, unlike the literature of Late Antique Christianity. The absence of hagiographies, except for the life of the Prophet, has been noted already. The characteristic literature of renunciation is not the biography but the collection of short sayings, like the *apophthegmata* of the Christian tradition. But the literary study of Islamic renunciation is still at a primitive stage.[101] Christian literature seems to have been divided between a mystical strand (e.g., Evagrius) and an ascetical, anti-mystical (e.g., Athanasius).[102] The Islamic tradition seems to take off from the latter, mystical expressions apparently dating only from the mid-ninth century.

To conclude, the holy man was everywhere on the landscape of Islam in the earlier eighth century. A century later, he was less conspicuous, to be found among the forerunners to the Sufis but little elsewhere. This came especially from the routinization of politics, as the charisma of the caliphs dwindled away, and the professionalization of law, as technical reasoning and encyclopaedic knowledge supplanted personal holiness as the basis of jurisprudential authority. To some extent, as Muslims ceased to be merely a thin stratum at the top of society, this shrinking of the holy man's sphere actually made the Islamic world more closely resemble the Byzantine, where holy men lived alongside bishops and imperial officials (and were themselves increasingly domesticated by enrollment into monastic organizations).[103] To some extent, also, it reflected the development of other elements more important in Iraq and Iran (peripheral to the Umayyads, central to their successors the ʿAbbāsids) than the holy men of Egypt and Syria and equally available to the Muslims. One of these elements is Rabbinic Judaism (probably alongside varieties of Judaism not known to us); another is Persian imperialism, extending from political theory to ideas of the cultured life and bureaucratic precedents.

101 R. Marston Speight's rhetorical studies have stressed hadith going back to the Prophet, but the patterns he finds are likewise characteristic of early renunciant literature: 'Rhetorical argumentation' and 'A look at variant readings'. Michael Cooperson has interpreted two bodies of sayings from the ninth century in terms of respectful rivalry between renunciants and jurisprudents: 'Ibn Ḥanbal and Bishr al-Ḥāfī' and *Classical Arabic biography*, chap. 5.

102 Louth, *Origins*, 100.

103 The case for important continuing Byzantine influence on Islamic high culture has been pressed by Jokisch, *Islamic imperial law*. It has not been well received by Byzantinists, but it will probably be some time before someone with primary expertise in Byzantine law troubles to learn Arabic and do the job right.

Chapter 7: Renunciants and politics

Aristocrats have ever had two justifications for living by the sweat of other men's brows: 'We are braver than other people' and 'We have better taste.' Activity in the conquests demonstrated the first for Muslims of the seventh century; Islam was their badge of cultural superiority. There are many other examples in history of combining distinctive piety with militance. One thinks of Cromwell and his Ironsides, for example. The renunciants of the eighth century continued to cultivate military virtues, such as hardihood and group loyalty. But the problem arose in the seventh century of which group with which leader to be loyal to, in the eighth century of how much loyalty was owed to leaders under whom only professional soldiers fought, who seemed ever more to be looking out for their own interests ahead of the whole community's. Some groups cultivated physical withdrawal, more groups varying degrees of moral withdrawal.

Renunciants and religio-political sects

The Prophet was the head of a state, the first in Arabia, as well as a religious community. Politics was a central concern of the early Muslims as Muslims. Salvation came from being a member of the chosen community, and one feature of the chosen community was that it was led by the right person. Early Islamic history is punctuated by the Four Civil Wars (*fitnahs*) over who should be caliph: over who should succeed ʿUthmān (d. 35/656), then who should succeed Yazīd ibn Muʿāwiyah (d. 64/683), then the series of revolts against the Umayyads of which the ʿAbbāsids' was finally successful (132/750), finally al-Maʾmūn's toppling of his half-brother al-Amīn (d. 198/813). It is often said that the First Civil War, apparently the origin of the Sunni-Shiʿi split, was merely political without religious significance, religious significance being a matter of later interpretation. Unfortunately, this is not the dispassionate historical analysis it sounds like, always rightly on guard against anachronism. Rather, it is precisely the Sunni dogmatic position, that all the Companions being righteous there could have been no significant disagreement over religion. The Shiʿi dogmatic position is that it was of course a disagreement over religion, the Companions being mostly a pack of scoundrels who knowingly disregarded the Prophet's testament. Modern historians will axiomatically reject the idea that any particular generation was uniquely virtuous or vicious, which means rejecting both Sunni and Shiʿi dogmatic positions. As to whether the First Civil War had a religious side to it, however, the Shiʿi interpretation must be right. The special point here is that early renunciants

https://doi.org/10.1515/9783110617962-008

were unlikely to avoid political involvements inasmuch as all Muslims felt themselves involved as Muslims in politics. We should expect to find notable renunciants attached to all political parties and renunciant themes in the propaganda of all parties.

Renunciants can indeed be found in all camps. For one thing, they were needed as transmitters of hadith.

> ʿAlī ibn al-Madīnī (d. Samarra, 234/849) told Yaḥyá ibn Saʿīd al-Qaṭṭān (d. Basra, 198/813) that ʿAbd al-Raḥmān ibn Mahdī (d. Basra, 198/814) had said 'I leave, among traditionists, everyone who was a chief in heresy.' Yaḥyá ibn Saʿīd laughed and said, 'What would he do with Qatādah? What would he do with ʿUmar ibn Dharr al-Hamdānī? What would he do with Ibn Abī Rawwād?" Yaḥyá counted off a great number of others, then said, "If ʿAbd al-Raḥmān left this sort, he left many.'[1]

Heretics though they were, they were plainly involved in a common religious culture. Renunciant concerns complemented their juridical and theological. Qatādah ibn Diʿāmah (Basran, d. 118/736–7?), longtime associate of al-Ḥasan al-Baṣrī (d. 110/728), appears in all of the Six Books. 'He advocated something of *qadar* (predestination)', according to Ibn Saʿd.[2] A Muʿtazili source quotes him as advocating a primitive, intermediate version: 'All things are predestined except sins.'[3] Admittedly, he is not particularly reputed as a renunciant (although he appears 20 times in the extant *Kitāb al-Zuhd* of Aḥmad ibn Ḥanbal as a transmitter, usually of stories of earlier prophets, and twelve times in the *Zuhd* of Ibn al-Mubārak), likewise ʿUmar ibn Dharr (Kufan Murjiʾ, d. 153/770?), a preacher (*qāṣṣ*) who appears in four of the Six Books. ʿAbd al-ʿAzīz ibn Abī Rawwād (Meccan Murjiʾ, d. 159/775–6?), who likewise appears in four of the Six Books, was a notorious Murjiʾ. Ibn Abī Rawwād did not look up to Heaven for 40 years.[4] He was blind for 20 years without his family's knowing it (showing how little he complained, also how little active he was in worldly affairs).[5] Asked what was the best form of worship, he said, 'Longstanding sadness, night and day.'[6] Ibn Abī Rawwād's son ʿAbd al-Majīd (d. 206/821–2) was likewise a Murjiʾ and likewise known for not lifting up his head to Heaven.[7]

---

1 Al-Khaṭīb al-Baghdādī, *Kifāyah*, 128–9 *156–7*; cf. Ibn Ḥajar, *Tahdhīb* 8:353.

2 Ibn Saʿd, *Ṭabaqāt* 7/2:1 *7:229*.

3 Abū al-Qāsim al-Balkhī, '*Bāb dhikr al-muʿtazilah*', 88. A similar position is attributed to al-Ḥasan himself: ʿAbd al-Razzāq, *Muṣannaf* 11:119.

4 Abū Nuʿaym, *Ḥilyah* 8:191.

5 Abū Nuʿaym, *Ḥilyah* 8:191.

6 Abū Nuʿaym, *Ḥilyah* 8:194.

7 Ibn Ḥajar, *Tahdhīb* 6:381.

If Qatādah was not himself a notable renunciant, others of the Qadarīyah were. ʿAbd Allāh ibn Abī Labīd (Medinese cl., d. *ca* 136/754) was known for being withdrawn (*munqaṭiʿ*) and given to strenuous devotions.[8] ʿAbd al-Wāḥid ibn Zayd (Basran, *fl.* earlier 8th cent.) was among the followers of al-Ḥasan al-Baṣrī rejected for advocating *qadar*. Among other things, he stayed up all night for 40 years, making his dawn prayer on the ablution of the evening.[9] The antipredestinarian Muʿtazilah were probably named 'withdrawers' for withdrawal from sinful society.[10] Their founding figure ʿAmr ibn ʿUbayd (Basran, d. 144/761–2) was another who stayed up all night for 40 years, making his dawn prayer on the ablution of the previous evening, and made 40 pilgrimages on foot.[11]

The Khawārij are clearly identified in the most hostile sources as the most outwardly renunciant of Muslims. Boundary maintenance has been identified as a theme of both Christian and Islamic asceticism.[12] It does seem to have functioned this way for the Khawārij *vis à vis* other Muslims, for their outstandingly strenuous devotional life is repeatedly conceded in the Sunni record. For example, the Prophet is quoted as saying,

> There will come out among you a group beside whose ritual prayer you will think little of your own, beside whose fasting likewise, and beside whose works likewise. They will recite the Qur'ān but it will not pass their windpipes. They will pass through the faith as an arrow passes through an animal.[13]

Ibn ʿAbbās described the Khawārij by their scarred faces from long prostration, hands like the calluses of camels, and washed garments.[14]

As for the Shiʿah, I have observed before that Imami collections of hadith from the late ninth and early tenth centuries are replete with renunciant sentiments, attributed of course to Shiʿi imams.[15] For example, I have quoted the Com-

---

8 Ibn Ḥajar, *Tahdhīb* 5:372.
9 Ibn Ḥajar, *Lisān* 4:80–1.
10 Stroumsa, 'The beginnings of the Muʿtazilah'.
11 Abū al-Qāsim al-Balkhī, '*Bāb Dhikr al-muʿtazilah*', 68; Ibn al-Murtaḍá, *Klassen*, 36.
12 Gaiser, Shurāt *legends*, 12–14, 29–30.
13 Mālik, *Muwaṭṭa'*, rec. Yaḥyá, *al-ṣalāh* 133, *mā jā'a fī al-Qur'ān*, no 545; rec. Abū Muṣʿab, *al-ṣalāh* 16, *jāmiʿ al-qirā'ah*, no 273; Bukhārī, *faḍā'il al-Qur'ān* 36, *bāb ithm man rā'a bi-qirā'at al-Qur'ān*, no 5058. Cf. Juynboll, *Encyclopedia*, 670–1, identifying this form of words with Yaḥyá ibn Saʿīd al-Anṣārī (Medinese qadi, d. 144/761–2?).
14 Mubarrad, *Kāmil*, 560 *3:1132*. Among other examples brought up by Abū al-Shabāb, *Khawārij*, 62–3.
15 Melchert, 'Renunciation (*zuhd*) in the early Shiʿi tradition'.

panion Abū Mūsá al-Ashʿarī (d. 50/670–1?) from Sunni sources as saying, 'O people, weep. If you do not weep, pretend to weep.'[16] Sunni sources attribute similar exhortations to the Prophet[17] and the Companion and first caliph Abū Bakr.[18] A major Shiʿi source attributes this to the sixth imam Jaʿfar al-Ṣādiq (d. Medina, 148/765).[19] I have also proposed that such quotations of the imams are more likely to be Shiʿi versions of earlier Sunni formulations than the other way around; but weeping, for example, was plainly a shared feature of early Sunni and Shiʿi piety both.

Imami biographical sources also mention adherents outstanding for renunciant values. ʿAlī ibn Mahziyār, a convert from Christianity to Shiʿism (*fl.* Ahwaz, early 9th cent.), would not raise his head until he had prayed for 1,000 of his brothers as well as himself. On his forehead was a mark (*sajjādah*) like a camel's knee.[20] Another Imami, Ṣafwān ibn Yaḥyá (Kufan cl., *fl.* early 9th cent.), prayed 500 sets a day, fasted three months of the year, and paid the alms tax three times a year, since he and two others had agreed that if one died, the others would pray his prayers, and if two died, the third would pray all their prayers.[21]

The sources refer to a distinctive party called the *qurrāʾ* in earliest Iraqi politics, who took part on all sides in the first two Civil Wars. In particular, a significant number of the *qurrāʾ* broke away from ʿAlī's army to join the Khawārij in 37/657.[22] The obvious interpretation is that they were the ultra-pious party, marked by their devotional recitation of the Qur'an. Norman Calder has suggested alternatively that *qāriʾ* originally referred to temporary or seasonal troops, serving for a *qarʾ* or *qurʾ* (period).[23] M. A. Shaban's identification of these *qurrāʾ* as people of villages (*qurá*) is evidently fanciful.[24] Later references to *qurrāʾ* must anyway refer in the first place to reciters of the Qur'an, in the second to renunciants generally, qur'anic recitation being so central a form of devotions that it became synonymous with *zuhhād* and *nussāk*. (There was even a group of 70 Companions who perished in the Prophet's own wars called the *qurrāʾ*. By one account, they

16 Ibn Saʿd, *Ṭabaqāt*, 4/1:81 *4:110*; Aḥmad., *Zuhd*, 199 *247*.
17 Ibn Mājah, *al-zuhd* 19, *bāb al-ḥuzn wa-al-bukāʾ*, no. 4196.
18 Ibn Abī Shaybah, *Muṣannaf* 14:7–8 *12:424*; Aḥmad, *Zuhd*, 108 *135*.
19 Kulaynī, *Kāfī* 2:483, *al-duʿāʾ*, *bāb al-raghbah wa-al-rahbah*.
20 Najāshī, *Rijāl*, 459 *548–9*.
21 Ṭūsī, *Fihrist*, 83.
22 For a basic survey, see Sayed, *Die Revolte des Ibn al-Ašʿaṯ*.
23 Calder, 'The *qurrāʾ*'.
24 Shaban, *Islamic history*, 50–1, supported by Juynboll, 'The qurrāʾ', then only partially in idem, 'The position of Qur'an recitation'. Cf. Shah, 'The quest for the origins of the *qurrāʾ*', 11–12.

spent their nights studying the Qur'an, by another performing the ritual prayer.[25])

Principles dear to the renunciants were at the heart of some sectarian positions. One was commanding right and forbidding wrong (*al-amr bi-al-maʿrūf wa-al-nahy ʿan al-munkar*). Mālik ibn Dīnār (Basran cl., d. *ca* 130/747–8) got a tax collector to release a merchant's boat and rebuked the governor of Basra, refusing to pray for him and pointing out how many wronged persons were cursing him.[26] Muḥammad ibn al-Munkadir (Medinese, d. 131/748–9?) gave a sermon mentioning something he had heard of the baths. In consequence, he and his associates (disciples? *aṣḥāb*) were brought before the governor and beaten for commanding right and forbidding wrong.[27] Aḥmad ibn Ḥanbal held that Ibn Abī Dhiʾb (Medinese, d. 159/775–6?) was better than Mālik (d. 179/795) because he had commanded and forbidden the caliph Abū Jaʿfar (al-Manṣūr, *r.* 136–58/754–75) whereas Mālik had been silent.[28] He complained that the caliph al-Mahdī was spending so much of the community's money on his travel.[29]

Commanding right and forbidding wrong was one of the five principles of the Muʿtazilah as formulated in the earlier 3rd/9th century, also of the early Murjiʾah (or even the not-so-early).[30] Salm ibn Sālim (d. Mecca? 194/810?) was a Murjiʾ who did not look up to Heaven for 40 years, never slept on a bed, and fasted continuously except for festivals (alternatively, on alternate days).[31] He was also known for commanding the right and forbidding the wrong, for which Hārūn al-Rashīd imprisoned him in al-Raqqah, although there is disagreement in the sources as to whether he was hauled away from Balkh or Mecca.[32] Ḥamdūn al-Qaṣṣār (d. Nishapur, 271/884–5), on being asked about the way of the Malāmatīyah, said, 'The fear of the Qadarīyah and the hope of the Murjiʾah.'[33] That is, he wished his Khurasani renunciants to be as fearful as the Qadarīyah, who believed in free will

25 For the larger story, see Kister, 'The expedition of Biʾr Maʿūna'. For their good works by night and day, see for example Ibn Saʿd, *Ṭabaqāt* 3/2:71 *3:514–15*, Muslim, *al-imārah* 41, *bāb thubūt al-jannah lil-shahīd*, no 1902, and Abū Nuʿaym, *Ḥilyah* 1:123–4.

26 Abū Nuʿaym, *Ḥilyah* 2:374, 384.

27 Fasawī, *Maʿrifah* 1:660.

28 Aḥmad, *ʿIlal* 1:509, 539 *1:188, 198*; Marrūdhī, *Akhbār*, 89, no 111.

29 Marrūdhī, *Akhbār*, 85–6, no 106; also said of Sufyān al-Thawrī: Marrūdhī, *Akhbār*, 76, nos 84–5; Abū Nuʿaym, *Ḥilyah* 6:378.

30 See Cook, *Commanding right*, 196–8, on early Muʿtazili doctrine (suitably cautious about attributions) and idem, 'Activism and quietism', on Murjiʾ doctrine.

31 Al-Khaṭīb al-Baghdādī, *Tārīkh* 9:141 *10:203*.

32 Ibn Saʿd, *Ṭabaqāt* 7/2:106 *7:374*; al-Khaṭīb al-Baghdādī, *Tārīkh* 9:9:141–2 *10:204*.

33 Sīrjānī, *Sufism, Black and white*, 401.

and therefore that Muslims were liable to be sent to Hell for their deliberate misdeeds, and as hopeful as the Murji'ah, who thought that everyone who believed, meaning all Muslims, would be saved regardless of their actions.

al-Jihād fī sabīl Allāh

Jihād, the holy war, was the predominant activity of the most zealous Muslims during the seventh century, when they conquered the largest empire the world had known till then. War complemented many renunciant values, which must be a major reason why, I would argue, *jihād* was naturally attractive to renunciants in the first place. The Qur'an refers to war as something toilsome that the Arabs would prefer to avoid. For example,

> O you who believe,
> what is the matter with you?
> When you are told, 'Go out in God's way',
> you sink heavily to the ground.
> Are you content with the life of this world
> rather than the world to come?
> The enjoyment of the life of this world is a little thing,
> compared with the world to come (Q. 9:38).

The warrior fights best when he does not care whether he lives or dies, so that indifference toward the world (*al-zuhd fī al-dunyā*) was the ideal attitude. Moreover, nomads are notoriously difficult to control. The verses following the one just quoted threaten those who did not come out to fight the unbelievers with consequences in the Afterworld, not now. (Compare the Song of Deborah, one of the oldest passages in the Old Testament [Judges 5], in which the tribes that had failed to come out suffer jeering but no material penalties.) The state was not sufficiently strong at this point to coerce tribesmen into fighting; nor did it become so, most likely, until the Marwānid period from the end of the seventh century. Eighth-century stories of how simply the early caliphs lived, as of 'Umar's rough clothing and simple diet, must be interpreted first as legends meant to discredit luxurious rulers of the eighth century; however, it seems very plausible that the early caliphs did rely heavily on their pious example to maintain the loyalty of their tribal armies.[34]

34 For 'Umar, see for example Ibn Sa'd, *Ṭabaqāt* 3/1:236–9 *3:327–30* (clothing), 3/1:229–31 *3:317–19* (food).

It is a familiar observation that Christian monks and nuns succeeded Christian martyrs when the era of persecution came to an end in the fourth century.[35] Solitaries like St Antony stood up to demonic assaults as earlier martyrs had stood up to human. It is a major argument of this book that renunciation succeeded *jihād* when the conquest period ran out near the beginning of the eighth century. In the seventh century, military expeditions were the obvious place for a zealous young Muslim. In the eighth century, as the military was professionalized and frontiers stabilized, something else was needed. In large part, renunciant literature represents an attempt to maintain the martial virtues of the seventh century in the changed circumstances of the eighth.

Hadith mentions various inducements to participate in *jihād*, most notoriously the martyr's prospect of marrying seventy-three houris in Paradise.[36] They consistently stress pleasing God and reward after death, though, not in this world. Indeed, the famous hadith report about actions and intentions makes fighting in *jihād* (the point of *hijrah*, leaving nomadic ways) its main example:

> Works are only by intention. A man has only what he intends. Whosever *hijrah* is to God and his Messenger, his *hijrah* is to God and his Messenger. Whosever *hijrah* is to a worldly good for him to get or a woman to marry (*yatazawwajuhā*), his *hijrah* is to what he emigrated to.

It is included in all of the Six Books (Bukhārī's *Ṣaḥīḥ* has slightly different versions in seven different books). Tirmidhī places it precisely in his book on the virtues of *jihād*.[37] The point is that only properly self-denying *jihād* has religious merit. Ibn Masʿūd is quoted as reviewing multiple motivations, to be recorded by angels: 'This one is fighting for a worldly good, this one is fighting for power (*mulk*), this one is fighting for renown (*dhikr*), and the like, while this one is fighting to please God (lit. seeking God's face). Whoever is killed seeking to please God, that one is in Paradise.'[38]

---

35 E.g., Brock, 'Early Syrian asceticism', 2.

36 Tirmidhī, *faḍā'il al-jihād* 25, *bāb fī thawāb al-shahīd*, no 1663.

37 Bukhārī, *bad' al-waḥy* 1, *bāb kayfa kāna bad' al-waḥy*, no 1; *al-īmān* 41, *bāb mā jā'a anna al-aʿmāl bi-al-nīyah wa-al-ḥisbah*, no 54; *al-ʿitq* 6, *bāb al-khaṭa' wa-al-nisyān*, no 2529; *manāqib al-anṣār* 45, *bāb hijrat al-nabī*, no 3898; *al-nikāḥ* 5, *bāb man hājara aw ʿamila khayran li-tazwīj imra'ah*, no 5070; *al-aymān wa-al-nudhūr* 23, *bāb al-nīyah fī al-aymān*, no 6689; *al-ḥiyal* 1, *bāb fī tark al-ḥiyal*, no 6953. Tirmidhī, *faḍā'il al-jihād* 16, *bāb mā jā'a fīmān yuqātilu riyā'an wa-lil-dunyā*, no. 1647.

38 Ibn al-Mubārak, *Jihād*, no 9. Cf. a Prophet hadith report in which a man is dispatched to Hell because he fought only to acquire a reputation for bravery, a second because he recited the Qur'an only to acquire a reputation for learning, and a third because he spent all his money on

Renunciants must have been attracted to *jihād* inasmuch as it was about imposing God's will on the world, just as they sought to impose God's will on themselves. Some sayings liken the struggle to subdue ones lower self (*nafs*) to fighting the holy war. At the Farewell Pilgrimage, the Prophet said *inter alia* that the *mujāhid* is he who struggles against his lower self in obedience to God.[39] Asked what was the best *jihād*, he said, 'Your *jihād* against yourself concerning your fancy (*hawá*).'[40] He said, 'The *mujāhid* is he who strives against himself by himself.'[41] Abū Dharr (d. 32/652–3) asked the Prophet what *jihād* was best. He said, 'That you fight against yourself (*an tujāhida nafsak*) and your fancy for the sake of God …'[42]

Ibrāhīm ibn Abī 'Ablah (Syrian, d. 152/769–70?) said to someone who was returning from raiding, 'You have come from the lesser *jihād*. What have you done about the greater *jihād* (*al-jihād al-akbar*)?' They said, 'O Abū Ismā'īl, what is the greater *jihād*?' He said, 'The *jihād* of the heart.'[43] Our surviving source for this is late, but it suggests that the prophetic formula of the lesser and greater *jihād*s developed from an earlier renunciant saying. The earliest attribution to the Prophet I have found is in one of the short works of al-Muḥāsibī (d. 243/857–8), which quotes this without context or *isnād*: 'You have returned from the lesser *jihād* to the greater *jihād*: struggling with your souls (*mujāhadat al-nafs*).'[44] Some of the renunciant anxiety not to let fighting be the main expected activity of pious Muslims comes out in a quotation of Mālik ibn Dīnār: 'They talk about *jihād*. I am on *jihād* against myself.'[45] If warfare continued to be the main activity of zealous Muslims, Islam threatened to become a young man's religion.[46]

---

charitable objects only to acquire a reputation for generosity: Muslim, *al-imārah* 43, *bāb man qātala lil-riyā' wa-al-sum'ah*, no 1905.

39 Ibn al-Mubārak, *Zuhd*, nos 826, 141 < Nu'aym; Aḥmad, *Musnad* 6:21, shorter versions at 6:20, 22 *39:381–2*, shorter versions at *39:375, 386–7*.

40 Al-Mu'āfá ibn 'Imrān, *Zuhd*, 303, no 217; anonymous asker.

41 Ibn al-Mubārak, *Jihād*, no 175; shorter version, Tirmidhī, *faḍā'il al-jihād* 2, *bāb mā jā'a fī faḍl man māta murābiṭan*, no 1621.

42 Abū Nu'aym, *Ḥilyah* 2:249, s.n. al-'Alā' ibn Ziyād (Basran, d. 94/712–13), next quoted for a similar report from 'Abd Allāh ibn 'Amr (d., 63/683?).

43 Ibn 'Asākir, *Tārīkh* 6:438.

44 Muḥāsibī, '*Kitāb al-Khalwah*', 480. Earlier cited, I have also discovered, by Gavin Picken, 'The "greater" jihad', 130–1.

45 Abū Nu'aym, *Ḥilyah* 2:363.

46 As Khārijism threatened to become, with its stress on martyrdom, according to Heck, 'Eschatological scripturalism', 140n, 151.

Encouragements to participate in *jihād*, common in some chapters of the Qur'an and classic collections of hadith, are actually not many in books of renunciation. Hannād ibn al-Sarī, *al-Zuhd*, has no separate chapter on *jihād*. A section on which works are encouraged does have this item: 'The Messenger of God was asked, "Which work is best?" He said, "Faith in God and his Messenger." "Then what, O Messenger of God?" He said, "*Jihād* in the path of God is the height of works." "Then what, O Messenger of God?" He said, "An accepted pilgrimage."'[47] The Prophet said, 'The like of the *mujāhid* on the path of God is the one who humbly fasts and keeps vigil without flagging until he returns.'[48] There are many such sayings that characterize *jihād* as equal to other manifestations of piety, not superior.[49] The value of martyrdom in warfare is diluted by extension of the status of martyr to persons who die in many additional ways.[50] Compare also A. J. Wensinck: 'When however the inner value of the new religion becomes a matter of keen interest and discussion, the question arises whether the highest place in Islām belongs exclusively to those who wage war. Is not the fulfilling of the other precepts of the Ḳor'ān a duty of equal inner value?'[51] Shorn of the suggestion that religions inevitably evolve more sublime forms, Wensinck's formulation plausibly points to the time, as the conquest period wound down and the military was professionalized, when 'those who wage war' came to be a dwindling minority of the articulate Muslims who elaborated the religion.

Renunciant hirelings

If renunciant literature tends to be only mildly encouraging of *jihād*, it tends to be strongly discouraging of involvement with rulers. The classic Sunni political position (i.e., from the later ninth century) is quietist; that is, accepting the rule of whoever comes to effectively maintain order. For example, al-Bukhārī quotes the Prophet,

---

47 Hannād, *Zuhd* 2:518–19; also Tirmidhī, *faḍā'il al-jihād* 22, *bāb mā jā'a fī ayy al-a'māl afḍal*, no 1658; sim., Dārimī, *Musnad*, 572.

48 Ibn al-Mubārak, *Jihād*, no 37; Mālik, *Muwaṭṭa'*, rec. Yaḥyá, *al-jihād* 1, *al-targhīb fī al-jihād*, no 1283 = rec. Abū Muṣ'ab, *al-jihād* 4, *al-targhīb fī al-jihād*, no 905.

49 A central theme of Denaro, *Dal martire allo* šahīd, esp. Part III, 65–124.

50 To begin with, see *EI*[2], s.v. 'shahīd', by Kohlberg, Cook, *Martyrdom*, chap. 6, 'Martyrs of love and epic heroes', and Denaro, 'Definitions'.

51 Wensinck, 'Oriental doctrine', 153.

> The Children of Israel had prophets to lead them. Whenever one perished, a prophet came after him. There is no prophet after me but there will be many caliphs. Fulfill your oaths of allegiance to them one after another, giving them their due. God will ask them about what they have been charged to watch over.[52]

An early Ḥanbali creed expressly calls for obedience to rulers both just and unjust:

> The caliphate belongs to the Quraysh so long as there are two persons. No one may struggle with them over it, nor rebel against them. We do not testify that it will belong to anyone else before the Hour. The holy war (*jihād*) goes on continually with the imams, whether pious or reprobate. It is not negated by the oppression of any oppressor or the justice of any just one. Friday, the two festivals, and the pilgrimage are with the *sulṭān* (reigning caliph), even if they are not pious, just, and godfearing. One pays the alms tax, the land tax, tithes, and the prescribed shares of booty to the commanders, whether they behave justly or unjustly. One submits to whomever God has appointed to rule over you. Not a hand is to be withdrawn from obedience to him, nor may you draw your sword against him in order that God should make for you a release and a way out. You may not rebel against the *sulṭān*. You must hearken and obey, not breaking your oath of loyalty. Whoever does that is an innovator, turning away and breaking with the community (*jamāʿah*).

There is no obedience in wrongdoing, but the creed quickly returns to obedience:

> If the ruler (*sulṭān*) gives you a command that is disobedience to God, you certainly may not obey him. Neither may you rebel against him or deny his right. Holding back in civil strife (*fitnah*) is the past *sunnah* and obligatory to do. If you are tried, put yourself before your religion without helping to generate strife by hand or tongue. Rather, restrain your hand, tongue, and fancy (*hawá*). God is the Helper.[53]

The Companion Ibn ʿUmar (d. Mecca, 73/692–3?) would pray behind any commander who came along and pay his alms tax to him. He said, ‘I will not fight in a civil war. I pray behind whoever wins.’[54] Salamah ibn al-Akwaʿ (d. 74/693–4?), asked why he did not distance himself from the Umayyad caliph, said, ‘I do not distance myself nor do I swear allegiance to him.’ He did pay his alms tax to them.[55] Many reports support neutrality.[56]

We have abundant reports of renunciants who mistrusted rulers and tried to avoid them. A surprisingly early example of tension is the story of Abū Dharr, said

---

52 Bukhārī, *aḥādīth al-anbiyāʾ* 5, *bāb mā dhukira ʿan Banī Isrāʾīl*, no 3455.
53 Ibn Abī Yaʿlá, *Ṭabaqāt al-ḥanābilah*, Creed I, at 1:26–7 *1:58*. Very likely this creed should be attributed to Ḥarb al-Kirmānī (d. 280/893–4), for which see Al-Sarhan, ‘The creeds of Aḥmad ibn Ḥanbal’, also Ḥarb al-Kirmānī, *Masāʾil*, 355–66.
54 Ibn Saʿd, *Ṭabaqāt* 4/1:100 *4:149*.
55 Ibn Saʿd, *Ṭabaqāt* 4/2:40 *4:307*.
56 Ibn Saʿd, *Ṭabaqāt* 4/2:40 *4:307*.

to be the fourth or fifth convert to Islam. After the conquest, he moved to Damascus where he made himself unpopular by applying Q. 9:34, 'Those who hoard gold and silver and do not spend it in God's way', to local Muslims. The then-governor of Damascus, the future caliph Muʿāwiyah, forbade people to sit with him in the mosque. Then he was recalled to Medina by the caliph ʿUthmān, who later exiled him (or permitted him to depart—reports vary) to Rabadhah, two hundred kilometres northeast of Medina, where he lived until his death.[57] Sufyān ibn ʿUyaynah (Kufan, transferred to Mecca, d. 198/814) named him among the three most outstanding avoiders of rulers, the others being Ṭāwūs (Yemeni cl., d. 106/725?) and Sufyān al-Thawrī (Kufan, d. 161/777?).[58] Given his troubles with ʿUthmān, it is unsurprising to find him among the few Companions lauded by Shiʿi biographers.[59] But the Sunni account uses his troubles mainly to stress the necessity of obedience to appointed rulers; for example, reporting the Prophet's advice not to rebel when rulers wrongly appropriate booty for themselves but 'Be patient until you meet me', and consenting to pray behind the governor of Rabadhah even though he was an Ethiopian slave, since he had been appointed by the caliph.[60] He is quoted as advising one Companion to accept a stipend (from the caliph) so long as it was a sufficiency to live on (*mutʿah*) although not if it had become a debt (something to be repaid), to another that it was all right to accept office inasmuch as he had not used his position to compete in building or to acquire agricultural property or flocks.[61] Such stories seem anachronistic for the conquest period but bespeak attitudes thought appropriate in the century after.

Ṭāwūs, a reputed Shiʿi sympathizer, is quoted in contempt of oppressive rulers: 'I am amazed that our brothers of the people of Iraq call al-Ḥajjāj a believer.'[62] The caliph Sulaymān ibn ʿAbd al-Malik (*r.* 96–9/715–17), then just heir apparent, summoned him at the instigation of Rajāʾ ibn Ḥaywah (Palestinian, d. 112/730–1). Among other things, Ṭāwūs told him, 'The most despicable of creation to God is someone whom God has given power (*sulṭān*), which he then uses in disobedience to him.' Rajāʾ said, 'I saw Sulaymān rub his head with his hand till I was afraid his nails would injure his head.'[63] Muḥammad ibn Yūsuf, brother to Ḥajjāj and Sulaymān's governor of Mecca, or his lieutenant Ayyūb ibn Yaḥyá once sent

57 Ibn Saʿd, *Ṭabaqāt* 4/1:166 *4:226*.
58 Ibn Ḥajar, *Tahdhīb* 5:5.
59 E.g., Kashshī, *Rijāl*, 27–31.
60 Ibn Saʿd, *Ṭabaqāt* 4/1:166–7 *4:226–7*; Abū Dāwūd, *al-sunnah* 30, *bāb fī al-khawārij*, no 4759; sim., ʿAbd al-Razzāq, *Muṣannaf* 11:334. Discussed by Crone, '"Even an Ethiopian slave"', 60–1.
61 Ibn Saʿd, *Ṭabaqāt* 4/1:169 *4:230*.
62 Ibn Saʿd, *Ṭabaqāt* 5:393 *5:540*. For his Shiʿism, see Ibn Abī Khaythamah, *Tārīkh* 1:310.
63 Marrūdhī, *Akhbār*, 88, no 109.

Ṭāwūs 500 or 700 dinars. He refused to accept it so the envoy threw the purse onto a windowsill. When the ruler heard something offensive to him, he sent his envoy back to reclaim the money. He found that it was all still there on the windowsill with a cobweb over it.[64]

Sufyān al-Thawrī is associated especially with contempt for the ʿAbbāsids.[65] If given a choice between having his vision filled with 'them' and going blind, he would prefer blindness, he said. He was against so much as reciting Q. 112 to rulers.[66] He went in to the caliph Abū Jaʿfar al-Manṣūr but would not salute him.[67] He refused to shake hands with someone who came up to him in his circle, explaining afterwards that this was the way to treat those who sat with 'them'.[68]

There are many general warnings against association with rulers. The Prophet said, 'A man does not increase his nearness to the ruler without increasing his distance from God. His followers do not increase without an increase of his satans. Neither does his wealth increase without an increase of his reckoning.'[69] Abū Hurayrah (d. 58/677–8?) would not ride out to join Muʿāwiyah's procession as it entered Mecca, saying he would ride only when God was his guarantor (i.e., on *jihād*).[70] ʿUbayd ibn ʿUmayr (Meccan, d. bef. 70/689–90) said, 'The closer one draws to the ruler, the further from God.'[71] Abū Wāʾil Shaqīq ibn Salamah (Kufan, d. 99/717–18?) told his slave girl Barakah not to accept any food from his son Wāʾil after he assumed the judgeship.[72] Muḥammad ibn Wāsiʿ (Basran, d. 123/740–1) said, 'A small amount of dust is better than approaching the caliph (*sulṭān*).'[73] To someone who asked him to intercede for him, he said, 'Woe betide you. Approaching them is to be slaughtered.'[74] Abū Salamah (al-Mughīrah) ibn Muslim (Madayini, *fl.* mid-8th cent.) ate some tasty vegetables (*buqūl*) but left and made himself vomit when he heard that they were from a certain person's garden—probably a ruler or someone close to him who did not have it by right.[75]

---

64 Aḥmad, *Zuhd*, 375 *449*; Abū Nuʿaym, *Ḥilyah* 4:14–15.
65 See Juynboll, *Muslim tradition*, 208–13, and Judd, 'Competitive hagiography in biographies of al-Awzāʿī and Sufyān al-Thawrī', esp. 31–4.
66 Marrūdhī, *Waraʿ*, 95 *77*; idem, *Akhbār*, 67.
67 Marrūdhī, *Akhbār*, 70.
68 Marrūdhī, *Akhbār*, 129, no 191.
69 Hannād, *Zuhd* 1:327 (Egyptian/Meccan *isnād*); shorter version in Abū Dāwūd, *al-ṣayd* 25, *bāb fī ittibāʿ al-ṣayd*, no 2860, and Aḥmad, *Musnad* 2:371 *14:430–1* (Kufan *isnād*).
70 Ibn al-Mubārak, *Zuhd*, no 18 < Nuʿaym; Aḥmad, *Zuhd*, 177 *221*.
71 Abū Nuʿaym, *Ḥilyah* 3:274.
72 Marrūdhī, *Aḥkām*, 119, no 173; sim., Aḥmad, *Zuhd*, 358 *429* (< ʿAl.); Abū Nuʿaym, *Ḥilyah* 4:103.
73 Abū Nuʿaym, *Ḥilyah* 2:352.
74 Marrūdhī, *Akhbār*, 49, no 22.
75 Marrūdhī, *Waraʿ*, 85 *67*.

A number of quotations suggest that rulers in the first place associated themselves with recitation of the Qur'an. Ṭāwūs is quoted as saying, 'The person with the best voice in reciting the Qur'an is the one who most fears God (mighty and glorious is he).'[76] In one version, he then adds, 'and is free of those.'[77] Al-Ḥasan al-Baṣrī inveighed against *qurrāʾ* he found at the governor's gate.[78] 'Do not answer a ruler's invitation, even if he invites you to recite before him a chapter of the Qur'an. You will not go out from him but worse than when you went in.'[79] Muḥammad ibn Sīrīn (Basran, d. 110/729) said, 'If a ruler bids you to recite the Qur'an to him, do not go to him.'[80] Ḥammād ibn Salamah (Basran, d. 167/783–4) said, 'If the ruler (*amīr*) bids you recite to him *qul huwa Allāh aḥad* (Q. 112), do not go to him.'[81] Perhaps it was precisely the preponderance of Qur'an recitation among services performed for rulers by men of religion that made *qāriʾ* a pejorative term, by contrast with *zāhid* and *nāsik*.

As a variant of concern for eating only licit food, there are many notices of anxiety to avoid drinking from rulers' wells. Ṭāwūs would drink only from ancient wells on the way to Mecca; that is, avoiding any drilled by recent rulers.[82] 'Amr ibn 'Ubayd would often thirst but would not drink until he had got home.[83] Bishr ibn Manṣūr (Basran, d. 180/796–7) would not drink from a well provided by Hārūn al-Rashīd's governor 'Īsá ibn Ja'far.[84] Al-Ḍaḥḥāk ibn 'Uthmān (Medinese, *fl.* later 8th cent.) would not drink 'their' water, which met with Aḥmad ibn Ḥanbal's approval.[85]

This story is told of Muḥammad ibn Wāsi' (d. 123/740–1?), illustrating both rulers' blandishments and some renunciants' resistance:

> One of the commanders in Basra distributed alms among the *qurrāʾ* of the people of Basra. He sent (alms) to Mālik ibn Dīnār, who accepted, whereas Muḥammad ibn Wāsi' refused. He said, 'O Mālik, have you accepted the ruler's rewards?' He said, 'He said for me to ask those who sit with me. They said, "O Abū Bakr, buy slaves with it and set them free."'

---

76 Aḥmad, *Zuhd*, 213 *262* (< 'Al.). Sim. attributed to Ṭalq ibn Ḥabīb (Basran, d. after 90/708–9), *ibid.*, 174 *217*.
77 Ibn Abī Shaybah, *Muṣannaf* 10:462–5 *10:210–11*.
78 Abū Nu'aym, *Ḥilyah* 2:150–1.
79 'Abd al-Razzāq, *Muṣannaf* 11:326.
80 Marrūdhī, *Akhbār*, 66; an alternative version, same page, says 'a chapter of the Qur'an'.
81 Marrūdhī, *Akhbār*, 67–8; Abū Nu'aym, *Ḥilyah* 6:251. Also attributed to Sufyān al-Thawrī: Abū al-Qāsim al-Baghawī, *Ja'dīyāt* 2:25; Ibn Abī Ḥātim, *Jarḥ* 1:89.
82 Marrūdhī, *Wara'*, 86 *69*.
83 'Abd al-Jabbār, *Faḍl al-i'tizāl*, 248.
84 Abū Nu'aym, *Ḥilyah* 6:239.
85 Marrūdhī, *Akhbār*, 141, no 230.

> Muḥammad said to him, 'I beseech you by God: is your heart disposed towards him now as it was before he rewarded you?' He said, 'O God, no.' He said, 'Do you see what has come over you?' Mālik said to those sitting with him, 'Mālik is only an ass. God is worshipped only by the like of Muḥammad ibn Wāsiʿ.'[86]

It is said that Muḥammad ibn Wāsiʿ was wanted for the judgeship but refused. His wife rebuked him for it, saying, 'You have dependants and you are needy.' He said, 'So long as you see me patient with vinegar and vegetables, don't tempt me in this matter.'[87] And rulers had ways of associating themselves with holy men in spite of their resistance. Ṭāwūs may have been famous for indifference toward the caliph, but Hishām ibn ʿAbd al-Malik (*r.* 105–25/724–43) contrived to lead the prayer at his funeral.[88]

To the contrary, however, there are also many stories of renunciants who did associate with rulers and accept their blandishments. Ibn ʿAwn (Basran, d. 150/767–8?) said of Ibrahim (al-Nakhaʿī, Kufan, d. 96/714?), 'He would go to the caliph (*sulṭān*) and ask them for prizes.'[89] Ibrahim took a prize from the general Ibrāhīm ibn al-Ashtar (d. 72/691) during the Second Civil War.[90] He received garments and a thousand dirhams from Zuhayr al-Azdī, governor of Ḥulwān.[91] (Later, he dissociated himself from rulers. Perhaps he was living by a rule attributed to him elsewhere, 'They used to seek the world; then when they reached 40 they would seek the afterlife.'[92]) Al-Aʿmash (Kufan, d. 148/765–6?) said that the prominent Companions Ibn ʿAbbās (d. 68/687–8) and Ibn ʿUmar (d. Mecca, 73/693?) both accepted presents from al-Mukhtār, the Shiʿi leader for whom Ibrāhīm ibn al-Ashtar worked for a time.[93] He is also said to have accepted money from one of al-Mukhtār's Umayyad enemies, ʿAbd al-ʿAzīz ibn Marwān, during the Civil War.[94] And it is said, 'Ibn ʿUmar never refused a bequest or a present from anyone except al-Mukhtār.'[95] Contradictory reports like these suggest that they had much to do with the politics of the next century, different parties marshalling venerable supporters of the past for whatever party interested them in

86 Abū Nuʿaym, *Ḥilyah* 2:353–4 (< ʿAl., *Zuhd*).
87 Abū Nuʿaym, *Ḥilyah* 2:353 (< ʿAl., *Zuhd*).
88 Ibn Saʿd, *Ṭabaqāt* 5:395 *5:542*.
89 Ibn Saʿd, *Ṭabaqāt* 6:193 *6:277*.
90 Ibn Saʿd, *Ṭabaqāt* 6:193 *6:277*. On Ibrāhīm ibn al-Ashtar, see Kennedy, *Armies of the caliphs*, 38.
91 Ibn Saʿd, *Ṭabaqāt* 6:193 *6:277*; short version, with approval, Shaybānī, *Āthār* 2:752–3, *bāb jawāʾiz al-ʿummāl*.
92 Ibn Abī al-Dunyā, *Dhamm al-dunyā*, 206.
93 Ibn Saʿd, *Ṭabaqāt* 4/1:111 *4:150*; Abū Nuʿaym, *Ḥilyah* 5:54.
94 Ibn Saʿd, *Ṭabaqāt* 4/1:115 *4:157* (Basran *isnād*).
95 Ibn Saʿd, *Ṭabaqāt* 4/1:115–16 *4:157* (Basran *isnād*).

the present. But they also seem likely evidence that eighth-century Muslims expected contending politicians to recruit prominent religious figures.

Finally, there are reports suggesting ambivalence about association with rulers. Abū Ḥāzim (Medinese cl., *qāṣṣ*, d. *ca* 142/760) advised a governor of Medina to whom he had gone, 'Look at the people by your door. If you bring near the people of goodness, the people of evil will go away. If you bring near the people of evil, the people of goodness will go away.'[96] Al-Aʿmash, on leaving a ruler, said, 'In our opinion, they are simply like gardens (*al-ḥushsh*): when we need them we go to them, when we do not need them, we leave them.'[97] One historiographical tradition stresses how far Muslims have expected rulers to follow clear religious guidelines; that actual governments have never found it possible to live by these guidelines; that, in consequence, challengers to constituted authority have always had powerful religious justifications at hand to reinforce their assaults.[98] Medieval Muslim political thinkers did not advocate continual revolution, to be sure, but rather tended to enjoin loyal obedience to the effective authority so long as it met a few minimal criteria—criteria they moreover reduced over time. But any challenger who promised to meet these criteria might likewise command obedience, so again it encouraged political instability. Renunciant piety tended to encourage low expectations of rulers, hence emerging Sunni quietism, keeping away from politics. The other chief response to disappointment with politics, Sunni internationalism, was mainly a matter of later developments, notably the schools of law and Sufi orders.

---

96 Abū Nuʿaym, *Ḥilyah* 3:240.
97 ʿIjlī, *Tārīkh al-thiqāt*, 204–5.
98 See Gardet, *La cité musulmane*.

Chapter 8: The economics of renunciation

During the conquest period, Muslims were supported directly by booty or indirectly by the provision of stipends, the state's redistribution of tribute from the conquered peoples. That system became unfeasible as the Muslim population increased, as urbanized Muslims failed to develop the military habits of pastoralists, and as the caliphs found professional soldiers more dependable supports. The alms tax (*zakāh*) laid down by the Qur'an as an essential duty, by interpretation a levy of one-fortieth of wealth above a certain amount, was one obvious redistributive mechanism. It seems to have played only a minor role in supporting holy men in the eighth century, though. Self-support by trading and craftsmanship were both recommended, but the lasting solution to the problem of supporting religious specialists was the development of *waqf* foundations in the ninth century.

The economic tradition

In the conquest period of the seventh century, politics and economics were closely related inasmuch as most Muslims were supported by plunder, either what could be brought back from new conquests at the frontier or, more substantially, what came as regular tribute from subject peoples. Crucially important was the caliphs' decision not to divide up the conquered territories among the conquering commanders but to maintain existing tax régimes and support the Muslims by shares of the tribute, redistributed by the central authority.[1] An obvious advantage to the caliphs was to keep the Muslims dependent on them. Settling the Muslims in garrison cities rather than existing population centres, at least outside Syria, also kept the troops separate from the Egyptians, Iraqis, and others, and so hindered the Muslims' cultural assimilation. Regional Muslim and non-Muslim élites joined in revolt against the central power at various points in the ninth century but seldom before then. Presumably, Arabic survived and spread partly in consequence of this long interval of living apart, as Islamic religious and political structures stabilized and the number of Arab (i.e., Arabophone) Muslims grew.

It is no new idea that the Islamic moral economy was in substantial continuity with the pre-Islamic. In 1962, Meïr M. Bravmann published a study of the

---

1 On the distinction between land- and tax-based states, see Wickham, *Land and power*, chaps 1–2, qualified in *idem*, *Framing the early Middle Ages*, 60.

https://doi.org/10.1515/9783110617962-009

words *ʿafw*, *faḍl*, *kasb*, and *fāʾidah* in early Islamic chronicles and poetry to establish that they came out of a tribal economy in which superiors were expected to distribute the surplus of their property to their inferiors; to find such a surplus by raiding if necessary.[2] Nomadic pastoralists are unusually exposed to sudden and complete ruin. Raiders can entirely sweep away a flock in a bad hour, reducing a family to destitution. Anthropologists have sometimes adduced this vulnerability to explain heightened cultivation of honour south of the Mediterranean as opposed to north of it. That is, it is more critical for pastoralists than agriculturalists to scare off would-be attackers by the threat of immediate, savage reprisal against any trespass. Similarly, it has been used to explain the persistence of polygamy south of the Mediterranean, where raiding more easily created gross disparities of wealth than where agriculture was comfortably predominant. However, vulnerability to raiding somewhat limits the accumulation of property, hence the institution of redistribution that Bravmann makes out. Bravmann suggests that it is at the origin of *zakāh*, the Islamic alms tax levied on Muslims' property above a certain level. Be that as it may, it must have seemed appropriate for seventh-century Muslims to be supported mainly by stipends from the state, ultimately acquired from without the community. Christian Décobert and Michael Bonner have also described the economy of redistribution in the early community.[3] Both stress how redistribution from patrons was used to integrate newcomers into an existing tribal unit.

After the conquest period

The old system whereby all the Muslims were supported by tribute from the conquered peoples could not outlast the conquest period. It had to be strained by the professionalization of the military, as stipends graded by date of conversion gradually gave way to straightforward salaries for military service.[4] It also had to be strained as the proportion of Muslims in the population grew by natural increase and conversion, so that tribute had to accommodate more receivers. One response to the strain was to encourage austerity in everyday life, in the city as formerly in the camp. Restraint on consumption must have tended to lessen the problem of resentment: the poor were encouraged to reconcile themselves to their poverty (by making a virtue of necessity); more importantly, at least some of the

2 Bravmann, 'The surplus of property'.
3 Décobert, *Le mendiant et le combattant*; Bonner, 'The *Kitāb al-Kasb*'; *idem*, 'Poverty and charity'.
4 Kennedy, *The armies of the caliphs*, chap. 3, esp. 76–7.

more prosperous, notably those able to spend time on scholarship, conspicuously refused to live it up.[5]

Some economic attitudes of the conquest period certainly lived on. The warrior's contempt for powerless peasants sometimes shows up in hadith disdainful of agriculture. By a Syrian *isnād*, al-Bukhārī relates that the Prophet, on seeing a mouldboard and other agricultural implements, said, 'This will not enter a people's house but that God will make humiliation enter it.'[6] By an Egyptian *isnād*, Abū Dāwūd relates that the Prophet said, 'If you sell by means of *ʿīnah*, take hold of oxen's tails, become satisfied with agriculture, and leave off the holy war, God will make humiliation prevail over you, which he will not remove until you return to your faith.'[7] One might interpret this as disdaining agriculture inasmuch as it entails leaving the holy war and no more, which fits the nomadic outlook on settled cultivators (i.e., weaklings easily bullied); however, the association seems random (if there is no connection between *ʿīnah* and agriculture, why should there be between agriculture and *jihād*?), making it just one more offence. A lingering aristocratic bias seems to underlie an attribution to Muḥammad ibn Wāsiʿ

5 Cf. Bonner, 'Definitions of poverty', esp. 343. Bonner distinguishes between a radical theory of almsgiving, stressing circulation of wealth and better suited to the conquest period, and a conservative version, accepting permanent stratification and better suited to what followed. *Isnād* analysis leads him to assign the former to Medina, the latter to Iraq, so that a generally Schachtian approach to hadith leads to a particular exception: Medinese doctrine on this point is not a reaction to Iraqi but genuinely archaic. Conceivably (my guess), universal conversion and caliphal largesse to the holy cities retarded the formation of a class of Muslim poor there by comparison with the garrison towns of Iraq. However, I have doubts we should rely on his characterization of Medinese doctrine. A section *bāb masʾalat al-nās* in ʿAbd al-Razzāq, *Muṣannaf* 11:90–6, includes sayings of both tendencies but with only somewhat more of the conservative variety Iraqi at the Follower level (9:6), only somewhat more of the radical Hijazi (3:2). The central conservative report by which the Prophet defines the *miskīn* most deserving of charity as him who is needy but goes unnoticed rather than beg is in the *Muwaṭṭaʾ* of Mālik (rec. Yaḥyá, *al-jāmiʿ* 27, *mā jāʾa fī al-masākīn*, no 2672; rec. Abū Muṣʿab, *al-jāmiʿ* 25, *bāb mā jāʾa fī al-miskīn*, no 1932; rec. Shaybānī, *jāmiʿ al-ḥadīth*, *bāb faḍl al-maʿrūf wa-al-ṣadaqah*, no 931). Its formulation is attributed directly to Mālik by Juynboll, *Encyclopedia*, 369. The *Muwaṭṭaʾ* does not give us the Medinese tradition so reliably as the Māliki tradition makes out, but it seems difficult to argue that it here espouses the Iraqi tradition against the earlier Hijazi.

6 Bukhārī, *al-ḥarth wa-al-muzāraʿah* 2, *bāb mā yuḥdharu min ʿawāqib al-ishtighāl bi-ālat al-zarʿ*, no 2321. On the basis mostly of later sources, this and related hadith reports are surveyed in Kister, 'Land property and *jihād*'. Kister stresses the humiliation of moving into the category of taxpayers for Muslims who buy agricultural land.

7 Abū Dāwūd, *al-buyūʿ* 54, *bāb al-nahy ʿan al-ʿīnah*, no 3462. *ʿĪnah* has been interpreted as a device to avoid interest by means of a double sales contract—say, 'I hereby sell you this pen for 50 dirhams, payable now, and buy that one from you for 55, payable in six months.'

(Basran, d. 123/740–1) identifying four possible characters of pure wealth: trade in the licit, inheritance by will, free-will donation from a Muslim brother, and a share of the booty from a just imam.[8] Manual labour is conspicuously missing. But resentment of agriculture expressly as distracting from the holy war can be found.

> Mālik ibn ʿAbd Allāh al-Khathʿamī and Ḥabīb ibn Maslamah [*fl.* 7th cent.] were in some commander's army. One of them said, 'O people, beware of besmirching God's religion.' The other one said ..., 'If you last, there will be a time when poor men go raiding while the rich hold back, preoccupied by agriculture and stock-raising. Those are the ones who besmirch God's religion.'[9]

The last words may be Aḥmad ibn Ḥanbal's comment.

Bonner cites a discussion in *Kitāb al-Kasb* ('Gain') that reviews hadith on either side, for trade or agriculture, and concludes that agriculture is ultimately better 'because its benefit is more general and because its *ṣadaqa* (charitable giving) is more apparent (*aẓhar*).'[10] *Kitāb al-Kasb* is a section of the massive Ḥanafi handbook of al-Sarakhsī (d. 483/1090–1?), *al-Mabsūṭ*.[11] Al-Sarakhsī states near the beginning that it is his commentary on a little-known work, *Kitāb al-Kasb*, related by Muḥammad ibn Samāʿah (Baghdadi, d. 233/847–8) from al-Shaybānī (d. 189/ 804–5).[12] It has been published several times as a separate work alternatively attributed directly to al-Shaybānī or Ibn Samāʿah.[13] Bonner thinks this passage goes back to its earliest layer, mainly al-Shaybānī himself. However, this passage, especially in consideration of its appeal to 'our shaykhs', looks like al-Sarakhsī to me. There is a section on agriculture in every legal handbook and topical hadith collection, largely setting out rules for different rental arrangements, and even nomads commonly practise cultivation on some scale. However, universally-valid Islam was a product mainly of urban culture, more strongly influenced by the ethos of nomadic warriors than great landowners, and preference for agriculture fits the time of al-Sarakhsī more easily than that of al-Shaybānī.

Dependence on stipends from tribute should have been congenial to renunciants as freeing them to pursue their devotions. Stories of army camps humming

---

8 Abū Nuʿaym, *Ḥilyah* 2:353.

9 Marrūdhī, *Waraʿ*, 151 *115–16*.

10 Bonner, 'The *Kitāb al-Kasb*', 417; similarly cited by Brunschvig, 'Métiers vils', 44; also Kister, 'Land property', 300–1.

11 Sarakhsī, *Mabsūṭ* 30:244–87.

12 Sarakhsī, *Mabsūṭ* 30:244; Shaybānī, *Kasb*, 65.

13 Bonner, 'The *Kitāb al-Kasb*', 413. My own article on this work stresses its documentation of hostility to austere living at the end of the eighth century: Melchert, 'Al-Shaybānī'.

like bee hives at night are about their ideal. Nevertheless, I have to admit that I have come across few stories that expressly mention a renunciant's living off his stipend (*ʿaṭāʾ*). Abū Wāʾil Shaqīq ibn Salamah (Kufan, d. *ca* 99/717–18) said, 'I prefer one dirham from trade to ten from my stipend.'[14] He did evidently take a stipend. Al-Ḥasan al-Baṣrī (d. 110/728) apparently enjoyed a stipend as a veteran of the conquest of Khurasan (probably small, since he was a non-Arab client).[15] The story is told that his stipend was once held up (*ḥubisa*). A man offered him 400 dinars but he refused. 'Whoever sits in my place and gets a consideration (*maʿrūf*) does not hope for any dignity from God.'[16] That is, regardless of his present need, he did not want to live on his reputation for piety. According to another story, he once took to distributing his stipend amongst other families until reminded by a son that he had dependants of his own.[17]

Décobert and Bonner's vision of continual recirculation of wealth does not closely fit surviving juridical discussions of either the alms tax (*zakāh*, *ṣadaqah*—the two were not clearly distinguished until the later ninth century) or the holy war, confirming that these discussions took place well after the old system had lapsed. The Qur'an appears to lay down the recipients: 'The alms are for the poor and the destitute, for those who work to collect them and those whose hearts are to be reconciled, to free slaves and debtors, in God's way and for the traveller' (Q. 9:60). 'Those whose hearts are to be reconciled' (*al-muʾallafah qulūbuhum*) traditionally refers to Meccans whom the Prophet needed to buy off to end the long war. The Medinese jurisprudent al-Zuhrī (d. 124/742?) is quoted as saying that it refers to Jews and Christians, rich or poor, who are to be induced to convert. Later eighth-century authorities are quoted as saying that the category lapsed already at the death of the Prophet.[18]

From a little later, the *Kitāb al-Amwāl* of Abū ʿUbayd (d. 224/838–9?) quotes a memorandum written by al-Zuhrī at the direction of the caliph ʿUmar ibn ʿAbd al-ʿAzīz (*r*. 99–101/717–20) setting out eight categories of recipients of *ṣadaqah* (eight doubtless after Q. 9:60).

---

14 Ibn Saʿd, *Ṭabaqāt* 6:68 *6:101*.

15 Van Ess, *Th.u.G.* 2:42 *2:47*.

16 Fasawī, *Maʿrifah* 2:51.

17 Aḥmad, *Zuhd*, 277–8 *338*; Hannād, *Zuhd* 1:338.

18 Ibn Abī Shaybah, *Muṣannaf* 3:223 *4:361–2*. Al-Shaybānī quotes Abū Ḥanīfah as saying of 'those whose hearts are to be reconciled', 'That was only in the time of the Prophet ..., when people needed to be reconciled to Islam and he would give them something of that. As for today, no': Shaybānī, *Aṣl* 2:142. Similarly, Mālik is quoted as saying, 'There is nothing for the *muʾallafah* today': Ibn Abī Zayd, *Nawādir* 2:280, citing Ibn al-Mawwāz < Aṣbagh, confirmed by Ibn Bashīr.

> One-half of the share meant for the poor is for those who are joining the battle for the first time having been assigned duties. They will take from the first grants issued. After this, they will not be entitled to take from the *ṣadaqa*, and their shares will come from the general booty.[19]

Another whole eighth is assigned to 'the path of God (*sabīl Allāh*)', meaning the holy war:

> A share is meant for God's cause. One-fourth of this will go to those soldiers to whom it is regularly assigned. The temporary soldiers and the poor will get another fourth (each). One-fourth of it will go to the war veteran in God's cause who is faced with a dire need.[20]

The alms tax, then, one of the pillars of Islam, did develop in part around the holy war as an employment opportunity supported by the state; but this was only one purpose among many, at least by the eighth century. When the *Muwaṭṭa'* of Mālik, for example, turns to *zakāh*, it is mainly concerned with the amount due on different categories of wealth, also with the *jizyah* levied on non-Muslim subjects. The common theme of the chapter is obviously an involuntary tax, not support for either the poor or warriors.[21] The *Umm* of al-Shāfiʿī says only a little more about support for the poor and warriors.[22] Encouragements to give in hadith do not particularly recommend as recipients either warriors or paragons of piety; for example, 'He who supports widows and the destitute (*miskīn*) is like one striving on the path of God or who fasts by day and keeps vigil at night.'[23] If they have any consistent stress, it is on the benefits to givers, not the interests of receivers, social justice, or even the strengthening of communal bonds.

In hadith on alms, there is considerable stress on the principle that charity begins at home, meaning here that one should begin with needy relatives. One report includes an apparent gloss by Ibn ʿUmar (d. Mecca, 73/692–3?), in reply to a letter from ʿAbd al-ʿAzīz ibn Hārūn bidding him ask for whatever he needed: 'I heard the Messenger of God ... say, "Begin with your dependants, the upper hand

---

19 Abū ʿUbayd, *Amwāl*, 764 *527*.
20 Abū ʿUbayd, *Amwāl*, 765 *528*.
21 Mālik, *Muwaṭṭa'*, *k. al-zakāh* in all recensions, although individual hadith reports seem to use *ṣadaqah* interchangeably.
22 Shāfiʿī, *Umm*, has a *k. al-zakāh* at 2:2–60 *3:5–180*, then *jimāʿ farḍ al-ṣadaqāt* at 2:60–80 *3:181– 230*. The latter section treats recipients; e.g., the conditions under which *ṣadaqāt* (here, required alms) may be moved from the locale where they have been collected to relieve want elsewhere (2:65–6 *3:193–4*). On the title of the latter section, see the editor's note at *3:181*.
23 Mālik, *Muwaṭṭa'*, rec. Abū Muṣʿab (not in rec. Yaḥyá), *al-ṣalāh* 17, *bāb isbāl al-rajul thawbah*, nos 1915–16; Bukhārī, *al-nafaqāt* 1, *bāb faḍl al-nafaqah ʿalá al-ahl*, no 5353, *al-adab* 25, *al-sāʿī ʿalá al-armalah*, no 6006.

being better than the lower hand." I count the upper hand as being the giver, the lower as the asker. I am not asking you nor will I refuse any provision that God sends me by means of you.'[24] Ibn 'Umar would not beg but he would not refuse a gift, either. Some renunciants were supported by relatives; for example, Miʿḍad al-ʿIjlī (Kufan, *fl.* early 8th cent.) gave himself to worship while his brother, who traded, supported him.[25] Presumably, the legal discussion does not line up with Bravmann and Bonner's picture of recirculation in the traditional Arab economy because the legal tradition treats conditions in the eighth century and after, which were not the same as in the seventh, and because it was the work of city people constructing an alternative to the old system of dependence on tribal political and military leaders.

Al-Zuhrī's letter to ʿUmar ibn ʿAbd al-ʿAzīz does apparently allow one opening for alms to renunciants.

> The share of those whose hearts have been reconciled ... will also be given to those who have been employed temporarily (*mushtariṭan*), are not paid a grant (*ʿaṭāʾ*), and are poor (*al-fuqarāʾ*). Part of it will go to those needy persons (*al-masākīn*) who come to the mosques, have no grants or shares (*sahm*), and who do not seek alms, God willing.[26]

Presumably, renunciants who congregated in mosques for their devotions might fit well the category of 'needy persons who come to the mosques'. ʿAbd al-Razzāq relates two reports by which the Kufan ʿAmr ibn Shuraḥbīl (Abū Maysarah, d. 63/682–3) would gather *zakāt al-fiṭr* (alms due at the end of Ramaḍān) in the mosque of his tribe, then divide it among Christian monks.[27] On the whole, still, the alms tax evidently would not serve to support a class of worshippers.

---

24 Ibn Saʿd, *Ṭabaqāt* 4/1:110–11 *4:150*. ʿAbd al-ʿAzīz ibn Hārūn was later governor of Iraq under the caliph Yazīd ibn al-Walīd, but at this time presumably just governor of Mecca. Another version (without mention of any letter) at Mālik, *Muwaṭṭaʾ*, rec. Yaḥyá, *al-jāmiʿ* 85, *mā jāʾa fī al-taʿaffuf ʿan al-masʾalah*, no 2851, rec. Abū Muṣʿab, *al-jāmiʿ* 77, *bāb al-taʿaffuf ʿan al-masʿalah*, no 2108, and Bukhārī, *al-zakāh* 18, *bāb lā ṣadaqah illā ʿan ẓahr ghiná*, no 1429, among other places. Observing that it appears in various contexts, G. H. A. Juynboll guesses that the saying about the upper hand was a pre-Islamic proverb: *Encyclopedia*, 255.

25 Ibn Abī Shaybah, *Muṣannaf* 13:417 *12:299*.

26 Abū ʿUbayd, *Amwāl*, 765 *528*.

27 ʿAbd al-Razzāq, *Muṣannaf* 4:113.

The occupations of renunciants

The danger of living on a stipend was above all, as developed in the previous chapter, the temptation to support corrupt rulers. Virtuous early rulers are quoted in favour of living by a trade.[28] We also have many reports of renunciants who lived by handicrafts rather than depend on a stipend or charity. Abū Wāʾil has been quoted already. Abū Dharr (d. Syria, 32/652–3?) is said to have supported himself by spinning wool.[29] Yazīd ibn Maysarah (Damascene, *fl.* late 7th cent.) told the governor to give his stipend to the poor. He also sold everything he had to give it away as alms, even the house he was living in. We are not told how he supported himself.[30] Mālik ibn Dīnār (Basran cl., d. *ca* 130/747–8) usually had only two dirhams, one to buy paper, the other to buy palm fronds for him to work with.[31] The paper (papyrus) was for copying the Qur'an, his second occupation for licit gain.[32] Kahmas (Basran muezzin, d. Mecca, 149/766–7) worked as plasterer for two *dānaq*s a day. In the evening, he would buy fruit with them for his mother.[33] ʿUtbah al-Ghulām (Basran, d. bef. 153/770) plaited palm fronds that he bought for a *fals* and sold for three, of which he used one for alms, one for food, and one for capital.[34] Sufyān al-Thawrī (Kufan, d. 161/777?) was sometimes supported by a sister's weaving.[35] Bishr ibn Manṣūr (Basran, d. 180/796–7), had 100,000 dirhams but taught his sons to weave palm fronds.[36] The oft-cited principle is to live by the gain of one's hand, as recommended by a Prophet hadith report: 'No one ever ate food better than eating by the gain of his hand. The prophet Dāwūd used to eat by the gain of his hand.'[37] Muḥammad ibn Masrūq (d. Alexandria, early 9th cent.) lived austerely, supported by a spinning slave girl.[38] Self-sufficiency was the point, on which more later.

---

28 Ibn al-Mubārak, *Jihād*, no 209.
29 Ibn Abī Shaybah, *Muṣannaf* 13:343 *12:246–7*.
30 Abū Zurʿah al-Dimashqī, *Tārīkh* 1:268–9.
31 Aḥmad, *Zuhd*, ed. Sharaf, 2:309 (< ʿAl.); Abū Nuʿaym, *Ḥilyah* 2:367.
32 Ibn Saʿd, *Ṭabaqāt* 7/2:11 *7:243*; Abū Nuʿaym, *Ḥilyah* 2:367, 368.
33 Abū Nuʿaym, *Ḥilyah* 6:212.
34 Abū Nuʿaym, *Ḥilyah* 6:229–31.
35 Abū Nuʿaym, *Ḥilyah* 7:67.
36 Abū Nuʿaym, *Ḥilyah* 6:240.
37 Bukhārī, *al-buyūʿ* 15, *bāb kasb al-rajul wa-ʿamalihi bi-yadih*, no 2072 (Syrian *isnād*); Marrūdhī, *Waraʿ*, 19 *23*; also Bukhārī, *aḥādīth al-anbiyāʾ* 37, *bāb wa-ātaynā Dāwūd zabūran*, no 3417; Hammām ibn Munabbih, *Ṣaḥīfat Hammām*, no 47.
38 Abū Bakr al-Mālikī, *Riyāḍ al-nufūs* 1:194.

The most common occupation named in the biographical dictionaries is trade.[39] Saʿīd ibn al-Musayyib (Medinese, d. 94/712–13?) refused his stipend and traded in oil with a capital of 400 dinars.[40] Muwarriq al-ʿIjlī (Basran, d. 105/723–4?) would make three to five-hundred dirhams in a week by trading, which, however, he would then give away.[41] Abū ʿAbd Rabbi (d. 112/730–1), although identified as a renunciant (*zāhid*), was also one of the richest people of Damascus. A story is told of his trading in Azarbaijan.[42] There are occasional references to someone's going to 'his market (*sūq*)', indicating the place in the market where he sat to trade. For example, Sufyān al-Thawrī recalled of his master ʿAmr ibn Qays (Kufan, d. 140s/758–68), 'I used to look for him in his market. If I did not find him in his market, I should find him at home, either praying or reading in a copy of the Qur'an.'[43]

Ibn al-Mubārak (Khurasani, d. 181/797) is important to us mainly as a collector of renunciant sayings. The earliest extant biography of him remarks his activity as an author and reciter of poetry encouraging renunciation and the holy war.[44] A more substantial biography from around 75 years later includes stories of his generosity to traditionists but still no express estimate of his wealth or its source.[45] He is quoted as saying, on being asked for a definition of humility, 'Haughtiness around the rich (*al-takabbur ʿalá al-aghniyāʾ*).'[46] Finally, in a substantial eleventh-century biography, there is some indication of the basis of his wealth, mainly a question about his bringing trade goods to Mecca.[47] Asked to explain why he spent so much in other places, none in his home town (Marw), he explained that this was to maintain knowledge of hadith, threatened to be lost if travellers in search of it were not supported.[48] His expenditure on the poor (*al-fuqarāʾ*) was reportedly 100,000 dirhams a year.[49] There is one story of his hidden expenditure on some Sufis who accompanied him to the frontier, but they

39 As generally for the men of religion, for which see Cohen, 'Economic background'.
40 ʿIjlī, *Tārīkh al-thiqāt*, 188.
41 Ibn Saʿd, *Ṭabaqāt* 7/1:157 *7:215*. He traded only for the sake of the poor according to Aḥmad, *Zuhd*, 314 *381*.
42 Abū Nuʿaym, *Ḥilyah* 5:160–1.
43 Abū Nuʿaym, *Ḥilyah* 5:100–1.
44 Ibn Saʿd, *Ṭabaqāt* 7/2:104–5 *7:372*.
45 Ibn Abī Ḥātim, *Jarḥ* 1:276–8.
46 Ibn Abī Ḥātim, *Jarḥ* 1:280.
47 Al-Khaṭīb al-Baghdādī, *Tārīkh* 10:159–60 *11:397*. The shifting biographical record is also surveyed in Denaro, 'From Marw to the *ṯuġūr*', with stress on the advantage of trade and travel for insulating Ibn al-Mubārak from politics.
48 Al-Khaṭīb al-Baghdādī, *Tārīkh* 10:160 *11:397*.
49 Al-Khaṭīb al-Baghdādī, *Tārīkh* 10:158 *11:395*.

have evidently come to participate in the holy war.[50] I bring up Ibn al-Mubārak partly because he has recently been made out by Feryal Salem as a major advocate of a completely inner-worldly asceticism compatible with great wealth, a normal appetite for good food, and so on. Her argument rests too heavily on the biographical tradition, I would say, and without due regard for the renunciant sayings Ibn al-Mubārak himself collected and transmitted.[51] But even the early biographical tradition seems reticent about his wealth. It also, by the way, tells us little of how renunciants were supported in the later eighth century, only traditionists and frontier raiders, except inasmuch as traditionists and frontier raiders were renunciants, too.

Some statements indicate distrust of trading. It might be a distraction from more important things. The famous Companion Abū al-Dardā' (d. Syria, early 30s/650s?) is widely quoted as saying, 'What a good cell for a man is his house. It screens his sight and tongue. Beware of the market, for it distracts and renders ineffectual (*tulhī wa-tulghī*).'[52] He himself traded in the Jāhilīyah but found he could not worship and trade as a Muslim, hence chose worship alone.[53] Apparently in answer to objections he explained that he had said God had allowed trading and forbidden usury (alluding to Q. 2:275) but that he preferred not to be distracted by trade from the recollection of God.[54] Salmān al-Fārisī (d. 36/656–7?) told his disciples that it was better to die on pilgrimage or raiding than living off trade or tribute.[55] Yazīd ibn Sharīk al-Taymī (Kufan, d. 65–86/685–705) made a 4,000-dirham profit on slaves brought from Basra but disdained to go back for more.[56]

Mujāhid ibn Jabr, famous Meccan Qur'an commentator (d. 103/721–2?), commented on Q. 4:32, 'Ask God of his favour', 'The aim is not this world.'[57] Al-Ḥasan al-Baṣrī was sceptical of licit accumulation: 'If it were said to them', he said of the pious, '"Will you not take your share of this wealth, which you may take licitly?"

---

50 Al-Khaṭīb al-Baghdādī, *Tārīkh* 10: 157–8 *11:394*.
51 Salem, *The emergence of early Sufi piety*.
52 Wakīʿ, *Zuhd* 2:516; Aḥmad, *Zuhd*, 135 *168*; Ibn al-Mubārak, *Zuhd*, no 14 < Nuʿaym; Ibn Abī Shaybah, *Muṣannaf* 13:309–10 *12:221*; Jāḥiẓ, *Bayān* 3:132; Abū Dāwūd, *Zuhd*, 127.
53 Aḥmad, *Zuhd*, 138 *172*; Hannād, *Zuhd* 2:353; Ibn Saʿd, *Ṭabaqāt* 7/2:117 *7:391–2*; Ibn Abī Shaybah, *Muṣannaf* 13:316 *12:226*; Abū Nuʿaym, *Ḥilyah* 1:209.
54 Aḥmad, *Zuhd*, 137 *170*.
55 Ibn al-Mubārak, *Jihād*, no 215.
56 Hannād, *Zuhd* 1:322; Aḥmad, *Zuhd*, 359 *430*.
57 Aḥmad, *Zuhd*, 381 *457*.

they would say, "No, we fear that taking it would corrupt our hearts."'[58] 'The dirham and dinar are poor companions', he said, 'for they do you no good until they depart.'[59] Al-Rabīʿ ibn Abī Rāshid (Kufan, *fl.* 1st half 8th cent.) said, 'The recollection of death has come between me and much trading.'[60] Presumably, he would trade enough to live but the prospect of death prevented him from aspiring to improve his condition. Ḥammād ibn Salamah (Basran, d. 167/783–4) would trade in clothing long enough to make one or two *dānaq*s, then close up shop.[61] Al-Ḥasan ibn Ṣāliḥ ibn Ḥayy (Kufan, d. 169/785–6) wept in the market over people's activity, praying 'See, O God, how they gather fruit (*yuʿallilūna*) until there comes to them death.'[62] Maryam al-Baṣrīyah (*fl.* late 8th cent.?) said she had not pursued her provision since she had heard God say, 'And in the sky is your sustenance' (Q. 51:22).[63]

Other quotations indicate suspicion that trading was outright wicked. The Prophet allegedly warned, 'What God most likes of cities is their mosques; what God most despises of cities is their markets.'[64] Ibrāhīm al-Nakhaʿī (Kufan, d. 96/714) said, 'They used to prefer the gain of one's hand to trade.'[65] Al-Ḥasan al-Baṣrī said, 'There is no good in the people of the market. I have heard that one of them will do his brother out of a dirham.'[66] Ṭalḥah ibn Muṣarrif (Kufan, d. 112/730–1 or after) disliked to make any profit off the Muslims, as by selling food.[67] ʿAbd Allāh ibn Abī Zakarīyā' (d. 119/717) never touched money.[68] Zubayd al-Yāmī (Kufan, d. 122/739–40 or after) likened dirhams to dung.[69] Mālik ibn Dīnār said, 'The market increases wealth but takes away *dīn* (religion).'[70] Ibrāhīm ibn Saʿd (*fl.* early 9th cent.?) and two others undertook to touch no silver or gold,[71] while the famous traditionist al-Bukhārī (Transoxanian, d. 256/870), although he lived largely by trade, said that he never touched money, having someone else buy ink and paper

58 Aḥmad, *Zuhd*, 262–3 *321*; sim., Abū Nuʿaym, *Ḥilyah* 2:149.
59 Abū Nuʿaym, *Ḥilyah* 2:155.
60 Abū Nuʿaym, *Ḥilyah* 5:78.
61 Abū Nuʿaym, *Ḥilyah* 6:250.
62 Abū Nuʿaym, *Ḥilyah* 7:329.
63 Sulamī, *Early Sufi women*, 84–5.
64 Muslim, *al-masājid* 52, *bāb faḍl al-julūs fī muṣallāhu baʿda al-ṣubḥ*, no 671.
65 Ibn Abī Shaybāh, *Muṣannaf* 7:269 *7:739*.
66 Aḥmad, *Zuhd*, 288 *351*; Fasawī, *Maʿrifah* 2:42.
67 Aḥmad, *Zuhd*, 365 *438* (< ʿAl.); Abū Nuʿaym, *Ḥilyah* 5:15.
68 Abū Nuʿaym, *Ḥilyah* 5:151.
69 Abū Nuʿaym, *Ḥilyah* 5:31; sim. said of al-Zuhrī, Abū Nuʿaym, *Ḥilyah* 3:371.
70 Abū Nuʿaym, *Ḥilyah* 2:385.
71 Abū Nuʿaym, *Ḥilyah* 10:156.

for him.[72] Bishr al-Ḥāfī (Baghdadi, d. 227/841) would also disapprove of trading in food.[73]

Some stories commend economic recklessness. For example, Zādhān Abū ʿUmar al-Kindī (Kufan Shīʿi, d. 83/702–3) would display the worse end of a garment he was selling.[74] Yūnus ibn ʿUbayd, a Basran cloth merchant (d. 139/756–7), bought a wrap (*izār*) for al-Ḥasan al-Baṣrī, giving a man eight after he had bargained him down to seven and a half because al-Ḥasan had forbidden taking *kisar* (fragments of dirhams, used to make small change).[75] Yūnus himself gave 125 dirhams for a silk dress when a slave girl offered it to him for 60 dirhams and a neighbour told him it was worth 120.[76] He would bargain upward and resist driving up prices in a distant place.[77] These are all examples of scrupulosity (*waraʿ*), but the fear is specifically to make an unfair profit. When the Kufan jurisprudent al-Aʿmash (d. 148/765–6?) said, 'We used to count the people of the market the worst of us, but today we count them the best of us',[78] he was probably lamenting the degeneration of renunciation rather than praising the life of trade.

Alms for renunciants

Living off alms from private persons was one way to avoid depending on rulers. It was certainly meritorious to give alms, as suggested above by stories of ʿUtbah al-Ghulām and Ibn al-Mubārak. Khaythamah ibn ʿAbd al-Raḥmān (Kufan, d. after 80/699) inherited 200,000 dirhams, which he gave to the *fuqarāʾ* and *fuqahāʾ* (poor persons and jurisprudents).[79] He prepared food and invited to eat the outstanding Kufan jurisprudent of his time Ibrāhīm al-Nakhaʿī and his associates.[80] Ibrāhīm al-Nakhaʿī himself is elsewhere reported to have said, on being seen in a white garment, 'Khaythamah clothed me.'[81] He paid 50 dirhams a month to the

72 Al-Khaṭīb al-Baghdādī, *Tārīkh* 2:9, 11–13 *2:327, 330–1.*
73 Al-Khaṭīb al-Baghdādī, *Tārīkh* 3:82 *4:140.*
74 Abū Nuʿaym, *Ḥilyah* 4:199 (< ʿAl., *Zuhd*).
75 Fasawī, *Maʿrifah* 2:50.
76 Ibn Ḥajar, *Tahdhīb* 11:444.
77 Abū Nuʿaym, *Ḥilyah* 3:15.
78 Abū Nuʿaym, *Ḥilyah* 5:50.
79 Abū Nuʿaym, *Ḥilyah* 4:113.
80 Abū Nuʿaym, *Ḥilyah* 4:113.
81 Abū Nuʿaym, *Ḥilyah* 4:113–14.

blind man al-Musayyab ibn Rāfiʿ (Kufan, d. 105/723–4) and bought him a servant.[82] Ḥabīb ibn Abī Thābit (Kufan, d. 119/737) spent 100,000 on *qurrāʾ* (Qur'an reciters).[83] ʿĀmir ibn ʿAbd Allāh (Medinese, d. 121/738–9) often gave away 10,000 dirhams in a day.[84] Muḥammad ibn al-Munkadir (Medinese, d. 130/747–8?) sent someone 40 dinars to support his worship, fed pilgrims, and had *qurrāʾ* gather around him.[85] Muslim ibn Yasār (Basran, active Mecca, d. 100/718–19?) told the story of a rich woman in Bahrein who bade him always stay with them, then lost her fortune, her sons, and her slave after the pattern of Job.[86] Al-Fuḍayl ibn ʿIyāḍ (d. 187/803) is said to have lived on a stipend from Ibn al-Mubārak and other pious persons.[87] Jarīr ibn ʿAbd al-Ḥamīd (Kufan, l. Ray, d. 188/804) said, 'In Kufa, I was offered 2,000 dirhams, which they would give me along with the *qurrāʾ*. I refused, but then I have come today seeking what they have.'[88]

On the other hand, Sunni hadith collections strongly discourage begging. For example, the Prophet is quoted as saying, 'One of you will keep begging until he meets God with not a bit of flesh on his face.'[89] Ibn ʿAbbās is quoted as saying, 'If the beggar knew what it involved, he would not beg.'[90] The Prophet, again, is widely reported to have said, 'That one of you should take a cord and gather a bundle of firewood and sell it so that God can save his face with it is better than that he should ask people, whether they give or refuse.'[91]

There are copious warnings against accepting alms from private persons as well. ʿĪsá told his disciples (*aṣḥāb*) on the night he was raised, 'Do not eat by the Book of God, for if you do not do that, God will seat you on stone mimbars, some

---

82 Abū Nuʿaym, *Ḥilyah* 4:114.
83 Abū Nuʿaym, *Ḥilyah* 5:61.
84 Abū Nuʿaym, *Ḥilyah* 3:166.
85 Abū Nuʿaym, *Ḥilyah* 3:149, also (pilgrims) ʿAbd al-Malik ibn Ḥabīb, *Tārīkh*, 161–2.
86 Aḥmad, *Zuhd*, 257 *314*; Abū Nuʿaym, *Ḥilyah* 2:295–6.
87 Dhahabī, *Siyar* 8:390.
88 Al-Khaṭīb al-Baghdādī, *Tārīkh* 7:258 *8:190*.
89 Muslim, *al-zakāh* 35, *bāb karāhat al-masʾalah lil-nās*, no 1040; Ibn Abī Shaybah, *Muṣannaf* 3:208 *4:338–9* (Basran/Medinese *isnād*).
90 Ibn Abī Shaybah, *Muṣannaf* 3:208 *4:339* (Kufan *isnād*); sim., Bukhārī, *al-zakāh* 52, *bāb man saʾala al-nās takāthuran*, no 1474 (Egyptian/Medinese *isnād*).
91 Bukhārī, *al-musāqāh* 13, *bāb bayʿ al-ḥaṭab wa-al-kalaʾ*, no 2373 (Basran/Meccan *isnād*); sim., Mālik, *Muwaṭṭaʾ*, rec. Yaḥyá, *al-jāmiʿ*, *bāb mā jāʾa fī al-taʿaffuf ʿan al-masʾalah*, no 285, rec. Abū Muṣʿab, *al-jāmiʿ* 77, *bāb al-taʿaffuf ʿan al-masʾalah*, no 2110; and Bukhārī, *al-zakāh* 50, *bāb al-istiʿfāf ʿan al-masʾalah*, no 1470 (Medinese *isnād*); Bukhārī, *al-buyūʿ* 15, *bāb kasb al-rajul*, no 2074, repeated *al-musāqāh* 13, *bāb bayʿ al-ḥaṭab wa-al-kalaʾ*, no 2374 (Egyptian/Medinese *isnād*); Bukhārī, *al-zakāh* 53, *bāb qawl Allāh lā yasʾalūna al-nās ilḥāfan*, no 1480 (Kufan *isnād*). G. H. A. Juynboll ascribes this report in its present form to Mālik: *Encyclopedia*, 369.

of which are better than the world and what is in it.' 'Abd al-Jabbār ibn 'Ubayd Allāh ibn Sulaymān, probably Abū 'Abd Rabbi, the Damascene renunciant, explained that this meant *maq'ad ṣidq* (Q. 54:55).[92] To 'eat by the Book of God' probably refers to reciting the Qur'an for alms. 'Abd Allāh ibn Muḥayrīz (Meccan, l. Jerusalem, d. 99/717–18?) refused a discount on account of who he was, saying, 'We came to buy with our dirhams, not our religion.'[93] Ṭalḥah ibn Muṣarrif (Kufan, d. 112/730–1?) said, 'If we eat by religion, we begin with vinegar, whereas if we do not eat by religion, we begin with the fat.'[94] Yūnus ibn 'Ubayd dismissed some youths who had come to hear Sufyān al-Thawrī on the ground that they had all sat with him in order to gain their living, probably in the form of presents for relating hadith.[95] 'Utbah al-Ghulām (Basran, *fl.* earlier 8th cent.) fainted, then on recovering prayed for mercy on one who lived by religion. He was found to have two *fals* on him.[96]

Sufyān al-Thawrī was against asking for so much as salt and water.[97] He reportedly refused to relate hadith at the time of his hiding in Basra, when a letter had reached him from his family, complaining of their distress (that is, wishing him to take money for relating hadith to pass on to them).[98] He rebuked a blind man from his circle for praying with people in Ramadan, so attracting clothes and money. Perhaps as an apology for appearing so harsh, he explained that he feared to be charged at the Resurrection with not having counselled someone who sat with him.[99] Ibn al-Mubārak said that the lowest are those who live by their religion.[100] Al-Fuḍayl ibn 'Iyāḍ said, ''*Ilm* (knowledge, particularly hadith) is the medicine of the faith, wealth is the plague of the faith, so if the one who has '*ilm* should draw the plague to himself, what will make others whole?'[101] Bishr al-Ḥāfī said, ''*Ilm* has now ended up with people who eat by it.'[102]

92 Ibn al-Mubārak, *Zuhd*, no 1447.
93 Aḥmad, *Zuhd*, 381 *456*; Ibn Abī Shaybah, *Muṣannaf* 13:577 *12: 415*.
94 Abū Nu'aym, *Ḥilyah* 5:20 (< Aḥ., *Zuhd*).
95 Abū Nu'aym, *Ḥilyah* 6:382.
96 Abū Nu'aym, *Ḥilyah* 6:234.
97 Abū Nu'aym, *Ḥilyah* 6:382.
98 Ibn Qutaybah, *'Uyūn* 2:368.
99 Abū Nu'aym, *Ḥilyah* 7:16.
100 Abū Nu'aym, *Ḥilyah* 8:167–8.
101 Abū Nu'aym, *Ḥilyah* 8:112.
102 Abū Nu'aym, *Ḥilyah* 8:341. For more on payment for hadith, see Melchert, 'The transmission of hadith', 235–9.

Another theme of hadith on almsgiving is to distinguish the deserving poor from the undeserving. One character of the deserving is precisely that they do not call attention to themselves.

> The Prophet once said, 'A pauper is not the man who wanders around begging from the people and getting one or two morsels, or one or two dates.' Those listening asked: 'But who then is a pauper, Messenger of God?' He answered: 'He who does not find anything to sustain him without the people realizing that so that he may receive charity, and who does not stand up to go begging.'[103]

In some versions, the Prophet goes on to quote Q. 2:273, 'that do not beg importunately from people'.[104] One might be encouraged by this to hang about in the mosque doing devotions in hopes of attracting alms without directly seeking them. Accepting anything offered is expressly encouraged.

> The Messenger of God sent a gift (*'aṭā'*) to 'Umar ibn al-Khaṭṭāb. 'Umar refused it. The Messenger of God asked him, 'Why did you refuse it?' He said, 'O Messenger of God, did you not tell us that it is better for one of us never to take anything from someone else?' The Messenger of God said, 'That has to do only with asking (*al-mas'alah*). As for what comes without asking, it is a provision that God provides you.' 'Umar ibn al-Khaṭṭāb said, 'Is it not then the case, by him in whose hand is my soul, that I will never ask anyone for anything while nothing will come to me without my asking but that I will accept it.'[105]

There is also some suggestion that the deserving poor were formerly easier to recognize. Ibrāhīm al-Nakhaʿī said, 'They did not use to beg except for one in need.'[106]

Positively, there is a heavy stress in hadith on independence. The Arabic word for 'poor' (*faqīr*, pl. *fuqarā'*) has the primary sense of 'needy'; the Arabic word for 'rich' (*ghanī*, pl. *aghniyā'*) means first of all 'self-sufficient'. The Qur'an preaches incessantly against feelings of self-sufficiency as opposed to dependence on God. 'Man is impious, Because he thinks that he is self-sufficient' (Q. 96:6–7). 'O men, you are the ones who are in need (*fuqarā'*) of God. God is the All-sufficient (*al-ghanī*) and the Laudable' (Q. 35:15). In hadith, by contrast, self-sufficiency is

103 Juynboll, *Encyclopedia*, 369, where this formulation is attributed to Mālik. Cf. Mālik, *Muwaṭṭa'*, rec. Yaḥyá, *al-jāmiʿ* 27, *mā jā'a fī al-masākīn*, no 2672; rec. Abū Muṣʿab, *al-jāmiʿ* 25, *bāb mā jā'a fī al-miskīn*, no 1932. See above, N. 5.

104 E.g., Bukhārī, *al-zakāh* 53, *bāb qawl Allāh wa-lā yas'alūna al-nās ilḥāfan*, no 1479; *al-tafsīr* 2, *ad* Q. 2:273, no 4539 (likewise with Medinese *isnāds*).

105 Mālik, *Muwaṭṭa'*, rec. Yaḥyá, *al-jāmiʿ* 85, *bāb mā jā'a fī al-taʿaffuf ʿan al-mas'alah*, no 2852 = rec. Abū Muṣʿab, *al-jāmiʿ* 77, *bāb mā jā'a fī al-taʿaffuf ʿan al-mas'alah*, no 2109.

106 ʿAbd al-Razzāq, *Muṣannaf* 4:109.

a laudable condition, stress having shifted to having no need of other people. A hadith report recommending gathering firewood to sell over begging has been mentioned already. One variant expressly recommends it as a means to self-sufficiency: 'That one of you should go and collect firewood on his back, to give alms with it and to become thereby independent of people (*wa-yastaghniya bihi min al-nās*), is better for him than that he should beg from a man, whether he gives him that or not.'[107] Other hadith reports strongly recommend self-sufficiency. For example, the Prophet is said to have explained to a group that their pledge of allegiance to him committed them to worshipping God alone, performing the five daily prayers, and obeying him. 'He said in a low voice, "Do not ask people for anything."' The Companion who reports this adds, 'I saw that a whip might fall from some of that group but not a one of them would ask anyone to hand it to him.'[108] In another story, the Prophet himself names the whip as an example of something not to ask for.[109] Ayyūb al-Sakhtiyānī (Basran, d. 131/749?) is quoted as saying it was better to stick to the market so as not to depend on people.[110] Stress on self-sufficiency justifies the break with dependence on stipends and even more the old system of *zakāh* and *jihād*. But whether it could practically sustain the old ideal of all-night devotional murmuring seems unlikely.

Repudiation of gain

The *Kasb* of al-Shaybānī or al-Sarakhsī also includes a passage directed against certain idiotic Sufis (*ḥamqá ahl al-taṣawwuf*) who say that gain is prohibited (*ḥarām*) except in case of necessity, like eating carrion. These Sufis offer two arguments. First, they cite a hadith report in favour of *tawakkul*, a qur'anic term for committing oneself to God: by an Egyptian *isnād*, the Prophet is quoted as saying, 'If you relied properly on God (*law annakum tatawakkalūna ʿalá Allāh ḥaqq tawakkulih*), he would provide for you as he provides for the birds. They go out with empty stomachs and return with full.'[111] It looks like a version of Matthew 6:26, 'Behold the fowls of the air: for they sow not, neither do they reap, nor gather into barns; yet your heavenly Father feedeth them.' Secondly, they assert that the

107 Muslim, *al-zakāh* 35, *bāb karāhat al-masʾalah lil-nās*, no 1042 (Kufan *isnād*).
108 Muslim, *al-zakāh* 35, *bāb karāhat al-masʾalah lil-nās*, no 1042 (Kufan *isnād*).
109 Aḥmad, *Musnad* 5:172 *35:401* (Syrian *isnād*).
110 Abū Nuʿaym, *Ḥilyah* 3:11.
111 Ibn al-Mubārak, *Zuhd*, no 559; Tirmidhī, *al-zuhd* 33, *bāb fī al-tawakkul ʿalá Allāh*, no 2344; Ibn Mājah, *al-zuhd* 14, *bāb al-tawakkul wa-al-yaqīn*, no 4164; Aḥmad, *Musnad* 1:30, 51 (twice) *1:332–3, 438, 439*.

Companions were praised for sitting in the mosque rather than being active elsewhere, as in seeking worldly gain.[112]

The Baghdadi renunciant writer al-Muḥāsibī (d. 243/857–8) names two Sufis who repudiated buying and selling, ʿAbd Allāh ibn Yazīd and ʿAbdak, perhaps in particular at the time of the Fourth Civil War (Amīn *vs* Maʾmūn, 195–98/810–13, much longer in Syria).[113] Certain Muʿtazilah are likewise identified with the repudiation of normal gain; among others, Abū ʿImrān al-Raqāshī (*fl.* early 9th cent.), Ibn al-Rāwandī (d. 298/910–11?), and al-Rummānī (d. 384/994).[114] And in the ninth century, the repudiation of normal gain became a distinctive doctrine of the Karāmīyah, who tended to absorb the Muʿtazilī renunciant tradition.[115] Al-Muḥāsibī attributes the repudiation of gain above all to Shaqīq ibn Ibrāhīm al-Balkhī (d. Kūlān, Transoxania, 194/809–10): 'According to what is related of him, Shaqīq asserted that effort (*ḥarakah*) in pursuit of gain is a sin.'[116] Ibrāhīm ibn Adham is quoted as remonstrating with Shaqīq against his repudiation of gain.[117] Baghdadi Sufis who reject gain are mentioned also by the Ḥanbali Abū Bakr al-Khallāl (d. 311/923).[118] A century later, the Nishapuran Sufi writer al-Khargūshī distinguishes the Nishapuran Malāmatīyah by their upholding lawful gain, by contrast with the Sufis of Iraq who reject it.[119] Rejection of gain is hard to find in works coming out of and documenting the classical Sufism of al-Junayd (d. 298/911?) and his circle. Al-Kalābādhī (d. 380/990–1?) asserts that the Sufis unanimously accept that pursuit of gain is licit, then offers an apparent qualification

112 Sarakhsī, *Mabsūṭ* 30:247; Shaybānī, *Kasb*, 81–2.

113 Muḥāsibī, *Makāsib*, 212 *64*.

114 See Ibn al-Murtaḍá, *Klassen*, 77 (Abū ʿImrān), Ibn al-Nadīm, *Fihrist* 1:603 (Ibn al-Rāwandī), and Sezgin, *GAS* 8:114 (Rummānī, *Taḥrīm al-makāsib*). For references to *ṣūfiyat al-muʿtazilah*, see Josef van Ess, *Th.u.G.* 3:130–45, 4:88–94, 5:328–30 *3:141–57*, *4:101–8*. Another study of this group is Yücesoy, 'Political anarchism'. Yücesoy supposes without argument that the Sufi Muʿtazilah rejected gain on political grounds, namely that the House of Unbelief (*dār al-kufr*) now comprised the whole world (70). There may be evidence for this in the title of the book just cited, *Fasād al-dār wa-taḥrīm al-makāsib* ('the decadence of the House and the prohibition of gain'), attributed to Ibn al-Rāwandī. Whatever the Sufi Muʿtazili reasoning, however, it does not fit the Sufis in this passage from Shaybānī (or Sarakhsī). See also Aydinli, 'Ascetic and devotional elements', and Sviri, *Perspectives*, 26–8.

115 See esp. van Ess, 'Lecture', 190, 192; *idem*, *Ungenützte Texte*, 30–2; Massignon, *Passion* 3:227. 'Karrāmīyah' has become the usual form, but some early poetry in praise of the movement's eponym requires 'Karām' or 'Kirām' to scan properly. See Ibn Ḥajar, *Tabṣīr al-mushtabih* 3:1191.

116 Muḥāsibī, *Makāsib*, 194 *61*; followed by Massignon, *Essay*, 173.

117 Abū Nuʿaym, *Ḥilyah* 8:37.

118 Khallāl, *Ḥathth*, 143–5.

119 Kharkūshī, *Tahdhīb al-asrār*, 40, 298–300 *25, 270–2*.

from Sahl al-Tustarī (d. 283/896?), who stood to the side of al-Junayd and his circle.[120] Therefore, the rejection of gain must be identified with a strand of the renunciant movement in the ninth century rejected by the contemporary hadith party and to which (in part) al-Junayd's Sufism was a reaction.

Charitable foundations

I have continually contended that the devotional life advocated by the early renunciant tradition, of spending nights in supererogatory ritual prayer and reciting the Qur'an, was an attempt to preserve the ethos of the conquest period. It presumed that Muslims belonged to a thin stratum at the top of society supported by tribute from below. It became impossible to maintain as the Muslims became a majority and most of them necessarily had to work for a living. To some extent, almsgiving could take the place of tribute if those with money to spare supported those who wished to spend their lives in devotions (or study). Abū Ḥafṣ al-Naysābūrī (d. 265/878?), founding leader of the Malāmati school, came to Baghdad in the company of a patron who had spent 100,000 dirhams on him, then added another 100,000 he had borrowed.[121] ʿAbd Allāh ibn Muḥammad al-Ḍabbī (d. 339/950–1) spent over 100,000 on the ulema and renunciants.[122] Ibn Nujayd (d. 365/975?), chief of the Malāmatīyah, spent his inherited wealth on the ulema and leading renunciants.[123]

Living off alms had to become easier with the development of formal institutions for it. The foundation (*waqf*; usually in earlier usage *ḥubs*, sometimes in later) is the principal form of charitable giving by Muslims apart from occasional almsgiving and the required alms tax (in time distinguished as respectively *ṣadaqah* and *zakāh* but continually used interchangeably in the early literature).[124] For example, someone may declare that a given building is now a *waqf*, its rent to pay first for an administrator and necessary repairs, then to be divided amongst his heirs and their heirs in perpetuity, unless they should die out, in which case it is to be rendered generally to the poor. This avoids the awkwardness of dividing up the building into shares on his death. (Historically, most *waqf* foundations seem to have been established for the benefit of close relations and descendants, which seems to qualify its charitable character; but we should remember the strong

120 Kalābādhī, *Taʿarruf*, 56–7 (Ar.), 80–1 (Engl.).
121 Sarrāj, *Lumaʿ*, 177.
122 Dhahabī, *Tārīkh* 25 (331–350 H.): 476, quoting al-Ḥākim al-Naysābūrī, *Tārīkh Naysābūr*.
123 Dhahabī, *Tārīkh* 26 (351–380 H.): 336, likewise quoting al-Ḥākim al-Naysābūrī.
124 See *EI*², s.vv. 'ṣadaḳa', by Weir and Zysow, and 'waḳf', § I, by Peters.

principle that charity begins at home. Early opposition to the institution seems to have come most commonly from unease at its potential to circumvent the normal inheritance rules.) The tradition unsurprisingly traces the institution back to the time of the Prophet; for example, eight properties in Medina are enumerated as having been dedicated by him as *ḥubs*.[125] But records of the earliest debates suggest that the classical form came about by fusion of several earlier ones, notably the *ḥubs fī sabīl Allāh*, a donation in favour of equipping fighters in the holy war.[126] The *Aṣl* of al-Shaybānī treats *waqf* by laying out hypothetical endowment deeds. The first half dozen are all for the benefit of someone's descendants; only then does al-Shaybānī treat a *waqf* directly for the poor and destitute. Other objects mentioned include pilgrims, warriors on the frontier, fountains, and cemeteries.[127]

Shaybānī does not mention a *waqf* for the benefit of religious scholars or worshippers, but I have remarked such a foundation in a report from Isfahan. In 281/894–5, some *murābiṭūn*, literally men living in a frontier outpost (*ribāṭ*), complained to a prominent scholar of delayed expenditures in their favour. This scholar complained of the qadi to the point of insult and got himself imprisoned for a time.[128] The term for a frontier outpost was eventually appropriated almost entirely for a Sufi lodge, synonymous with *khānaqāh* and other terms. From lack of continuous evidence, the chronology of this appropriation is unclear.[129] But it seems likely at this point that the *murābiṭūn* are mainly occupied by devotions rather than keeping ready with horses and weapons for frontier warfare. Their discontent would focus on the qadi because he was in charge of supervising *waqf* properties, although this particular qadi, Abū Bakr ibn Abī ʿĀṣim (d. 287/900?), had been associated with 'the Sufis of the mosque' back in Basra before his appointment.[130] The historical significance of this report is that it documents the emergence of a regular mechanism for supporting pious specialists at just the time when classical Sufism emerges. The law of pious foundations was likely one of the preconditions.

---

125 Khaṣṣāf, *Aḥkām al-awqāf*, 2.

126 My understanding of the historical development of the law of *waqf* comes especially from Schacht, 'Early doctrines on *waqf*', Hennigan, *Birth of a legal institution*, and Oberauer, 'Early doctrines on *waqf*'.

127 Shaybānī, *Aṣl* 12:66–102.

128 Abū al-Shaykh, *Ṭabaqāt* 3:380–1.

129 See *EI*[2], s.v. 'ribāṭ', by Chabbi, and *EI*[3], s.v. 'k̲ānaqāh', by Böwering and Melvin-Koushki.

130 On Abū Bakr ibn Abī ʿĀṣim, his Sufism and his juridical and theological positions, see further Melchert, 'Baṣran origins', 236–8.

Chapter 9: Opposition to renunciation

The language of the early renunciants tends to suggest that all the Muslims should live as they do. For example, Khulayd al-ʿAṣarī (Basran, *fl.* early 8th cent.) said, 'The believer should not be met with save in three: a mosque he enlivens, a house that screens him, or a worldly need that has no harm in it.'[1] Al-Ḥasan al-Baṣrī (d. 110/728) and others have already been quoted about how believers will be always sad. This was likely to grate when Muslims had become the majority, as articulated in a saying attributed to an obscure Companion, al-Ḥārith ibn Jarīr: 'Among the *qurrāʾ* (Qur'an reciters), the ones I like are those who smile and laugh much. As for the one who meets your cheer with a scowl and makes you feel inferior by his works, may God not multiply his like among the Muslims.'[2] Many later sayings suggest at least that the whole religious élite should set an example of austere living. We hear from Bishr al-Ḥāfī (Baghdadi, d. 227/841), 'I went in to Ḥammād ibn Zayd [Basran traditionist, d. 179/795] and saw in his house a carpet that displeased me. This is not how the ulema are.'[3] And there are many warnings that the learnèd élite must practise what they preach; for example, the quotation by which Abū al-Dardāʾ (d. Damascus, early 30s/650s?) said, 'One is not learnèd (*ʿālim*) until he has learnt, nor is one learnèd until he is working (*ʿāmil*) in accordance with his knowledge.'[4] These are opposed by reports extolling knowledge over worship. For example, Abū al-Dardāʾ is quoted as relating from the Prophet, 'The superiority of the scholar to the worshipper is like that of the moon over the rest of the stars. The ulema are the heirs of the prophets.'[5] Muṭarrif ibn al-Shikhkhīr (Basran, d. 95/713–14) allegedly told his son, 'Knowledge is better than works (*al-ʿilm khayr min al-ʿamal*).'[6] These represent the counterattack of an increasingly distinct scholarly class against an increasingly distinct renunciant class.

---

1 Aḥmad, *Zuhd*, 237 *290* (< ʿAl.).

2 Muḥāsibī, *Riʿāyah*, 243 *389*.

3 Al-Khaṭīb al-Baghdādī, *Tārīkh* 7:69 *7:547*.

4 Ibn Saʿd, *Ṭabaqāt* 2/2:114 *2:357*.

5 Aḥmad, *Musnad* 5:196 36:45–9; Dārimī, *Musnad*, 165; Abū Dāwūd, *al-ʿilm* 1, *bāb alḥathth ʿalá ṭalab al-ʿilm*, no 3641; Tirmidhī, *al-ʿilm* 19, *mā jāʾa fī faḍl al-fiqh ʿalá al-ʿibādah*, no 2682; Ibn Mājah, *al-sunnah* 17, *bāb faḍl al-ʿulamāʾ*, no 223.

6 Dārimī, *Musnad*, 166; *al-ʿilm* 17, *bāb fī faḍl al-ʿilm wa-al-ʿālim*.

https://doi.org/10.1515/9783110617962-010

The importance of inward and outward dispositions

The Islamic tradition is of two minds about inward dispositions, or rather about the value of outward appearances that do not match inward dispositions. The Qur'an barely recognizes ambiguity: one is either faithful or faithless.[7] The tradition sometimes indicates that only inward attitude determines the value of any action. The very first report in al-Bukhārī's *Ṣaḥīḥ* is famously *innamā al-aʿmāl bi-al-nīyāt*, 'Actions are only by intentions. Every man has just what he intends. Whosever emigration is to a worldly good for him to get, or a woman for him to marry, his emigration is to what he has emigrated to.'[8] There is no otherworldly reward, here, for an outward action not matched by the proper inward disposition.

Some reports indicate that inward disposition will be rewarded by itself, regardless of outward action. Alternatively, a bad inward disposition will be overlooked so long as it does not issue in a bad outward action. One famous report runs so:

> God has recorded the good and bad deeds, then clarified that. Whoever thinks of a good deed but does not do it, God records it as a complete good deed. If he thinks of it, then does it, God records it as ten good deeds to 700 or more. If he thinks of a bad deed but does not do it, God records it as a complete good deed. If he thinks of it, then does it, God records it as a single bad deed.[9]

Previously noted has been the Prophet's directive to those who hear the Qur'an being recited: 'Weep; and if you do not weep, pretend to weep.'[10]

---

7 As observed by Donner, *Narratives*, 75–6. His whole section on qur'anic piety (64–85) is highly recommended.

8 Bukhārī, *bad' al-waḥy* 1, *kayfa kāna bad' al-waḥy*, no 1; repeated with variations at *al-ʿitq* 6, *bāb al-khaṭa' wa-al-nisyān*, no 2529, *manāqib al-anṣār* 45, *bāb hijrat al-nabī*, no 3898, *al-nikāḥ* 5, *bāb man hājara aw ʿamila khayran li-tazwīj imra'ah*, no 5070, *al-aymān wa-al-nudhūr* 23, *bāb al-nīyah fī al-aymān*, no 6689, *al-ḥiyal 1*, *bāb fī tark al-ḥiyal*, no 6953. In the quoted example, 'for him to marry', *yankiḥuhā*, might equally mean 'for him to enjoy coitus with'; however, other versions have *yatazawwajuhā*, which must refer to marriage. Cf. Muslim, *al-imārah* 45, *bāb qawluhu ... innamā al-aʿmāl bi-al-nīyah*, no 1907.

9 Translation after the 37th of Nawawī's *Forty hadith*, for which see Pouzet, *Herméneutique*, 56. For variants, see for example Muslim, *al-īmān* 59, *bāb idhā hamma al-ʿabd bi-ḥasanah kutibat*, no 128, in which God says this is what he will do, no 129, in which these are God's instructions to his angels, and no 131, in which these are the words of the Prophet himself. Attributed to Sufyān ibn ʿUyaynah by Juynboll, *Encyclopedia*, 611.

10 Among other places, Hannād, *Zuhd* 1:270, *Aḥmad*, *Zuhd*, 27 36.

The tradition highly values outward appearance and communal solidarity. I have often mentioned al-Ghazālī's discussion of permissible lying. If someone asks, 'Are you an adulterer?' it is the Muslim's duty, he says, to answer 'No.' Adultery is one of the cardinal sins and very much better to avoid, of course; but if one commits adultery regardless, it constitutes a second offence to encourage another Muslim to follow one's bad example.[11] Al-Bukhārī quotes the Prophet thus:

> All my nation will be forgiven except for those who act openly (*al-mujāhirīn*). Acting openly is that a man does a work by night, then in the morning, God having screened him, says, 'O so-and-so, last night I did such-and-such.' All night his Lord screened him, then in the morning he pulls away God's screen from himself.[12]

What they don't know will not hurt you.

There is certainly no tradition of belittling right inward dispositions. At most, outward actions are sufficient to indicate acceptable or unacceptable inward dispositions. For example, Ibn Masʿūd (d. 32/652–3?) thought it the chief of humility to sit at the meanest part of a session and salute first whomever one meets.[13] ʿAlī (d. 40/661) commented on Q. 23:2, '(those) who are humble (*khāshiʿūn*) in their prayers', that humility is indicated by not turning to the side in the ritual prayer (i.e., facing forward throughout).[14] Qatādah (Basran, d. 117/735–6?) said, 'Hypocrites seldom stay up nights.'[15]

To the contrary, we also have warnings that inward dispositions are not reliable indicators of one's status; for example, Bukhārī relates in four different contexts that the Prophet said, 'A man may do the work of one of the people of Paradise, as it appears to people, when he is among the people of the Fire; and a man may do the work of the people of the Fire, as it appears to people, when he is among the people of Paradise.'[16] Ibn Baṭṭāl (Cordovan, d. 449/1057) comments,

> There is a subtle and far-reaching wisdom in God's concealing their ends from his servants. If one knew the end of his work, he would become pleased and lazy who knew he would end up with faith, while whoever knew he would end up with unbelief would go even further in straying, oppression, and unbelief. God provokes with that knowledge in order that

---

11 Ghazālī, *Iḥyāʾ ʿulūm al-dīn* 24, k. *āfāt al-lisān, bayān mā rukhkhiṣa fīhi min al-kadhib.*

12 Bukhārī, *al-adab* 60, *bāb satr al-muslim ʿalá nafsih*, no 6069; sim., Muslim, *al-zuhd* 8, *bāb al-nahy ʿan hatk al-insān satr nafsih*, no 2990 (both with Medinese *isnād*s).

13 Aḥmad, *Zuhd*, 210 *259* (< ʿAl.).

14 Ibn al-Mubārak, *Zuhd*, no 1148.

15 Ibn al-Mubārak, *Zuhd*, no 93; Abū Nuʿaym, *Ḥilyah* 2:338 (< Aḥ., *Zuhd*).

16 Bukhārī, *al-jihād* 77, *bāb lā yaqūlu fulān shahīd*, no 2989; *al-maghāzī* 39, *bāb ghazwat Khaybar*, nos 4202, 4207; *al-riqāq* 33, *bāb al-aʿmāl bi-al-khawātīm*, no 6493; *al-qadar* 5, *bāb al-ʿamal bi-al-khawātīm*, no 6607.

> his servants be between fear and hope. The one who obeys God is not pleased by his work, nor does the sinner despair of his mercy.[17]

This is why traditionalists insisted into the ninth century that one answer the question 'Are you a believer?' by saying 'Yes, God willing': not to connote positive doubt in one's salvation but rather lack of complacency as to one's standing with God. Abū al-Dardā' said, 'A man does not become secure in his faith save that he is bereaved of it.'[18] Abū Idrīs al-Khawlānī (Syrian, d. 82/701–2) said, 'There is no man on the face of it who does not fear that his faith should go away but that it has already gone.'[19]

Fear that outward signs of renunciation are for show, masking inward indifference to the Afterworld, presumably goes back almost as far as renunciation itself. Consider, for example, the prophecy of Zechariah: 'And it shall come to pass in that day, that the prophets shall be ashamed every one of his vision, when he hath prophesied; neither shall they wear a rough garment to deceive' (Zech. 13:4, KJV). Therefore, there is nothing necessarily anachronistic or otherwise surprising about the reproach quoted of Abū al-'Āliyah (Basran, d. 90/709) toward someone wearing wool in public, 'this being the garb of the monks: when Muslims visit one another, they put on comely clothes.'[20] Sometimes the same figure is quoted both for and against outward austerities. For example, al-Ḥasan al-Baṣrī, on seeing Farqad al-Sabakhī (d. 131/748–9?) in a woollen cloak, told him, 'Farqad, piety is not in these clothes. Piety is only what lodges in the heart, verified by doing and acting.'[21] He also reportedly said that Mūsá wore wool and that the Prophet Muḥammad (as examples of humility) rode an ass, wore wool, licked his fingers, and ate on the floor.[22] Shaqīq al-Balkhī (d. 194/809–10) said he wore wool for twenty years on repenting, although not understanding that clarity actually came of moral transformation till it was explained by 'Abd al-'Azīz ibn Abī Rawwād (Meccan, d. 159/775–6).[23] Ibn Abī Rawwād was accused of being a Murji' and Shaqīq was close to the nascent Ḥanafi school in Iraq. The relation between inward dispositions and outward actions was discussed in theological

17 Ibn Baṭṭāl, *Sharḥ* 10:203–4, *ad* no 6493.

18 Ibn al-Mubārak, *Zuhd*, no 1547.

19 Ibn al-Mubārak *Zuhd*, no 1548.

20 Ibn Sa'd, *Ṭabaqāt* 7/1:83 *7:115*; Abū Nu'aym, *Ḥilyah* 2:217.

21 Aḥmad, *Zuhd*, 267 *327*; Jāḥiẓ, *Bayān* 3:153; Ibn Qutaybah, *'Uyūn* 2:372.

22 Abū Nu'aym, *Ḥilyah* 2:137; Ibn al-Mubārak, *Zuhd*, no 995 (< Ḥu.). Abū al-'Āliyah is also quoted on both sides, relating that a woollen garment was among just three possessions 'Īsá left on being raised: Abū Nu'aym, *Ḥilyah* 2:221.

23 Abū Nu'aym, *Ḥilyah* 8:59.

as well as pious contexts. Where Sunni traditionalists insisted that faith comprised both profession and outward actions, particularly performance of the ritual prayer, the Murji'ah proposed that outward actions are not faith itself, which lodges in the heart, but confirm it.

Against outward austerity

Hadith literature includes many warnings against collecting knowledge for the wrong reasons but not disdain for knowledge itself.[24] Disdain for outward austerity itself, not just its combination with inward avarice, seems to have appeared in about the last quarter of the eighth century. The habit of projecting back all wisdom to the earliest authorities of course interferes with our dating any such development. For example, the early qur'anic commentator al-Ḍaḥḥāk ibn Muzāḥim (d. 106/724–5?) reportedly disliked musk. He was told that Muḥammad's Companions had perfumed themselves but said, 'We know more than they did.'[25] Does this reveal the arrogance of the Followers, presuming themselves better than the Companions? Or does it document just the hostility of the tenth-century Muʿtazili, Abū al-Qāsim al-Balkhī (d. 319/931?), from whom it is known to us as part of a polemic against the probity of eighth-century traditionists? Of course, it may go back to any time between al-Ḍaḥḥāk and Abū al-Qāsim, too.

Similarly, Farqad al-Sabakhī was reported to Ibrāhīm al-Nakhaʿī (Kufan, d. 96/714) as not eating meat or such-and-such. Ibrāhīm protested, 'The Companions of Muḥammad were better than he. They ate meat, clarified butter (*samn*), and such-and-such and such-and-such.'[26] Farqad is more often opposed to al-Ḥasan al-Baṣrī. One example has been cited already, about clothing. Al-Ḥasan once asked Farqad, 'Do you like *khabīṣ* (a sweet)?' He said, 'No, by God: I like neither it nor anyone else who likes it.' Al-Ḥasan said, 'Is he mad? Is he mad?'[27] The effect is to make Farqad a representative of excessive outward austerity—obviously excessive for going beyond what the Companions had practised.

Some discomfort with the renunciation of an earlier generation is indicated by a report that ʿAwn ibn ʿAbd Allāh (Kufan, d. bef. 120/737–8) quoted the Companion ʿAbd Allāh ibn Masʿūd as saying, 'The servant does not achieve true faith till he reaches his summit (or maturity; *dhirwah*). He has not reached his summit

---

24 E.g., Dārimī, *Musnad*, 169–74, *al-ʿilm* 19, *bāb al-tawbīkh li-man yaṭlubu al-ʿilm li-ghayr Allāh*.
25 Abū al-Qāsim al-Balkhī, *Qabūl*, 262.
26 Ibn Abī Shaybah, *Muṣannaf* 14:39 *12:446–7*.
27 Aḥmad, *Zuhd*, 327–8 *395*. Longer version in ʿUqaylī, *Ḍuʿafāʾ* 3:459.

until he prefers poverty to riches, prefers humility to prominence, and considers alike the one praising him and the one blaming him.' Then he commented, "Abd Allāh's companions interpreted this as, "until he prefers poverty with lawfulness to riches with illicitness, prefers humility in obedience to God to prominence in disobedience to God, and considers alike the one truthfully praising him and the one truthfully blaming him."'[28] Somebody thought that Ibn Masʿūd's definitions went too far. The attribution to Ibn Masʿūd is questionable, partly because similar statements are attributed to the Companion Muʿādh ibn Jabal (d. 18/639–40),[29] more because such considerations seem unlikely so early in the conquest period. The comment should then be from one of the transmitters between ʿAwn and Aḥmad ibn Ḥanbal, namely al-Masʿūdī (ʿAbd al-Raḥmān ibn ʿAbd Allāh, d. 160/776–7?) or Yazīd (ibn Hārūn, d. 206/821–2). At any rate, the interpretation clearly betrays uneasiness with the apparent disparagement of riches in themselves and indignation at being slandered.

Sufyān al-Thawrī (Kufan, d. 161/777?) is often quoted in favour of inner-worldly renunciation; that is, renunciation as an inward attitude of detachment not needing to be matched by outward austerity. 'Renunciation of the world is shortness of hope, not eating what is rough or wearing a hood (*ʿabāyah*).'[30] Asked, 'Can a man be a renunciant if he has wealth?' he said 'Yes, if, when he is tried, he is patient and, when he is given, he is thankful.'[31] A similar authority is Sufyān ibn ʿUyaynah (d. Mecca, 198/814), who said, for example, 'Renunciation concerns what God has forbidden. As for what God has allowed, he has made it indifferent to you. The prophets married, rode, and ate, but when God forbade them something, they refrained from it and so were renunciant concerning it.'[32] He told Aḥmad ibn Abī al-Ḥawārī (Syrian, d. 246/860?) that the renunciant of the world was 'He who, when he is blessed, is thankful, and when he is tried is patient.'[33] He related through the Basran Ayyūb al-Sakhtiyānī (d. 131/749?) that the

---

28 Aḥmad, *Zuhd*, 158 *197*.

29 Ibn al-Mubārak, nos 188–9 < Nuʿaym.

30 Wakīʿ, *Zuhd* 1:222; Ibn Abī al-Dunyā, *Qiṣar al-amal*, 42; Abū Nuʿaym, *Ḥilyah* 6:386; Ibn Qutaybah, *ʿUyūn* 3:356; sim. Ibn Abī Shaybah ('wearing wool'), *Muṣannaf* 14:6 *12:456*. Cited by Kinberg, 'What is meant by *zuhd*', 34.

31 Abū Nuʿaym, *Ḥilyah* 6:387–8. Sim., asked, 'What is thanksgiving?' Sufyān said, 'That you avoid what God has forbidden': Ibn al-Aʿrābī, *K. fīhi maʿná al-zuhd*, 58, through Ibn Abī al-Ḥawārī.

32 Abū Nuʿaym, *Ḥilyah* 7:297.

33 Ibn Abī al-Dunyā, *Dhamm al-dunyā*, 46, no 116; Abū Nuʿaym, *Ḥilyah* 7:273; Bayhaqī, *Zuhd*, 77, no 65. Quoted by Kinberg, 'What is meant by *zuhd*', 38. Sim. attributed to Sufyān al-Thawrī by Abū Nuʿaym, *Ḥilyah* 6:387–8.

Prophet was told by some travelling companions that one of their number performed the ritual prayer whenever they were stopped, recited the Qur'an whenever they were riding, and fasted continuously. The Prophet told them that they who did only the required devotions were better than he.[34] Sufyān had a significant reputation for austere living, too; for example, he is said to have fed on barley bread for sixty years (or forty, by another account).[35] Presumably, such austerity was part of his authority to downplay it.

To be sure, many figures of the eighth century are quoted in favour of inward renunciation, particularly equanimity before good or bad fortune. Al-Ḥasan al-Baṣrī himself said, 'Islam? What is Islam? that you surrender your heart to God (be he exalted) and that every Muslim and *dhū ʿahd* (non-Muslim subject) be safe from you.'[36] Al-Zuhrī (Medinese, d. 124/742?) said, 'The *nāsik* is nothing but whosever patience overcomes the forbidden, whose thanks overwhelm the licit.'[37] Abū Ḥāzim (Medinese cl., *qāṣṣ*; d. *ca* 142/760) said, 'Whoever knows the world will not be joyful at anything in it of ease nor saddened by tribulation.'[38] According to a Shiʿi source, Mūsá al-Kāẓim (d. 183/799) wrote to a Sikkīn al-Nakhaʿī, 'As for what you have said about his leaving women, you know what the Messenger of God had by way of women. As for what you have said about good food, the Messenger of God would eat meat and honey. As for your saying that fear entered into him such that he could not raise his head to heaven, let him recite often these verses, "The patient, the truthful,, the obedient, those who spend and those who seek pardon in the mornings (Q. 3:17)."'[39] Al-Fuḍayl ibn ʿIyāḍ (d. Mecca, 187/803), on being asked to define *zuhd*, said, 'Contentment is *zuhd* and self-sufficiency (*ghiná*).'[40] Yūsuf ibn Asbāṭ (l. Antioch, d. 195/810–11), on being asked what was the extreme of *zuhd*, said, 'Do not be joyful over what comes nor saddened over what has turned away.'[41] To be sure, he is also quoted very much in favour of traditional outward renunciation: on being asked 'What is *zuhd*?' he said 'That

34 Ibn al-Mubārak, *Jihād*, no 214.
35 Abū Nuʿaym, *Ḥilyah* 7:272–3.
36 Ibn al-Mubārak, *Zuhd*, no 658; longer variant in Abū Nuʿaym, *Ḥilyah* 2:152.
37 Jāḥiẓ, untitled epistle, 297.
38 Abū Nuʿaym, *Ḥilyah* 3:238.
39 Kashshī, *Rijāl*, 316–17; al-Ṭūsī Shaykh al-Ṭāʾifah, *Ikhtiyār*, 370–1.
40 Ibn Abī al-Dunyā, *Zuhd*, 136.
41 Abū Nuʿaym, *Ḥilyah* 8:238. Muḥammad ibn Ṣubayḥ ibn al-Sammāk, a Kufan preacher (d. 183/799–800), is quoted similarly: 'The *zāhid* is the one who is not made joyful by what he is given of it (the world) nor saddened by what misses him of it': *Ḥilyah* 8:204.

you should be renunciant with regard to what God has allowed. As for what God has forbidden, if you do it, God will punish you.'[42]

Qur'an recitation was such a common occupation of renunciants that *qārī'*, 'reciter', became a synonym for *zāhid*, 'renunciant', or *'ābid*, 'worshipper'. When al-Jāḥiẓ relates that Abū 'Amr ibn al-'Alā' (Basran, d. Kufa, 154/770–1?), one of the famous seven readers of the Qur'an, burnt his books when he devoted himself entirely to worship, he uses the word *yataqarra'u*, meaning literally to take up recitation.[43] The Andalusian Māliki jurisprudent al-Bājī (d. 474/1081) explains that when 'Umar said, 'I like to look on a *qārī'* with white clothing', *qārī'* may be interpreted to mean *'ābid*, as in their saying, "Whoever is not good at attaining certainty will not be good at renunciation (*man lam yuḥsin yutqinu lam yuḥsin yaqra'*)", meaning that he has not worshipped.'[44]

However, *qārī'* is a word that worsened over time, for it came to designate bad renunciants as opposed to good ones. Most often, perhaps, there are said to be good ones and bad; for example, when Mālik ibn Dīnār (Basran cl., d. *ca* 130/747–8) says,

> Among the *qurrā'* are some with two faces: when they meet kings, they enter with them into whatever they are up to, whereas when they meet the people of the hereafter, they enter with them into whatever they are up to. Therefore, you should be among the *qurrā'* of the Most Merciful.[45]

But the bad ones apparently predominate in, for example, the Prophet's denunciation, 'Most of the hypocrites of this community are its *qurrā'*.'[46] Sufyān al-Thawrī said, 'The *qurrā'* of this time of ours have its evil but no piety.'[47] The transformation became complete in the Sufi period, as when Bundār ibn al-Ḥusayn (Persian, d. 353/964–5) distinguished between the *mutaṣawwif* as the one

---

42 Abū Nu'aym, *Ḥilyah* 8:237.

43 Jāḥiẓ, *Bayān* 1:321. This interpretation is confirmed by the version of Ibn al-Jazarī, using the word *tanassaka*: *Ghāyah* 1:290.

44 Bājī, *Muntaqá* 7:220. For the hadith report in question, see Mālik, *Muwaṭṭa'*, rec. Yaḥyá, *al-jāmi'* 15, *mā jā'a fī lubs al-thiyāb lil-jamāl bihā*, no 2645; rec. Abū Muṣ'ab, *al-jāmi'* 15, *bāb mā jā'a fī lubs al-thiyāb al-muṣabbaghah wa-al-dhahab*, no 1905.

45 Abū Nu'aym, *Ḥilyah* 2:345.

46 Aḥmad, *Musnad* 2:175, 4:151, 155 *11:209–13, 28:268–9 597*; Ibn al-Mubārak, *Zuhd*, no 451; Ibn Abī Shaybah, *Muṣannaf* 13:228 *12:161*. Also attributed to 'Uqbah ibn 'Āmir al-Juhanī (d. *ca* 60/679–80): Ibn al-Mubārak, *Zuhd*, no 64 < Nu'aym.

47 Abū Nu'aym, *Ḥilyah* 7:21; another version at 7:68.

who has chosen God and been forgiven by contrast with the *mutaqarri'* 'who has burdened himself, showing off his renunciation while hiding his desire.'[48]

Mālik and al-Shaybānī against excessive renunciation

More securely dated than scattered stories and quotations set in the seventh and eighth centuries are strictures against renunciant activities from the Medinese jurisprudent Mālik ibn Anas (d. 179/795) and the Baghdadi Muḥammad ibn al-Ḥasan al-Shaybānī (d. 189/804–5). As for Mālik, some of his disapproval is evident from hadith included in the principal and earliest extant collection of hadith he related and his juridical opinions, the *Muwaṭṭa'*. The *Muwaṭṭa'* includes, for example, a hadith report from the Medinese client Ismā'īl ibn Abī Ḥakīm (d. 130/747–8)

> that the Messenger of God ... heard a woman praying by night. He asked, 'Who is this?' He was told, 'This is al-Khawlā' bint Tuwayt who does not sleep at night.' The Messenger of God ... disliked that. His dislike was recognizable on his face. Then he said, 'God (be he blessed and exalted) does not become tired till you become tired. Take on as much work as you have the capacity for.'[49]

There are plentiful other hadith reports in opposition to taking on too strenuous a régime of supererogatory devotions in favour of whatever one will be able to maintain. This one in Mālik's collection stands out for the Prophet's anger and the assumption that this unseen woman would soon weaken.[50] Another well-known hadith report in the *Muwaṭṭa'* is this:

> The Prophet saw a man standing in the sun, so he said, 'What is this about?' They said, 'He has vowed not to speak, not to shade himself from the sun, not to sit, and to fast.' The Prophet ... said, 'Command him to speak, shade himself, and sit. Let him complete his fast.'[51]

---

48 Sulamī, *Ṭabaqāt*, 491–2.
49 Mālik, *Muwaṭṭa'*, rec. Yaḥyá, *al-ṣalāh* 71, *mā jā'a fī ṣalāt al-layl*, no 311; rec. Abū Muṣ'ab, *al-nidā'* 19, *bāb mā jā'a fī ṣalāt al-layl*, no 288. Bukhārī quotes two versions not through Mālik with the woman unnamed: Bukhārī, *al-īmān* 32, *bāb aḥabbu al-dīn ilá Allāh adwamuh*, no 43; *al-tahajjud* 18, *bāb mā yukrahu min al-tashdīd fī al-'ibādah*, no 1151.
50 Cf. the Prophet's straightforward warning to 'Abd Allāh ibn 'Amr, 'Do not be like so-and-so who used to stay up nights but left off staying up nights': Bukhārī, *al-tahajjud* 19, *bāb mā yukrahu min tark qiyām al-layl li-man kāna yaqūmuh*, no 1152; Ibn al-Mubārak, *Zuhd*, no 1211; Ibn Sa'd, *Ṭabaqāt* 4/2:11 *4:265*.
51 Mālik, *Muwaṭṭa'*, rec. Yaḥyá, *al-nudhūr wa-al-aymān* 4, *bāb mā lā yajūzu min al-nudhūr fī ma'ṣiyat Allāh*, no 1363; rec. Abū Muṣ'ab, *al-nudhūr wa-al-aymān* 8, *bāb mā lā yajibu min al-*

The Prophet makes no attempt to determine the man's intention, nor does he pronounce on it. He just rules out excessive austerities.

Much more distrust of contemporary renunciant practice is quoted of Mālik by later writers in his school. He is said to have preferred *mudhākarah* concerning jurisprudence, meaning to sit in a group recalling earlier legal opinions, to supererogatory ritual prayer.[52] 'Mālik most strongly disliked supplication on entering the mosque and leaving it, since it is an innovation.'[53] That it was actually an innovation seems highly doubtful; that Mālik's dislike bespoke a struggle to reserve the mosque for jurisprudents as (increasingly) distinct from renunciants seems highly probable. Mālik disapproved of extending one's hands in the course of his supplication, then wiping his face with them when he has finished.[54] By one contrary report, the Prophet would always wipe his face with his hands after raising them to pray.[55] It was reportedly the practice of al-Ḥasan al-Baṣrī as he supplicated in the course of his ritual prayer.[56] According to 'Abd al-Razzāq (Yemeni, d. 211/827), 'They say that those in the past would supplicate, then return their hands to their faces in order to return the supplication and blessing. I myself saw Ma'mar supplicate with his hands to his chest, then return his hands and wipe his face with them.'[57] Again, Mālik was apparently opposing well-established practice.

Qaṣaṣ, informal preaching (i.e., apart from the *khuṭbah* on Friday), was a natural activity for renunciants. Of 109 reputed *quṣṣāṣ* (preachers) surveyed by Lyall Armstrong, 43 are conservatively counted as 'identified as having ascetic tendencies'.[58] *Qāṣṣ* (preacher) might still be complimentary in the middle of the ninth

---

nudhūr fī ma'ṣiyat Allāh, no 2214. Sim., Bukhārī, *al-aymān wa-al-nudhūr* 31, *bāb al-nadhr fīmā lā yamliku wa-fī ma'ṣiyah*, no 6704 (Basran/Medinese *isnād*); 'Abd al-Razzāq, *Muṣannaf* 8:434–7, where the man is sometimes named Abū Isrā'īl, perhaps suggesting (improbably) that his excessive austerities were of Jewish inspiration. Remarked by Goldziher, 'Ascétisme', 165–6.

52 Qarāfī, *Dhakhīrah* 13:347.

53 Qarāfī, *Dhakhīrah* 13:347, quoting the author of *al-Bayān*, meaning Ibn Rushd al-Jadd (d. 520/1126).

54 Ibn Abī Zayd, *Nawādir* 1:530, citing *al-Majmū'ah*, a work by the Qayrawani Ibn Bashīr (d. 260/873–4?), on whom see Sezgin, *GAS* 1:473–4.

55 Tirmidhī, *al-da'awāt* 11, *bāb mā jā'a fī raf' al-aydī 'inda al-du'ā'*, no 3386.

56 'Abd Allāh, *Masā'il*, 91.

57 'Abd al-Razzāq, *Muṣannaf* 2:253, referring to Ma'mar ibn Rāshid (Basran, transferred to Yemen, d. 153/770?).

58 Armstrong, *Quṣṣāṣ*, 285–314. As for conservatism, Armstrong includes four Companions, for example, whom he does not mark as having ascetic tendencies who have sections to themselves in Ibn Abī Shaybah, *Muṣannaf*, *al-zuhd*. See also 'Athamina, 'Qasas'.

century. For example, al-Jāḥiẓ' section 'Mention of the *quṣṣāṣ*' is entirely admiring.[59] Later still, Ibn al-Jawzī (d. 597/1201), a notable preacher himself, wrote an important survey arranged biographically, generally favourable, although the survey of Zayn al-Dīn al-ʿIrāqī (d. 806/1414), a notable Egyptian traditionist, is hostile.[60] The Prophet was quoted against it: 'No one preaches (*lā yaquṣṣu*) but a ruler, someone under orders (*maʾmūr*), or someone conceited (*mukhtāl*).'[61] One strongly suspects professional jealousy. Mālik also was said to be opposed: 'I have heard that Saʿīd ibn al-Musayyib, al-Qāsim ibn Muḥammad, and Khārijah ibn Zayd would not sit for the preacher to the assembly (*qāṣṣ al-jamāʿah*).'[62] Another term for preaching was *tadhkīr*, 'bringing to mind'. Asked about what the Companion ʿUmar had said to Abū Mūsá, 'Remind us of our Lord (*dhakkirnā bi-rabbinā*)', Mālik said, 'I have never heard of this.'[63] Asked about renunciation of the world, Mālik said, 'Purity of income and shortness of hope (*ṭīb al-maksib wa-qiṣar al-amal*)', enouncing a minimally world-rejecting inward piety.[64]

As for al-Shaybānī, the principal evidence of his views on renunciation is the sketch of a work he made at the end of his life, *Kitāb al-Kasb* ('gain'), mentioned in the previous chapter. It appears to be mainly a polemic against *inkār al-kasb*, 'the repudiation of gain'. In the first or second generation after al-Shaybānī, the Muʿtazili Abū ʿImrān al-Raqāshī (*fl.* early 9th cent.) is associated with the repudiation of normal gain.[65] That is, he considered it best to withdraw from labour and live on alms. Still later in the ninth century, the repudiation of normal gain became a distinctive doctrine of the Karāmīyah, who tended to absorb the Muʿtazili renunciant tradition, and our *Kitāb al-Kasb* expressly argues against them in a

---

59 Jāḥiẓ, *Bayān* 1:366–9.
60 Ibn al-Jawzī, *Quṣṣāṣ*; ʿIrāqī, *Bāʿith*.
61 Abū Dāwūd, *al-ʿilm* 13, *bāb fī al-qaṣaṣ*, no 3665 (Syrian *isnād*); sim., Ibn Mājah, *al-adab* 40, *bāb al-qaṣaṣ*, no 3753 (Kufan *isnād*), and Dārimī, *Musnad*, 665; *al-raqāʾiq* 62, *bāb fī al-nahy ʿan al-qaṣaṣ*, with 'hypocrite' instead of 'someone conceited'.
62 Ibn Rushd, *Bayān* 17:296–7, naming three of the Seven Jurisprudents of Medina, all Followers, for which see Qarāfī, *Dhakhīrah* 13:343. The Māliki tradition of seven jurisprudents was opposed by alternatives naming just four, for which see Aḥmad, *ʿIlal* 2:410–11 *1:349*. See also Schacht, *Origins*, 243–4.
63 Ibn Abī Zayd, *Nawādir* 1:529. Alternatively, ʿUmar is quoted as bidding Abū Mūsá to recite the Qur'an to him; e.g., Ibn Saʿd, *Ṭabaqāt* 4/1:91 *4:109*.
64 Bājī, *Sunan*, 599, citing Mālik's disciple Zayd ibn Dāwūd al-Anṣārī, on whom see al-Qāḍī ʿIyāḍ, *Tartīb* 3:163. For more on Mālik's hostility, see Melchert, 'Mālik'.
65 See Ibn al-Murtaḍá, *Klassen*, 77.

later passage obviously not from al-Shaybānī.[66] Our main witness to the early controversy over gain is a book by the Baghdadi renunciant al-Muḥāsibī (d. 243/857–8). As observed earlier, he names two early Sufis who repudiated buying and selling, ʿAbd Allāh ibn Yazīd and ʿAbdak, perhaps in particular at the time of the Fourth Civil War (Amīn *vs* Maʾmūn, 195–8/810–13, much longer in Syria).[67] But al-Muḥāsibī attributes the doctrine above all to the Khurasani renunciant Shaqīq ibn Ibrāhīm al-Balkhī (d. 194/809–10): 'According to what is related of him, Shaqīq asserted that effort (*ḥarakah*) in pursuit of gain is a sin.'[68] Elsewhere, Ibrāhīm ibn Ad'ham (d. 163/779–80?) is quoted as remonstrating with Shaqīq against his repudiation of gain.[69]

Shaqīq al-Balkhī is fairly strongly associated with the early Ḥanafi tradition in Khurasan. Ḥanafi sources assert that he was disciple to Abū Yūsuf, before whom he read *Kitāb al-Ṣalāh*.[70] Al-Dhahabī quotes someone's testimony that he said he had learnt jurisprudence from Abū Ḥanīfah's Basran associate Zufar (d. 158/774–5).[71] He was a significant source of biographical information in al-Muwaffaq al-Khwārizmī (d. 568/1172–3), *Manāqib al-imām al-aʿẓam Abī Ḥanīfah*.[72] The Karāmīyah were mainly Ḥanafi in law, and may have got their repudiation of gain from a Ḥanafi tradition going back to Shaqīq al-Balkhī.[73] It is possible, then, that al-Shaybānī's *Kasb* was largely an intra-Ḥanafi polemic against a Khurasani school within the larger grouping. The Ḥanafi school of the ninth century was still, of course, inchoate by comparison with the Ḥanafi guild school that developed in the tenth century. But the Karāmīyah were also prominent rejecters of gain. The books on *kasb* of al-Ḥakīm al-Tirmidhī (d. *ca* 295/907–8?) and, indeed, this section of Sarakhsī's commentary would then be later contributions to the same intra-Ḥanafi polemic.[74]

Al-Shaybānī's second main theme seems to be defence of teaching.

---

66 On the Karāmi position, see van Ess, 'Lecture', 190, 192; *idem*, *Ungenützte Texte*, 30–2; Massignon, *Passion* 3:227. On the Karāmīyah in *al-Kasb*, see Sarakhsī, *Mabsūṭ* 30:250–1; Shaybānī, *Kasb*, 96–101; also Bonner, 'The *Kitāb al-Kasb*', 413–15.

67 Muḥāsibī, *Makāsib*, 212 *64*.

68 Muḥāsibī, *Makāsib*, 194 *61*; followed by Massignon, *Essay*, 173.

69 Abū Nuʿaym, *Ḥilyah* 8:37. On Shaqīq, see Gramlich, *Alte Vorbilder* 2:13–62.

70 See Ibn Abī al-Wafāʾ, *Jawāhir* 2:254–5.

71 Dhahabī, *Tārīkh* 13 (191–200 H.): 230; shorter version, Dhahabī, *Siyar* 9:315.

72 Al-Muwaffaq ibn Aḥmad, *Manāqib*.

73 For the Karāmīyah and Ḥanafism, see Maqdisī, *Aḥsan al-taqāsīm*, 365. Cf. Zysow, 'Two unrecognized Karrāmī texts', 580.

74 Al-Ḥakīm al-Tirmidhī, *Bayān al-kasb*. Unfortunately, al-Ḥakīm follows another Ḥanafi tradition in leaving his opponents anonymous, so it is difficult to say against precisely whom he is arguing.

> If the people left the seeking of knowledge, truth would not be distinguished from falsity, the right from the wrong, filial piety from estrangement. Distinguishing between truth and falsity is the root of religion. It is not achieved except by knowledge. [Teaching] is incumbent on the learnèd whenever there reaches them something from those before them in which is benefit to the people.[75]

Here also there is probably an element of intra-Ḥanafi polemic. Dāwūd al-Ṭāʾī (d. 165/781–2?) famously sat with Abū Ḥanīfah but then became disillusioned by his circle's worldliness and withdrew to his house. The earliest extant biographical dictionary of the Ḥanafi school quotes Ibn Kaʾs (d. 324/935): 'There was once no one in Abū Ḥanīfah's circle whose voice was louder than Dāwūd al-Ṭāʾī's. Then he renounced the world, withdrew from them, and turned to worship.'[76] The Kufan qadi Ḥafṣ ibn Ghiyāth (d. 195/811?) said, 'Dāwūd al-Ṭāʾī sat with us by Abū Ḥanīfah until he excelled in *raʾy*. Then he rejected that and rejected hadith, although he had gone far in it, and stuck to worship and avoiding people.'[77] In the later Sufi tradition, Dāwūd preferred al-Shaybānī to Abū Yūsuf (d. 182/798), the other most celebrated disciple to Abū Ḥanīfah, because al-Shaybānī had started rich and made himself poor in pursuit of religious learning, whereas Abū Yūsuf had started poor and made himself rich.[78] Whatever his regard for al-Shaybānī, his withdrawal from Abū Ḥanīfah's circle was a rebuke to the jurisprudents, while al-Shaybānī's *Kasb* defends the jurisprudents against qualms about devoting oneself to worship instead.

Finally, al-Shaybānī several times defends moderate self-indulgence against extreme self-denial; for example, 'Wherever eating is a duty, eating is subject to reward, for it is tantamount to a command. By its means, one is enabled to fulfil his duties by way of fasting and ritual prayer. It is equivalent to hurrying to fulfil the Friday assembly and ritual purity to fulfil the duty of ritual prayer.'[79] I have seen no direct report that some renunciants of his time were actually failing to fast and pray from self-imposed starvation. At most, I have found clay-eating.[80]

---

75 Sarakhsī, *Mabsūṭ* 30:261; Shaybānī, *Kasb*, 154–5.

76 Ṣaymarī, *Akhbār*, 109. For more on Dāwūd al-Ṭāʾī, see Dhahabī, *Siyar* 7:422–5 with further references. Another early Ḥanafi biographical dictionary is Saʿdī, *Faḍāʾil Abī Ḥanīfah*. Although the editor prefers an early date, it is actually very uncertain whether it belongs to the tenth century or the eleventh. It offers another story of Dāwūd al-Ṭāʾī's dropping out of Abū Ḥanīfah's circle at 246.

77 Ṣaymarī, *Akhbār*, 116.

78 Hujvīrī, *Kashf*, 136 *110*.

79 Sarakhsī, *Mabsūṭ* 30:275; Shaybānī, *Kasb*, 203.

80 See Abū Nuʿaym, *Ḥilyah* 7:381, on Ibrāhīm ibn Adʾham; but Ibrāhīm is one of the eighth-century figures who most attracted back projection of later ideas, and the considerably more

Much later, the Sufi al-Sarrāj (d. 378/988) says that he has seen many who have made do with little, eaten grass, and refused to drink water to the point that they did miss prayers. Others ate little, stayed up nights, and recollected God continuously to the point that they lost consciousness and required days of care before they could again perform the required prayers.[81] By contrast, Sahl al-Tustarī (Basran, 283/896?) told his disciples to eat meat once a week so as not to be too weak for worship.[82] However, al-Sarrāj also reports that Sahl would eat once in 15 days, once a month in Ramadan.[83] Whether or not to the degree that al-Shaybānī argues against, there plainly were calls in his time, a century before Sahl, to extreme austerity of clothing and diet, making *Kitāb al-Kasb* the earliest evidence we have of this extreme. Otherwise, repudiation of gain is attested mainly in the next century, as by, most notably, the *Makāsib* of al-Muḥāsibī. Secondly, inasmuch as al-Shaybānī argues generally against the renunciant tradition in favour of an inward, world-embracing piety, his work confirms other evidence of a turn against outward, world-rejecting piety in the late eighth century.[84]

Al-Muḥāsibī against excessive renunciation

Al-Muḥāsibī has been mentioned before. He is identified with the nascent Shāfiʿi school in law, and his *Kitāb Fahm al-Qurʾān* is largely about how to infer rules.[85] He barely touches on legal questions in his magnum opus, *al-Riʿāyah li-ḥuqūq Allāh* ('watching out for the claims of God'), but its respect for Qur'an, *sunnah*, and consensus as the basis of the law, to be interpreted as necessary by *tamthīl* and *qiyās*, are consistent with the preclassical Shāfiʿism of his time.[86] His *Kitāb al-ʿAql* posits that reason is not how we know the rules but how we recognize our

numerous stories stressing pure food seem more plausible. Stories are told of his eating sand for periods of eight or fifteen days in Mecca, also of its turning into wheat flour in his mouth: Ibn ʿAsākir, *Tārīkh* 6:301, 302, 326.

81 Sarrāj, *Lumaʿ*, 417–18.

82 Sarrāj, *Lumaʿ*, 417.

83 Sarrāj, *Lumaʿ*, 163.

84 For more on Shaybānī's position, see Melchert, 'Al-Shaybānī'.

85 See Metzler, *Den Koran verstehen*, which includes an edited text, translation, and study of *Fahm al-Qurʾān*; also Melchert, 'Qur'anic abrogation', and van Ess, *Theologie* 4:203–4 *4:230–2*, for a theological discussion.

86 Muḥāsibī, *Riʿāyah*, 222 *357*. Later on the same page, Muḥāsibī refers to *qiyās* and *naẓar* as faculties of the qualified jurisconsult, suggesting that *tamthīl* means something like 'analogy' while *qiyās* is still being used for something like 'reason'.

obligation to follow the rules revealed by God.[87] He suffered at the end of his life from adherents of the nascent Ḥanbali school for involvement in *kalām*, dialectical theology, even if it was in defence of Sunni positions.[88] (A list in the *Riʿāyah* of erroneous views, such as advocacy of agnosticism [*waqf*, particularly over the createdness of the Qur'an] and the pronunciation [of the Qur'an, particularly conceding that it is create], denial of predestination and the beatific vision, does to the contrary agree closely with ninth-century traditionalist doctrine.[89]) A prolific writer especially on renunciant themes, he was hailed by the later Sufis as an important precursor. Many modern writers have called him a Sufi, but there is no evidence that he was ever called one in his lifetime.

Al-Muḥāsibī does not cast doubt on common renunciant devotional practices, as Mālik does. Rather, *al-Riʿāyah li-ḥuqūq Allāh* goes over at great length the many sorts of conceit and complacency to which the worshipper is liable. It includes many warnings against concentration on supererogatory works to the point of neglecting required works.[90] But it also warns against, for example, performing the required ritual prayers for fear of attracting disapproval, not just to do one's duty to God, and neglecting dependants and relatives for the sake of seeking hadith.[91] It permits keeping vigil or weeping in company with a group, not at home by oneself, if one finds one does it for God, not to be seen by the group.[92]

> A group believes that renunciation of the world is to destroy wife and children, leaving on journeys without provision, being contented and pleased with tribulation when it befalls the Muslims, forbidding medicine and prayer, abandoning hope that sins have not been, preoccupation with God (mighty and glorious is he) by leaving off required and supererogatory works, claiming insight and the illumination of their hearts by asserting knowledge of the unsee .... They argue for that by means of reports such as his (the Prophet's) saying ..., 'The believer sees by the light of God.'[93]

87 See de Crussol, *Le rôle de la raison*.
88 For various accounts of what provoked Ḥanbali ire, also the trouble it made for him (exile from Baghdad, private funeral), see Melchert, 'Adversaries', 242–4. For a longer review of the evidence, see Picken, 'Ibn Ḥanbal and al-Muḥāsibī', concluding anew that the dispute was mainly about the legitimacy of *kalām*.
89 Muḥāsibī, *Ri`āyah* 243–4 *389–90*.
90 E.g., 'An increasingly large party of *qurrāʾ* have pursued supererogatory works, as they claim, while leaving off the required': Muḥāsibī, *Riʿāyah*, 57 *113*.
91 Muḥāsibī, *Riʿāyah*, 56, 124 *111, 215*.
92 Muḥāsibī, *Riʿāyah*, 178–9 *296–7*.
93 Muḥāsibī, *Riʿāyah*, 47 *97–8*.

Unlike Mālik and al-Shaybānī, al-Muḥāsibī is concerned with antinomian mysticism, on which more in the next chapter.

As for the question of *kasb*, al-Muḥāsibī rules out the rejection of gain. Abū al-Dardā' may have found it impossible to pursue both trade and worship, but he said, '"I have left off trading": he did not say, "I should not like to trade, gaining fifty dinars a day to give as alms, without being distracted by that from the recollection of God."'[94] A short work of al-Muḥāsibī's directed just to the question of gain, *al-Mākāsib*, has been quoted already for naming several persons who rejected it. As in the *Ri'āyah*, al-Muḥāsibī fears failure to perform required works.

> Whoever bids the people to hunger has disobeyed God, knowing that hunger kills. Many have done that to the destruction of reason, until they left the required duties (*farā'iḍ*). Among them was one who went for a knife and slaughtered himself. Another changed his nature, becoming ill-tempered.[95]

In the *Makāsib*, though, al-Muḥāsibī seems especially concerned with *tawakkul*, a qur'anic term for committing one's affair to God.[96] It is an obligation for all believers and therefore must be compatible with economic activity. He cites a Prophet hadith report, 'The best of what a man eats is from his gain' (i.e., what he has earned by his labour), and the examples of various past prophets and Companions.[97] Those who reject the active pursuit of gain, after the advice of Shaqīq al-Balkhī and others, may accept alms from dubious patrons.[98] If the almsgivers are held to be giving from what they have acquired licitly, then it must be licit to pursue gain.[99] Yet al-Muḥāsibī does not necessarily reject such *tawakkul*. Rather, he hopes that refusing to work for gain may be accepted if indeed it is not embarked on for the sake of worldly repute.[100] Ibn al-Jawzī berates him precisely for endorsing the rejection of gain.[101] In short, the works of al-Muḥāsibī testify to the growth of extreme renunciation in the first half of the ninth century. However, unlike Mālik and al-Shaybānī, he cannot be held to advocate a world-affirming

94 Muḥāsibī, *Ri'āyah*, 163 *274*.
95 Muḥāsibī, *Makāsib*, 227 *104*.
96 An important study is Reinert, *Lehre*.
97 Muḥāsibī, *Makāsib*, 183–4, 195, 199 *48–9, 62, 63–4*.
98 Muḥāsibī, *Makāsib*, 194 *61*.
99 Muḥāsibī, *Makāsib*, 195 *63*.
100 Muḥāsibī, *Ri'āyah*, 188 *310*.
101 Ibn al-Jawzī, *Talbīs*, 230–2; *Devil's delusion*, *Islamic culture* 10 (1936): 636–8. Based on a long quotation in Ghazālī, *Iḥyā' 'ulūm al-dīn*, however, conceivably attributed to al-Muḥāsibī by mistake (although the same may be said of *al-Makāsib*). See also Massignon, *Essay*, 167–8.

piety, nor modest austerity as opposed to extreme; rather, with dogged insistence, he wants all works to be dedicated purely to God, in complete indifference (*zuhd*—why not?) to social approval or disapproval.

Traditionalists against extreme renunciation

I have hitherto stressed specialization as the reason for increasing opposition to renunciation across the eighth century, as jurisprudents became differentiated from renunciants, at the same rate becoming rivals for domination of the mosques.[102] But there was also resistance to developing renunciant piety in the ninth century from the traditionalist party, which largely resisted specialization itself—they equally resented distinction between expertise in law and hadith. Various renunciants are said to have been prevented from paying proper attention to hadith by their devotional lives; for example, Ibn Ḥibbān said of Yazīd ibn Abān al-Raqāshī (Basran, d. 110s/728–38),

> He was among the best of the worshippers of God among those who wept by night in deserted places .... He was among those who neglected the trade of hadith and memorizing it, being distracted by worship ... until he would invert the talk of al-Ḥasan and make it come from Anas ibn Mālik from the Prophet without his knowing.[103]

He said of ʿAbd al-Wāḥid ibn Zayd (Basran, *fl.* earlier 8th cent.), another disciple to al-Ḥasan al-Baṣrī, 'He was among those overcome by worship to the point that he neglected certainty as to what he related, so disreputable things multiplied in his narration.'[104] Sufyān al-Thawrī reputedly opposed specialization in either seeking knowledge or devotions.[105] When someone told Aḥmad ibn Ḥanbal (d. Baghdad, 241/855) that it was impossible both to seek hadith and to worship at the mosque, Aḥmad said both were incumbent on him.[106]

Some writers have attributed growing doubts about austerity to the rise of a wealthy trading class. 'Renunciation of worldly goods was always the main current in Islam, and traditions favouring property and wealth arose only as a concession to the ruling economic power of the bourgeoisie.'[107] This seems plausible,

102 Sim., Melchert, 'Early renunciants as *ḥadīth* transmitters', but cf. 'The piety of the hadith folk'.
103 Ibn Ḥibbān, *Majrūḥīn* 3:98.
104 Ibn Ḥibbān, *Majrūḥīn* 2:155.
105 Abū Nuʿaym, *Ḥilyah* 7:12.
106 Ibn Abī Yaʿlá, *Ṭabaqāt* 1:23 *1:50–1.*
107 Kinberg, 'Compromise', 195; sim., Goitein, 'Rise'.

at least as one reason. I would urge that we consider it a matter of a bourgeoisie arising alongside an aristocracy, inasmuch as the Muslims were effectively all aristocrats living off tribute from the subject peoples at the beginning of the eighth century, the renunciant tradition being then an attempt to preserve the ethos of the conquest period.[108]

There is also something here of a problem that Michael Cooperson has identified with relation, first, to Aḥmad ibn Ḥanbal:

> First, Ibn Ḥanbal's ambitious project is doomed to failure because he cannot fully emulate a man who himself emulated no one. The Prophet lived spontaneously, and spontaneity by definition lies beyond the reach of imitation. ... Second, as Ibn Ḥanbal's contemporaries appear to have furtively conceded, the complete success of his project would broach the scandalous possibility that he could come to replace the Prophet.[109]

So for the leading traditionist and jurisprudent of his generation, so equally for contemporary renunciants: whereas worldly athletes are allowed to improve on the performances of their forebears, religious ascetics are forbidden by definition to improve on the models of the first generation. There was necessarily something impious about mortifying the self and denying the world more than the Prophet and his Companions had done.

Finally, there is something in the nature of moralism necessarily hostile to extremes of austerity. A moral demand is necessarily the same for everyone, in every place, at every time. For example, adultery is not sometimes forbidden, sometimes allowed, but always forbidden; supporting one's family is not sometimes required, sometimes omissible, but always required. If someone did something not everyone might do, such as never worrying about his provision for the morrow, it was evidently not in response to a moral demand from God. It rather had the nature of a stunt—'Look what I can do.' As such, it necessarily appeared to the likes of Aḥmad ibn Ḥanbal as frivolity, a reprehensible distraction from the performance of universal religious duties.[110] It took the spread of a mystical sensibility in the later ninth century to make unusual self-mortification acceptable as a proper activity for Sunnis; that is, adherents of the great community (*al-jamāʿah* = *ekklēsía*).

---

108 See Stark, 'Upper class asceticism', for a survey of other religious traditions but mostly medieval Latin Christianity, arguing that ascetics normally came from the aristocracy.
109 Cooperson, 'Ibn Ḥanbal', 78.
110 More on this tension in Melchert, 'Piety of the hadith folk'.

Chapter 10: The transition to Sufism

Sufism is widely defined as Islamic mysticism, particularly the form that took shape around the Baghdadi master al-Junayd (d. 298/911?). A good summary of the history as presently understood is Ahmet T. Karamustafa, *Sufism: the formative period*. Distinguishing characteristics of the new Sufism were especially, he says, devotion to experiential knowledge of God, the idea of a spiritual path, and the special camaraderie and status of the friends of God.[1] There were persons called Sufis before al-Junayd's time, but they were mainly marginal, disreputable figures not identified as forbears by the later Sufi biographers. There is no evidence that they were mystics, either. It will be useful to separate the two problems: how 'Sufi' came to designate a respectable Sunni group as it had not to begin with and how mysticism arose to become the predominant form of piety, at least among pious specialists.

Previous chapters have pointed out a rising tide of opposition to the renunciant programme of the early eighth century. Economically, it became unfeasible to demand that faithful Muslims spend their days and nights in devotions once the Muslims were a majority and no longer supported by tribute from non-Muslims, rather needing to work for a living themselves. Socially, an increasingly differentiated élite of jurisprudents (increasingly traditionists as well) resented competition for attention from pious preachers, worshippers, and others. At the same time, it appears that some renunciants were pushing their austerities to a new extreme, as in refusing to work for gain or setting out on journeys with no provisions, expecting to be sustained accidentally; that is, by divine provision alone.

There are roughly two solutions to the problem of maintaining a rigorous piety and allowing the believers to make a living. One is to turn piety inward, reducing demands for outward observances such as time-consuming rituals to what is practical for most persons. This is roughly the Protestant solution in the Christian tradition, that of the 'Hadith Folk' in the Islamic.[2] The other is to create a specialist caste of full-time religious, supported by alms from ordinary believers. This is the monastic solution in the Christian and Buddhist traditions, among others, to a great extent the Sufi solution in the Islamic. As it crystallized around

1 Karamustafa, *Sufism*, 19–24.
2 See Melchert, 'Piety of the hadith folk'.

https://doi.org/10.1515/9783110617962-011

al-Junayd, Sufism repudiated the most extreme forms of austerity in favor of inward dependence on God.[3] As mystics, the Sufis found it easy to be generous toward nonspecialist Muslims and hopeful of their prospects for salvation, taking some of the offence out of their élitism. This seems to be the characteristic Sunni position.

Mysticism

'Mysticism' is a term with a fairly clear history in Christian usage, meaning experiential knowledge of God. (It has further extensions, too. A popular Anglican hymn refers to the church's 'mystic sweet communion/With those whose rest is won'.[4] In Christian Arabic, *al-asrār al-sabʿah* are the seven gifts of the Spirit.) It is sometimes connected with a dominical saying, 'And he said unto them, Unto you it is given to know the mystery of the kingdom of God: but unto them that are without, all these things are done in parables' (Mark 4:11), hence esotericism.[5] Some Christian writers have tried to keep it Christian, distinguishing between true forms that approach God through Jesus Christ and delusory forms that do not. Resistance to the term 'mysticism' from Muslims largely has to do with traditional reluctance to liken anything Islamic to anything non-Islamic. Exclusive definitions such as these are completely unhelpful to comparative religious scholarship and will not be heeded here. Some universalists have also perceived mysticism as the essential core of all religions, effectively the one true religion. Their theory has the obvious disadvantage of contradicting what nearly all mystical writers say about their own traditions. Let it suffice here to observe that identifying true and false religion is not a concern of historical scholarship, such as this book.

The closest Arabic term to 'mysticism' is *maʿrifah*, 'knowing', contrasted with *ʿilm*, knowledge passed on orally by human teachers, as when al-Junayd speaks, for example, of being 'transported by gnosis (*maʿrifah*) whither knowledge (*ʿilm*) never transported them—to an infinite aim.'[6] This is a technical usage not characteristic of the period before classical Sufism. The Arabic *taṣawwuf* (Sufism) refers to the wearing of wool, not religious experience. Nevertheless, it is just to describe Sufism as 'Islamic mysticism', at most with the qualification that some

3 See Reinert, *Lehre vom tawakkul*.

4 Samuel John Stone (d. 1900), 'The church's one foundation'.

5 See Bouyer, 'Mysticism', for a treatment of the term among early Christian writers (and a few yet earlier non-Christian).

6 Junayd, *Dawāʾ al-arwāḥ*, 220 (Ar.), 226 (trans.).

Islamic mystical forms are found outside Sufism and, of course, that not everything every Sufi does is suffused with mysticism.[7] A predominantly mystical piety seems to emerge in the literary record in the mid-ninth century, in the generation before al-Junayd. In a few generations, the particular Junaydi version evidently absorbed parallel movements from Khurasan to Egypt and beyond.

Effectively beginning with Max Weber, sociologists of religion have defined 'asceticism' as the piety that stresses obedience to transcendent deity. They contrast it with 'mysticism', the piety that stresses communion with immanent deity.[8] Here are some oppositions:

Asceticism	Mysticism
obedience	communion
Θ transcendent	Θ immanent
imposing Θ's will on the world	finding Θ revealed in the world
times and places equal	some times and places special
divinity personal	divinity impersonal
divine omniscience	divine omnipotence
pessimism	optimism
salvation from sin	salvation from death
fear alternating with chosenness	abundant grace
'faith' = 'loyalty'	'faith' = 'confidence'
egalitarian sect	hierarchical church

Most religious traditions comprise elements of each, but it should be possible to put them at different points of a spectrum. For example, Protestantism tends to be more ascetical than Roman Catholicism, but within Protestantism Calvinism is more ascetical than Lutheranism, while Roman Catholicism is more ascetical than Greek Orthodoxy. The two are in tension with each other, and religious history is often about the successive predominance of one or the other.

The Muslim renunciants quoted in the preceding chapters are clearly on the side of asceticism. They do not refer to unitive experience, rather to fear at the

7 Tomb visitation, highly mystical in its recognition of special times and places, also involvement with miracles, is an example of a practice rightly distinguished from Sufism by Christopher Taylor, *In the vicinity*. Julian Baldick mentions as an example the Islamic continuation of Greek philosophy: *Sufism*, 4. A famous study bringing out the relatively ascetical character of Moroccan Sufism (for example) is Geertz, *Islam observed*.

8 I am much indebted for conceptual clarity to Mueller, 'Asceticism and mysticism'.

prospect of seeing God at the Last Judgement. They do not refer to *dhikr* as conducing to communion with God, rather to its being recorded in their favour for future reward. They express uneasiness with worldly hierarchies, whether within the study group in the mosque or observing the splendour of the court. As obedience is required of everyone at all times and in all places, so they assume that their régime is for all the Muslims to follow. When Dhū al-Nūn (d. 245/860?) refers to God's select servants whose bodies are in the world but spirits hung up in the kingdom, we seem to have moved to the territory of mysticism, all the more when a disciple to Abū Yazīd al-Bisṭāmī (d. 261/874–5?) asks him about a groan that he had seen tear the veil between him and God, to which Abū Yazīd responds by lauding the groan that means there is no veil to tear.[9] About the mid-ninth century, there seems to be something new.

Two short treatises attributed to Shaqīq al-Balkhī (d. 194/809–10) have been held to illustrate earliest Islamic mysticism. Sara Sviri says, 'I shall assume the understanding that mysticism is a current within religions and cultures, associated with voluntary efforts, usually beyond and in addition to traditional religious practices, aimed at gaining an intensified experience of the sacred.'[10] I wish she dealt directly with the opposition to asceticism (is it mystical by her definition if someone cultivates intense fear of meeting God?), but let me pass to her interpretation of a passage from one of these treatises (the first paragraph her translation, the second her commentary), describing the seeker who has reached the stage of longing for Paradise:

> He (i.e. the practitioner) then becomes one who yearns (*al-mushtāq*), who loves ardently (*al-shadīd al-ḥubb*), a knower and a stranger (*al-ʿālim al-gharīb*), constantly behaving kindly (*al-dāʾim al-iḥsān*), one who does not hasten to acquire possessions (*alladhī lā yarūḥu il-kasb al-māl*). ... When you see him, he is always smiling, pleased with what he possesses. ... He is the one continuously fasting, the one continuously praying (*al-ṣawwām al-qawwām*).
> The transformation occurs in this life and is not confined to a 'reward and punishment' in the afterlife theology. It described a state of being while in the world. Though Shaqīq's programme contains 'ascetical' elements, they are not its main characteristics. *Al-ṣawwām al-qawwām*—'one continuously fasting, continuously praying'—may even be understood as an ironical reference to those who are immersed in fasting and praying at the expense of proceeding towards higher states.[11]

9 Abū Nuʿaym, *Ḥilyah* 9:349 (Dhū al-Nūn),10:38 (Abū Yazīd).
10 Sviri, *Perspectives*, 24.
11 Sviri, *Perspectives*, 45, first paragraph translated from Shaqīq, *Ādāb*, 20.

I tend to doubt the attribution of this short text to Shaqīq. These treatises are not attributed to him in any medieval biography, nor do they sound the least similar to the earliest extant Sufi collection of his sayings, the biography of al-Sulamī.[12] At most, one might find that not hastening to acquire possessions agrees with al-Muḥāsibī's report that Shaqīq upheld *inkār al-kasb*. I would allow it to be from the generation of his disciples. Does it testify to mysticism in either the eighth or ninth century, as Sviri thinks? I am unconvinced. Longing (*ishtiyāq*) is a felt lack, not possession, nor something attributed to God. 'What he possesses' more likely refers to whatever the worshipper has in the world, having renounced the pursuit of worldly possessions because the most he could obtain is so palpably little compared with the prospect of Paradise. I do not see at all that 'He is the one continuously fasting, the one continuously praying' can refer to others, not the one longing for Paradise. And note the word *ʿālim* for 'knowing', not the diagnostic *ʿārif*.

Al-Muḥāsibī (d. Baghdad? 243/857–8) is aware of developing mysticism, as observed in the previous chapter ('claiming insight and the illumination of their hearts by asserting knowledge of the unseen'), which alarms him for its potential antinomianism; however, his warnings are overwhelmingly to fellow renunciants. He refers several times to ignorant *qurrāʾ* and *mutaṣawwifah*, occasionally mistaken *mutaqashshifīn*, such as those who call for someone who has memorized the Qur'an from a copy acquired with illicit funds to forget it, once to mistaken *qurrāʾ* and *nussāk* who consider a ritual prayer nullified if performed in forbidden clothing (presumably starting with silk or embroidery on men).[13] These are still advocates of extreme austerity, not mystics. Other *qurrāʾ* and *mutaṣawwifah* appear to hold reasonable views, such as those who agree with Sufyān al-Thawrī that one should divest oneself of an inheritance built up by oppression and fraud.[14] (Al-Muḥāsibī himself was said to have refused to inherit anything from his father on account of theological deviance.[15]) He clearly endorses social hierarchy: 'The Muslims are agreed that whoever undertakes the caliphate, rulership, judgeship, supplicating God (mighty and glorious is he), and giving juridical opinions, he is saved and better than all the (rest of) the people.'[16] Sufi élitism would be about exalting those closest to God. Al-Muḥāsibī accepts that there will

12 Sulamī, *Ṭabaqāt*, 54–9.
13 Muḥāsibī, *Makāsib*, 222–3 *98–9*.
14 Muḥāsibī, *Makāsib*, 212 *84*.
15 Abū Nuʿaym, *Ḥilyah* 10:75, evidently drawing on the Sufi biographer Jaʿfar al-Khuldī, who quotes al-Junayd. See van Ess, *Gedankenwelt*, 2–4.
16 Muḥāsibī, *Riʿāyah*, 163 *274*.

be separate specialists in law and piety, but he still conceives of the latter as calling on God, not communing with him.

Later Sufi mystics were given to introspection and naturally found al-Muḥāsibī's heavy stress on it congenial. Where ascetics characteristically deprecate mystics' self-absorption, mystics deprecate ascetics' complacency, just like al-Muḥāsibī. But this does not make al-Muḥāsibī a mystic. For example, he calls at length for the contemplation of death and its horrors, but the end of that is, by the help of God, 'that he shortens his hope, observes his term, and becomes ready by repentance to meet his Lord.'[17] (Another of al-Muḥāsibī's short works, *al-Tawahhum*, is all about contemplation of Judgement and the Afterworld. The attribution is admittedly not certain.) He may refer to *maʿrifah* but not in opposition to *ʿilm*, the transmitted knowledge of the ulema. For example, one of his short works is called *Sharḥ al-maʿrifah*, 'explanation of knowing', but whereas it begins with *maʿrifat Allāh*, the knowledge of God, it goes on to *maʿrifat ʿadūw Allāh Iblīs*, the knowledge of God's enemy Iblīs, then *maʿrifat nafsika al-ammārah bi-al-sūʾ*, the knowledge of your lower soul, urging to evil, and so on. *Maʿrifah* is not opposed to *ʿilm* and seems to mean something close to *recognition*.[18] Even *Kitāb al-Maḥabbah* ('the book of love'), apparently reproduced or at least excerpted by Abū Nuʿaym al-Iṣbahānī, identifies love (*ḥubb*) with longing (*shawq*), not a mutual relationship with God as later Sufis characterize love.[19]

At most, al-Muḥāsibī does point to the most probable path, at the experiential level, from renunciation to mysticism, mainly single-minded concentration on God; for example, 'cutting off every distraction that distracts from God', although this is not for him an end stage.[20] Before him, the Syrian Abū Sulaymān al-Dārānī (d. 215/830–1) is quoted as reviewing different definitions of renunciation (*zuhd*) current in Iraq. 'Some say it is leaving off meeting people, some say it is leaving off desires, and some say it is leaving off satiety. Their definitions are similar to one another. I think that renunciation is leaving off whatever distracts you from God.'[21]

This is to go against some modern scholars who conceive of Sufism as an unchanging essence above historical change. For example, speaking of al-Muḥāsibī, here is Atif Khalil:

---

17 Muḥāsibī, *Riʿāyah*, 82–3 *149*.

18 Muḥāsibī, *Sharḥ al-maʿrifah*, 30–5.

19 Abū Nuʿaym, *Ḥilyah* 10:76–80. Recently, Sara Sviri also has made a point of acknowledging that al-Muḥāsibī himself does not write as a mystic: *Perspectives*, 144.

20 Abū Nuʿaym, *Ḥilyah* 10:77.

21 Abū Nuʿaym, *Ḥilyah* 9:258.

> Julian Baldick's contention that 'he was neither a Sufi nor a mystic, but a moralizing theologian'—in line with the general revisionist thrust of his work on the early tradition—appears to reflect an ignorance of the nature and scope of medieval Sufi literature, most of which was concerned not with ecstatic, paranormal, and supernatural experiences, but with the everyday virtues that the mystics sought to perfect in order to ascend into the divine presence.[22]

This talk of 'ecstatic, paranormal, and supernatural experiences' is, note, a strawman definition of Sufi mysticism projected onto Baldick, not enounced by him. Khalil's formulation is a conversation stopper and I can only respond by saying that I am working in a different tradition from his.

It has often been alleged but never convincingly demonstrated that Shiʿism was decisively important to the emergence of Sufism. Sometimes it is alleged that the esoteric element of Sufism depended on Shiʿi precedents, such as finding allusions to ʿAlī and his house in the Qur'an. Sometimes it is alleged that whenever Sufi sources quote a Shiʿi imam, especially Jaʿfar al-Ṣādiq, it betrays a Shiʿi background, no matter how Sunni the quotation sounds. Sometimes it is alleged that Sufi ideas of charismatic individuals must have been modelled on early Shiʿi ideas. The weakness of the case is ever and again the lack of Shiʿi literature securely dated before the emergence of Sufi mysticism in the mid-ninth century, so that alleged Shiʿi precedents can only be assumed, not demonstrated. Extant Shiʿi literature from the late ninth and early tenth centuries (al-Barqī, al-Ahwāzī, Ibn Hammām al-Iskāfī, and al-Kulaynī) present Shiʿi versions of Sunni renunciant sayings. Early Shiʿi books do not present Shiʿi versions of later Sufi sayings, unless extravagant Shiʿi claims for imams are (unnecessarily) taken as the basis of extravagant later claims for Sufi saints.[23]

Mysticism does show up in claims of experience that aroused hostility for infringing on divine transcendence. Abū Sulaymān al-Dārānī was expelled from Damascus for saying that he had seen angels and been addressed by them.[24] Ibn Abī al-Ḥawārī (Syrian, d. 230/844–5) was later forced to flee from the same city for saying he preferred the friends (of God; *awliyā'*) to the prophets.[25] Possibly led by a Māliki jurisprudent, the people of Old Cairo repudiated Dhū al-Nūn and accused him of secret unbelief.[26] Aḥmad ibn Ḥanbal accused Sarī al-Saqaṭī (d. Baghdad,

---

22 Khalil, *Repentance*, 125, citing Baldick, *Mystical Islam*, 34.

23 E.g., Morris, 'Revisiting'.

24 Ibn al-Jawzī, *Talbīs*, 218; *Devil's delusion, Islamic culture* 10 (1936): 359, citing al-Sulamī, presumably *Miḥan al-ṣūfiyah*.

25 Ibn al-Jawzī, *Talbīs*, 218; *Devil's delusion, Islamic culture* 10 (1936): 359.

26 Ibn al-Jawzī, *Talbīs*, 218; *Devil's delusion, Islamic culture* 10 (1936): 359. Ibn al-Jawzī names ʿAbd Allāh ibn ʿAbd al-Ḥakam as leader of the opposition to Dhū al-Nūn, but he seems very early

253/867?) of unbelief.[27] Abū Yazīd was expelled from Bisṭām for saying that he had made a heavenly ascension like the Prophet's, and went into exile for several years.[28] Abū Ḥamzah (d. Baghdad, 269/882–3) was expelled from Tarsus for recognizing the voice of God in the cawing of a crow.[29] Al-Kharrāz (d. Cairo, 277/890–1?) was driven from Old Cairo for some things he wrote of mystical experience, of Mecca for slighting the goodness of ordinary believers.[30] Even Sahl al-Tustarī (d. Basra, 283/896?) was forced to flee from Tustar to Basra, where he died, on account of relating conversations with angels, jinn, and devils.[31]

The advent of Sunni Sufis

Wearing wool as a sign of otherworldly piety, to which the term *ṣūfī* refers, goes back to long before Islam. The first Muslim to be called a Sufi, although not the first to wear wool as a sign of otherworldly piety, is famously one Abū Hāshim of Kufa (d. 150/767–8?).[32] Someone called Ibrāhīm ibn Bashshār al-Ṣūfī acted as servant to Ibrāhīm ibn Ad'ham (d. 163/779–80?).[33] Some Sufis accompanied Ibn al-Mubārak (d. 181/797) on an expedition to the frontier, apparently expecting to

---

(d. 214/829). Probably, his yet more prominent son, Muḥammad (d. 268/882), was the leader in question. Sulamī, *Sufi inquiries*, 55, mentions denunciation to the *sulṭān* but provides no details. However, this appears to be the end of a longer account quoted from Sulamī, *Miḥan al-ṣūfiyah*, mentioning ʿAbd Allāh ibn ʿAbd al-Ḥakam that is quoted by Dhahabī, *Tārīkh* 18 (241–250 H.): 267. To the contrary, al-Khaṭīb al-Baghdādī relates only stories of friendly exchanges between Dhū al-Nūn and al-Mutawakkil: *Tārīkh* 8:394–7 *9:375–8.*

27 Yaʿqūb al-Ḥanbalī, *K. al-Ḥurūf, apud* Ibn Ḥajar, *Lisān* 3:14; Ibn al-Jawzī, *Talbīs*, 221; *Devil's delusion, Islamic culture* 10 (1936): 362.

28 Ibn al-Jawzī, *Talbīs*, 218; *Devil's delusion, Islamic culture* 10 (1936): 359–60; Dhahabī, *Mīzān* 2:347, citing Sulamī. In another version as it appears of *Miḥan al-ṣūfiyah*, Sulamī relates only that Abū Yazīd aroused anger by talking of the states of prophets and saints: *Sufi inquiries*, 56–7.

29 Abū Nuʿaym, *Ḥilyah* 10:321; Ibn al-Jawzī, *Talbīs*, 221; *Devil's delusion, Islamic culture* 10 (1936): 362.

30 For Egypt, see Dhahabī, *Siyar* 13:421, quoting Sulamī, presumably *Miḥan al-ṣūfiyah*. For Mecca, see Ibn ʿAsākir, *Tārīkh* 5:136–7.

31 Ibn al-Jawzī, *Talbīs*, 219; Böwering, *Mystical Vision*, 59–63. Alternatively, on false accusations of unbelief initially provoked merely by his saying, 'Repentance is a servant's duty with every breath', see Sulamī, *Sufi inquiries*, 56.

32 Nicholson, 'Historical enquiry', 305; Massignon, *Essay*, 105.

33 Abū Nuʿaym, *Ḥilyah* 7:346, 370. Also remarked by Massignon, *Essay*, 105. Ibrāhīm ibn Bashshār is frequently named as a transmitter of sayings from Ibrāhīm; e.g., seven of ten sayings at Abū Nuʿaym, *Ḥilyah* 8:16–18. Someone called ʿAbd Allāh al-Ṣūfī quotes him at *Ḥilyah* 8:21.

go raiding with him.[34] Quite a number were notable for their disrespect of rulers: al-ʿAbbās ibn al-Muʾammal al-Ṣūfī, imprisoned by Hārūn for 'ordering the good'; rowdies in Alexandria who 'ordered the good' and rejected the governor's authority in the year 200/815–16; someone who rebuked the caliph al-Maʾmūn (who successfully defended himself rather than punish the man); Sufis in the entourage of the Egyptian qadi ʿĪsá ibn al-Munkadir (d. Baghdad, after 215/830–1), who was himself later taken away to Iraq to die in prison for defying the governor's authority; and the Sufis who, in alliance with the local Zaydīyah, took over Kūfa for a few weeks on behalf of two Ḥasanids in 255/869.[35] There was also a group called 'the Sufis of the Muʿtazilah', probably so called in the first place for their austere living (the Muʿtazilah, 'withdrawers', having started out as a renunciant movement more than a theological) but very likely also because of their devotion to one of the five outstanding principles of the Muʿtazilah, 'commanding good and forbidding evil'.

Sufi writers of the tenth and eleventh centuries implicitly expound a history whereby Sufism developed out of an earlier renunciant movement, the subject of the previous chapters. They mostly ignore the disreputable Sufis of the early ninth century and before, such as these various commanders of good and forbidders of evil. There are some exceptions. The *rūḥānīyah* ('spiritualists') are denounced by the heresiographer al-Malaṭī (d. 377/987–8), perhaps quoting the earlier Egyptian heresiographer Khushaysh ibn Aṣram (d. 253/867). He names two advocates of adultery and drinking alcohol, among other enormities: Rabāḥ and Kulayb.[36] The latter is presumably the same as the Kulayb on al-Jāḥiẓ' short list of Sufi renunciants (*al-ṣūfīyah min al-nussāk*).[37] One may doubt whether heresiographical invective is good evidence for their actual doctrine, but it is good evidence of Sufis in disrepute for antinomianism. 'Rabāḥ' presumably indicates Riyāḥ ibn ʿAmr al-Qaysī (d. 170s/787–97?), a Basran sometimes associated with Rābiʿah al-ʿAdawīyah.[38] The critic Abū Zurʿah (d. Ray, 264/878) accepted him as a well-intentioned (*ṣadūq*) traditionist but Abū Dāwūd (d. Basra, 275/889) accused him of *zandaqah* (secret unbelief).[39] He nevertheless appears in Abū Nuʿaym's *Ḥilyat al-awliyāʾ* and some other surveys of the retrospectively legitimate

34 Al-Khaṭīb al-Baghdādī, *Tārīkh Baghdād* 10:157–8 *11:394*.

35 Abū Nuʿaym, *Ḥilyah* 10:159; al-Kindī, *Governors*, 162; Masʿūdī, *Murūj* 4:314–16; *Wakīʿ*, *Akhbār al-quḍāh* 3:240; Ṣūlī, *Awrāq*, 366.

36 Malaṭī, *Widerlegung*, 73–4 *93–4*; also Massignon, *Recueil*, 7.

37 Jāḥiẓ, *Bayān* 1:366.

38 For the name, see Ibn Ḥajar, *Tabṣīr* 2:588. For biographies, see Dhahabī, *Siyar* 8:174–5, with further references.

39 Ibn Ḥajar, *Lisān* 2:469.

precursors to the classical Sufis. There is no record that he was called a Sufi, but he shows that the literature of the Sufi period does not entirely suppress the memory of disreputable eighth-century renunciants.

There was at least one Sufi among the disciples of Aḥmad ibn Ḥanbal (d. 241/855): Abū Ḥamzah al-Baghdādī (d. 263/877?), whom Aḥmad would ask, 'What do you say about it, Sufi?' Later, his was the second circle of Sufis in the Friday mosque of Baghdad.[40] Other disciples of Aḥmad's were at least important to the later Sufis, if not Sufis themselves, although more prominent were disciples who continued the old renunciant tradition, including his named successor, ʿAbd al-Wahhāb (d. 251/865?).[41] They are evidence of Sufis, so called, increasingly prominent in Sunni circles in the mid-ninth century.

The earliest unambiguously Sunni Sufis seem to have formed the circle around Abū Ḥātim al-ʿAṭṭār (Basran, d. 260s/874–84). Ibn al-Aʿrābī names four of his followers, whom he characterizes as 'Sufis of the mosque, adherents of the *sunnah* and hadith, given to austerity (*nusuk*) and commanding good and forbidding evil. They had weight and prestige in the city.'[42] 'Commanding good and forbidding evil' connects them with the rowdy pre-classical Sufis but Abū Ḥātim's innovative talk of *ishārāt* ('allusions', a Sufi technical term) and his consistently interiorizing piety, as in calling for wandering by the heart (*al-siyāḥah bi-al-qulūb*), suggest the quietist Sufism to come.[43] There are some intersections between it and the circle of al-Junayd in Baghdad in the late ninth century. By one report, Abū Ḥātim al-ʿAttār was even one of al-Junayd's teachers.[44] Significantly, Abū Ḥātim al-ʿAṭṭār's circle did not attract the hostility from traditionalist Sunnis that was about to make trouble for Sufi mystics in Baghdad.

> In the mosque was a group of people who repudiated the people love (*ahl al-maḥabbah*) on account of what they heard of them by way of confusion (*takhlīṭ*). They were adherents of hadith, all taking dictation from Abū Ḥātim and pleased by his talk on account of its softness and on account of his advocating the *sunnah* and opposing the Ghassānīyah.[45]

---

40 Ibn Abī Yaʿlá, *Ṭabaqāt* 1:268–9 *2:234–6*; Dhahabī, *Siyar* 12:581, based on Ibn al-Aʿrābī, *Ṭabaqāt al-nussāk*.

41 See Melchert, 'Ḥanābila', esp. 355–9.

42 Dhahabī, *Tārīkh* 20 (261–280 H.): 212.

43 Dhahabī, *Tārīkh* 20:212, evidently quoting Ibn al-Aʿrābī for *siyāḥah* and expressly al-Sulamī for *ishārāt*, evidently in *Tārīkh al-ṣūfiyah*, since Abū Ḥātim is not mentioned in *Ṭabaqāt al-ṣūfiyah*. On wandering from place to place in the renunciant tradition, disapproved of by middle-of-the-road Sunnis of the late ninth century, see Melchert, 'Three qur'anic terms', 90–6. On *ishārah* as a technical term, see Sarrāj, *Lumaʿ*, 223–4, 337–8.

44 Sulamī, *apud* Dhahabī, *Tārīkh* 20:212. See further Melchert, 'Baṣran origins', 234–40.

45 Ibn al-Aʿrābī, *apud* Dhahabī, *Tārīkh* 20:212.

The confusion referred to will be of God and creation, on which more to come. 'Softness' (*riqqah*) commonly refers to the opposite of hardness, mainly of hearts—the point here, I take it, is that Abū Ḥātim's preaching stirred up feelings of penitence. 'Ghassānīyah', finally, seems to be a textual corruption, obviously naming some rejected sect but precisely which I am not sure.

Abū al-Ḥasan al-Būshanjī (d. 348/959–60) famously said of 'Sufism', 'It is a name without a reality. It used to be a reality without a name.'[46] The historian's problem of having only names to deal with means that a reality without a name, such as *mysticism*, may be difficult to pin down. It also indicates the problem of transition periods, when names such as *Sufism* will be applied inconsistently to different things.

Al-Būshanjī's regard for a past reality without a name brings up a third historiographical difficulty. Mystics are used to having grace come at them through things of the world. I have told students that a mystic will find meaning in a telephone directory. Sufis such as al-Būshanjī easily found earlier teaching useful to them and interpreted earlier writers as Sufis like themselves. There is nothing surprising in, say, al-Sulamī's including in his biographical dictionary of Sufis (*Ṭabaqāt al-ṣūfīyah*) various early renunciants who were not known as Sufis in their lifetimes. It seems to me self-evident that careful historical scholarship will avoid applying the term 'Sufi' to such persons as al-Muḥāsibī and the Egyptian Dhū al-Nūn who were not known as Sufis in their own lifetimes, however much their teaching and examples were valued by the later Sufi tradition. Intersection must be distinguished from congruence.

The Inquisition of Ghulām Khalīl

Mystical claims provoked new hostility from ascetics. The most spectacular manifestation of hostility was the Sufi Inquisition of Ghulām Khalīl (d. 275/888), a Basran traditionist and popular preacher who came from Wasit to Baghdad at the beginning of 264/Fall 877 and whose Inquisition took place the same year.[47] A conflict was already under way in Basra between traditionalist renunciants (*nussāk, ahl al-ḥadīth*), used to enjoining the good and forbidding the bad, and 'the people of love' (*ahl al-maḥabbah*). The people of love asserted that their love of

---

46 See Karamustafa, *Sufism*, 100, 111n.

47 See Gramlich, *Alte Vorbilder* 1:383–5, s.v. Abū al-Ḥusayn al-Nūrī. The date is from Dhahabī, *Siyar* 14:71, quoting Abū Nuʿaym, although the date is not in *Ḥilyah* 10:250, nor the same passage as quoted by al-Khaṭīb al-Baghdādī, *Tārīkh* 5:133–4 *6:335–6*.

God was such that fear had fallen away from them.[48] In Baghdad, Ghulām Khalīl began to preach against the people of love, asserting that one might love fellow creatures but that God must be feared. (Al-Sulamī reports an exculpatory story by which he was taken in by a women whom Sumnūn ibn Ḥamzah [d. *ca* 298/910–11] had refused to marry, who accused the Sufis of meeting with her every night to do the forbidden.[49]) He appealed to both the court and the general, who admired him for his austerity.[50] At last, Ghulām Khalīl prevailed on the mother-in-law of the shadow caliph, al-Muwaffaq, to make the *muḥtasib* follow his orders, so he provided him with a list of seventy-odd Baghdadis to be arrested. Most of them hid, some were arrested and imprisoned for a time. Al-Junayd himself escaped arrest by asserting that he was not a Sufi at all but a student of Abū Thawr's jurisprudence.[51] Abū al-Ḥusayn al-Nūrī (d. Baghdad, 295/907–8), famous for saying, 'I love God and God loves me (*aʿshaqu Allāh wa-Allāh yaʿshaqunī*)', was among those arrested.[52] Stories are told of al-Nūrī's addressing the qadi so graciously that he became unwilling to execute them, then addressing the caliph such that he released them altogether.[53] The happy ending is cast in doubt by al-Nūrī's leaving Baghdad to reside in al-Raqqah for fourteen years, as we shall see: either he deeply feared re-arrest or the story of his graceful address is a fiction.

Classical Sufism

Although no one was put to death, the round-up had to be scary. Al-Junayd went on to develop a language to deal with mystical experience that would not offend more old-fashioned ascetics. Abū Ḥātim al-ʿAṭṭār sounds mystical when quoted as saying, 'You need to repent of your repentance and worship God for him, not for you.'[54] This is a far cry from the call for continuous awareness of one's sin that

48 This account of the Inquisition and its Basran antecedents based mainly on Ibn al-Aʿrābī, *Ṭabaqāt al-nussāk*, *apud* Dhahabī, *Tārīkh* 20 (261–280 H.): 212, 277; cf. Dhahabī, *Siyar* 13:284.

49 Sulamī, *Sufi inquiries*, 55.

50 Ibn al-Nadīm lists Ghulām Khalīl among the renunciants and Sufis in his *Fihrist* 1:663, while al-Khaṭīb al-Baghdādī reports that he was vegetarian, *Tārīkh* 5:80 *6:248*.

51 Ibn al-Jawzī, *Talbīs*, 225; *Devil's delusion*, *Islamic culture* 10 (1936): 367. There seems to be independent confirmation of Junayd's study under Abū Thawr. See Sulamī, *Ṭabaqāt*, 141; Abū Nuʿaym, *Ḥilyah* 10:255; al-Khaṭīb al-Baghdādī, *Tārīkh* 7:242 *8:169*. However, it is doubted by Halm, *Ausbreitung*, 40–1.

52 Sarrāj, *Pages*, 5.

53 Gramlich summarizes five versions: *Alte Vorbilder* 1:384. There are similar stories of Dhū al-Nūn before the caliph al-Mutawakkil; e.g., al-Khaṭīb al-Baghdādī, *Tārīkh* 8:393–5 *9:374–7*.

54 Dhahabī, *Tārīkh* 20 (261–280 H.): 211.

characterizes renunciant thought in the previous century. But Abū Ḥātim also worked at a trade (selling perfume) and would say that there was a saying appropriate to every state.[55] It may have been a willingness to say different things to different audiences and his devotion to allusive speech (Sulamī is quoted as saying that he was the first in Iraq to speak of that science) that kept in his circle both Sufis and those who opposed 'the people of love'.[56] Al-Junayd is sometimes accused of being double-faced. Notably, al-Nūrī is quoted as telling him, 'You have cheated them, and so they have given you the place of honour. I addressed them sincerely, and so they threw stones at me.'[57]

The more usual characterization of al-Junayd has been to credit him with developing a Sufism of sobriety as against Abū Yazīd's drunken style. The tradition goes back to Hujvīrī (d. Lahore, 465/1072–3?).[58] It has been objected that al-Junayd admired Abū Yazīd and lectured on his *shaṭaḥāt*.[59] Al-Sarrāj quotes a series of his explanations for Abū Yazīd's apparently scandalous sayings.[60] What I would stress as historically important is not mainly that al-Junayd was comfortable with Abū Yazīd's mysticism but that he undertook to make it unthreatening to ascetics.

A. J. Arberry says of al-Junayd's writing, 'His style is involved to the point of obscurity.'[61] This obscurity, along with heavy reliance on allusions, also presumably helped shield him from criticism by non-mystics. Notably, al-Junayd also proposed triads like separation-union-separation (*farq-jamʿ-farq*) and subsistence-annihilation-subsistence (*baqāʾ-fanāʾ-baqāʾ*) to replace the old dichotomies (e.g., *farq-jamʿ*). One spoke of the first sobriety, seeing the world in common daylight, followed by the drunkenness of ecstatic absorption by God, followed by the second sobriety, in which one was conscious of the world again but in a way transformed by the experience of drunkenness. Thus a mystic could speak of his union with God in a way that recognized the validity of his experience but also reassured the ascetical-minded that he recognized divine transcendence. Al-Junayd also pushed mysticism in an inward direction, offering a style of mystical piety that would not interfere so clearly with the collection of hadith, the study of jurisprudence, making a living, and so on. Tension between mystics and ascetics

55 Dhahabī, *Tārīkh* 20 (261–280 H.): 212.
56 Dhahabī, *Tārīkh* 20 (261–280 H.): 212.
57 Abū Nuʿaym, *Ḥilyah* 10:251–2; Massignon, *Passion* 1:79.
58 Hujvīrī, *Kashf al-maḥjūb*, 230, 235 *185*, *189*.
59 Sarrāj, *Lumaʿ*, 346, remarked by Ernst, *Words of ecstasy*, 11, 50. See also Mojaddedi, 'Getting drunk with Abū Yazīd'.
60 Sarrāj, *Lumaʿ*, 380–7.
61 *EI*², s.v. 'Djunayd', by Arberry.

did not go away, and the prominent Sufis al-Ḥallāj and Ibn ʿAṭāʾ were put to death in 309/922. However, whereas al-Junayd was molested in the Inquisition of Ghulām Khalīl, he was left alone when al-Ḥallāj was first arrested.[62]

The Sufi biographer Abū Saʿīd ibn al-Aʿrābī (d. Mecca, 340/952?) relates a discussion of terminology that passed between him and al-Nūrī in 270/883–4, six years after the Inquisition of Ghulām Khalīl, when al-Nūrī was still a refugee in al-Raqqah. Al-Nūrī asked about al-Junayd, so Ibn al-Aʿrābī told him of the new talk of second separation and sobriety. Al-Nūrī affirmed that the so-called second separation was really an aspect of joining. In other words, al-Junayd had merely coined new words to describe the familiar mystical experience.[63]

Another eight years later (278/891–2), Ibn al-Aʿrābī and two friends spotted al-Nūrī in Baghdad. The older mystic was initially reluctant to associate with Sufis. Memories of betrayal at the Inquisition must have rankled. However, they eventually persuaded him to come to their mosque, where they spent the night. On the next Friday, they took a boat to where al-Junayd was. At first, everyone welcomed al-Nūrī, and he and al-Junayd traded reminiscences and joked with each other. Then all the Sufis sat for a formal discussion. Al-Junayd urged al-Nūrī to address the first question, but al-Nūrī declined, saying, 'I am just come, and prefer to listen.' Al-Junayd and the others spoke a while longer, then again pressed al-Nūrī to talk, but he said, 'You have used terms (*alqāb*) that I do not know, and talk in a fashion I am not used to. Let me listen and get to know what you mean.' Al-Junayd's terminology was unfamiliar to him.

At last, someone asked him about the separation (*farq*) that comes after the joining (*jamʿ*), what its signs were, and what was the difference between it and the first separation. Al-Nūrī resorted to ambiguity: 'It is not one aspect of joining,' he said, 'nor is it sobering up from joining, but they return to what they know.' The Sufis Ruwaym and Ibn ʿAṭāʾ complained that al-Nūrī was asserting something and its contrary. Al-Junayd begged them not to be unkind to al-Nūrī, who might have become senile. In the upshot, concludes Ibn al-Aʿrābī,

> Abū al-Ḥusayn (al-Nūrī) withdrew from all of them and spurned them. He became ill and went blind. He stuck to the deserts and graveyards. ... I have heard a number say that for

62 Ḥallāj has attracted much attention. Massignon, *Passion*, looks at his life from a religious point of view. Ernst, *Words*, 102–10, proposes a political interpretation of his prosecution. Arjomand, 'Crisis', stresses Shiʿism.

63 This and the following based on Dhahabī, *Siyar* 14:74–5, based in turn on Ibn al-Aʿrābī, *Ṭabaqāt al-nussāk*.

> anyone who had seen al-Nūrī since his return from al-Raqqah without having seen him before that might as well not have seen him at all, on account of his changing (God have mercy on him).

Such was the pitiful end of a mystic who could speak only of joining and drunkenness, not knowing how to speak the sophisticated new language of the second separation, the second sobriety, and so on.

Loose ends

The transition from early renunciation to Sufism was inevitably uneven. For a start, it may be useful to consider continuity and discontinuity. A notable point of continuity was austere living: Sufis were known for 'eating little, speaking little, sleeping little, and withdrawal from people', all typical activities of the early renunciants as well. When Ruwaym asked for some water on a hot day, a slave girl exclaimed, 'A Sufi who drinks during the day!' and threw down the jug of water she was carrying. Ever after, Ruwaym fasted by day, evidently living up to the normal expectation.[64] Moderate austerity remained until modern times an important part of ideal deportment among all Muslims. And of course respect for the law continued to be a feature of Sufism as of renunciant piety before it. As al-Junayd says, echoing al-Muḥāsibī, 'they fear lest, knowing what they are required to do for God (*wājib al-ḥuqūq*), they may suffer some vain conceit to enter into the performance of their dues.'[65] I remember an Egyptian woman's explaining to me what it meant to be *mutaṣawwifah*—in effect, 'scrupulously observant', as in always wearing long sleeves.

As for discontinuity, mysticism meant more tolerance of hierarchy: masters and disciples, full- and part-time devotees, initiates and non-initiates. The expectation of communion with God was a greater point of discontinuity, which explains why it was precisely this issue over which Sufis were attacked at the Inquisition of Ghulām Khalīl. So were some Sufi practices, notably 'audition' (*samāʿ*), the cultivation of rapture by listening to music, which seems to have burgeoned from about the middle of the ninth century. More significant is the theoretical elaboration of the mystical path. The renunciants of old collected stories and sayings, but it was especially the Sufis who seem to have sat about trading definitions of technical terms and only Sufis (except for al-Muḥāsibī, it appears) who wrote treatises.

---

64 Sarrāj, *Lumaʿ*, 163; cf. Qushayrī, *Epistle*, 48.
65 Junayd, *Dawāʾ al-arwāḥ*, 224 (Ar.), 230 (trans.).

Although they reportedly had masters and disciples in common and are quoted complementarily, al-Junayd is sometimes opposed in the tradition to Abū al-Ḥusayn al-Nūrī. For example, al-Nuri is quoted as saying, 'I wanted to see one of these miracles. I took a cane from some boys and stood between two boats. Then I said, "By your mightiness, if a three-pound fish does not come out to me, let me drown myself." Then there came out to me a fish weighing three pounds.' When al-Junayd heard of this, he said, 'It should have been a snake come out to him in order to bite him.'[66] Al-Junayd is wary, here, that miracle-working may encourage self-importance.

To the contrary tendency, we are told that one day

> Nūrī said to Junayd, who had decided reluctantly to speak in public and was lecturing in a theoretical mystical vocabulary, while he, Nūrī, was preaching out of fraternal devotion: 'You defraud them, and they have let you sit in their pulpits, but as for me, who wanted to warn their souls, they have thrown me into the rubbish heap.'[67]

Al-Junayd visited al-Nūrī when he was ill; later al-Nūrī visited al-Junayd when he was ill—but then al-Nūrī not only sat by his bedside, he also laid his hand on his forehead and cured him.[68] Ahmet T. Karamustafa suggests that al-Nūrī represents a more populist, demonstrative line of Sufi teaching and practice, perhaps continuing the line of al-Kharrāz a little before him and anticipating ʿAbd Allāh-i Anṣārī (d. 481/1089) and others after him.[69]

As for the spread of Sufism, two parties of the pious seem to have contested supremacy in Nishapur (today in northeastern Iran) in the later ninth century, the undemonstrative Malāmatīyah and the more populist Karāmīyah. Sufism, so-called, was evidently introduced from Baghdad by Abū Bakr al-Wāsiṭī (d. after 320/932), although his teaching was soon reinforced by Nishapurans who had travelled to Baghdad and back, notably Abū ʿAlī al-Thaqafī (d. Nishapur, 328/940).[70] By the early eleventh century, it had absorbed the Malāmati tendency and

66 Sarrāj, *Lumaʿ*, 327; Qushayrī, *Epistle*, 369. On Sufi suspicion of miracles, see Geoffroy, 'Attitudes contrastées'.

67 Massignon, *Passion* 1:79, quoting from Kalābādhī, *Taʿarruf*, 112.

68 Al-Khaṭīb al-Baghdādī, *Tārīkh* 5:132 *6:333–4*, apparently drawing on Sulamī, *Tārīkh al-ṣūfīyah*.

69 Karamustafa, *Sufism*, 93–6, 101–6.

70 Who introduced Sufism to Khurasan according to Qushayrī, *Epistle*, 63 (but disagreeing with Knysh's translation: he has 'It was during his lifetime that Sufism appeared in Nishapur', whereas I take *wa-bihi ẓahara al-taṣawwuf fī Naysābūr* to indicate active responsibility).

perhaps the Karāmi as well, inasmuch as the *khānaqāh* began as a Karāmi institution but continued as a central Sufi one from the eleventh century.[71] At the beginning of the tenth century, Khurasani writers al-Sulamī and al-Khargūshī distinguish between the doctrines of the Khurasanis and the Baghdadis, Malāmatīyah and Sufis, but later in the century al-Sīrjānī and al-Qushayrī do not. The first Andalusian to be called a Sufi was an ʿAbd Allāh ibn Naṣr (d. 315/927–8).[72] Biographers mention miracle workers in North Africa from early on but not Sufis until much later.[73]

In Basra, Sahl al-Tustarī seems to have stood apart from Abū Ḥātim al-ʿAṭṭār and his circle.[74] Sahl's doctrine was maintained and extended for a time by Ibn Sālim (d. 350s/961–70) and the Sālimi school. Abū Ṭālib al-Makkī (d. 386/996), *Qūt al-qulūb*, probably represents the culmination of Sālimi doctrine. The school seems to have been absorbed by Baghdadi Sufism after him. The magnificent synthesis of al-Ghazālī (d. 505/1111), *Iḥyāʾ ʿulūm al-dīn*, is heavily reliant on the *Qūt* in many places (without acknowledgement).

Sahl al-Tustarī and the Basran tradition after him make a good example of the distorting effect of Sufi spread and consolidation, for Sufi writers like al-Sarrāj quote Sahl as though he had been at the centre of the Sufi movement of his time, not its periphery. (Massignon inferred rather that al-Sarrāj was himself a leading Sālimi, implying that he was an outsider who saw something attractive in Sufism.[75]) The effect of such quotation is to disguise disagreement. Overlooking disagreement came easily to Sufi historians, who as mystics were used to discovering meaning in almost everything and so could easily see the affinity of Sahl's teaching with their own ideas. However, it forces responsible modern scholars to read Sufi histories against the grain.

To conclude, the Sufis managed to absorb and continue the earlier renunciant tradition by making renunciation an early stage in the progress of a Sufi and a continuing outward observance of all Sufis. Circumstances forced some such adjustment of the original renunciant programme. With the expansion of the

---

71 The Karāmīyah owe their fame first to Massignon, *Essay*, 171–83, the Malāmatīyah to ʿAfīfī (his student), *al-Malāmatīyah*. Their rivalry with the Karāmīyah was developed by Chabbi, 'Remarques'. See also Melchert, 'Sufis and competing movements in Nishapur', with references to other studies, to which add Thibon, *Oeuvre*, Silvers, *Soaring minaret*, and Sviri, *Perspectives*, chap. 5.

72 Marín, 'Early development', 85.

73 See for a start Cornell, *Realm of the saint*.

74 For discussions of what distinguished his doctrine from that of al-Junayd and the Baghdadis, see Baldick, *Mystical Islam*, 39–40, and Karamustafa, *Sufism*, 38–43.

75 Massignon, *Passion* 2:130.

community and differentiation of roles within it, single-minded, unremitting seriousness ceased to be viable as the one model of Islamic piety. Doubtless the Sufi literary tradition is far richer than the renunciant tradition before it. But the renunciant tradition certainly put its stamp on the foundational literature of Islam, the Qur'an and hadith, and its attraction is strong even today. (On my last trip to Damascus, I came across three editions of Aḥmad ibn Ḥanbal, *al-Zuhd*, in bookstores, none of any collection of his legal opinions.) Making it a subordinate part of Sufism, Muslims preserved it as a possibility for those attracted to a piety of single-minded, unremitting seriousness. But of course it means something different when it is not a majority pursuit. The Islamic State in northern Iraq from 2014 attempted to restore a conquest society but it was horrible in new ways because its context was so different. Max Weber observed that modern conditions are not conducive to saintliness. This evidently goes for those Muslims who nonetheless aim at saintliness in the renunciant and Sufi traditions alike.

Works cited

Primary sources

ʿAbd al-Jabbār, al-Qāḍī (d. Ray? 415/1025?). *Faḍl al-iʿtizāl*. Pages 129–350 in Fuʾād Sayyid, editor and compiler. *Faḍl al-iʿtizāl wa-ṭabaqāt al-muʿtazilah*. Tunis: al-Dār al-Tūnusīyah lil-Nashr, 1393/1974.

ʿAbd Allāh ibn Aḥmad (d. Baghdad, 290/903). *Masāʾil al-imām Aḥmad ibn Ḥanbal*. Edited by Zuhayr al-Shāwīsh. Beirut: al-Maktab al-Islāmī, 1401/1981.

ʿAbd Allāh ibn Aḥmad. *Kitāb al-Sunnah*. Edited by ʿAbd Allāh ibn Ḥasan ibn Ḥusayn. Mecca: al-Maṭbaʿah al-Salafīyah, 1349. Also edited by Abū ʿAbd Allāh ʿĀdil ibn ʿAbd Allāh Āl Ḥamdān. Silsilat kutub al-sunnah wa-al-iʿtiqād 1. N.p.: n.p., 1437. References to the latter edition in *italic*.

ʿAbd al-Malik ibn Ḥabīb (d. Cordova, 238/853?). *Kitāb al-Taʾrīj*. Edited by Jorge Aguadé. Fuentes arábico-hispanas 1. Madrid: Consejo Superior de Investigaciones Cientificas, Instituto de Cooperación con el Mundo Árabe, 1991.

ʿAbd al-Razzāq (d. 211/827). *Al-Muṣannaf*. Edited by Ḥabīb al-Raḥmān al-Aʿẓamī. Min manshūrāt al-Majlis al-ʿIlmī 39. 11 vols. Beirut: Majlis Ilmi, 1390–2/1970–2.

ʿAbd al-Razzāq. *Al-Tafsīr*. Edited by ʿAbd al-Muʿṭī Amīn Qalʿajī. 2 vols. Beirut: Dār al-Maʿrifah, 1411/1991

Abū al-ʿArab (d. Qayrawan, 333/945). *Classes des savants de l'Ifrîqîya*. Edited by Mohammed ben Cheneb. Publications de la Facultée des lettres d'Alger, Bulletin de Correspondance africaine, 51. Paris: Leroux, 1915.

Abū al-ʿArab. *Kitāb al-Miḥan*. Edited by Yaḥyá Wahīb al-Jabbūrī. Beirut: Dār al-Gharb al-Islāmī, 1403/1983. Reprinted 1408/1988.

Abū al-Qāsim al-Baghawī (d. 317/929). *Al-Jaʿdīyāt*. Edited by Rifʿat Fawzī ʿAbd al-Muṭṭalib. 2 vols. Cairo: Maktabat al-Khānjī, 1415/1994.

Abū al-Qāsim al-Balkhī (d. Balkh, 319/931?). *'Bāb Dhikr al-muʿtazilah'*. Pages 57–119 in *Faḍl al-iʿtizāl wa-ṭabaqāt al-muʿtazilah*. Compiled and edited by Fuʾād Sayyid. Tunis: al-Dār al-Tūnusīyah, 1393/1974.

Abū al-Qāsim al-Balkhī. *Qabūl al-akhbār wa-maʿrifat al-rijāl*. Edited by Abū ʿAmr al-Ḥusaynī ibn ʿUmar ibn ʿAbd al-Raḥīm. 2 vols. Beirut: Dār al-Kutub al-ʿIlmīyah, 1421/2000.

Abū al-Shaykh (d. 369/979). *Kitāb al-ʿAẓamah*. Edited by Riḍā Allāh Muḥammad Idrīs al-Mubārakafūrī. 5 vols. Riyadh: Dār al-ʿĀṣimah, 1411–19.

Abū al-Shaykh. *Ṭabaqāt al-muḥaddithīn bi-Iṣbahān*. Edited by ʿAbd al-Ghafūr ʿAbd al-Ḥaqq Ḥusayn al-Balūshī. 4 vols. Beirut: Muʾassasat al-Risālah, 1987–92.

Abū Bakr al-Mālikī (d. Qayrawan, *ca* 463/1061–2). *Kitāb Riyāḍ al-nufūs fī ṭabaqāt ʿulamāʾ al-Qayrawān wa-Ifrīqīyah*. Edited by Bashīr al-Bakkūsh. Supervised by Muḥammad al-ʿArūsī al-Muṭṭawwī. 3 vols. Beirut: Dār al-Gharb al-Islāmī, 1401–3/1981–3.

Abū Dāwūd (d. Basra, 275/889). *Kitāb Masāʾil al-imām Aḥmad*. Edited by Muḥammad Bahjah al-Bayṭār. Cairo: Dār al-Manār, 1353/1934. Reprinted Beirut: Muḥammad Amīn Damj, n.d.

Abū Dāwūd. *Al-Sunan*. Edited by Muḥammad Muḥyī al-Dīn ʿAbd al-Ḥamīd. 4 vols. Cairo: Maṭbaʿat Muṣṭafá Muḥammad, 1354.

Abū Dāwūd. *Al-Zuhd*. Edited by Muṣṭafá Maḥmūd Ḥusayn. Tanta: Maktabat Dār al-Ḍiyāʾ li-Taḥqīq al-Turāth, 1424/2003.

https://doi.org/10.1515/9783110617962-012

Abū Khaythamah Zuhayr ibn Ḥarb (d. 234/849?). *Kitāb al-ʿIlm*. Pages 109–49 in *Min kunūz al-sunnah: rasāʾil arbaʿah*. Edited by Muḥammad Nāṣir al-Dīn al-Albānī. Damascus: al-Maṭbaʿah al-ʿUmūmīyah, 1966. Reprinted separately Beirut: al-Maktab al-Islāmī, 1403/1983.

Abū Nuʿaym al-Iṣbahānī (d. Isfahan, 430/1038). *Geschichte Iṣbahāns nach der Leidener Handschrift*. Edited by Sven Dedering. 2 vols. Leiden: E. J. Brill, 1931, 1934.

Abū Nuʿaym al-Iṣbahānī. *Ḥilyat al-awliyāʾ wa-ṭabaqāt al-aṣfiyāʾ*. 10 vols. Cairo: Maṭbaʿat al-Saʿādah and Maktabat al-Khānjī, 1352–7/1932–8. '< Aḥ., *Zuhd*' and '< ʿAl., *Zuhd*' indicate passages apparently quoted from lost sections of Aḥmad ibn Ḥanbal, *al-Zuhd*, or an addition to it by its redactor, ʿAbd Allāh ibn Aḥmad.

Abū Nuʿaym al-Iṣbahānī. *Maʿrifat al-ṣaḥābah*. Edited by Muḥammad Ḥasan Muḥammad Ḥasan Ismāʿīl and Musʿad ʿAbd al-Ḥamīd al-Saʿdanī. 5 vols. Beirut: Dār al-Kutub al-ʿIlmīyah, 1422/2002.

Abū Nuʿaym al-Iṣbahānī. *Al-Musnad al-mustakhraj ʿalá Ṣaḥīḥ al-imām Muslim*. Edited by Muḥammad Ḥasan Muḥammad Ḥasan Ismāʿīl al-Shāfiʿī. 4 vols. Beirut: Dār al-Kutub al-ʿIlmīyah, 1417/1996.

Abū ʿUbayd al-Qāsim ibn Sallām (d. Mecca, 224/838–9?). *Kitāb al-Amwāl*. Edited by Muḥammad Khalīl al-Harrās. Cairo: Maktabat al-Kullīyāt al-Azharīyah, 1388/1968. Also published as *The book of revenue*. Translated by Imran Ahsan Khan Nyazee. Reading: Garnet, 2003. References to the latter edition in *italic*.

Abū ʿUbayd al-Qāsim ibn Sallām. *Faḍāʾil al-Qurʾān*. Edited by Marwān al-ʿAṭīyah, Muḥsin Kharābah, and Wafāʾ Taqī al-Dīn. Damascus: Dār Ibn Kathīr, 1415/1995.

Abū ʿUbayd al-Qāsim ibn Sallām. *Gharīb al-ḥadīth*. Edited by Muḥammad ʿAbd al-Muʿīd Khān. 4 vols. Al-Silsilah al-jadīdah min maṭbūʿāt dāʾirat al-maʿārif al-ʿuthmānīyah 92. Hyderabad: Maṭbaʿat Majlis Dāʾirat al-Maʿārif al-ʿUthmānīyah, 1396/1976. Reprinted Beirut: Dār al-Kitāb al-ʿArabī, n.d.

Abū ʿUbayd al-Qāsim ibn Sallām. *Al-Khuṭab wa-al-mawāʿiẓ*. Edited by Ramaḍān ʿAbd al-Tawwāb. Maktabat Abī ʿUbayd al-Qāsim ibn Sallām 1. Cairo: Maktabat al-Thaqāfah al-Dīnīyah, 1406/1986.

Abū Yūsuf (d. Baghdad, 182/798?). *Kitāb al-Kharāj*. Bulaq: al-Maṭbaʿah al-Mīrīyah, 1302. In margin: al-Shaybānī, *al-Jāmiʿ al-ṣaghīr*.

Abū Zurʿah al-Dimashqī (d. Damascus, 280/893–4). *Al-Tārīkh*. Edited by Shukr Allāh Niʿmat Allāh al-Qawjānī. 2 vols. Damascus: Majmaʿ al-Lughah al-ʿArabīyah, 1980.

Aḥmad ibn Ḥanbal (d. Baghdad, 241/855). *Kitāb al-ʿIlal wa-maʿrifat al-rijāl*. Edited by Waṣī Allāh ibn Muḥammad ʿAbbās. 4 vols. Beirut: al-Maktab al-Islāmī, 1988. The recension of ʿAbd Allāh ibn Aḥmad, also published as part of *Kitāb al-Jāmiʿ fī al-ʿilal wa-maʿrifat al-rijāl* (1:69–354 and 2). Edited by Muḥammad Ḥusām Bayḍūn. 2 vols. Beirut: Muʾassasat al-Kutub al-Thaqāfīyah, 1410/1990. References to the latter edition in *italic*. Additions noted from the redactor, ʿAbd Allāh ibn Aḥmad.

Aḥmad ibn Ḥanbal. *Musnad imām al-muḥaddithīn*. 6 vols. Cairo: al-Maṭbaʿah al-Maymanīyah, 1313/1895. Also published as *Musnad al-imām Aḥmad ibn Ḥanbal*. Edited by Shuʿayb al-Arnaʾūṭ, &al. 50 vols. Beirut: Muʾassasat al-Risālah, 1413–21/1993–2001. References to the latter edition in *italic*. Additions noted from the redactor, ʿAbd Allāh ibn Aḥmad.

Aḥmad ibn Ḥanbal. *Al-Zuhd*. Edited by ʿAbd al-Raḥmān ibn Qāsim. Mecca: Maṭbaʿat Umm al-Qurá, 1357, reprinted Beirut: Dār al-Kutub al-ʿIlmīyah, 1396/1976. Also reprinted with different pagination Beirut: Dār al-Kutub al-ʿIlmīyah, 1403/1983. References to the latter edition in *italic*. A slightly different recension edited by Muḥammad Jalāl Sharaf. 2 vols.

Beirut: Dār al-Nahḍah al-ʿArabīyah, 1401/1981. Additions noted from the redactor, ʿAbd Allāh ibn Aḥmad.
Al-Ahwāzī. See under al-Iskāfī.
Al-Bājī (d. Almeria, 474/1081). *Al-Muntaqá*. Edited by Muḥammad ibn ʿAbbās ibn Shaqrūn. 7 vols in 4. Cairo: Maṭbaʿat al-Saʿādah, 1331–2. Reprinted n.p.: Dār al-Fikr al-ʿArabī, n.d.
Al-Bājī. *Sunan al-ṣāliḥīn wa-sanan al-ʿābidīn*. Edited by Ibrāhīm Bājis ʿAbd al-Majīd. 2 vols. Beirut: Dār Ibn Ḥazm, 1424/2003.
Al-Barqī (d. 280/893–4?). *Kitāb al-Maḥāsin*. Edited by Jalāl al-Dīn al-Ḥusaynī. Tehran: Dār al-Kutub al-Islāmīyah, 1370. Reprinted Najaf: al-Maṭbaʿah al-Ḥaydarīyah, 1384/1964.
Al-Bayhaqī (d. Nishapur, 458/1066). *Kitāb al-Zuhd al-kabīr*. Edited by ʿĀmir Aḥmad Ḥaydar. Beirut: Dār al-Janān and Muʾassasat al-Kutub al-Thaqāfīyah, 1408/1987. Also translated by Roger Deladrière. *L'anthologie du renoncement:* Kitāb al-Zuhd al-Kabīr = *Le livre du renoncement*. Collection 'Islam spirituel'. Lagrasse: Verdier, 1995. References to the latter edition in *italic*.
Al-Bukhārī (d. Khartank, 256/870). *Al-Adab al-mufrad*. Edited by Muḥammad ʿAbd al-Qādir ʿAṭā. Beirut: Dār al-Kutub al-ʿIlmīyah, 1417/1996.
Al-Bukhārī. *Kitāb al-Tārīkh al-kabīr*. 4 vols in 8. Hyderabad: Maṭbaʿat Dāʾirat al-Maʿārif al-Niẓāmīyah, 1941–5. Reprinted Hyderabad: Maṭbaʿat Dāʾirat al-Maʿārif al-ʿUthmānīyah, 1377/1958. Reprinted with added index volume, Beirut: Dār al-Kutub al-ʿIlmīyah, n.d.
Al-Dārimī (d. Nishapur, 253/867?). *Al-Musnad al-jāmiʿ*. Edited by Nabīl ibn Hāshim ʿAbd Allāh al-Ghamrī. Beirut: Dār al-Bashāʾir al-Islāmīyah, 1434/2013.
Al-Dhahabī (d. Damascus, 748/1348?). *Siyar aʿlām al-nubalāʾ*. Edited by Shuʿayb al-Arnaʾūṭ, &al. 25 vols. Beirut: Muʾassasat al-Risālah, 1401–9/1981–8.
Al-Dhahabī. *Tārīkh al-islām*. Edited by ʿUmar ʿAbd al-Salām Tadmurī. 52 vols. Beirut: Dār al-Kitāb al-ʿArabī, 1407–21/1987–2000.
Farīd al-Dīn ʿAṭṭār (*fl.* 12th cent.?). *The Tadhkiratu 'l-awliya ("Memoirs of the saints")*. Edited by Reynold A. Nicholson. 2 vols. London: Luzac, 1905–7.
Al-Fasawī (d. Basra, 277/890). *Kitāb al-Maʿrifah wa-al-tārīkh*. Edited by Akram Ḍiyāʾ al-ʿUmarī. 4 vols. 3rd edition. Medina: Maktabat al-Dār, 1410/1989.
Al-Ghazālī, Abū Ḥāmid (d. Tus, 505/1111). *Iḥyāʾ ʿulūm al-dīn*. 4 vols. N.p.: ʿĪsá al-Bābī al-Ḥalabī wa-Shurakāʾuh, n.d.
Al-Ḥakīm al-Tirmidhī (d. *ca* 295/907–8?). *Bayān al-kasb*. With *Ādāb al-murīdīn*. Edited by ʿAbd al-Fattāḥ ʿAbd Allāh Barakah. Maktabat al-Ḥakīm al-Tirmidhī. N.p.: Maṭbaʿat al-Saʿādah, n.d.
Al-Ḥakīm al-Tirmidhī. *The concept of sainthood in early Islamic mysticism: two works by al-Ḥakīm al-Tirmidhī*. Edited and translated by Bernd Radtke and John O'Kane. Curzon Sufi series. Richmond: Curzon, 1996.
Hammām ibn Munabbih (attributed; d. 131/748–9?). *Ṣaḥīfat Hammām ibn Munabbih*. Edited by Muḥammad Ḥamīd Allāh. *Revue de l'Académie Arabe de Damas* 28 (1953/1372–3): 96–116, 270–81, 443–67.
Hannād ibn al-Sarī (d. Kufa, 243/857). *Kitāb al-Zuhd*. Edited by ʿAbd al-Raḥmān ibn ʿAbd al-Jabbār al-Farīwāʾī. 2 vols. Kuwayt: Dār al-Khulafāʾ lil-Kitāb al-Islāmī, 1406/1985.
Ḥarb al-Kirmānī (d. 280/893–4). *Masāʾil al-imām Aḥmad ibn Muḥammad ibn Ḥanbal wa-Isḥāq ibn Rāhūyah*. Edited by Nāṣir ibn Suʿūd ibn ʿAbd Allāh al-Salāmah. Riyadh: Maktabat al-Rushd, 1425/2004.
Hujvīrī (d. Lahore, 465/1072–3?). *Kashf al-maḥjūb*. Edited by Valentin Zhukovskii. Leningrad: Gosydarstvennaya Akademicheskaya Telegrafeya, 1926. Reprinted n.p.: Muʾassasah-i

Maṭbūʿātī Amīr-i Kabīr, n.d. Translated by Reynold A. Nicholson. *The Kashf al-maḥjúb: The Oldest Persian Treatise on Ṣúfism*. Leiden: E. J. Brill and London: Luzac & Co., 1911. References to the latter edition in *italic*.

Ibn Abī al-Dunyā (d. Baghdad, 281/894). *Kitāb Dhamm al-dunyā*. Edited by Ella Almagor. The Max Schloessinger memorial series, texts, 6. Institute of Asian and African Studies, the Hebrew University of Jerusalem. Jerusalem: Magnes Press, 1984.

Ibn Abī al-Dunyā. *Al-Jūʿ*. Edited by Muḥammad Khayr Ramaḍān Yūsuf. Beirut: Dār Ibn Ḥazm, 1417/1997.

Ibn Abī al-Dunyā. *Muḥāsabat al-nafs*. Edited by Majdī al-Sayyid Ibrāhīm. Cairo: Maktabat al-Qurʾān, n.d.

Ibn Abī al-Dunyā. *Kitāb Mujābī al-daʿwah*. With *Qiṣaṣ al-ṣāliḥīn*. Bombay: al-Dār al-Qayyimah, 1391/1972. Also edited by Majdī al-Sayyid Ibrāhīm. Cairo: Maktabat al-Qurʾān, 1987. References to the latter edition in *italic*.

Ibn Abī al-Dunyā. *Qiṣar al-amal*. Edited by Muḥammad Khayr Ramaḍān Yūsuf. Beirut: Dār Ibn Ḥazm, 1416/1995.

Ibn Abī al-Dunyā. *Al-Riqqah wa-al-bukāʾ*. Edited by Musʿad ʿAbd al-Ḥamīd Muḥammad al-Saʿdānī. Maktabat Ibn Abī al-Dunyā. Cairo: Maktabat al-Qurʾān, n.d.

Ibn Abī al-Dunyā. *Kitāb al-Tahajjud wa-qiyām al-layl*. Edited by Muṣliḥ ibn Jazāʾ ibn Fadghūsh al-Ḥārithī. Riyadh: Maktabat al-Rushd, 1418/1998.

Ibn Abī al-Dunyā. *Al-Tawāḍuʿ wa-al-khumūl*. Edited by Muḥammad ʿAbd al-Qādir ʿAṭā. Beirut: Dār al-Kutub al-ʿIlmīyah, 1409/1989.

Ibn Abī al-Wafāʾ (d. Cairo, 775/1373). *Al-Jawāhir al-muḍīyah fī ṭabaqāt al-ḥanafīyah*. Edited by ʿAbd al-Fattāḥ Muḥammad al-Ḥulw. 5 vols. Cairo: Dār Iḥyāʾ al-Kutub al-ʿArabīyah, 1398–1408/1978–88. Reprinted Giza: Hajr, 1413/1993.

Ibn Abī Ḥātim (d. Ray, 327/938). *Kitāb al-Jarḥ wa-al-taʿdīl*. 9 vols. Hyderabad: Jamʿīyat Dāʾirat al-Maʿārif al-ʿUthmānīyah, 1360–71. Reprinted Beirut: Dār Iḥyāʾ al-Turāth al-ʿArabī, n.d.

Ibn Abī Khaythamah (d. Baghdad, 279/892?). *Al-Tārīkh al-kabīr*. Edited by Ṣalāḥ ibn Fatḥī Halal. 2 vols. Cairo: al-Fārūq al-Ḥadīthah, 1424/2004.

Ibn Abī Shaybah, Abū Bakr (d. Kufa, 235/849). *Kitāb al-Muṣannaf*. Edited by ʿAbd al-Khāliq Khān al-Afghānī. 14 vols. Hyderabad: al-Maṭbaʿah al-ʿAzīzīyah, 1386/1966 (1) and Bombay: al-Dār al-Salafīyah, n.d.-1403/1983 (2–15). Also edited by Ḥamad ʿAbd Allāh al-Jumʿah and Muḥammad Ibrāhīm al-Luḥaydān. 16 vols. Riyadh: Maktabat al-Rushd, 1425/2004. References to the latter edition in *italic*.

Ibn Abī Yaʿlá ibn al-Farrāʾ (d. Baghdad, 526/1133). *Ṭabaqāt al-ḥanābilah*. Edited by Muḥammad Ḥāmid al-Fiqī. 2 vols. Cairo: Maṭbaʿat al-Sunnah al-Muḥammadīyah, 1371/1952. Also edited by ʿAbd al-Raḥmān ibn Sulaymān al-ʿUthaymīn. 3 vols. N.p.: al-Amānah al-ʿāmmah lil-iḥtifāl bi-murūr miʾat ʿām ʿalá taʾsīs al-mamlakah, 1419/1999. References to the latter edition in *italic*.

Ibn Abī Zayd al-Qayrawānī (d. Qayrawan, 386/996?). *Kitāb al-Jāmiʿ*. Edited by Muḥammad Abū al-ʿAjfān and ʿUthmān Bittīkh. Min turāthinā al-islāmī 17. Beirut: Muʾassasat al-Risālah and Tunis: al-Maktabah al-ʿAtīqah, 1402/1982.

Ibn Abī Zayd al-Qayrawānī. *Al-Nawādir wa-al-ziyādāt*. Edited by ʿAbd al-Fattāḥ al-Ḥulw, &al. 15 vols. Beirut: Dār al-Gharb al-Islāmī, 1999.

Ibn al-Aʿrābī (d. Mecca, 340/952?). *Kitāb fīhi maʿná al-zuhd wa-al-maqālāt wa-ṣifāt al-zāhidīn*. Edited by Khadījah Muḥammad Kāmil with ʿĀmir al-Najjār. Cairo: Dār al-Kutub, 1998.

Ibn al-Jawzī (d. Baghdad, 597/1201). *Manāqib al-imam Aḥmad ibn Ḥanbal*. Edited by Muḥammad Amīn al-Khānjī al-Kutubī. Cairo: Maṭbaʿat al-Saʿādah, 1349. Also edited by

ʿAbd Allāh ibn ʿAbd al-Muḥsin al-Turkī and ʿAlī Muḥammad ʿUmar. Cairo: Maktabat al-Khānjī, 1979. Reprinted Cairo: Hajr, 1409/1988. References to the latter edition in *italic*.

Ibn al-Jawzī. *Al-Muntaẓam fī tārīkh al-mulūk wa-al-umam*. Edited by Muḥammad ʿAbd al-Qādir ʿAṭā and Muṣṭafá ʿAbd al-Qādir ʿAṭā, with Naʿīm Zarzūr. 18 vols. Beirut: Dār al-Kutub al-ʿIlmīyah, 1412/1992.

Ibn al-Jawzī. *Al-Quṣṣāṣ wa-al-mudhakkirīn*. Edited and translated by Merlin L. Swartz. Buḥūth wa-dirāsāt bi-idārat Maʿhad al-ādāb al-sharqīyah. Beirut: Dār al-Mashriq, 1971.

Ibn al-Jawzī. *Kitāb Ṣifat al-ṣafwah*. 4 vols. Hyderabad: Maṭbaʿat Majlis Dāʾirat al-Maʿārif al-ʿUthmānīyah, 1355–6.

Ibn al-Jawzī. *Talbīs Iblīs*. Edited by ʿIṣām Fāris al-Ḥarastānī. Beirut: al-Maktab al-Islāmī, 1414/1994. Translated by D. S. Margoliouth as *"The Devil's delusion" by Ibn al-Jauzi*, *Islamic culture* 9 (1935): 1–21, 187–208, 377–99, 533–57; 10 (1936): 29–39, 169–92, 339–68, 633–47; 11 (1937): 267–73, 393–403, 529–33; 12 (1938): 108–18, 235–40, 352–64, 447–58; 19 (1945): 69–81, 171–88, 272–89, 376–83; 20 (1946): 58–71, 181–90, 297–310, 408–22; 21 (1947): 73–9, 172–83, 394–402; 22 (1948): 75–86.

Ibn al-Jazarī (d. Shiraz, 833/1429). *Ghāyat al-nihāyah fī ṭabaqāt al-qurrāʾ*. Edited by Gotthelf Bergsträßer, indexes by Otto Pretzl. 3 vols. Cairo: Maktabat al-Khānjī, 1351–2/1932–3. Reprinted Baghdad: Maktabat al-Muthanná, n.d. Also reprinted Beirut: Dār al-Kutub al-ʿIlmīyah, 1400/1980.

Ibn al-Mubārak (d. Hit, 181/797). *Kitāb al-Jihād*. Edited by Nazīh Ḥammād. Beirut: Dār al-Nūr, 1391/1971. Reprinted with different pagination but the same item numbers Beirut: al-Maktabah al-ʿAṣrīyah, 1409/1988.

Ibn al-Mubārak. *Al-Zuhd wa-al-raqāʾiq*. Edited by Ḥabīb al-Raḥmān al-Aʿẓamī. Malegaon: Majlis Iḥyāʾ al-Maʿārif, 1386. Reprinted with different pagination but the same item numbers Beirut: Dār al-Kutub al-ʿIlmīyah, 1419/1998. Additions noted from the redactor al-Ḥusayn ibn al-Ḥasan, likewise items found only in the recension of Nuʿaym ibn Ḥammād.

Ibn al-Murtaḍá (d. Dhofar, 840/1437). *Die Klassen der Muʿtaziliten*. Edited by Susanna Diwald-Wilzer. Bibliotheca Islamica 21. Wiesbaden: Franz Steiner, 1961.

Ibn al-Nadīm (d. 380/990?). *Kitāb al-Fihrist*. Edited by Ayman Fuʾād Sayyid. 4 vols. Silsilat al-nuṣūṣ al-muḥaqqaqah. 2nd edition. London: Muʾassasat al-Furqān lil-Turāth al-Islāmī, 1435/2014.

Ibn ʿAsākir (d. Damascus, 571/1176). *Tārīkh madīnat Dimashq*. Edited by Muḥibb al-Dīn Abū Saʿīd ʿUmar ibn Gharāmah al-ʿAmrawī. 80 vols. Beirut: Dār al-Fikr, 1415/1995.

Ibn Baṭṭāl, ʿAlī ibn Khalaf (d. 449/1057). *Sharḥ* Ṣaḥīḥ *al-Bukhārī*. Edited by Abū Anas Ibrāhīm ibn Saʿīd al-Ṣabīḥī and Abū Tamīm Yāsir ibn Ibrāhīm. 11 vols. Riyadh: Maktabat al-Rushd, 1423/2003.

Ibn Ḥajar al-ʿAsqalānī (d. Cairo, 852/1449). *Lisān* al-Mīzān. 7 vols. Hyderabad: Majlis Dāʾirat al-Maʿārif, 1329–31. Reprinted Beirut: Muʾassasat al-Aʿlamī, 1406/1986.

Ibn Ḥajar al-ʿAsqalānī. *Tabṣīr al-muntabih bi-taḥrīr* al-Mushtabih. Edited by ʿAlī Muḥammad al-Bijāwī, supervised by Muḥammad ʿAlī al-Najjār. Turāthunā. 4 vols. Cairo: al-Dār al-Miṣrīyah lil-Taʾlīf wa-al-Tarjamah, 1964?–7. Reprinted Beirut: al-Maktabah al-ʿIlmīyah, n.d.

Ibn Ḥajar al-ʿAsqalānī. *Kitāb Tahdhīb* al-Tahdhīb. 12 vols. Hyderabad: Majlis Dāʾirat al-Maʿārif al-Niẓāmīyah, 1325–7. Reprinted Beirut: Dār Ṣādir, n.d.

Ibn Hāniʾ al-Naysābūrī (d. Baghdad, 275/888–9). *Masāʾil al-imām Aḥmad ibn Ḥanbal*. Edited by Zuhayr al-Shāwīsh. 2 vols. Beirut: al-Maktab al-Islāmī, 1400.

Ibn Ḥibbān (d. Bust, 354/965). *Kitāb al-Majrūḥīn*. Edited by Maḥmūd Ibrāhīm Zāyid. 3 vols. Aleppo: Dār al-Waʿy, 1396.

Ibn Ḥibbān. *Al-Thiqāt*. Edited by Muḥammad ʿAbd al-Muʿīd Khān. 9 vols. Hyderabad: Maṭbaʿat Dāʾirat al-Maʿārif al-ʿUthmānīyah, 1393–1403/1973–83.

Ibn Hishām (d. Old Cairo, 218/833). *Al-Sīrah al-nabawīyah*. Edited by Ṭāhā ʿAbd al-Raʾūf Saʿd. 4 vols. Cairo: Maktabat al-Kullīyāt al-Azharīyah, 1974. Translated by A. Guillaume as *The life of Muhammad*. London: Godfrey Cumberledge and Oxford University Press, 1955.

Ibn Mājah (d. Qazvin, 273/887). *Al-Sunan*. Edited by Muḥammad Fuʾād ʿAbd al-Bāqī. 2 vols. Cairo: Dār Iḥyāʾ al-Kutub al-ʿArabīyah, 1952–4.

Ibn Māzah, Burhān al-Dīn (d. 616/1219–20). *Al-Muḥīṭ al-burhānī fī al-fiqh al-nuʿmānī*. Edited by ʿAbd al-Karīm Sāmī al-Jundī. 9 vols. Beirut: Dār al-Kutub al-ʿIlmīyah, 2004/1424.

Ibn Qutaybah (d. Baghdad, 276/889?). *Taʾwīl mukhtalif al-ḥadīth*. Edited by Muḥammad Zuhrī al-Najjār. Cairo: Maktabat al-Kullīyāt al-Azharīyah, 1386/1966.

Ibn Qutaybah. *ʿUyūn al-akhbār*. 4 vols. Cairo: Dār al-Kutub al-Miṣrīyah, 1343–9/1925–30.

Ibn Saʿd (d. Baghdad, 230/845). *Kitāb al-ṭabaqāt al-kabīr*. Edited by Eduard Sachau, &al. 9 volumes in 15. Leiden: E. J. Brill, 1904–40. Also published as *al-Ṭabaqāt al-kubrá*. 9 vols. Beirut: Dār Ṣādir, 1957–68. References to the latter edition in *italic*.

Ibn Saʿd. *Al-Ṭabaqāt al-kubrá: al-qism al-mutammim li-tābiʿī ahl al-Madīnah wa-man baʿdahum*. Edited by Ziyād Muḥammad Manṣūr. Silsilat iḥyāʾ al-turāth 6. Medina: al-Jāmiʿah al-Islāmīyah and al-Majlis al-ʿIlmī, 1403/1983.

Al-ʿIjlī (d. Tripoli, 261/874–5). *Tārīkh al-thiqāt*. Arranged by ʿAli ibn Abī Bakr al-Haythamī (d. Cairo, 807/1405). Additions by Ibn Ḥajar al-ʿAsqalānī (d. Cairo, 852/1449). Edited by ʿAbd al-Muʿṭī Qalʿajī. Beirut: Dār al-Kutub al-ʿIlmīyah, 1405/1984.

Al-ʿIrāqī, Zayn al-Dīn (d. Cairo, 806/1414). *Al-Bāʿith ʿalá al-khalāṣ min ḥawādith al-quṣṣāṣ*. Edited by Muḥammad ibn Luṭfī al-Ṣabbāgh. Riyadh: Dār al-Warrāq , 1422/2001.

Al-Iskāfī, Ibn Hammām (d. 336/948). *Al-Tamḥīṣ*. With al-Ḥusayn ibn Saʿīd al-Ahwāzī (*fl.* first half, 9th cent.), *al-Muʾmin*. Qum: Madrasat al-Imām al-Mahdī, 1404/1363 sh.

Ismāʿīl ibn Isḥāq (d. Baghdad, 282/893). *Al-Juzʾ min aḥādīth Ayyūb al-Sakhtiyānī*. Edited by Sulaymān ibn ʿAbd al-ʿAzīz al-ʿUraynī. Riyadh: Maktabat al-Rushd, 1418/1998.

ʿIyāḍ, al-Qāḍī (d. Marrakech, 544/1149). *Tartīb al-madārik wa-taqrīb al-masālik li-maʿrifat aʿlām madhhab Mālik*. Edited by Muḥammad ibn Tāwīt al-Ṭanjī (1), ʿAbd al-Qādir al-Ṣaḥrāwī (2–4), Muḥammad ibn Sharīfah (5), and Saʿīd Aḥmad Aʿrāb (6–8). 8 vols. Ribāṭ, &c.: Maṭbaʿat Faḍālah, &c., 1966–83.

Al-Jāḥiẓ (d. Basra, 255/868–9). *Al-Bayān wa-al-tabyīn*. Edited by ʿAbd al-Salām Muḥammad Hārūn. Maktabat al-Jāḥiẓ 2. 4 vols. Cairo: Maṭbaʿat Lajnat al-Taʾlīf wa-al-Tarjamah wa-al-Nashr, 1367–9/1948–50.

Al-Jāḥiẓ. Untitled epistle. Edited by Charles Pellat. *Al-Machriq* 47 (1953): 281–303.

Al-Junayd (d. Baghdad, 298/910?). *Dawāʾ al-arwāḥ*. Edited and translated by A. J. Arberry as 'The book of the cure of souls', *Journal of the Royal Asiatic Society* 69/2 (1937): 219–31.

Al-Kalābādhī, Abū Bakr (d. 380/990–1?). *Kitāb al-Taʿarruf li-madhhab ahl al-taṣawwuf*. Edited by A. J. Arberry. Cairo: Maktabat al-Khānjī, 1352/1933. Reprinted 1415/1994. Also translated by Arthur John Arberry as *The doctrine of the Sufis*. Cambridge: University Press, 1935.

Al-Kashshī (d. *ca* 340/951). *Al-Rijāl*. Edited by Aḥmad al-Ḥusaynī. Karbalāʾ: Muʾassasat al-Aʿlamī lil-Maṭbūʿāt, n.d.

Kawsaj, Isḥāq ibn Manṣūr (d. Nishapur, 251/865). *Masāʾil al-imām Aḥmad ibn Ḥanbal wa-Isḥāq ibn Rāhawayh*. Edited by Abū al-Ḥusayn Khālid ibn Maḥmūd al-Rabāṭ, Wiʾām al-Ḥawshī, and Jumʿah Fatḥī. 2 vols. Riyadh: Dār al-Hijrah, 1425/2004.

Khalīfah ibn Khayyāṭ (d. Basra? 240/854–5?). *Kitāb al-Ṭabaqāt*. Edited by Suhayl Zakkār. Damascus: Wizārat al-Thaqāfah, 1967. 2nd edition Beirut: Dār al-Fikr, 1414/1993.

Khalīfah ibn Khayyāṭ. *Al-Tārīkh*. Edited by Suhayl Zakkār. Iḥyā' al-turāth al-qadīm 19. 2 vols. Damascus: Wizārat al-Thaqāfah, 1968.

Al-Khalīlī (d. Qazvīn? 446/1055). *Al-Irshād fī ma'rifat 'ulamā' al-ḥadīth*. Abridged by al-Silafī (d. Alexandria, 576/1180). Edited by 'Āmir Aḥmad Ḥaydar. Mecca: al-Shāmīyah, 1993/1414.

Al-Khallāl (d. Baghdad, 311/923). *Kitāb al-Ḥathth 'alá al-tijārah*. Edited by Abū 'Abd Allāh Maḥmūd ibn Muḥammad al-Ḥaddād. Riyadh: Dār al-'Āṣimah, 1407.

Al-Kharkūshī (d. Nishapur, 407/1016?). *Kitāb Tahdhīb al-asrār*. Edited by Bassām Muḥammad Bārūd. Abu Dhabi: al-Majma' al-Thaqāfī, 1999. Also edited by Sayyid Muḥammad 'Alī. Beirut: Dār al-Kutub al-'Ilmīyah, 2006/1427. References to the latter edition in *italic*.

Al-Khaṣṣāf (d. Baghdad, 261/874). *Kitāb Aḥkām al-awqāf*. N.p.: Maṭba'at Dīwān 'Umūm al-Awqāf al-Miṣrīyah, 1322/1904.

Al-Khaṭīb al-Baghdādī (d. Baghdad, 463/1071). *Kitāb al-Kifāyah fī 'ilm al-riwāyah*. Hyderabad: Dā'irat al-Ma'ārif al-'Uthmānīyah, 1357. Also edited by Aḥmad 'Umar Hāshim. Beirut: Dār al-Kitāb al-'Arabī, 1985. References to the latter edition in *italic*.

Al-Khaṭīb al-Baghdādī. *Tārīkh Baghdād aw Madīnat al-Salām*. 14 vols. Cairo: Maktabat al-Khānjī, 1349/1931. Reprinted Cairo: Maktabat al-Khānjī and Beirut: Dār al-Fikr, n.d. Also published as *Tārīkh Madīnat al-Salām wa-akhbār muḥaddithīhā wa-dhikr quṭṭānihā al-'ulamā' min ghayr ahlihā wa-wāridīhā*. Edited by Bashshār 'Awwād Ma'rūf. 17 vols. Beirut: Dār al-Gharb al-Islāmī, 1422/2001. References to the latter edition in *italic*.

Al-Khuttalī (d. *ca* 260/873–4). *Kitāb al-Maḥabbah lillāh*. Pages 45–194 in *Materialien zur alten islamischen Frömmigkeit*. Edited by Bernd Radtke. Basic texts of Islamic mysticism 2. Leiden: Brill, 2009.

Al-Kindī (d. Old Cairo, 350/961?). *The governors and judges of Egypt*. Edited by Rhuvon Guest. E. J. W. Gibb memorial series 19. Leiden: E. J. Brill, 1912.

Al-Kulaynī (d. Baghdad, 329/941?). *Al-Kāfī*. Edited by 'Alī Akbar al-Ghaffārī, corrected by Muḥammad al-Ākhundī. 8 vols. Tehran: Dār al-Kutub al-Islāmīyah, 1389, 1391.

Al-Malaṭī (d. Ashkelon, 377/987–8). *Die Wiederlegung der Irrgläubigen und Neuerer*. Edited by Sven Dedering. Bibliotheca Islamica 9. Istanbul: Staatsdruckerei, 1936. Also published as *al-Tanbīh wa-al-radd 'alá ahl al-ahwā' wa-al-bida'*. Edited by Muḥammad Zāhid ibn al-Ḥasan al-Kawtharī. (Cairo:) Maktab Nashr al-Thaqāfah al-Islāmīyah, 1368/1949. Reprinted Cairo: al-Maktabah al-Azharīyah lil-Turāth, 1418/1997. References to the latter edition in *italic*.

Al-Maqdisī (Muqaddasī; *fl.* 375/985). *Aḥsan al-taqāsīm fī ma'rifat al-āqālīm*. Edited by M. J. De Goeje. Bibliotheca geographorum Arabicorum 3. Leiden: E. J. Brill, 1877.

Al-Marrūdhī (d. 275/888). *Akhbār al-shuyūkh wa-akhlāqihim*. Edited by 'Āmir Ḥasan Ṣabrī. Silsilat al-ajzā' wa-al-kutub al-ḥadīthīyah 35. Beirut: Dār al-Bashā'ir al-Ḥadīthīyah, 1426/2005.

Al-Marrūdhī. *Kitāb al-Wara'*. Edited by Zaynab Ibrāhīm al-Qārūṭ. Beirut: Dār al-Kutub al-'Ilmīyah, 1403/1983. Also edited by Muḥammad al-Sayyid Basyūnī Zaghlūl. Beirut: Dār al-Kitāb al-'Arabī, 1409/1988. References to the latter edition in *italic*.

Al-Mas'ūdī (d. Old Cairo, 345/956–7?). *Murūj al-dhahab wa-ma'ādin al-jawhar*. Edited by C. A. C. Barbier de Meynard and B. M. M. Pavet de Courteille. Revised by Charles Pellat. Manshūrāt al-Jāmi'ah al-lubnānīyah, qism al-dirāsāt al-tārīkhīyah, 11. Beirut: al-Jāmi'ah al-Lubnānīyah, 1973–4.

Al-Māwardī (d. Baghdad, 450/1058). *Al-Ḥāwī al-kabīr*. Edited by Maḥmūd Maṭrajī, &al. 24 vols. Beirut: Dār al-Fikr, 1414/1994.

Al-Māwardī. *Al-Nukat wa-al-ʿuyūn*. Edited by al-Sayyid ibn ʿAbd al-Maqṣūd ibn ʿAbd al-Raḥīm. 6 vols. Beirut: Dār al-Kutub al-ʿIlmīyah and Muʾassasat al-Kutub al-Thaqāfīyah, n.d.

Muʿāfá ibn ʿImrān (d. 185/801–2?). *Kitāb al-Zuhd*. With *al-Musnad*. Edited by ʿĀmir Ḥasan Ṣabrī. Silsilat al-ajzāʾ wa-al-kutub al-ḥadīthīyah 12–13. 2 volumes in 1. Beirut: Dār al-Bashāʾir al-Islāmīyah, 1420/1999.

Al-Mubarrad (d. Baghdad, 285/898?). *Al-Kāmil*. Edited by W. Wright. Leipzig: G. Kreysing, 1864. Also edited by Muḥammad Aḥmad al-Dālī. 3 vols. Beirut: Muʾassasat al-Risālah, 1406/1996. References to the latter edition in *italic*.

Al-Muḥāsibī (d. Baghdad? 243/857–8). *'Kitāb al-Khalwah'*, edited by Ighnāṭiyūs ʿAbduh Khalīfah, *al-Mashriq* 48 (1954): 182–191, 49 (1955): 43–54, 451–90.

Al-Muḥāsibī. *Al-Makāsib*. Pages 171–234 in *al-Masāʾil fī aʿmāl al-qulūb*. Edited by ʿAbd al-Qādir Aḥmad ʿAṭā. Cairo: ʿĀlam al-Kutub, 1969. Also published as *al-Makāsib*. Edited by ʿAbd al-Qādir ʿAṭā. Beirut: Muʾassasat al-Kutub al-Thaqāfīyah, 1407/1987. References to the latter edition in *italic*.

Al-Muḥāsibī. *Kitāb al-Riʿāya liḥuqūq Allāh*. Edited by Margaret Smith. E. J. W. Gibb memorial series, new series, 15. London: Luzac & Company, 1940. Also published as *al-Riʿāyah li-ḥuqūq Allāh*. Edited by ʿAbd al-Qādir ʿAṭā. Beirut: Dār al-Kutub al-ʿIlmīyah, n.d. References to the latter edition in *italic*.

Al-Muḥāsibī. *Sharḥ al-maʿrifah*. With *Badhl al-naṣīḥah*. Edited by Ṣāliḥ Aḥmad al-Shāmī. Damascus: Dār al-Qalam and Beirut: al-Dār al-Shāmīyah, 1413/1993.

Al-Muḥāsibī. *Kitab al-Tawahhum*. Edited by Arthur J. Arberry. Cairo: Association of Authorship, Translation and Publication Press, 1937. Also published as pages 387–443 in *al-Waṣāyā*. Edited by ʿAbd al-Qādir ʿAṭā. Beirut: Dār al-Kutub al-ʿIlmīyah, 146/1986.

Muslim (d. Nishapur, 261/875). *Al-Jāmiʿ al-ṣaḥīḥ*. Edited by Muḥammad Fuʾād ʿAbd al-Bāqī. 5 vols. Cairo: ʿĪsá al-Bābī al-Ḥalabī wa-Shurakāʾuh, 1374–5/1955–6.

Muwaffaq ibn Aḥmad al-Bakrī Khaṭīb Khwārizm (d. Khwārizm, 568/1172–3). *Manāqib al-imām al-aʿẓam Abī Ḥanīfah*. 2 vols. Hyderabad: Maṭbaʿat Majlis Dāʾirat al-Maʿārif al-Niẓāmīyah, 1321.

Al-Nasāʾī (d. al-Ramlah? 303/915?). *Al-Mujtabá*. Edited by Muḥammad ʿAṭāʾ Allāh al-Fūjayānī al-Amritsarī. Lahore: al-Maktabah al-Salafīyah, 1376, reprinted 1976.

Al-Nasāʾī. *Kitāb al-Sunan al-kubrá*. Edited by ʿAbd al-Ghaffār Sulaymān al-Bundārī and Sayyid Kisrawī Ḥasan. 7 vols. Beirut: Dār al-Kutub al-ʿIlmīyah, 1411/1991. Also edited by Ḥasan ʿAbd al-Munʿim Shalabī, supervised by Shuʿayb al-Arnaʾūṭ. 12 vols. Beirut: Muʾassasat al-Risālah, 1421/2001. Abbreviated as *SK*. References to the latter edition in *italic*.

Al-Qāḍī al-Nuʿmān (d. Cairo, 363/974). *Daʿāʾim al-islām*. Edited by ʿĀṣif ibn ʿAlī Aṣghar Fayḍī. 2 vols. Cairo: Dār al-Maʿārif, 1951, reprinted 1969.

Al-Qarāfī (d. Dayr al-Ṭīn, near Old Cairo, 684/1285). *Al-Dhakhīrah*. Edited by Muḥammad al-Ḥajjī (1, 8, 13), Saʿīd Aʿrāb (2, 6), and Muḥammad Būkhubzah (3–5, 7, 9–12). 14 vols. Beirut: Dār al-Gharb al-Islāmī, 1994.

The Qurʾān. Translated by Alan Jones. N.p.: Gibb Memorial Trust, 2007.

Al-Qurṭubī (d. Munyat Banī Khaṣīb, Upper Egypt, 671/1273?). *Al-Jāmiʿ li-aḥkām al-Qurʾān*. Edited by ʿAbd al-Razzāq al-Mahdī. 20 vols in 10. Beirut: Dār al-Kitāb al-ʿArabī, 1418/1997.

Al-Qushayrī (d. Nishapur, 465/1072). *Al-Qushayri's Epistle on Sufism = al-Risala al-qushayriyya fī ʿilm al-tasawwuf*. Translated by Alexander D. Knysh. Reviewed by Muhammad Eissa. Great books of Islamic civilisation. Reading: Garnet, 2007.

Al-Sa'dī, Abū al-Qāsim 'Abd Allāh ibn Muḥammad (*fl.* 11th cent.?). *Faḍā'il Abī Ḥanīfah wa-akhbāruhū wa-manāqibuh*. Edited by Laṭīf al-Raḥmān al-Bahrā'ijī al-Qāsimī. Mecca: al-Maktabah al-Imdādīyah, 1431/2010.

Al-Sam'ānī (d. Marv, 562/1166). *Kitāb al-Ansāb*. Edited by Muḥammad Aḥmad Ḥallāq. 4 vols. Beirut: Dār Iḥyā' al-Turāth al-'Arabī, 1419/1999.

Al-Sarakhsī, Muḥammad ibn Aḥmad (d. 483/1090–1?). *K. al-Mabsūṭ*. Edited by Muḥammad Rāḍī al-Ḥanafī. 30 vols in 13. Cairo: Maṭba'at al-Sa'ādah, 1324–31.

Al-Sarrāj (d. Nishapur? 378/988). *The Kitáb al-Luma' fi 'l-taṣawwuf*. Edited by Reynold Alleyne Nicholson. E. J. W. Gibb memorial series 22. Leiden: E. J. Brill and London: Luzac & Co., 1914. To be supplemented by *Pages from the* Kitāb al-Luma'. Edited by A. J. Arberry. London: Luzac, 1947.

Al-Ṣaymarī (d. Baghdad, 436/1045). *Akhbār Abī Ḥanīfah wa-aṣḥābih*. Silsilat al-maṭbū'āt 13. Hyderabad: Maṭba'at al-Ma'ārif al-Sharqīyah, 1394/1974. Reprinted Beirut: Dār al-Kitāb al-'Arabī, 1976.

Al-Shāfi'ī (d. Old Cairo, 204/820). *Al-Risālah*. Edited by Aḥmad Muḥammad Shākir. Cairo: Maṭba'at Muṣṭafá al-Bābī al-Ḥalabī wa-Awlādih, 1358/1940. Reprinted Beirut: n.p., n.d.

Al-Shāfi'ī. *Kitāb al-Umm*. 7 vols in 4. Bulaq: al-Maṭba'ah al-Kubrá al-Amīrīyah, 1321–5. Also edited by Rif'at Fawzī 'Abd al-Muṭṭalib. 11 vols. Al-Manṣūrah: Dār al-Wafā', 1422/2001. References to the latter edition in *italic*.

Shaqīq ibn Ibrāhīm (d. Kūlān, 194/809–10). *Ādāb al-'ibādāt*. Pages 15–22 in *Trois oeuvres inédites de mystiques musulmans, Šaqīq al-Balḫī, Ibn 'Aṭā, Niffarī*. Edited by Paul Nwyia. Recherches publiées sous la direction de l'Institut de lettres orientales de Beyrouth, Nouvelle série, A. Langue arabe et pensée islamique, 7. Beirut: Dar el-Machreq, 1973.

Al-Shaybānī (d. Ranbūyah, 189/804–5). *Kitāb al-Aṣl*. Edited by Mehmet Boynukalın. 13 vols. Beirut: Dār Ibn Ḥazm, 1433/2012.

Al-Shaybānī. *Kitāb al-Āthār*. Edited by Khālid al-'Awwād. Waqfīyat al-Muzaynī. 2 vols. Kuwayt: Dār al-Nawādir, 1429/2008. Reprinted 1432/2011.

Al-Shaybānī (attributed). *Kitāb al-Kasb*. With Ibn Taymīyah (d. Damascus, 728/1328), *Risālat al-ḥalāl wa-al-ḥarām*. Edited by 'Abd al-Fattāḥ Abū Ghuddah. Beirut: Dār al-Bashā'ir al-Islāmīyah and Aleppo: Maktab al-Maṭbū'āt al-Islāmīyah, 1417/1997. Reprinted Beirut: Maktab al-Maṭbū'āt al-Islāmīyah 1426/2005.

Sīrjānī (*fl.* first half 11th cent.). *Sufism, black and white: a critical edition of* Kitāb al-Bayāḍ wa-l-sawād *by Abū l-Ḥasan al-Sīrjānī (d. ca. 470/1077)*. Edited by Bilal Orfali and Nada Saab. Islamic history and civilization, studies and texts, 94. Leiden: Brill, 2012.

Al-Subkī, Taqī al-Dīn (d. Damascus, 756/1355?). *Al-Fatāwá*. 2 vols. Cairo: Maktabat al-Qudsī, n.d.

Sufyān al-Thawrī (d. Basra, 161/777?). *Al-Tafsīr*. Beirut: Dār al-Kutub al-'Ilmīyah, 1403/1983.

Al-Sulamī (d. Nishapur, 412/1021). *Early Sufi women: Dhikr an-niswa al-muta'abbidāt aṣ-Ṣūfiyyāt*. Edited and translated by Rkia Elaroui Cornell. Louisville, Ky.: Fons Vitae, 1999.

Al-Sulamī. *Sufi inquiries and interpretations*. With Ismā'īl ibn Nujayd (d. 366/976–7), *A treatise of traditions*. Edited by Bilal Orfali and Gerhard Bowering. Islamic studies. 2nd edition. Beirut: Dar el-Machreq, 2012.

Al-Sulamī. *Kitāb Ṭabaqāt al-ṣūfiyya*. Edited by Johannes Pedersen. Leiden: E. J. Brill, 1960.

Al-Ṣūlī (d. Basra, 336/947?). *Kniga listov* (*Kitāb al-Awrāq*). Edited by Anas Khalidov. Pamiatniki kul'tury Vostoka, Sankt-Peterburgskaia nauchnaia seriia 5. St. Petersburg: Tsentr 'Peterburgskoe Vostokovendenie', 1998.

Al-Thaʿlabī, Aḥmad ibn Muḥammad (d. Nishapur, 427/1035). *Die vom Koran Getöteten: aṯ-Ṯaʿlabīs* Qatlā l-Qurʾān *nach der Istanbuler und den Leidener Handschriften*. Edited and translated by Beate Wiesmüller. Arbeitsmaterialien zum Orient 12. Würzburg: Ergon 2002.

Al-Tirmidhī (d. Tirmidh, 279/892?). *Al-Jāmiʿ al-ṣaḥīḥ*. Edited by Aḥmad Muḥammad Shākir, Muḥammad Fuʾād ʿAbd al-Bāqī, and Ibrāhīm ʿAṭwah ʿAwaḍ. 5 vols. Cairo: Muṣṭafá al-Bābī al-Ḥalabī wa-Awlāduh, 1356–95/1937–75. Later reprinted with vols 4 and 5 (by ʿAwaḍ) replaced by a fourth volume edited by Kamāl Yūsuf al-Ḥūt. Beirut: Dār al-Kutub al-ʿIlmīyah, n.d.

Al-Ṭūsī Shaykh al-Ṭāʾifah (d. Najaf, 460/1067?). *Ikhtiyār maʿrifat al-rijāl*. Edited by Ḥasan al-Muṣṭafawī. Mashhad: Dānishgāh-i Mashhad, 1348.

Al-ʿUqaylī (d. Hijaz, 322/934). *Kitāb al-Ḍuʿafāʾ al-kabīr*. Edited by ʿAbd al-Muʿṭī Amīn Qalʿajī. 4 vols. Beirut: Dār al-Kutub al-ʿIlmīyah, 1404/1984.

Wakīʿ (d. Baghdad, 306/918). *Akhbār al-quḍāh*. Edited by ʿAbd al-ʿAzīz Muṣṭafá al-Marāghī. 3 vols. Cairo: Maṭbaʿat al-Istiqāmah, 1366–9/1947–50.

Wakīʿ ibn al-Jarrāḥ (d. Fayd, 197/812?). *Al-Zuhd*. Edited by ʿAbd al-Raḥmān ibn ʿAbd al-Jabbār al-Farīwāʾī. 3 vols in 2. Medina: Maktabat al-Dār, 1404/1984. Reprinted Riyadh: Dār al-Ṣumayʿī, 1415/1994.

Zayd ibn ʿAlī (d. Kufa, 120/738?). *Corpus iuris di Zaid ibn ʿAlī (VIII sec. cr.)*. Edited by Eugenio Griffini. Milan: Ultrico Hoepli, 1919.

Secondary sources

Abū al-Shabāb, Aḥmad ʿAwaḍ. *Al-Khawārij*. Beirut: Dār al-Kutub al-ʿIlmīyah, 2005/1426.

ʿAfīfī, Abū al-ʿAlāʾ. *Al-Malāmatīyah wa-al-ṣūfīyah wa-ahl al-futūwah*. Muʾallafāt al-Jamʿīyah al-Falsafīyah al-Miṣrīyah 5. Cairo: ʿĪsá al-Bābī al-Ḥalabī, 1364/1945.

Ahmed, Shahab. 'Ibn Taymiyyah and the Satanic Verses'. *Studia Islamica*, no 87 (1998), 67–124.

Andrae, Tor. 'Zuhd und Mönchtum. Zur Frage von den Beziehungen zwischen Christentum und Islam'. *Le monde oriental* 25 (1931): 296–327.

Akasoy, Anna, James E. Montgomery, and Peter E. Pormann, editors. *Islamic crosspollinations: interactions in the medieval Middle East*. N.p.: Gibb Memorial Trust, 2007.

Al-Sarhan, Saud. 'The creeds of Aḥmad ibn Ḥanbal'. Pages 29–44 in *Books and bibliophiles: studies in honour of Paul Auchterlonie on the bio-bibliography of the Muslim world*. Edited by Robert Gleave. N.p.: Gibb Memorial Trust, 2014.

Amir-Moezzi, Mohammad Ali. *The spirituality of Shiʿi Islam: beliefs and practices*. London: I. B. Tauris, 2011.

Ammann, Ludwig. *Vorbild und Vernunft: Die Regelung von Lachen und Scherzen im mittelalterlichen Islam*. Arabische Texte und Studien 5. Hildesheim: Georg Olms, 1993.

Arjomand, Said Amir. 'The crisis of the imamate and the institution of occultation in Twelver Shiʿism: a sociohistorical perspective'. *International journal of Middle East studies* 28 (1996): 491–515.

Armstrong, Lyall R. *The* quṣṣāṣ *of early Islam*. Islamic history and civilization, studies and texts, 139. Leiden: Brill, 2016.

ʿAthamina, Khalil. 'Al-Qasas: its emergence, religious origin and its socio-political impact on early Muslim society'. *Studia Islamica*, no 76 (1992), 53–74.

Aydinli, Osman. 'Ascetic and devotional elements in the Muʿtazilite tradition: the Sufī [*sic*] Muʿtazilites'. *Muslim world* 97 (2007): 174–89.
Baldick, Julian. *Mystical Islam*. London: I. B. Tauris, 1989.
Berg, Herbert. *The development of exegesis in early Islam: the authenticity of Muslim literature from the formative period*. Curzon studies in the Qurʾān. Richmond, Surrey: Curzon, 2000.
Bonner, Michael. 'Definitions of poverty and the rise of the Muslim urban poor'. *Journal of the Royal Asiatic Society*, series 3, 6 (1996): 335–44.
Bonner, Michael. 'The *Kitāb al-Kasb* attributed to al-Shaybānī: poverty, surplus, and the circulation of wealth'. *Journal of the American Oriental Society* 121 (2001): 410–27.
Bonner, Michael. 'Poverty and charity in the rise of Islam'. Pages 13–30 in *Poverty and charity in Middle Eastern contexts*. Edited by Michael Bonner, Mine Ener, and Amy Singer. SUNY studies in the social and economic history of the Middle East. Albany: State University of New York Press, 2003.
Bouyer, Louis. 'Mysticism/an essay on the history of the word'. Pages 42–55 in *Understanding mysticism*. Edited by Richard Woods. London: The Athlone Press, 1981.
Bowker, J. W. 'Intercession in the Qur'an and the Jewish tradition'. *Journal of Semitic studies* 11 (1966): 69–82.
Bravmann, Meïr M. '"The surplus of property": an early Arab social concept'. *Der Islam* 38 (1962): 28–50.
Brock, S. P. 'Early Syrian asceticism'. *Numen* 20 (1973): 1–19.
Brown, Jonathan A. C. *Hadith: Muhammad's legacy in the medieval and modern world*. Oxford: Oneworld, 2009.
Brown, Peter. *Power and persuasion in Late Antiquity*. Madison: University of Wisconsin Press, 1992.
Brown, Peter. 'The rise and function of the holy man in Late Antiquity'. *Journal of Roman studies* 61 (1971): 80–101.
Brown, Peter. 'The rise and function of the holy man in Late Antiquity, 1971–1997'. *Journal of early Christian studies* 6 (1998): 353–76.
Brown, Peter. 'The saint as exemplar in Late Antiquity'. *Representations* 1/2 (Spring 1983): 1–25.
Brunschvig, Robert. 'Métiers vils en Islam'. *Studia Islamica*, no 16 (1962), 41–60.
Calder, Norman. 'Ikhtilâf and ijmâʿ in Shâfiʿī's Risâla'. *Studia Islamica*, no 58 (1983), 55–81.
Calder, Norman. *Islamic jurisprudence in the Classical era*. Edited by Colin Imber. Cambridge: University Press, 2010.
Calder, Norman. 'The *qurrāʾ* and the Arabic lexicographical tradition'. *Journal of Semitic studies* 36 (1991): 297–307.
Calder, Norman. *Studies in early Muslim jurisprudence*. Oxford: Clarendon Press, 1993.
Calder, Norman. '*Tafsīr* from Ṭabarī to Ibn Kathīr: problems in the description of a genre, illustrated with reference to the story of Abraham'. Pages 101–40 in *Approaches to the Qurʾān*. Edited by G. R. Hawting and Abdul-Kader A. Shareef. Routledge/SOAS series on contemporary politics and culture in the Middle East. London: Routledge, 1993.
Caspar, R. 'Râbiʿa et le pur amour de Dieu'. *IBLA* (Tunis) 121 (1968): 71–95.
Chabbi, Jacqueline. 'Remarques sur le développment historique des mouvements ascétiques et mystiques au Khurasan'. *Studia Islamica*, no 46 (1977), 5–72.
Chaumont, Éric. 'Tout chercheur qualifié dit-il juste?' Pages 11–27 in *La controverse religieuse et ses forms*. Edited by Alain Le Boulluec. Patrimoines. Paris: Éditions du Cerf, 1995.

Chittick, William C. 'Weeping in classical Sufism'. Pages 132–44 in *Holy tears: weeping in the religious imagination*. Edited by Kimberley Christine Patton and John Stratton Hawley. Princeton: University Press, 2005.

Cohen, Hayyim J. 'The economic background and the secular occupations of Muslim jurisprudents and traditionists in the classical period of Islam (until the middle of the eleventh century)'. *Journal of the economic and social history of the Orient* 13 (1970): 16–61.

Colby, Frederick S. *Narrating Muḥammad's night journey*. Albany: State University of New York Press, 2008.

Conrad, Lawrence I. 'Medicine and martyrdom: some discussions of suffering and divine justice in early Islamic society'. Pages 212–36 in *Religion, health and suffering*. Edited by John R. Hinnells and Roy Porter. London: Kegan Paul International, 1999.

Cook, David. *Martyrdom in Islam*. Themes in Islamic history. Cambridge: University Press, 2007.

Cook, Michael. 'Activism and quietism in Islam: the case of the early Murjiʾa'. Pages 15–23 in *Islam and power*. Edited by Alexander S. Cudsi and Ali E. Hillal Dessouk. Croom Helm series on the Arab world. London: Croom Helm, 1981.

Cook, Michael. Commanding right and forbidding wrong in Islamic thought. Cambridge: University Press, 2000.

Cook, Michael. *The Koran*. Very short introductions 13. Oxford: University Press, 2000.

Cook, Michael. *Muhammad*. Past masters. Oxford: University Press, 1983.

Cooperson, Michael. *Classical Arabic biography*. Cambridge studies in Islamic civilization Cambridge: University Press, 2000.

Cooperson, Michael. 'Ibn Ḥanbal and Bishr al-Ḥāfī: a case study in biographical traditions'. *Studia Islamica*, no 86 (1997), 71–101.

Cornell, Vincent J. *Realm of the saint: power and authority in Moroccan Sufism*. Austin: University of Texas Press, 1998.

Crone, Patricia, and Martin Hinds. *God's caliph: religious authority in the first centuries of Islam*. University of Cambridge Oriental publications 37. Cambridge: University Press, 1986.

Crone, Patricia, and Fritz Zimmermann. *The epistle of Sālim ibn Dhakwān*. Oxford Oriental monographs. Oxford: University Press, 2001.

Crone, Patricia. '"Even an Ethiopian slave": the transformation of a Sunnī tradition'. *Bulletin of the School of Oriental and African Studies* 57 (1994): 59–67.

Crone, Patricia. *Medieval Islamic political thought*. Edinburgh: University Press, 2004.

Décobert, Christian. *Le mendiant et le combattant: l'institution de l'islam*. Paris: Éditions du Seuil, 1991.

De Crussol, Yolande. *Le rôle de la raison dans la réflexion éthique d'Al-Muḥāsibī: ʿaql et conversion chez al-Muḥāsibī (165–243/782–857)*. Paris: Consep, 2002.

De Jong, Frederick, and Bernd Radtke, editors. *Islamic mysticism contested: thirteen centuries of controversies and polemics*. Islamic history and civilization, studies and texts, 29. Leiden: Brill, 1999.

Denaro, Roberta. *Dal martire allo* šahīd*: fonti, problem e confronti per una martirografia islamica*. Centro alti studi in scienze religiose 4. Rome: Edizioni de Storia e Letteratura, 2006.

Denaro, Roberta. 'Definitions and narratives of martyrdom in Sunni hadith literature'. Pages 82–96 in *Twenty-first century jihad: law, society and military action*. Edited by Elisabeth Kendall and Ewan Stein. London: I. B. Tauris, 2015.

Denaro, Roberta. 'From Marw to the *ṯuġūr*: Ibn al-Mubārak and the shaping of a biographical tradition'. *Eurasian studies* 7 (2009): 125–44.

Donner, Fred M. *Muhammad and the believers: at the origins of Islam*. Cambridge, Mass.: Belknap Press of Harvard University Press, 2010.
Donner, Fred M. *Narratives of Islamic origins: the beginnings of Islamic historical writing*. Studies in Late Antiquity and early Islam 14. Princeton: Darwin Press, 1998.
Douglas, Mary. *Natural symbols: explorations in cosmology*. New York: Pantheon Books, 1970.
Douglas, Mary. *Purity and danger: an analysis of concepts of pollution and taboo*. London: Routledge & Kegan Paul, 1966.
During, Jean. 'Musique et rites: le *samāʿ*'. Pages 157–72 in *Les voies d'Allah: les ordres mystiques dans l'islam des origines à aujourd'hui*. Edited by Alexandre Popovic and Gilles Veinstein. Paris: Fayard, 1996.
Ebstein, Michael. 'D̲ū l-Nūn al-Miṣrī and early Islamic mysticism'. *Arabica* 61 (2014): 559–612.
Encyclopaedia Iranica (abbreviated *EIr*), s.vv. '*abdāl*', by J. Chabbi, and '*k̲ānaqāh*', by Gerhard Böwering and Matthew Melvin-Koushki.
Encyclopaedia Islamica, s.v. '*abdāl*', by Hussein La-Shay', translated by Farzin Negahban.
The encyclopaedia of Islam, new edn (abbreviated as *EI*²), s.vv. '*abdāl*', by I. Goldziher, slightly amended by H. J. Kissling, 'D̲junayd', by A. J. Arberry, 'ribāṭ', by J. Chabbi, '*ṣadaḳa*', by T. H. Weir and A. Zysow, '*s̲h̲ahīd*', by E. Kohlberg, '*taṣawwuf*', by B. Radtke, and '*waḳf*', § I., by R. Peters. *The encyclopaedia of Islam*, 3rd edn (abbreviated as *EI*³), s.v. 'asceticism', by Christopher Melchert.
The encyclopaedia of the Qurʾān (abbreviated as *EQ*), s.v. 'Intercession', by Valerie J. Hoffman.
Ernst, Carl W. *The Shambhala guide to Sufism*. Boston, Mass.: Shambhala, 1997.
Ernst, Carl W. *Words of ecstasy in Sufism*. Albany: State University of New York Press, 1985.
Ess, Josef van. 'Une lecture à rebours de l'histoire du muʿtazilisme'. *Revue des études islamiques* 46 (1978): 163–240, 47 (1979): 16–69.
Ess, Josef van. 'Le *miʿrāǧ* et la vision de Dieu'. Pages 99–116 in *Le voyage initiatique en terre d'Islam*. Directed by Mohammad Ali Amir-Moezzi. Bibliothèque de l'École des hautes études, section des sciences religieuses, 113. Louvain: Peeters, 1996.
Ess, Josef van. *Theologie und Gesellschaft im 2. und 3. Jahrhundert Hidschra. Eine Geschichte des religiösen Denkens im frühen Islam*. 6 vols. Berlin: Walter de Gruyter, 1991–95. Also *Theology and society in the second and third centuries of the Hijra: a history of religious thought in Early Islam*. Translated by John O'Kane and Gwendolin Goldbloom. 4 vols to date. Leiden: Brill, 2017. References to the latter edition in *italic*.
Ess, Josef van. *Ungenützte Texte zur Karrāmīya*. Sitzungsberichte der Heidelberger Akademie der Wissenschaften, philosophisch-historische Klasse; Jahrg. 1980, 6. Abhandlung. Heidelberg: Winter, 1980.
Al-Fayḍī, Muḥammad ibn Sālim ibn Sulaymān. *Al-Ṣūfīyah: nashʾatuhā wa-taṭawwuruhā*. N.p.: Ṣawt al-Qalam al-ʿArabī, 1431/2010.
Fenton, Paul B. 'La hiérarchie des saints dans la mystique juive et dans la mystique islamique'. Pages 48–73 in *ʿAlei shefer: studies in the literature of Jewish thought*. Edited by Moshe Ḥallamish. Ramat Gan: Bar-Ilan University Press, 1990.
Freidenreich, David M. 'Holiness and impurity in the Torah and the Quran: differences within a common typology'. *Comparative Islamic studies* 6 (2010): 5–22.
Gaddis, Michael. *There is no crime for those who have Christ: religious violence in the Christian Roman Empire*. Transformation of the Classical heritage 39. Berkeley: University of California Press, 2005.
Gaiser, Adam R. Shurāt *legends Ibāḍī identities*. Studies in comparative religion. Columbia: University of South Carolina Press, 2016.

Gardet, Louis. *La cité musulmane: vie sociale et politique*. Etudes musulmanes 1. Paris: Librarie philosophique J. Vrin, 1954.
Gauvain, Richard. 'Ritual rewards: a consideration of three recent approaches to Sunni purity law'. *Islamic law and society* 12 (2005): 333–93.
Geertz, Clifford. *Islam observed: religious development in Morocco and Indonesia*. Terry lectures. New Haven: Yale University Press, 1968.
Gellner, Ernest. *Saints of the Atlas*. London: Weidenfeld & Nicolson, 1969.
Geoffroy, Éric. 'Attitudes contrastées des mystiques musulmans face au miracle'. Pages 301–16 in *Miracle et* karāma. Hagiographies médiévales comparées 2. Bibliothèque de l'École des hautes études, sciences religieuses, 104. Turnhout: Brepols, 2000.
Gerhardsson, Birger. *Memory and manuscript*. Acta seminarii neotestamentici Upsaliensis 22. Upsala: Universiteit Nytestamentlige Seminar, 1961.
Gilliot, Claude. 'Coran 17, *isrā'*, 1 dans la recherche occidentale'. Pages 1–26 in *Le voyage initiatique en terre d'Islam*. Directed by Mohammad Ali Amir-Moezzi. Bibliothèque de l'École des hautes études, section des sciences religieuses, 113. Louvain: Peeters, 1996.
Gilliot, Claude. 'Les «informateurs» juifs et chrétiens de Muḥammad'. *Jerusalem studies in Arabic and Islam*, no 22 (1998), 84–126.
Goitein, Shelomo Dov. 'The rise of the Near-Eastern bourgeoisie in early Islamic times'. *Journal of world history* 3 (1956): 583–604.
Goldziher, Ignaz. 'De l'ascétisme aux premiers temps de l'Islam'. *Revue de l'histoire des religions* 37 (1898): 159–69.
Goldziher, Ignaz. *Introduction to Islamic theology and law*. Translated by Andras and Ruth Hamori. Modern classics in Near Eastern studies. Princeton: University Press, 1981.
Goodman, Lenn E. *Jewish and Islamic philosophy: crosspollinations in the classic age*. New Brunswick: Rutgers University Press, 1999.
Gramlich, Richard. *Alte Vorbilder des Sufitums* 1: *Scheiche des Westens* and 2: *Scheiche des Ostens*. Akademie der Wissenschaften und der Literatur, Mainz, Veröffentlichungen der Orientalischen Kommission, 42/1, 2. Wiesbaden: Harrassowitz, 1996.
Gramlich, Richard. *Weltverzicht: Grundlagen und Weisen islamischer Askese*. Akademie der Wissenschaften und der Literatur, Mainz, Veröffentlichungen der Orientalischen Kommission 43. Wiesbaden: Harrassowitz, 1997.
Gramlich, Richard. *Die Wunder der Freunde Gottes*. Freiburger Islamstudien 11. Wiesbaden: Franz Steiner, 1987.
Green, Nile. 'The religious and cultural roles of dreams and visions in Islam'. *Journal of the Royal Asiatic Society*, 3rd series, 13 (2003): 287–313.
Gribetz, Arthur. 'The *samā'* controversy: Sufi vs. legalist'. *Studia Islamica*, no 74 (1991), 43–62.
Gril, Denis. 'Les fondements scriptuaires du miracle en Islam'. Pages 237–49 in *Miracle et* karāma. Hagiographies médiévales comparées 2. Bibliothèque de l'École des hautes études, sciences religieuses, 104. Turnhout: Brepols, 2000.
Gril, Denis. 'Le miracle en Islam, critère de la sainteté?' Pages 69–81 in *Saints orientaux: Hagiographies médiévales comparées* 1. Directed by Denise Aigle. Paris: De Boccard, n.d.
Gruber, Christiane, and Frederick Colby, editors. *The Prophet's ascension: cross-cultural encounters with the Islamic* mi'rāj *tales*. Bloomington: Indiana University Press, 2010.
Haider, Najam. *Shīʿī Islam: an introduction*. New York: Cambridge University Press, 2014.
Hallaq, Wael B. *The origins and evolution of Islamic law*. Themes in Islamic law 1. Cambridge: University Press, 2005.

Halm, Heinz. *Die Ausbreitung der šāfi'itischen Rechtsschule von den Anfängen bis zum 8./14. Jahrhundert*. Beihefte zum Tübinger Atlas des vorderen Orients, B (Geisteswissenschaften), 4. Wiesbaden: Ludwig Reichert, 1974.
Hamori, A. 'Ascetic poetry (*zuhdiyyāt*)'. Pages 265–74 in *'Abbasid belles-lettres*. Edited by Julia Ashtiany, T. M. Johnstone, J. D. Latham, R. B. Serjeant, and G. Rex Smith. Cambridge history of Arabic literature. Cambridge: University Press, 1990.
Hansbury, Mary. 'Remembrance of God and its relation to Scripture in Isaac III including insights from Islamic and Jewish traditions'. Pages 93–121 in *The Syriac writers of Qatar in the seventh century*. Edited by Mario Kozah, Abdulrahim Abu-Husayn, Saif Shaheen al-Murikhi, and Haya al-Thani. Eastern Christian studies 38. Piscataway: Gorgias Press, 2014.
Heck, Paul L. 'Eschatological scripturalism and the end of community'. *Archiv für Religionsgeschichte* 7 (2005): 137–52.
Hennigan, Peter C. *The birth of a legal institution: the formation of the waqf in third-century A.H. Ḥanafī legal discourse*. Studies in Islamic law and society 18. Leiden: Brill, 2004.
Hillenbrand, Carol. 'A short history of jihad'. Pages 25–42 in *Twenty-first century jihad*. Edited by Elisabeth Kendall and Ewan Stein. London: I. B. Tauris, 2015.
Hodgson, Marshall G. S. *The Venture of Islam: Conscience and History in a World Civilization*. 3 vols. Chicago: University of Chicago Press, 1974.
Howard-Johnson, James, and Paul Antony Howard, editors. The cult of saints in Late Antiquity and the Middle Ages: essays on the contribution of Peter Brown. Oxford: University Press, 1999.
Jackson, Sherman. 'The second education of the *muftī*'. *Muslim world* 82 (1992): 201–17.
Jamil, Nadia. 'Caliph and quṭb'. Pages 11–57 in *Bayt al-maqdis: Jerusalem and early Islam*. Edited by Jeremy Johns. Oxford studies in Islamic art 9/2. Oxford: University Press, 1999.
Jarrar, Maher. 'Bišr al-Ḥāfī und die Barfüßigkeit im Islam', *Der Islam* 71 (1994): 191–240.
Jeffery, Arthur. *The foreign vocabulary of the Quran*. Gaekwad's Oriental series 79. Baroda: Oriental Institute, 1938.
Jihad, Kadhim. *Le livre des prodiges: anthologie des Karâmât des saints de l'islam*. La petite bibliothèque de Sindbad. N.p.: Sindbad, 2003.
Jokisch, Benjamin. *Islamic imperial law: Harun-al-Rashid's codification project*. Studien zur Geschichte und Kultur des islamischen Orients, neue Folge, 19. Berlin: Walter de Gruyter, 2007.
Judd, Steven C. 'Competitive hagiography in biographies of al-Awzāʿī and Sufyān al-Thawrī'. *Journal of the American Oriental Society* 122 (2002): 25–37.
Juynboll, G. H. A. *Encyclopedia of canonical ḥadīth*. Leiden: Brill, 2007.
Juynboll, G. H. A. *Muslim tradition: studies in chronology, provenance and authorship of early* ḥadīth. Cambridge studies in Islamic civilization. Cambridge: University Press, 1983.
Juynboll, G. H. A. 'The position of Qur'an recitation in early Islam'. *Journal of Semitic studies* 20 (1974): 240–51.
Juynboll, G. H. A. 'The qurrāʾ in early Islamic history'. *Journal of the economic and social history of the Orient* 16 (1973): 113–29.
Karamustafa, Ahmet T. *God's unruly friends: dervish groups in the Islamic later middle period, 1200–1550*. Salt Lake City: University of Utah Press, 1994.
Karamustafa, Ahmet T. *Sufism: the formative period*. The new Edinburgh Islamic surveys. Edinburgh: University Press, 2007.
Katz, Marion Holmes. *Body of text: the emergence of the Sunnī law of ritual purity*. Albany: State University of New York Press, 2002.

Katz, Marion Holmes. 'The ḥajj and the study of Islamic ritual'. *Studia Islamica*, nos 98–9 (2004), 95–129.

Katz, Marion Holmes. 'The study of Islamic ritual and the meaning of *wuḍū'*'. *Der Islam* 82 (2005): 106–45.

Kennedy, Hugh. *The armies of the caliphs*. Warfare and history. London: Routledge, 2001.

Khalil, Atif. *Repentance and the return to God:* tawba *in early Sufism*. Albany: State University of New York Press, 2018.

Khoury, R. G. 'Quelques réflexions sur les citations de la Bible dans les premières générations islamiques du premier et du deuxième siècles de l'hégire'. *Bulletin d'études orientales*, no 29 (1977), 269–78.

Kinberg, Leah. 'Compromise of commerce: a study of early traditions concerning wealth and poverty'. *Der Islam* 66 (1989): 193–212.

Kinberg, Leah. 'What Is Meant by *zuhd*'. *Studia Islamica*, no 61 (1985), 27–44.

King, Richard. 'Mysticism and spirituality'. Pages 323–38 in *The Routledge companion to the study of religion*. Edited by John R. Hinnels. 2nd edition. London: Routledge, 2010.

Kister, M. J. 'The expedition of Bi'r Ma'ūna'. Pages 337–57 in *Arabic and Islamic studies in honor of Hamilton A. R. Gibb*. Edited by George Makdisi. Leiden: E. J. Brill, 1965.

Kister, M. J. 'Land property and *jihād*: a discussion of some early traditions'. *Journal of the economics and social history of the Orient* 34 (1991): 270–311.

Koertner, Mareike. '*Dalā'il al-nubuwwa* literature as part of the medieval scholarly discourse on prophecy'. *Der Islam* 95 (2018): 91–109.

Livne-Kafri, Ofer. 'Early Muslim ascetics and the world of Christian monasticism'. *Jerusalem studies in Arabic and Islam*, no 20 (1996), 105–29.

Louth, Andrew. *The origins of the Christian mystical tradition: from Plato to Denys*. Oxford: Clarendon Press, 1981.

Lucas, Scott C. 'Where are the legal *ḥadīth*? A study of the *Muṣannaf* of Ibn Abī Shayba'. *Islamic law and society* 15 (2008): 283–314.

Maghen, Ze'ev. 'Much ado about *wuḍū'*'. *Der Islam* 76 (1999): 205–52.

Marín, Manuela. 'The early development of *zuhd* in al-Andalus'. Pages 83–96 in *Shi'a Islam, sects and Sufism*. Edited by Frederick De Jong. Utrecht: M. Th. Houtsma Stichting, 1992.

Massignon, Louis. *Essai sur les origines du lexique technique de la mystique musulmane*. Paris: Paul Geuthner, 1922. Revised edition Paris: J. Vrin, 1954. Translated by Benjamin Clark as *Essay on the origins of the technical language of Islamic mysticism*. Notre Dame, Ind.: University Press, 1997.

Massignon, Louis. *The passion of al-Hallāj, mystic and martyr of Islam*. Translated by Herbert Mason. Bollingen series 98. 4 vols. Princeton: University Press, 1982.

Massignon, Louis. *Recueil de textes inédits concernant l'histoire de la mystique en pays d'Islam*. Collection de textes inédits relatifs á la mystique musulmane 1. Paris: Paul Geuthner, 1929.

Melchert, Christopher. 'Abū Nu'aym's sources for *Ḥilyat al-awliyā'*, Sufi and traditionist'. Pages 145–60 in *Les maîtres soufis et leurs disciples: IIIe–Ve siècles de l'hégire (IXe–XIe s.): enseignement, formation et transmission*. Edited by Geneviève Gobillot and Jean-Jacques Thibon. Études arabes, médiévales et modernes (PIFD 273). Beirut: Presses de l'IFPO, 2012.

Melchert, Christopher. 'The adversaries of Aḥmad Ibn Ḥanbal'. *Arabica* 44 (1997): 234–53.

Melchert, Christopher. 'Aḥmad ibn Ḥanbal's book of renunciation'. *Der Islam* 85 (2008): 345–59.

Melchert, Christopher. 'Apocalypticism in Sunni hadith'. Pages 267–89 in *Apocalypticism and eschatology in Late Antiquity: encounters in the Abrahamic religions, 6th-8th centuries.* Edited by Hagit Amirav, Emmanouela Grypeou, and Guy Stroumsa. Late antique history and religion 17. Leuven: Peeters, 2017.

Melchert, Christopher. 'Başran origins of classical Sufism'. *Der Islam* 82 (2005): 221–40. Slightly corrected version at pages 169–85 in *Ḥadith, piety and law: selected studies.* Resources in Arabic and Islamic studies 3. Atlanta: Lockwood Press, 2015.

Melchert, Christopher. 'Before *ṣūfiyyāt*: female Muslim renunciants in the 8th and 9th centuries CE'. *Journal of Sufi studies* 5 (2016): 115–39.

Melchert, Christopher. 'The controversy over reciting the Qurʾān with tones (*al-qirāʾah bi-'l-alḥān)*'. Forthcoming in *Journal of the International Qur'anic Studies Association.*

Melchert, Christopher. 'Early renunciants as *ḥadīth* transmitters'. *The Muslim world* 92 (2002): 407–18.

Melchert, Christopher. 'Exaggerated fear in the early Islamic renunciant tradition'. *Journal of the Royal Asiatic Society*, series 3, 21 (2011): 283–300.

Melchert, Christopher. 'The Ḥanābila and the early Sufis'. *Arabica* 48 (2001): 352–67.

Melchert, Christopher. 'Ibn al-Mubārak, traditionist'. Forthcoming in *Modern hadith studies.* Edited by Belal Alabbas, Michael Dann, and Christopher Melchert. Edinburgh University Press.

Melchert, Christopher. 'Ibn al-Mubārak's *Kitāb al-Jihād* and early renunciant literature'. Pages 49–69 in *Violence in Islamic thought from the Qurʾān to the Mongols.* Edited by Robert Gleave and István Kristó-Nagy. Legitimate and illegitimate violence in Islamic thought 1. Edinburgh: University Press, 2015.

Melchert, Christopher. 'The Islamic literature on encounters between Muslim renunciants and Christian monks'. Pages 135–42 in *Medieval Arabic thought: essays in honour of Fritz Zimmermann.* Edited by Rotraud Hansberger, M. Afifi al-Akiti, and Charles Burnett. Warburg Institute studies and texts 4. London: Warburg Institute, 2012.

Melchert, Christopher. 'Khargūshī, *Tahdhīb al-asrār*'. *Bulletin of the School of Oriental and African Studies* 73 (2010): 29–44.

Melchert, Christopher. 'Locating Hell in early renunciant literature'. Pages 103–23 in *Locating Hell in Islamic traditions.* Edited by Christian Lange. Islamic history and civilization, studies and texts, 119. Leiden: Brill, 2016.

Melchert, Christopher. 'Mālik and early renunciant piety'. Forthcoming among selected papers of the Union Européenne des Arabisants et Islamisants, 2018.

Melchert, Christopher. 'The *Musnad* of Aḥmad ibn Ḥanbal: how it was composed and what distinguishes it from the Six Books'. *Der Islam* 82 (2005): 32–51.

Melchert, Christopher. 'The piety of the hadith folk'. *International journal of Middle East studies* 34 (2002): 425–39.

Melchert, Christopher. 'Quotations of extra-qur'anic scripture in early renunciant literature'. Pages 97–107 in *Islam and globalisation: historical and contemporary perspectives. Proceedings of the 25th congress of l'Union Européenne des Arabisants et Islamisants.* Edited by Agostino Cilardo. Orientalia Lovaniensia analecta 226. Leuven: Peeters and Departement Oosterse Studies, 2013.

Melchert, Christopher. 'Qur'anic abrogation across the ninth century'. Pages 75–98 in *Studies in Islamic legal theory.* Edited by Bernard Weiss. Islamic law and society 15. Leiden: Brill, 2002.

Melchert, Christopher. 'Renunciation (*zuhd*) in the early Shiʿi tradition'. Pages 271–94 in *The study of Shiʿi Islam: history, theology and law*. Edited by Farhad Daftary and Gurdofarid Miskinzoda. The Institute of Ismaili Studies Shi'i heritage series 2. London: I. B. Tauris, 2014. Slightly corrected version at pages 209–33 in *Ḥadith, piety and law: selected studies*. Resources in Arabic and Islamic studies 3. Atlanta: Lockwood Press, 2015.

Melchert, Christopher. 'Al-Shaybānī and contemporary renunciant piety'. *Journal of Abbasid studies* 6 (2019): 52–85.

Melchert, Christopher. 'Three qur'anic terms (*siyāḥa*, *ḥikma* and *ṣiddīq*) of special interest to the early renunciants'. Pages 89–116 in *The meaning of the word: lexicography and qur'anic exegesis*. Edited by S. R. Burge. London: Oxford University Press, 2015.

Melchert, Christopher. 'Transfer of knowledge and women in the early Islamic tradition'. Forthcoming in a collection of essays edited by Almut-Barbara Renger, & al.

Melchert, Christopher. 'The transition from asceticism to mysticism at the middle of the ninth century C.E.'. *Studia Islamica* 83 (1996): 51–70. Slightly corrected version at pages 119–37 in *Ḥadith, piety and law: selected studies*. Resources in Arabic and Islamic studies 3. Atlanta: Lockwood Press, 2015.

Melchert, Christopher. 'The transmission of hadith: changes in the ninth and tenth centuries C.E.' Pages 229–46 in *Arabic and Islamic studies in Europe and beyond. Proceedings of the 26th congress of the Union Européenne des Arabisants et Islamisants, Basel 2012*. Edited by Maurus Reinkowski and Monika Winet with Sevinç Yasar Gil. Orientalia Lovaniensia analecta 248. Leuven: Peeters, 2016.

Melchert, Christopher. 'When not to recite the Qur'an'. *Journal of qur'anic studies* 11/1 (2009): 141–51.

Messick, Brinkley. 'The mufti, the text and the world: legal interpretation in Yemen'. *Man: the journal of the Royal Anthropological Institute*, new series, 21 (1986): 102–19.

Metzler, Berenike. *Den Koran verstehen: das* Kitāb Fahm al-Qurʾān *des Ḥāriṯ b. Asad al-Muḥāsibī*. Diskurse der Arabistik 22. Wiesbaden: Harrassowitz, 2016.

Mikati, Rana. 'On the identity of the Syrian *abdāl*'. *Bulletin of the School of Oriental and African Studies* 80/1 (2017): 21–43.

Moin, A. Azfar. 'Partisan dreams and prophetic visions: Shiʿi critique in al-Masʿūdī's history of the Abbasids'. *Journal of the American Oriental Society* 127 (2007): 415–27.

Mojaddedi, Jawid A. 'Getting drunk with Abū Yazīd or staying sober with Junayd: the creation of a popular typology of Sufism'. *Bulletin of the School of Oriental and African Studies* 66 (2003): 1–13.

Molé, Marijan. *Les mystiques musulmanes*. Mythes et religions. Paris: Presses universitaires de France, 1965.

Morris, James Winston. 'Revisiting religious Shiʿism and early Sufism: the fourth/tenth-century dialogue of the sage and the young disciple'. Pages 102–16 in *Reason and inspiration in Islam*. Edited by Todd Lawson. London: I. B. Tauris, 2005.

Motzki, Harald, with Nicolet Boekhoff-van der Voort and Sean Anthony. *Analysing Muslim traditions: studies in legal, exegetical and* maghāzī ḥadīth. Islamic history and civilization, studies and texts, 78. Leiden: Brill, 2010.

Motzki, Harald. 'Dating Muslim traditions: a survey'. *Arabica* 52 (2005): 204–53.

Motzki, Harald. *The origins of Islamic jurisprudence: Meccan fiqh before the classical schools*. Translated by Marion H. Katz. Islamic history and civilization, studies and texts, 41. Leiden: Brill, 2002.

Mueller, Gert H. 'Asceticism and mysticism. A contribution towards the sociology of faith'. Pages 68–132 in *International yearbook for the sociology of religion* 8: *Sociological theories of religion/religion and language*. Edited by Günter Dux, Thomas Luckmann, and Joachim Matthes. Opladen: Westdeutscher Verlag, 1973.

Neusner, Jacob. 'Judaism'. Pages 1–30 in *Sacred texts and authority*. Edited by Jacob Neusner. Pilgrim library of world religions. Cleveland: Pilgrim Press, 1998.

Neuwirth, Angelika, Nicolai Sinai, and Michael Marx, editors. *The Qur'ān in context: historical and literary investigations into the Qur'ānic milieu*. Texts and studies on the Qur'ān 6. Leiden: Brill, 2010.

Nicholson, Reynold A. 'An historical enquiry concerning the origin and development of Sufism'. *Journal of the Royal Asiatic Society*, no 38 (1906), 303–48.

Nürnberg, Rosemarie. *Askese als sozialer Impuls: monastisch-asketische Spiritualität als Wurzel und Triebfeder sozialer Ideen und Aktivitäten der Kirche in Südgallien im 5. Jahrhundert*. Hereditas: Studien zur alten Kirchengeschichte 2. Bonn: Borengässer, 1988.

Oberauer, Norbert. 'Early doctrines on *waqf* revisited: the evolution of Islamic endowment law in the 2nd century AH'. *Islamic law and society* 20 (2013): 1–47.

Ogén, Göran. 'Did the term "*ṣūfī*" exist before the Sufis?' *Acta Orientalia* 43 (1983), 33–48.

Pagani, Samuela. 'L'invention des *ādāb*: «innovations» soufies et monachisme dans l'exégèse du verset 57:27 du Coran'. Pages 223–75 in *Ethics and spirituality in Islam: Sufi* adab. Edited by Francesco Chiabotti, Eve Feuillebois-Pierunek, Catherine Mayeur-Jaouen, and Luca Patrizi. Islamic literatures 1. Leiden: Brill, 2017.

Pavlovich, Pavel. *The formation of the Islamic understanding of* kalāla *in the second century AH (718–816 CE): between scripture and canon*. Islamic history and civilization, studies and texts, 126. Leiden: Brill, 2016.

Picken, Gavin. 'The "greater" jihad in classical Islam'. Pages 126–38 in *Twenty-first century jihad: law, society and military action*. Edited by Elisabeth Kendall and Ewan Stein. London: I. B. Tauris, 2015.

Picken, Gavin. 'Ibn Ḥanbal and al-Muḥāsibī: a study of early conflicting methodologies'. *Arabica* 55 (2008): 337–61.

Pietruschka, Ute. 'Apophthegmata Patrum in muslimischem Gewand: Das Beispiel Mālik ibn Dīnār'. Pages 160–71 in *Begegnungen in Vergangenheit und Gegenwart. Beiträge dialogischer Existenz. Eine freundschaftliche Festgabe zum 60. Geburtstag von Martin Tamcke*. Edited by Claudia Rammelt, Cornelia Schlarb, and Egbert Schlarb. Berlin: Lit, 2015.

Pouzet, Louis. *Une herméneutique de la Tradition islamique: le commentaire des 'Al-Arba'īn al-Nawawīya'*. Recherches, n.s. A. Langue arabe et pensée islamique 13. Beirut: Dar el-Machreq, 1982.

Rapp, Claudia. '"For next to God, you are my salvation": reflections on the rise of the holy man in Late Antiquity'. Pages 63–81 in *The cult of saints in Late Antiquity and the Middle Ages: essays on the contribution of Peter Brown*. Edited by James Howard-Johnson and Paul Antony Howard. Oxford: University Press, 1999.

Rapp, Claudia. *Holy bishops in Late Antiquity*. The transformation of the Classical heritage 37. Los Angeles: University of California Press, 2005.

Reinert, Benedikt. *Die Lehre vom* tawakkul *in der klassischen Sufik*. Studien zur Sprache, Geschichte und Kultur des islamischen Orients, new series, 3. Berlin: Walter de Gruyter, 1968.

Reinhart, A. Kevin. *Before revelation: the boundaries of Muslim moral thought*. SUNY series in Middle Eastern studies. Albany: State University of New York Press, 1995.

Reinhart, A. Kevin. 'Impurity/No Danger'. *History of religions* 30 (1990): 1–24.
Robinson, Chase F. *'Abd al-Malik*. Makers of the Muslim world. Oxford: Oneworld, 2005.
Robinson, Chase F. 'Prophecy and holy men in early Islam'. Pages 241–62 in *The cult of saints in Late Antiquity and the Middle Ages: essays on the contribution of Peter Brown*. Edited by James Howard-Johnson and Paul Antony Howard. Oxford: University Press, 1999.
Ṣādir, Yūḥannā. *Ruhbān ʿarab fī baʿḍ siyar al-mutaṣawwifah al-muslimīn*. Beirut: Dār Ṣādir, 1427/2005.
Sahner, Christian C. '"The monasticism of my community is jihād": a debate on asceticism, sex, and warfare in early Islam'. *Arabica* 64 (2017): 149–83.
Salem, Feryal. *The emergence of early Sufi piety and Sunnī scholasticism: ʿAbdallāh b. al-Mubārak and the formation of Sunnī identity in the second Islamic century*. Islamic history and civilization, studies and texts, 125. Leiden: Brill, 2016.
Sayed, Redwan. *Die Revolte des Ibn al-Ašʿaṯ und die Koranleser: ein Beitrag zur Religions- und Sozialgeschichte der frühen Umayyadenzeit*. Islamkundliche Untersuchungen 45. Freiburg im Breisgau: Klaus Schwarz, 1977.
Schacht, Joseph. 'Early doctrines on waqf'. Pages 443–52 in *60. doğum yılı münasebetiyle Fuad Koprülü armağan*. Istanbul: Osman Yalçın Matbaası, 1953.
Schacht, Joseph. *The origins of Muhammadan jurisprudence*. Oxford: Clarendon Press, 1950.
Schimmel, Annemarie. *Mystical Dimensions of Islam*. Chapel Hill: University of North Carolina Press, 1975.
Scholem, Gershom. *On the Kabbalah and its symbolism*. Translated by Ralph Manheim. London: Routledge and Kegan Paul, 1965.
Sezgin, Fuat. *Geschichte des arabischen Schrifttums*. 15 vols to date. Leiden: E. J. Brill, 1967–2010.
Shaban, M. A. *Islamic history: a new interpretation* 1: *Islamic history A.D. 600–750 (A.H. 132)*. Cambridge: University Press, 1971.
Shah, Mustafa. 'The quest for the origins of the *qurrāʾ* in the classical Islamic tradition'. *Journal of qur'anic studies* 7/2 (2005): 1–35.
Silvers, Laury. *A soaring minaret: Abu Bakr al-Wasiti and the rise of Baghdadi Sufism*. Albany: State University of New York Press, 2010.
Sirriyeh, Elizabeth. *Sufis and anti-Sufis: the defence, rethinking and rejection of Sufism in the modern world*. Curzon Sufi series. Richmond: Curzon, 1999.
Sizgorich, Thomas. *Violence and belief in Late Antiquity*. Divinations: rereading Late Ancient religion. Philadelphia: University of Pennsylvania Press, 2009.
Speight, R. Marston. 'A look at variant readings in the *ḥadīth*'. *Der Islam* 77 (2000): 169–9.
Speight, R. Marston. 'Rhetorical argumentation in the hadith literature of Islam'. *Semeia* 64 (1993): 73–92.
Spitaler, Anton. *Die Verszählung des Koran nach islamischer Überlieferung*. München: Verlag der Bayerischen Akademie der Wissenschaften, 1935.
Stark, Rodney. 'Upper class asceticism: social origins of ascetic movements and medieval saints'. *Review of religious research* 45 (2003): 5–19.
Sterk, Andrea. *Renouncing the world yet leading the church: the monk-bishop in late antiquity*. Cambridge, Mass.: Harvard University Press, 2004.
Stroumsa, Sarah. 'The beginnings of the Muʿtazilah, reconsidered'. *Jerusalem studies in Arabic and Islam*, no 13 (1990), 265–93.
Sviri, Sara. *Perspectives on early Islamic mysticism: the world of al-Ḥakīm al-Tirmidhī and his contemporaries*. Routledge Sufi series. London: Routledge, 2020.

Sviri, Sara. '*Wa-rahbānīyatan ibtadaʿūhā*: an analysis of traditions concerning the origin and evaluation of Christian monasticism'. *Jerusalem studies in Arabic and Islam*, no 13 (1990), 195–208.
Taylor, Christopher S. *In the vicinity of the righteous:* ziyāra *and the veneration of Muslim saints in late medieval Egypt.* Islamic history and civilization, studies and texts, 22. Leiden: Brill, 1999.
Thibon, Jean-Jacques. *L'œuvre d'Abū ʿAbd al-Raḥmān al-Sulamī (325/937–412/1021) et la formation du soufisme.* Damascus: Institut français du Proche-Orient, 2009.
Tottoli, Roberto. 'Origin and use of the term *isrâʾîliyyât* in Muslim literature'. *Arabica* 46 (1999): 193–210.
Vööbus, Arthur. *History of asceticism in the Syrian Orient. A contribution to the history of culture in the Middle East.* 2 vols. Louvain: Secrétariat du Corpus SCO, 1958–60.
Waardenburg, J. D. J. 'Official and popular religion as a problem in Islamic studies'. Pages 340–86 in *Official and popular religion: analysis of a theme for Religious Studies.* Edited by Pieter Hendrick Vrijhof and Jacques Waardenburg. Religion & Society 19. The Hague: Mouton, 1979.
Walker, Joel Thomas. *The legend of Mar Qardagh: narrative and Christian heroism in Late Antique Iraq.* Transformation of the Classical heritage 40. Berkeley: University of California Press, 2006.
Wansbrough, John E. *Quranic studies: sources and methods of scriptural interpretation.* London Oriental series 31. Oxford: University Press, 1977.
Wansbrough, John E. *The sectarian milieu: content and composition of Islamic salvation history.* London Oriental series 34. Oxford: University Press, 1978.
Watt, W. Montgomery. *Bell's introduction to the Qur'ān.* Islamic surveys 8. Edinburgh: University Press, 1970
Watt, W. Montgomery. *Muhammad at Mecca.* Oxford: Clarendon Press, 1953.
Watt, W. Montgomery. *Muhammad at Medina.* Oxford: Clarendon Press, 1956.
Weipert, Reinhard, and Stefan Weninger. 'Die erhaltenen Werke des Ibn Abī d-Dunyā. Eine vorläufige Bestandsaufnahme'. *Zeitschrift der Deutschen Morgenländischen Gesellschaft* 146 (1996): 415–55.
Weiss, Bernard G. *The spirit of Islamic law.* The spirit of the laws. Athens: University of Georgia Press, 1998.
Wensinck, A. J., &al. *Concordance et indices de la tradition Musulmane.* 7 vols. Leiden: E. J. Brill, 1936–69.
Wensinck, A. J. *A handbook of early Muhammadan tradition.* Leiden: E. J. Brill, 1927.
Wensinck, A. J. 'The Oriental doctrine of the martyrs'. Pages 147–74 in *Mededeelingen der Koninklike Akademie van Wetenschappen.* Afdeeling etterkunde deel 53, series A, no 6. Amsterdam: n.p., 1921.
Wickham, Chris. *Framing the early Middle Ages: Europe and the Mediterranean, 400–800.* Oxford: University Press, 2005.
Wickham, Chris. *Land and power: studies in Italian and European social history, 400–1200.* London: British School at Rome, 1994.
Yanagihashi, Hiroyuki. *Studies in legal hadith.* Studies in Islamic law and society 47. Leiden: Brill, 2019.
Yücesoy, Hayrettin. 'Political anarchism, dissent, and marginal groups in the early ninth century: the Ṣūfīs of the Muʿtazila revisited'. Pages 61–84 in *The lineaments of Islam: studies*

in honor of Fred McGraw Donner. Edited by Paul M. Cobb. Islamic history and civilization, studies and texts, 95. Leiden: Brill, 2012.
Zaehner, R. C. *Hindu and Muslim mysticism*. N.p.: University of London, Athlone Press, 1960.
Zysow, Aron. 'Two unrecognized Karrāmī texts'. *Journal of the American Oriental Society* 108 (1988): 577–87.

Index

Aaron (Hārūn)
– his supplication 83
ʿAbadan 55
ʿabāyah 164
ʿAbbās ibn al-Muʾammal al-Ṣūfī, al- 185
ʿAbbāsids 124, 125, 136
ʿAbdak 155–6, 170
ʿAbd al-ʿAzīz ibn Hārūn 145
ʿAbd al-ʿAzīz ibn Marwān 138
ʿAbd al-Bāqī, Muḥammad Fuʾād viii
ʿAbd al-Ḥamīd, Muḥammad Muḥyī al-Dīn viii
ʿAbd Allāh ibn ʿAbd al-Ḥakam 183n.
ʿAbd Allāh ibn Abī Labīd 127
ʿAbd Allāh ibn Abī Zakarīyāʾ
– intercession of saints 112
ʿAbd Allāh ibn Aḥmad 7
ʿAbd Allāh ibn al-Zubayr *see* Ibn al-Zubayr
ʿAbd Allāh ibn ʿAmr
– considered self-castration 34
– for withdrawal 49
– secret devotions 63
– took warning from fire 105
ʿAbd Allāh ibn Dīnār 83
ʿAbd Allāh ibn Lahīʿah
– explanation of ritual prayer 80
ʿAbd Allāh ibn Masʿūd see Ibn Masʿūd
ʿAbd Allāh ibn Muḥammad al-Ḍabbī 157
ʿAbd Allāh ibn Muḥayrīz
– refused alms 152–3
ʿAbd Allāh ibn Naṣr 193
ʿAbd Allāh ibn Rawāḥah al-Anṣārī
– weeping from uncertainty 47
ʿAbd Allāh ibn Saʿīd
– miraculous food 121
ʿAbd Allāh ibn Shaddād
– for wool 38
ʿAbd Allāh ibn Thaʿlabah
– against laughter 59, 61
ʿAbd Allāh ibn Ubayy 3
ʿAbd Allāh ibn ʿUmar see Ibn ʿUmar
ʿAbd Allāh ibn Wāqid 77
ʿAbd Allāh ibn Yazīd 155–6, 170
ʿAbd Allāh ibn Zakarīyāʾ
– cheerful 62
– never touched money 150
– to learn silence 55
ʿAbd Allāh-i Anṣārī 192
ʿAbd al-Majīd ibn Abī Rawwād 126
ʿAbd al-Malik ibn Marwān 37
ʿAbd al-Muṭṭalib
– dependence on God 42
ʿAbd al-Raḥmān ibn Abī Laylá
– secret ritual prayer 77
ʿAbd al-Raḥmān ibn Abī Nuʿm
– eating little 25
ʿAbd al-Raḥmān ibn al-Aswad
– supererogatory prayers at home 78–9
ʿAbd al-Raḥmān ibn Khālid 66
ʿAbd al-Raḥmān ibn Mahdī 126
– against laughter 61
– recited half the Qur'an nightly 97
ʿAbd al-Raḥmān ibn Sābiṭ
– for recollection at home 100
ʿAbd al-Raḥmān ibn Yazīd 65
ʿAbd al-Razzāq 2, 110, 142n., 168
ʿAbd al-Wahhāb 189
ʿAbd al-Wāḥid ibn Zayd 127
– for eating little 26
– incompetent traditionist 175
– married woman who wore wool 39
– paralysed except at prayer time 120
– rebuked in dream 95
– weeping 47
abdāl 39, 113–18, 121
ʿābid 11–12, 166
Abraham (Ibrāhīm) 113, 117
– self-reliance 52
abrār 50
ʿAbthar Abū Zabīd 30
Abū ʿAbd Rabbi
– against begging 152
– traded although rich 148
Abū ʿAbd Allāh ʿUrwah ibn Marwān al-ʿIrqī Ṭarābulusī
– vegetarian 28
Abū al-Aḥwaṣ
– on recollection of conquest army 103–4
Abū al-ʿAlāʾ
– for secret ritual prayer 77–8

https://doi.org/10.1515/9783110617962-013

Abū al-ʿĀliyah
– against wool 162
– for secret almsgiving 86
– purification from sin 71
– studied secretly 65
Abū al-Dardā' 29n.
– against mark of prostration 75
– against complacency 162
– contemplation 105
– for practising what one preaches 159
– for recollection of death 106
– for staying home 50
– for weeping 46
– poverty, illness, death 42
– preferred praising God to giving alms 68n., 99
Abū al-Ḥasan al-Būshanjī 187
Abū al-Jawzāʾ al-Rabʿī
– avoided cursed food 54
Abū al-Khalīl Ṭalq ibn Ḥabīb
– fear of God 44n.
Abū al-Qāsim al-Balkhī 163
Abū al-Ṣahbāʾ 31
Abū al-Sawwār al-ʿAdawī
– whipped for commanding ruler 109
Abū al-Tayyāḥ
– for secret devotions 88
ʿAbd al-Wāḥid ibn Zayd
– wept on seeing al-Ḥasan al-Baṣrī 43
– wore wool under other clothes 63
Abū al-Zinād
– on *abdāl* 117, 118
Abū ʿAlī al-Rāzī 61
Abū ʿAlī al-Thaqafī 192
Abū ʿAmr ibn al-ʿAlāʾ 166
Abū Bakr al-Khallāl 156
Abū Bakr ibn ʿAbd Allāh ibn Abī Maryam
– *mujtahid* 79
Abū Bakr al-Ṣiddīq 11, 120
– against food from illicit sources 28–9
– did not eat refined flour 28
– for poetry 58
– weeping 47, 93n., 94, 128
Abū Bakr al-Wāsiṭī 192
Abū Bakr ibn Abī ʿĀṣim al-Nabīl
– conflict with *murābiṭūn* 158
– light used without permission 41
Abū Bakr ibn ʿAyyāsh
– fasted 70 years 87
– no bed 31
Abū Bakr ibn Muḥammad ibn ʿAmr ibn Ḥazm
– no bed 31
Abū Bilāl Mirdās
– sexual abstinence 34
Abū Dāwūd al-Sijistānī vii, 2n., 142, 188
Abū Dharr 29n.
– for weeping 46
– trouble with rulers 134–5
Abū Ḥafṣ al-Naysābūrī 157
Abū Ḥafṣ ʿUmar ibn ʿAbd Allāh al-Fattāl 16
Abū Ḥamzah 23
Abū Ḥamzah al-Baghdādī (Muḥammad ibn Ibrāhīm) 184, 186
Abū Ḥamzah Muḥammad ibn Maymūn al-Sukkarī al-Marwazī
– eating little 26
Abū Ḥanīfah 171
– against chess 67
– sleeping little 30
Abū Hāshim 39, 184
Abū Ḥātim al-ʿAṭṭār 186–9, 193
Abū Ḥātim al-Rāzī
– knew greatest name of God 121
Abū Ḥāzim 139
Abū Hurayrah
– against poetry 57n.
– against supplicating with two fingers 82–3
– for praising God 68
– night vigil in shifts 73n.
– predicted future 120
– recollection observed in Heaven 100
– weeping 45
– would not greet Muʿāwiyah 136
Abū Idrīs al-Khawlānī
– against complacency 162
– for making one's concern one 42
Abū ʿImrān al-Jawnī
– weeping 47
Abū ʿImrān al-Raqāshī 156, 169
Abū Isḥāq al-Sabīʿī
– fasting 88
– on marks of prostration 74–5

– staying awake 32
Abū Ja'far
– fasted alternate days 87
Abū Khaythamah 22
Abū Lubābah ibn 'Abd al-Mundhir 3
Abū Maysarah
– prolonged prayer 74
– uncertainty whether saved 45
Abū Mu'āwiyah al-Aswad
– miraculously nullified catapults 120
Abū Muḥammad ibn Ḥayyān 8
Abū Mūsá al-Ash'arī
– asked to preach 169
– for weeping 47, 94n., 127–8
– qur'anic recitation 92
– wool 37–8
Abū Muslim al-Khawlānī
– avoidance of society 49
– constant recollection aloud 103
– devotional routine with his wife 99–100
– made woman go blind 120
– sleeping little 30, 31
– walked on water 121
Abū Nu'aym al-Faḍl ibn Dukayn
– joked 62
Abū Nu'aym al-Iṣbahānī 9, 115, 116, 182
– hadith tradition 6–7
– *Ḥilyat al-awliyā'* 7–8, 14, 185
Abū Qilābah
– against raised voice 56
Abū Sa'īd cl. of Abū Usīd 84
Abū Salamah (al-Mughīrah) ibn Muslim
– against food from illicit sources 136
Abū Sulaymān al-Dārānī 37
– celibacy 34–5
– expelled from Damascus 183
– on renunciation 182
Abū Ṭālib al-Makkī
– *Qūt al-qulūb* 193
Abū Thawr 188
Abū 'Ubayd al-Qāsim ibn Sallām 58
– *Amwāl, al-* 144–5
Abū 'Ubaydah ibn 'Abd Allāh ibn Mas'ūd
– for praising God over almsgiving 68
– silent recollection 102–3
Abū Umāmah
– against supererogatory prayer in mosque 78
Abū 'Uthmān al-Nahdī 84
Abū Wā'il Shaqīq ibn Salamah
– 'How are you?' 54
– preferred trade to stipend 144, 147
– stillness in ritual prayer 76
– would not accept food from a qadi 136
Abū Yaḥyá al-Rāzī 8
Abū Yazīd al-Bisṭāmī 180, 184, 189
Abū Yūsuf 171
– *Ṣalāh, al-* 170
Abū Zur'ah al-Rāzī 185
adab
– literary tradition 3–4, 7, 48
Adam (Ādam) 88, 113
– did not laugh for 100 years 60
'afw 141
agriculture 141
– contempt of 142–3
ahl al-ḥadīth 187
ahl al-maḥabbah 186, 187
Aḥmad ibn Abī al-Ḥawārī 37, 164
Aḥmad ibn al-Mu'adhdhal
– no shade on pilgrimage 89–90
Aḥmad ibn Ḥanbal vii, 35n., 58, 82, 109, 113, 137, 164, 176, 183
– against agriculture 143
– against chess 66–7
– against plastering 23
– against satiety 27
– and *wari'īn* 48
– and wiping face 82
– Creed I 134n.
– Creed V 45n.
– cured cripple 121
– danced 107
– depended on as intercessor 112
– fasting 88
– for balance between hadith, worship 175
– hadith tradition 6–7
– *Musnad, al-* 7, 115
– on Baghdadi *abdāl* 116
– on commanding and forbidding 129
– patched clothing 38
– pilgrimage 89

– recited Qur'an twice weekly or more 98
– Sufi associates 186
– *Zuhd, al-* 7, 9, 13, 126, 194
Aḥmad ibn Ḥarb 116
– interpreted pilgrimage 90–1
Aḥmad ibn Hilāl al-ʿAbartānī
– pilgrimages on foot 89
Aḥmad ibn Salamah al-Naysābūrī 35n.
ahwāl al-qiyāmah 45
Ahwāzī, al- 183
a'immah 50
ʿĀ'ishah 21, 31, 52n.
– against satiety 24
– against supplicating with two fingers 83
– for silent recollection 102
– scrupulosity 40
ʿajab 58
ʿAlā' ibn al-Ḥaḍramī, al-
– miraculous provision of ablution water 120
ʿAlā' ibn Ziyād, al-
– eating little 25
– for praying in subdued voice 56
– recollection of death 106
alcohol 27, 185
Alexandria 185
ʿAlī ibn ʿAbd Allāh ibn al-ʿAbbās
– 1,000 prostrations a day 73
ʿAlī ibn Abī Ṭālib 88, 115, 128
– against chess, backgammon 66
– against novel food 24
– allusions to in the Qur'an 183
– considered self-castration 34
– for poetry 58
– for stillness in ritual prayer 75
– for suppressing anger, laughing little 59
– humility 161
– sadness 43
ʿAlī ibn Bakkār
– slept little by night 33
ʿAlī ibn al-Fuḍayl ibn ʿIyāḍ 61
ʿAlī ibn al-Madīnī 126
ʿAlī ibn Mahziyār 128
ʿAlī ibn Ṣāliḥ ibn Ḥayy 73
ʿAlī Zayn al-ʿĀbidīn, ibn al-Ḥusayn
– against laughter 59
– his example normative 111
– secret almsgiving 63, 85
– supererogatory prayer 73
ʿālim 11, 159, 181
alms 67, 69, 85–6, 142n.
– compared with pilgrimage 90
– compared with praising God 99n.
– secret 63, 86, 95
– support of renunciants 144, 151–5, 157–8
alqāb 190
ʿAlqamah ibn Qays
– for lack of renown 65
– recited entire Qur'an in a night 97–8
ʿamal 79–80
Aʿmash, al- 67, 138, 151
– for using rulers 139
– prayed in first row 73
– when to finish reciting Qur'an 96
ʿāmil 159
āmīn 101
Amīn, al- 125, 155
ʿĀmir ibn ʿAbd Allāh
– almsgiving 67, 151–2
ʿĀmir ibn ʿAbd Qays
– against food from illicit sources 29
– celibacy 34
– his supplication 83
– marks of prostration 74
– sleeping little 31
– to make his concern one 42
– weeping 45
ʿĀmir ibn Ṭufayl 119
Amir-Moezzi, Mohammad Ali 114n.
amr bi-al-maʿrūf, al- (*see also* commanding) 65
ʿAmr ibn Maymūn al-Awdī
– pilgrimage 88
– recollection on entering mosque 100
– sleeping little 30
ʿAmr ibn Qays
– either in market or at home 148
ʿAmr ibn Shuraḥbīl
– alms to monks 146
ʿAmr ibn ʿUbayd
– repeated one verse all night 97

- would not drink from rulers' wells 137
'Amr ibn 'Utbah
- celibacy 34
- *mujtahid* 78–9
- protected by lion 120
- secrecy 63
Amritsarī, Muḥammad 'Aṭā' Allāh al-Fūjayānī al- viii
anachronism 1, 2
Anas ibn Mālik 25, 38, 175
'Anbas ibn 'Uqbah al-Taymī
- stillness in ritual prayer 76
Andalusia 35
angels 74, 77, 104, 112, 184
Anṣār 71
Anthony, Sean 2n.
Antichrist 2
Antony, Saint 131
apatheia 11
apocalypticism 18
apophthegmata 124
'aql 27
Arabia 10, 13, 29, 114
Arabic language 10, 16, 18, 66, 79, 140, 178
Arabs 10, 29
Aramaic 13
Arberry, A. J. 189
'ārif 181
Armstrong, Lyall 168
Arna'ūṭ, al-, Shu'ayb viii
Asad ibn Muhallab
- died at hearing Qur'an 94
'As'as ibn Salāmah 58
asceticism, ascetics 10, 12, 127, 168, 176
- as opposed to mysticism, mystics 179–80, 182, 188–9
aṣḥāb 129
'Āṣim ibn 'Amr 24
'Āṣim ibn 'Umar ibn al-Khaṭṭāb 24
askētēs 11
'Āṣim viii
asses 39, 42, 162
Aswad ibn Yazīd al-Nakha'ī, al-
- eating little 25, 86
- frequency of reciting Qur'an 97
- pilgrimage 88–9
'aṭā' 144
'Aṭā' al-Khurāsānī 117
- reciting Qur'an in prayer 93
'Aṭā' al-Salīmī
- against laughter 60
- fainted for fear 45
- stayed in bed 51
'Aṭā' ibn Abī Rabāḥ
- no bed 31
- restricted speech 54–5
Athanasius 124
Athene 114
Atlas 108
awliyā' 113, 183
'Awn ibn 'Abd Allāh ibn 'Utbah 11, 163
- against reciting Qur'an while sitting 93
- against withdrawal 53
- for recollection among heedless 104
- gave away estate 36
- his preaching, singing slave girl 107
- recollected before Umm al-Dardā' 102
- wore wool 38, 39
'Awn ibn Mu'ammar 61
awthān
- identified with chess 66
Awzā'ī, al- 8, 57n, 112, 119
- against laughter 60
ayyām al-bīḍ 88
Ayyūb al-Sakhtiyānī 77, 164–5
- for hiding renunciation 26
- for self-reliance 155
- pilgrimage 89
- stayed up nights 95–6
- weeping 47
Ayyūb ibn Yaḥyá 135
A'ẓamī, Ḥabīb al-Raḥmān al- 7
Azarbaijan 148

backgammon 66–7
badal, badīl 113n.
badhā' 53
Baghdad 1, 4, 55, 157, 186, 187–8, 190
Bahrein 152
baḥth 80
Bājī, al- 166
Bakkār ibn Muḥammad said of 'Abd Allāh ibn 'Awn 55

Bakr ibn ʿAbd Allāh 21–2
– against laughter 60
Baldick, Julian 14n., 16, 183
Balkh 129
Banī Qurayẓah 3
baqāʾ 189
Barakah 136
barefootedness 39
Barqī, al- 183
basham 25
Basra 10, 41, 66, 137, 184, 187, 193
bath 72
bāṭil 66
bayān 53
begging 86, 142n., 152, 153–4
Berg, Herbert 2n.
Bilāl ibn Saʿd 11, 64
– supererogatory prayer 73
bishops 111n
Bishr al-Ḥāfī 116
– against eating by *ʿilm* 153
– against food from illicit sources 29
– against luxury among ulema 159
– against trading in food 150
– depended on as intercessor 112
– doubted pilgrimage 90
– eating, speaking little 26–7, 55
Bishr ibn al-Mufaḍḍal
– supererogatory prayer, fasting 73, 87
Bishr ibn Manṣūr
– taught his sons to weave palm fronds 147
– would not drink from rulers' wells 137
Bishrah 107n.
Bisṭām 184
biṭnah 60
Boekhoff-van der Voort, Nicolet 2n.
Bonner, Michael 141, 142n, 143, 144, 146
bourgeoisie 175–6
borrowing 12–13
Bravmann, Meïr M. 140–1, 146
Brown, Jonathan A. C. 8
Brown, Peter 108–9, 118, 122
budalāʾ 113
Buddhists, Buddhism 16, 177
Bukhārī, al- vii, 119, 131, 133, 142, 160, 161
– never touched money 150
Bundār ibn al-Ḥusayn
– against *qurrāʾ* 166–7
Bundārī, al-, ʿAbd al-Ghaffār viii
burdah 37
Byzantine
– Empire 10
– history 2, 16

Calder, Norman 128
caliphs, caliphate 8n, 10, 123, 124, 130, 133, 138, 140, 142n., 181, 188
callus 127
camel 42n., 127
celibacy 33–5, 123
cemetery 49, 72, 158
Chabbi, Jacqueline 4n., 113–14
'checkmate' 66
chess 66–7, 103
Children of Israel 53, 133
Christians, Christianity 13–14, 72, 84, 111, 121, 122, 124, 127, 131, 144, 176n, 177, 178
– and Islamic renunciant tradition 16, 118
chronicles 141
clothing 37–9, 181
commanding and forbidding 51, 54, 65, 108–9, 122, 129, 185–7
Companions 2, 6, 13, 56, 63, 67, 110, 155, 163, 168, 176
– reliability of quotations 3
– wool 37–8
concubines 111
consensus 172
construction, against 22–3
consumer capitalism 18–19
Cook, Michael 109
Cooperson, Michael 176
Cornell, Rkia 17n.
Cromwell, Oliver 125
Crone, Patricia 20n., 114
cursing 54

Ḍaḥḥāk ibn Muzāḥim, al-
– forgetting from sin 27
– knew more than Companions 163
Ḍaḥḥāk ibn ʿUthmān, al-

– would not drink from rulers' wells 137
Damascus 55, 134, 183, 194
dār al-kufr 156n.
ḍarāwah 27
dāriʿah 38
dates, hijri and common era vii
Dāwūd ibn Abī Hind
– fasted secretly 88
Dāwūd al-Ṭāʾī
– against supererogatory prayers in mosque 78
– appearance 64
– celibacy 35
– left Abū Ḥanīfah's circle 171
– moved from room to room 22
– no bed 32
– stayed home 51
– would not be distracted 77
David (Dāwūd) 32
– fast of 87
– lived by the gain of his hand 147
– weeping 46–7
death, contemplation of 105–6, 150
Décobert, Christian 141, 144
Dhahabī, al- 170
dhākir 104
dhikr 92, 98–106, 131, 180
Dhū al-Nūn al-Miṣrī 183, 188n.
– back projection 6
– mysticism 180
– not a Sufi 187
Dijlat al-ʿAwrāh 29
Ḍirār ibn Murrah 44
dog 120
dream interpretation 119
duʿāʾ 56, 80–5, 98
During, Jean 107

eating 24–9
ecstasy 189
ekklēsía 176
Egypt 10, 11, 29, 104, 124, 140, 179
– monasticism 14n.
Encyclopaedia Iranica 113
Encyclopaedia of Islam vii, 113
Ernst, Carl 15n.
eschaton 18
Ethiopia 34
Euphrates 29
Evagrius 124

Faḍālah ibn ʿUbayd
– for secret study 65
faḍl 141
fāʾidah 141
fālūdhaj 24
famine 121, 122
fanāʾ 189
faqīh, fuqahāʾ 11n., 57, 151
faqīr, fuqarāʾ 22, 36, 85, 107, 146, 148, 151
– 'needy' 154
farāʾiḍ 174
Farewell Pilgrimage 132
Farīd al-Dīn ʿAṭṭār 6n.
Farīwāʾī, ʿAbd al-Raḥmān ibn ʿAbd al-Jabbār 15–16
farq 189, 190
Farqad al-Sabakhī
– against satiety 26
– opposed to Ibrāhīm al-Nakhaʿī, al-Ḥasan al-Baṣrī 163
– wore wool 162
fārr 104
fasād 50
fasting 12, 25, 30, 33, 73, 95, 98, 102, 112, 127, 145, 167, 171
– secret 64, 88
– supererogatory 86–8, 92, 129
Fatḥ al-Mawṣilī
– daughter's clothing 22
Fātiḥah, al- 80, 101
Fāṭimah bint ʿAbd al-Malik 35
fatwá 114
Fayḍī, Muḥammad ibn Sālim ibn Sulaymān, al- 16n.
fear 43–8, 95, 165
Fertile Crescent 13
fighting 56, 103
fikr 104–5
fingers 82–3
firāsh 31, 32
Fire see Hell
First Civil War 115, 125, 128

fitnah 98, 134
fiṭrah 71
Followers 67, 142n., 163
food from illicit sources 28–9, 122, 136–7, 172n
food, miraculous 121–2
fountains 158
Fourth Civil War 155, 170
frivolity 65–6, 103, 176
Fuḍayl ibn ʿIyāḍ, al- 71
– against laughter, sleeping all night 61
– against trading knowledge for money 153
– for inward renunciation 165
– recipient of alms 152
fujūr 63
funeral 56, 103

Gabriel 113
Gellner, Ernest 108
gestures to accompany supplication 81–3
ghāfil 50, 104
ghaflah 100
ghanī, *ghinā* 154, 165
Ghassānīyah 186–7
Ghazālī 94, 161
– *Iḥyā' ʿulūm al-dīn* 193
Ghazwān ibn Ghazwān
– against laughter 59
ghībah 70
Ghulām Khalīl 187–8, 191
ghusl 69
Gnosticism 13
Gospels 119
Gothic language 10
Gramlich, Richard 10
Greek language 16
Greek Orthodoxy 179
group recollection 100–2
group supplication 83–5

Ḥabīb al-Fārisī
– miraculous grain 122
Ḥabīb ibn Abī Thābit
– almsgiving 151
– stillness in ritual prayer 76
Ḥabīb ibn Maslamah 143
ḥadhr 40
hadith 16, 18, 57, 80, 173, 175, 186, 194
– eating little good for 27
– literary tradition 3, 123, 143
– provoked weeping 47–8
Hadith Folk 177
ḥadīth qudsī 88
Ḥafṣ viii
Ḥafṣ ibn Ghiyāth 171
hair 64, 91
Ḥajjāj ibn Farāfiṣah
– eating, sleeping little 26
Ḥajjāj ibn Yūsuf, al- 77, 135
ḥakīm 38n
Ḥakīm al-Tirmidhī, al- 170
Ḥakīm ibn ʿUmayr
– mark of prostration 74
Ḥallāj, al- 90, 189–90
Ḥamdūn al-Qaṣṣār 129
Ḥammād ibn Abī Sulaymān 51
Ḥammād ibn Zayd 159
Hammām ibn al-Ḥārith
– against reciting Qur'an for rulers 137
– sleeping little 30
Ḥammād ibn Salamah
– limited his income 150
– never laughed 61
Hammām ibn Nāfiʿ
– pilgrimage 89
hams 56
Ḥanafi school 72
Ḥanbalism 114
hands
– to pick up blessings 82
Hannād ibn al-Sarī 8, 70, 132
– austerities 35
– hadith tradition 6–7
ḥaqīqah 91
Ḥārith ibn Jarīr, al- 162
Ḥārith ibn Qays, al-
– would not sit with two 65
Hārūn ibn Ri'āb
– secrecy 64
– wool 37
Hārūn al-Rashīd 129, 137
Ḥasan, Sayyid Kisrawī viii

Ḥasan al-Baṣrī, al- 21, 24, 25, 28, 33, 38, 74, 78, 98, 151, 175
- acceptable pilgrimage 90
- against Farqad al-Sabakhī 163
- against laughter 18, 59n., 60
- against good works in public 64
- against outward show of piety 162
- against reciting Qur'an for rulers 137
- almsgiving 67, 85–6
- distrusted market 150
- eating little 25
- fasting 87–8
- fear 44, 47
- for contemplation 105
- for limiting one's income 149–50
- for making one's concern one 42
- for restricted speech 57
- for subdued voice in prayer 56
- for staying home 50, 122
- his example normative 111
- 'How are you?' 46
- lack of furniture 22
- looked up in supplication 82
- maintaining ritual purity 70
- minimal definition of 'Islam' 165
- sadness 43, 159
- secret weightier than public 63–4
- stipend 144
- stayed up nights 127
- warned of impending death 106
- weeping 47, 62
- wiping face 82, 168
Ḥasan ibn ʿAlī, al-
- prayer in shifts 73n.
Ḥasan ibn Ṣāliḥ ibn Ḥayy, al-
- nightly qur'anic recitation 73, 98
- wept over activity in market 150
Ḥassān ibn Abī Sinān 117, 118
- alms to beggar woman 67
- leaving what did not concern him 40
- scrupulosity 41
- secret ritual prayer 78
Ḥassān ibn ʿAṭīyah
- his supplication with a monk 83
- recollection in mosque 100
hawá 132
ḥayā' 53
ḥayf 50
ḥayr 49
Hebrew 12
Hell (the Fire) 28, 36, 43, 45–8, 59, 74, 91, 111, 121, 131n., 161
Hellenism 13
Hijaz 142n.
hijrah 131
Hilāl ibn Yisāf 64
Hillenbrand, Carol 20n.
Ḥilyat al-awliyā' 8–9, 110
Hind ibn ʿAwf
- no bed 32
Hinds, Martin 114
Hishām al-Dastuwā'ī
- against laughter 60
- recollection of death 106
Hishām ibn ʿAbd al-Malik 138
Hishām ibn Ḥassān
- weeping 47–8
Hodgson, Marshall 69
holiness 108
houris 131
ḥubb 182
ḥubs 157, 158
ḥubwah 57
Hujvīrī 189
Ḥulwān 138
Ḥusayn ibn ʿAlī al-Juʿfī, al- 27–8
- against laughter 61–2
- celibate 34
Ḥusayn ibn al-Ḥasan, al- 7
Ḥusayn ibn ʿAlī, al- 97
- gestures of supplication 81
- prayer in shifts 73n.
Hushaym ibn Bashīr
- not sleeping by night 33
hypocrisy 56

ʿī 53, 57
ʿibādah 12, 49
Ibn ʿAbbās
- accepted present from al-Mukhtār 138
- against begging 152
- gestures of supplication 81–2
Ibn ʿAbd Rabbih 3
Ibn Abī al-Dunyā 4

Ibn Abī al-Ḥawārī 183
Ibn Abī al-Zinād, ʿAbd al-Raḥmān 111
– against laughter 61
Ibn Abī Dhiʾb
– commanding and forbidding 129
– *ijtihād* 79
Ibn Abī Rawwād, ʿAbd al-ʿAzīz 126, 162
Ibn Abī Shaybah 2, 74, 110
– hadith tradition 6–7
Ibn al-Aʿrābī, Abū Saʿīd 4, 186, 190
Ibn al-ʿArīf 79–80
Ibn al-Jawzī 8n., 91, 107, 169, 174
Ibn al-Mubārak 116, 151
– against food from illicit sources 29
– against living by religion 153
– almsgiving 148, 152, 187–8
– and poetry 57
– hadith tradition 6–7

Jihād, al- 115
– on the effect of sleeping little 30
– *Riqāq, al-* 48
– trader 148–9
– *Zuhd, al-* 7, 40, 71, 115, 126
Ibn al-Rāwandī 156
Ibn al-Zubayr 98
– fasting, not changing clothes 86
– for supplicating with one finger 83
– his poverty 21
– recited Qur'an in prayer 92
– stillness in ritual prayer 75–6
Ibn ʿAmr 23
Ibn ʿAsākir 115, 116
Ibn ʿAṭāʾ 189–90
Ibn ʿAwn, ʿAbd Allāh 138
– restricted speech 55
Ibn Bābawayh 8
Ibn Baṭṭāl 161–2
Ibn Ḥajar viiin
Ibn Hammām al-Iskāfī 183
Ibn Ḥibbān 175
Ibn Hishām 119
Ibn Isḥāq 119
Ibn Khabbāzah 107
Ibn Mājah viii
Ibn Masʿūd 60n., 78
– against frivolous speech 53–4, 65
– against group praise of God 85
– against laughter 59
– against poetry 57n.
– against reciting Qur'an in less than three 96
– against withdrawal 53
– considered self-castration 34
– for humility 161
– for poverty 163–4
– for secret prayer, almsgiving 63, 95
– for sleeping little 30
– forgetting from sin 27
– indifference to family's condition 121
– intercessors 113
– motivations for *jihad* 131
– praising God better than alms 99n
– praising God better than freeing slaves 68n., 99
– recited Qur'an every three days 95
– stillness in ritual prayer 75
– subdued recollection 103
– undistracted worship 42
– wool 39
Ibn Muḥayrīz
– restricted public prayer 63
Ibn Nujayd 157
Ibn Qutaybah 4
Ibn Saʿd vii, 74, 116, 119, 126
Ibn Sālim 193
Ibn Samāʿah see Muḥammad ibn Samāʿah
Ibn Shubrumah 121
Ibn Sīrīn see Muḥammad ibn Sīrīn
Ibn ʿUmar 11
– against austere clothing 64
– against fourteen 66
– against mark of prostration 75
– against *qāṣṣ* raising hands 85
– against reciting Qur'anin a night 96
– against supplicating with two fingers 83
– against withdrawal 53
– agitated in prayer 77
– alms to whom 145–6
– and al-Mukhtār 138
– cursing 54
– eating little 25
– maintained ritual purity 70

– neutrality in civil strife 134
– no building 23
– on laughter 62
– pilgrimage 88
– sold ass 42
– subdued voice in prayer 55
– wept over qur'anic verse 94
Ibn Wahb
– frightened to death 45
Ibrāhīm al-Nakhaʿī
– accepted prizes from rulers 138
– against building 23
– against Farqad al-Sabakhī 163
– fasted alternate days 87
– for handicrafts over trade 150
– giver, recipient of alms 151
– restricted speech 56–7
– ritual ablutions after improper speech 70
– secret Qur'an reading 63
– suspicion of begging 154
– weeping from uncertainty 45–6
Ibrāhīm al-Taymī
– stillness in ritual prayer 76
Ibrāhīm ibn Abī ʿAblah 132
Ibrāhīm ibn Ad'ham 171n., 184
– against having dependants 36
– against repudiation of gain 156, 170
– back projection 6
– doubted pilgrimage 90
Ibrāhīm ibn al-Ashtar 138
Ibrāhīm ibn Bashshār al-Ṣūfī 184
Ibrāhīm ibn Hāniʾ 116
Ibrāhīm ibn Ismāʿīl ibn Abī Ḥabībah
– fasted 60 years 87
Ibrāhīm ibn Saʿd
– would not touch gold or silver 150
Ibrāhīm ibn Yazīd al-Taymī
– eating little 25
– recollection of death 106
ibtihāl 81
iftā' 109
ijtihād 12, 78–80
ikhlāṣ 81
ʿIkrimah 28
ʿilm 80, 153, 178, 182
imam 118
ʿimāmah 39
ʿImrān ibn al-Ḥuṣayn 5
ʿīnah 142
influence 12
inkār al-kasb 169, 181
inshāʾ 71n.
intercession 95, 108, 111–18, 122
Iran 123
Iraq 10, 54, 77, 108, 115, 116, 124, 135, 142n., 156, 162, 182, 185, 189, 194
Isfahan 6
ʿĪsa ibn al-Munkadir 185
ʿĪsá ibn Jaʿfar 137
Isḥāq ibn Rāhūyah 58
ishārāt 186
ishtiyāq 181
Islam, study of 16, 19
Islamic State 194
Islamization 75
Ismāʿīl ibn Abī Ḥakīm 167
Ismāʿīl ibn Rabāḥ
– for indifference to family 36
Ismāʿīl ibn ʿUlayyah
– against laughing, smiling 61
isnād analysis 142n.
Israelites
– miraculous clouds 123
– pilgrimage 89
Israfel 113
isrāʾīlīyāt 13
iʿtibār 104–5
iʿtikāf 51, 90
istikhārah 81

Jābir ibn Zayd
– alms better than repeat pilgrimages 90
Jaʿfar al-Ḍubaʿī 43
Jaʿfar al-Khuldī 4
Jaʿfar al-Ṣādiq 17, 79, 183
– against chess, backgammon 66
– for contemplation 105
– for staying awake 32
– for withdrawal 50
– for group supplication 85
– for weeping 94n., 128
– how often to recite Qur'an 96
– wool 37, 64

Jahannam 20, 31. 100
jāhil 11
jāhilīyah 58, 149
Jāḥiz, al- vii, 4, 113, 166, 169, 185
jam' 189, 190
jamā'ah 50, 134, 176
jamrah 38
Jarīr ibn 'Abd al-Ḥamīd
– recipient of alms 152
Jesus (*'Īsá*) 21, 162n., 178
– against begging 152
– against laughter 58
– celibacy 33
– fear of Last Judgement 45
– for secret fasting 64
– for staying awake 58
– for withdrawal 51
– not to ride 42
– wool 39
Jews, Judaism 3, 13–14, 71–2, 79, 82, 87, 110, 123, 124, 144, 168n.
jihād 20, 47, 68, 130–3, 134, 136, 155
jinn 94, 184
jizyah 145
John the Baptist (Yaḥyá) 21
– wore skins 39
Jones, Alan vii
Joseph (Yūsuf) 10, 34
jubbah 37, 39
Junayd, al- 1, 4, 156, 177–9, 186, 188–91
jurisprudence 49, 80, 188
Juynboll, G. H. A. 71, 116, 146n.

ka'ābah 43
Ka'b al-Aḥbār 70, 77
– fear of perdition 44
– weeping better than almsgiving 67–8
Ka'bah 3, 12, 72, 84, 97, 98n., 105
kaffārah 45n
Kahmas ibn al-Ḥasan
– lived as plasterer 147
– lost coin 40–1
Kalābādhī, al- 156
kalām 16, 173
Karāmīyah 192–3
– repudiation of gain 156, 169–70
Karamustafa, Ahmet T. 192
Sufism: the formative period 177
Katz, Marion 70, 71
Khaḍir, al- 58, 61
khafīf al-ḥādhdh 36
khā'if 44
Khālid ibn Ma'dān
– for recollection as one goes to sleep 100
– mark of prostration 74
– *mutaḥābbūn* 115n
Khalīfah ibn Khayyāṭ vi
Khalil, Atif 182–3
khānaqāh 158, 193
Khargūshī 5, 156, 193
Khārijah ibn Zayd 169
Khārijism, Khawārij 20, 37, 84, 123, 128, 132n
– known for strenuous devotions 127
Kharrāz, al- 184, 192
khāshi' 162
Khawlā' bint Tuwayt, al- 170
Khaythamah ibn 'Abd al-Raḥmān 39
– almsgiving 151
Khulayd al-'Aṣarī
– for withdrawal 159
– recollection 100, 102
Khurasan 116, 144, 192n.
Khushaysh ibn Aṣram 185
Kinberg, Leah 10n.
kisar 151
Kister, M. J. 142n.
Kufa 10, 35, 66, 152, 185
Kulayb 185
Kulaynī, al- 183
Kulthūm ibn 'Amr al-'Attābī
– wool 39
Kurdīyah bint 'Amr 30
Kurz ibn Wabarah
– miraculous cloud 120
– miraculously cured qadi 121

la''ān 54
lāghī 103
Last Day 113
Last Judgement 18, 44, 45, 70, 74, 111, 180
laughter 17–18, 58–60, 116, 159

law, Islamic 12, 14n., 18, 51, 57, 72, 78, 104, 124, 143, 146, 191
- food touched by fire 28
- *iftā'* as mediation 108–9
Layth ibn Sa'd, al-
- not eating alone 26
- vegetarianism 26, 27
leaving what does not concern one 40, 52
Library of Congress vii
look up 82
Luqmān
- against satiety 24
- for secrecy 64

Ma'dān 116
Magians 2, 16
Mahdī, al- 129
majāz 91
Makḥūl al-Shāmī
- for withdrawal 49, 50
Malāmatīyah 129, 156, 157, 192–3
Malaṭī, al- 185
Mālik ibn 'Abd Allāh al-Khath'amī 143
- fasted 60 years 86
Mālik ibn Anas 26, 70n., 80, 129, 145, 174
- against chess, fourteen 66, 67
- against excessive renunciation 167–9
- against unauthorized preaching 169
- against wiping face after prayer 168
- fasted alternate days 87
- for silent recollection 103
- preferred *mudhākarah* to supererogatory prayer 168
Muwaṭṭa' 80, 142n., 167
Mālik ibn Dīnār 14n., 117
- against market 150
- against *qurrā'* who associate with kings 166
- against wealth 22
- answered prayer 117–18
- commanding and forbidding 129
- for indifference to wife 36
- for sorrow 43–4
- for silence, asking forgiveness, and withdrawal 50
- group invocation 101
- *jihād* against self 132
- lived by copying Qur'an 147
- proper clothing 38
- rebuked for accepting prize from ruler 137–8
- simple diet 25–6
- wool 39
Ma'mar ibn Rāshid 52n.
- wiped face after supplication 168
Ma'mūn, al- 125, 155, 185
manāsik 12
mankhūl 28
Manṣūr, Abū Ja'far al- 129, 136
Manṣūr ibn al-Mu'tamir
- stillness in ritual prayer 76
Manṣūr ibn Zādhān
- recited Qur'an in course of prayer 92–3, 98
ma'rifah 178, 182
Marín, Manuela 35
market
- distrust of 149, 150
martyrs 113, 131
ma'rūf 144
Ma'rūf al-Karkhī
- celibate 34
Marwah, al- 12
Marwān ibn 'Abd al-Raḥmān
- would marry fallen women 35
Ma'rūf al-Karkhī 116
Marw 148
Mary (Maryam umm 'Īsá)
- fear of God 44
Maryam al-Baṣrīyah
- did not pursue provision 150
- recited one verse all night 97
mas'alah 82, 154
Mashriq 54
Masrūq ibn al-Ajda'
- against poetry 57n.
- restricted sex 35
- ritual prayer 73–4
- silent recollection 102
- slept only in prostration 31, 89
Massignon, Louis 15, 193
Mas'ūdī, al- 164

Māwardī, al- 3, 67
Maymūn ibn Mihrān
- scrupulosity 40
- wool 37, 64
Maymūnah bint al-Ḥārith
- against mark of prostration 75
maysir
- identified with chess 66
Mecca 13, 69, 91, 92, 98, 129, 136, 137, 144, 148, 184
Medina 13, 34, 52, 111, 119, 121, 134, 135, 142n., 157
Mediterranean 141
Michael 113
Miʿḍad al-ʿIjlī
- supported by brother 146
Middle East 13, 16
Mikati, Rana 115
miracles 63, 118–22, 191–2, 193
Misʿar ibn Kidām
- recited half the Qur'an nightly 97
miskīn, *masākīn* 22, 38, 85, 142n., 145, 146
Mizzī, al- viii
monasticism 14n., 125, 131
- Islamic equivalents 50
- Muslims called *rāhib*, *ruhbān* 35, 64, 106n.
Monday
- fast day 87–8
monks 55, 64, 83, 122, 162
- receivers of alms 146
monotheism 14, 53, 82
moralism 176
Moses (Mūsá) 4, 21, 58, 70, 89, 113
- celibacy 35
- fear of God 44
- his supplication 83
- wool 39, 162
mosque 31, 34, 47, 50, 54, 68, 72–3, 100, 118, 158, 175, 180, 186
- for restricted speech in 51, 55–7
- group prayer in 78
- group recitation in 101–2
- locus of almsgiving 146
Motzki, Harald 2, 110n.
Mount Lebanon 4
Muʿādh ibn Jabal 57
- against reciting Qur'an in less than three 96
- for group recollection 101
- for poverty 164
- for restricted laughter, sleeping, eating 59
Muʿādhah al-ʿAdawīyah
- no bed 31
- on being widowed 37
- refused to sleep 31–2
mu'allafah qulūbuhum, al- 144
Muʿāwiyah 38, 65, 134, 136
Muʿawwidhatayn, al- 80
mudhākarah 168
muezzins 72
muftī 109
muḥābbūn, *mutaḥābbūn* 113
Muḥammad al-Bāqir 8, 11, 28
- for recollecting death 106
Muḥammad ibn ʿAbd Allāh ibn ʿAbd al-Ḥakam 184n.
Muḥammad ibn al-Ḥanafīyah
- against withdrawal 53
Muḥammad ibn al-Munkadir
- almsgiving 152
- commanding and forbidding 129
- miraculous food 122
- pilgrimage 89
Muḥammad ibn al-Naḍr al-Ḥārithī
- sleeping little 30
- speaking little 55
Muḥammad ibn Juḥādah
- recited Qur'an in course of prayer 93
Muḥammad ibn Kaʿb
- against chess 66
- how to recite Qur'an 96–7
Muḥammad ibn Masrūq
- lived off slave girl's spinning 147
Muḥammad ibn Samāʿah 143
Muḥammad ibn Sīrīn
- against food from illicit sources 29
- against reciting Qur'an for rulers 137
- against supplicating with two fingers 83
- coins without name of God 41
- fasted alternate days 87

- laughter 62, 67
- recollection in market 100, 103
Muḥammad ibn Ṣubayḥ ibn al-Sammāk 165n.
Muḥammad ibn Sūqah
- weeping 44
- pilgrimage 89
Muḥammad ibn Wāsiʿ 26, 64, 118
- among *abdāl* 116–17
- face like a woman's who has lost her child 43
- fasted perpetually 88
- for avoiding rulers 136, 137–8
- licit wealth 142–3
- refused judgeship 139
- supplicated with two fingers 83
Muḥammad ibn Yūsuf 77, 135
Muḥammad ibn Yūsuf al-Iṣbahānī
- speaking little 55
Muḥāsibī, al- 132, 191
- *ʿAql, al-* 172–3
- concerned with mysticism 173–4, 181–3
- *Fahm al-Qurʾān* 172
- *Maḥabbah, al-* 182
- *Makāsib, al-* 172, 174
- not a Sufi 173, 187
- on repudiation of gain 155–6, 170, 172, 174
- *Riʿāyah li-ḥuqūq Allāh, al-* 172, 173–4
- *Sharḥ al-maʿrifah* 182
- *Tawahhum, al-* 182
- wool 38
muḥtasib 188
mujāhadat al-nafs 132
mujāhid 132
Mujāhid ibn Jabr 89, 149
- against mark of prostration 75
- against raised voice 56, 103
mujtahid 11, 78–9
mukhaḍram 25
Mukhtār, al- 138
mulk 131
munqaṭiʿ 127
muqaṣṣir 11
muqātil 104
muqlawlin 77
murābiṭ 158
Murjiʾah 129–30, 162–3
- commanding and forbidding 129
Murrah ibn Sharāḥīl
- marks of prostration 74
- recited Qur'an daily 98
Mūsa al-Kāẓim
- against outward austerity 165
Mūsá ibn Maysarah 103
Musāwir al-Maghribī 55
Musayyab ibn Rāfiʿ, al- 65
music 107
Muslim ibn al-Ḥajjāj viii, 6, 79
Muslim ibn Yasār 152
- against cursing 54
- stillness in ritual prayer 76
- would not be distracted 76–7
musūh 37
mutabādhilūn 113
mutʿah 135
mutaqarriʾ 167
mutaqashshif 181
Muṭarrif ibn al-Shikhkhīr
- group invocation 101
- preferred knowledge to works 159
- withdrawal 49, 51
- wool 38
mutaṣādiqūn 113
mutaṣawwif, mutaṣawwifah 166, 181, 191
mutawāṣilūn 113
Muʿtazilah, Muʿtazilism 49, 114, 126, 127, 129, 163
- repudiation of gain 156, 169–70
Muwaffaq, al- 188
Muwaffaq al-Khwārizmī
- *Manāqib al-imām al-aʿẓam Abī Ḥanīfah* 170
Mutawakkil, al- 184n., 188n.
Muwarriq al-ʿIjlī
- leaving what did not concern him 40
- secret devotions 63
- traded for the sake of almsgiving 67, 148
mysticism, mystics 1, 5–6, 11, 124, 174, 176, 177–84
- Indian 16

Naḍr ibn Shumayl, al-
– for some poetry 58
Nāfī‘, client of Ibn ‘Umar 103
Nāfi‘ ibn ‘Abd al-Raḥmān 93
nafs 132
Nasā’ī, al- viii
nāsik, nussāk 12, 137, 165, 181, 185, 187
Nasīyah bint Salmān 17
Naṣr al-Ṣāmit
– pilgrimage 89
Nawawī, al- 40
naẓar 172n.
Nishapur 192–3
Noah (Nūḥ) 21
– wept 300 years 93–4
nomads 9–10, 130, 141, 143
North Africa 10, 193
not to look up 60, 62, 82, 126, 129, 165
Nu‘aym ibn Ḥammād, 7, 40
Nūrī, Abū al-Ḥusayn al- 188–90, 191–2
nusk, nusuk 27, 58

Old Cairo 10, 183, 184
Old Testament 130

paideia 3
Palestine 116
Paradise 45, 46, 48, 60, 63, 91, 93, 131, 161, 180–1
Paul 79
Pavlovitch, Pavel 2n.
Persia, Persians 10, 16, 124
Persian language 24, 66
philosophy 179n.
Pietruschka, Ute 16n.
piety, components of 69
pilgrimage, pilgrims 12, 71, 88–92, 158
Platonism 16
poetry 57–8, 107, 141
pork 66, 67
polygamy 141
poverty, voluntary 21–3, 163–4
predestination 126, 161, 173
principle of dissimilarity 9
Prophet vii, 1, 2, 3, 9, 11, 13–14, 17, 25, 38, 44n., 71, 87, 125, 131n., 144, 157, 160n., 161, 175
– against agriculture 142
– against begging 86, 142n., 152, 153–4
– against building 23
– against chess 66, 103
– against eloquent speech 53–4
– against lying for the sake of laughter 65
– against markets 150
– against poetry 57
– against *qurrā’* 166
– against satiety 24
– against some poetry 58
– against staying up all night 86n., 167
– against unauthorized preaching 169
– against vow to stay in sun 167
– alms to whom 145–6
– and weeping 46, 48, 93, 128
– ascension 184
– best recollection 98–9, 103
– commentary on ritual ablutions 70
– did not practise outward austerity 165
– for celibacy in 200s 36
– for constant recollection aloud 103n.
– for consistent devotions 167
– for contemplation 105
– for fasting instead of self-castration 33
– for group prayer 78
– for group recitation 101
– for living by the gain of one’s hand 147, 174
– for nighttime devotions 32–3
– for required works only 165
– for scrupulosity 40
– for secret prayer 77
– for secret recitation 63, 98n.
– for self-reliance 52, 154–5
– for supplicating with one finger 82
– for *tawakkul* 155
– for three days of weekly fasting 88
– for weeping 48, 93, 160
– gift to ‘Umar 154
– his poverty 21, 31
– how he recited Qur’an 96
– humility 162
– inimitable 176
– intercession 111–13
– laughter 62

- miracles 119, 120n.
- model prayers 81, 99, 101
- on recollection of death 105
- on rulers 133, 135
- on seven who supplicate 115n.
- predestination 161
- preferred scholar to worshipper 159
- proper *mujāhid* 132, 133
- reliability of quotations 3
- seeing by the light of God 173
- settling quarrels 108
- spitting on hands 82n.
- suffering 48
- wiped face after supplication 168
- wool 37, 39
- would eat anything 28
- would not turn head 77
- would smile, not laugh 58–9, 77

prophets, pre-Muḥammadan 13, 44, 72, 112, 113, 133, 164, 183
Protestantism, Protestants 177, 179
Psalms 119

qadar 2, 126
Qadarīyah 127, 129
qalansuwah 39, 64, 90
qamīṣ 38
qāriʾ 38, 137, 166
qaṣāʾid 107
Qāsim ibn Muḥammad, al- 169
Qāsim ibn Mukhaymirah, al- 24
Qāsim ibn Musālim ibn ʿAbd Allāh, al- 111
qāṣṣ, quṣṣāṣ, qaṣaṣ 56, 74, 85, 126, 168–9
Qatādah ibn Diʿāmah 96n., 126, 127
- sleeping little 31, 161

qaylūlah 30
Qayrawan 36, 116
Qays ibn al-Sakan
- tongue as wild animal 55

Qays ibn ʿUbād
- for subdued voice 55–6, 103

qiblah 81
qiṣar al-amal 169
qiyās 172

Qur'an viii, 3, 9, 12, 14n., 16, 18, 30, 35, 54, 60, 66, 70, 71, 73, 82n., 87, 101, 109, 112, 128, 136, 140, 149, 150, 152, 160, 161, 166, 172, 181, 194
- against feeling of self-sufficiency 154
- alms to whom 144, 154
- and austerities 20
- and Bible 13, 119
- and poetry 57, 58
- and withdrawal 49
- barefootedness 89
- devotional recitation 92–8, 127, 148, 157, 165, 166
- for secret almsgiving 86
- frequency of recitation 96–8
- hypocritical recitation 131n.
- in Sunni theology 173
- mark of prostration 74
- on intercession 111
- on war 130
- postures while reciting 93
- recitation before rulers 136–7
- recitation better than *jihād* 68
- recitation in course of ritual prayer 80, 92–3, 95, 97
- *sābiqūn* 113n.
- secret recitation and study 63, 65, 95
- should split hearts 44
- Sufism and contemplation of 15
- weeping and recitation 93–5

qurrāʾ 62, 64, 137, 151, 152
- Companions 128–9
- disparaged 159, 166–7, 181
- in first two Civil Wars 128

Qurṭubī, al- 12, 104
Qushayrī, al- 11, 193
Qutaybah ibn Muslim 83

Rabadhah 135
Rabāḥ 185
rabbis 13, 110, 111n.
Rabīʿ, al-, and Ribʿī ibnā Ḥirāsh
- resisted laughing 59

Rabīʿ ibn Abī Rāshid, al-
- against gossip 57
- recollecting death 106n., 150

Rabīʿ ibn Khuthaym, al-

- acceptable speech 54, 56, 65
- for recollection death 106
- for withdrawal 49
- recited single verse all night 95
- sleeping little 31n.
- stillness in ritual prayer 75
- supererogatory prayers at home 78
- wept over qur'anic verse 94
- would not be distracted 76

Rabīʿ ibn Ṣabīḥ, al-
- regretted appearance of desiring 36

Rābiʿah al-ʿAdawīyah 185
- not a mystic 6

Rābiʿah bint Ismāʿīl
- sexless marriage 37

rāghib 11

rahbah 81

rahbānīyah see monasticism

rāhib 106n.

rain 121

Rajāʾ ibn Ḥaywah 135

rakʿah 97

Ramaḍān 30, 51, 69, 85, 96–8, 146, 153, 172

Raqqah, al- 129, 188, 190

raʾy 171

recollection 56, 70, 92, 98–106, 149
- silent or subdued 102–4

Reinhart, A. Kevin 114

renunciants 177, 179, 181
- and ritual ablutions 71–2
- distinguished from Sufis 15
- rivalry with jurisprudents 175, 177
- sadness at prospect of judgement 95
- sceptical of hierarchy 72, 180

renunciation 10, 12, 173
- literature of 124

repudiation of gain 155–6, 169–70

restricted speech 53–8

Resurrection 61, 66, 79, 90, 153

ribāṭ 158

riqqah 187

rituals 12–13, 69–92, 107
- and miracles 120
- circular 84
- pilgrimage explained 91
- prayer explained 80

riyāḍah 11n.

Riyāḥ ibn ʿAmr al-Qaysī 5n., 185–6

riyāsah 65

rizq 103

Robinson, Chase F. 123

Roman Catholicism 179

rūḥānīyah 185

Rummānī, al- 156

Ruwaym 190, 191

rural settlement 122–3

sabbāḥah 82

sābiqūn, subbāq 113

sacrifice 12

Saʿd ibn Abī Waqqāṣ 82
- against mark of prostration 75
- short prayer in public, long in private 63

Saʿd ibn Mālik
- silent recollection 102

ṣadaqah 90, 144, 145, 157

Saʿdī, al-
- *Faḍāʾil Abī Ḥanīfah* 171n.

sadness 30, 43–8, 94–5, 159

Ṣadr al-Shahīd ibn Māzah, al- 80–1

Saʿdūn ibn Ismāʿīl
- celibate 35

ṣadūq 185

Ṣafā, al- 12

Ṣafīyah bint Ḥuyayy
- for weeping at hearing Qur'an 94n.

Ṣafwān ibn Muḥriz 21
- withdrawal, weeping 50

Ṣafwān ibn Sulaym
- no bed 31

Ṣafwān ibn Yaḥyá
- supererogatory prayer, fasting, alms 73, 128

sāhī 103

Sahl al-Tustarī 156, 172, 184, 193

Saḥnūn
- almsgiving 86

Saʿīd ibn ʿAbd al-ʿAzīz
- weeping 47

Saʿd ibn ʿAbd Allāh
- his singing slave girl 107

Saʿīd ibn Abī Hind 103

Saʿīd ibn Ḥayyān 54
Saʿīd ibn Muḥammad
- poor food 28
Saʿīd ibn al-Musayyib 102, 123
- *dhikr* 100
- for poetry 58
- for restricted speech in mosque 56
- for withdrawal 49
- pilgrimage 89
- prayed in mosque 72
- preferred trade to stipend 148
- whipped for defying caliph 109
- wool 37
- would not stay for sermon 169
Saʿīd ibn Jubayr
- for recollecting death 106n.
- for subdued voice 56n.
- frequency of reciting Qur'an 97
- pilgrimage 89
- stillness in ritual prayer 76
sāj 77
sajjādah 128
ṣalāh 13
Salām ibn Abī Muṭīʿ
- stillness in ritual prayer 76
Salamah ibn al-Akwaʿ 134
Salem, Feryal 149
Ṣāliḥ ibn Aḥmad ibn Ḥanbal 107
Sālim ibn ʿAbd Allāh ibn ʿUmar
- for vegetarianism 27
- self-reliance 52
Sālimi school 193
Salm ibn Sālim
- did not look up, sleep on bed 129
Salmān al-Fārisī 29n
- distrusted trade, tribute 149
- for extending hands in supplication 81
salvation 125
samāʿ 107, 191
Samurah ibn Jundub 26
- against overeating 24–5
sarab 50
Sarakhsī, al-
- *Mabsūṭ, al-* 143, 170
Sarī al-Saqaṭī 183–4
- depended on as intercessor 112
Sarrāj, al- 172, 189, 193
Sasanian empire 1, 10
Satanic Verses 9
Schacht, Joseph 9, 110, 142n.
Scholem, Gershom 114n.
Second Civil War 98, 125, 128, 138
self-reliance 52
sermons 3
Seven Jurisprudents of Medina 110, 169n.
Seven Sleepers of Ephesus 49
Shaban, M. A. 128
Shaʿbī, al-
- against mark of prostration 75
- against noise in mosque 51
- for poetry 58
- for vegetarianism 27
- laughed in private 62
Shāfiʿī, al- 96
- against chess, backgammon 67
- *Umm, al-* 145
Shāfiʿi school 172
Shahr ibn Ḥawshab
- gestures in supplication 82
Shalabī, Ḥasan ʿAbd al-Munʿim viii
Shaqīq al-Balkhī
- for limited socializing 50
Shahr ibn Ḥawshab 60
Shaqīq ibn Ibrāhīm al-Balkhī
- mysticism 180–1
- repudiation of gain 156, 170, 174
- wool 162
shaṭaḥāt 189
shawq 182
Shaʿwānah
- for weeping 48
- sleeping little 30
Shaybānī, al- 174
- against chess, fourteen 66
- against excessive renunciation 167, 169–72
- *Aṣl, al-* 158
- for teaching 170–1
- *Kasb, al-* 143, 155, 169–71
sheep 39
Shīʿah 13, 17–18, 43, 50, 127–8, 135
- against hot food 28
- dog bit only them 120
Shiʿi hadith 8

Shiʿism 113–14, 125, 183
Shuʿayb ibn Ḥarb
– dressing poorly 22
Shuʿbah ibn al-Ḥajjāj
– dressing cheaply 22
– prayer he promulgated 71
Shufayy ibn Mātiʿ al-Aṣbaḥī
– for speaking little 55, 57
shuhrah 64
Shumayṭ ibn ʿAjlān
– for recollecting death 106
Shurayḥ
– scrupulosity 40n.
ṣiddīq 54
Ṣiffīn, Battle of 115
Sikkīn al-Nakhaʿī 165
Ṣilah ibn Ashyam 37
Ṣilah ibn Zufar
– indifference to family 36
sīmā 74
sin and unbelief 45n.
sirāṭ, al- 60
Sīrjānī, al- 193
Six Books 110, 131
siyāḥah 186
sleeping little 26, 30–3
Solomon (Sulaymān)
– told to sleep little at night 30
Song of Deborah 130
staff 38
stipends 143–4, 147, 155
subḥāna 'Llāh 85
Subkī, Taqīal-Dīn, al- 110
Sufis, Sufism 1, 3, 10n., 18, 89, 107, 110, 113–14, 118, 139, 148–9, 158, 166, 171, 172, 173, 177–94
– 'a name without a reality' 187
– and repudiation of gain 155–6
– and Shiʿism 183
– commanding right and forbidding wrong 109, 185, 186
– developed from renunciant tradition 4, 15, 39, 92, 124, 185
– internal or external development 14–15
– literary tradition 3–5, 7, 48, 79
– persecuted 186–8, 190
– repudiation of gain 155
ṣūfiyat al-muʿtazilah 156n., 185
Sufyān al-Thawrī vii, 94, 113, 123, 148, 181
– against begging 153
– against building 23
– against laughter 18, 59n., 60–1
– against overeating 60
– against present-day *qurrā'* 166
– avoided rulers 135
– contempt for ʿAbbāsids 136
– difficulty of renouncing leadership 65
– doubted pilgrimage 90
– dream interpretation 119
– dropped coin 41
– explanation of ritual prayer 80
– fell from contemplation 105
– for balance between hadith, renunciation 175
– for eating little 26
– for inward renunciation 164
– for reciting Qur'an in one day 97
– for withdrawal 49n., 50–2
– 'How are you?' 57
– reciting Qur'an in course of ritual prayer 92
– reciting Qur'an better than *jihad* 68
– supported by sister 147
– temptation of dependants 36
Sufyān ibn ʿUyaynah 135, 160n.
– for inward renunciation 164–5
Sulamī, al- 4, 188, 189
– *Ṭabaqāt al-ṣūfiyah* 4n., 187
Sulaym ibn Aswad al-Muḥāribī 75
Sulaymān al-Shaybānī 67n.
Sulaymān al-Taymī 81n.
– fasted alternate days 87
– man's hand withered 120
– no bed 32
– not sleeping by night 33, 87
Sulaymān ibn ʿAbd al-Malik 37, 135
Sulaymān ibn Yasār
– sexual abstinence 34
sulṭān 134, 135, 136, 138
Sumnūn ibn Ḥamzah 188
Sunan al-kubrá, al- viii
sunnah 172
Sunni hadith 8

Sunnis, Sunnism 13, 17, 45, 114, 125, 135, 139, 163, 173
supererogatory works 12, 31, 40, 70–1, 73–4, 111, 165
- supererogatory prayer in secret 77–81
supplication 71, 80–5, 93
sūq 148
ṣūrah 75
Sviri, Sara 11n., 12, 180–1, 183n.
Syria 10, 42, 108, 115, 116, 124, 140, 156
Syriac language 16
Syrian monasticism 14

taʿawwudh 82
Ṭabarī, al- 10
tabattul 81
taḍarruʿ 81
tadhkīr 169
tafakkur 104–5
tafriqat al-qalb 42
taḥrīm 73
takhlīṭ 186
Ṭalḥah ibn Muṣarrif
- against laughter 60
- against living by religion 153
- disliked to make profit off Muslims 150
Ṭalḥah ibn ʿUbayd Allāh
- gave away 700,000 42
Ṭalq ibn Ḥabīb
- best voice for reciting Qur'an 137n.
tamarrud 25
Tamīm al-Dārī
- for reciting Qur'an in all postures 93
- made pilgrimage trotting 89
- recited whole Qur'an in one prayer 97
tamthīl 172
tanabbuh 104
Tarsus 184
taṣawwuf 178
tashahhud 80, 82
tawakkul 155, 174
Ṭāwūs 138
- avoided rulers 135
- best voice for reciting Qur'an 136–7
- disdain for wealth and children 21
- mark of prostration 74
- sleeplessness 31
- stayed home 50
- would not be distracted 77
- would not drink from rulers' wells 137
ṭaylasān 77
Taym 54, 56
Thābit al-Bunānī 42
- fasted perpetually, recited Qur'an daily 98
- group recollection 102
- recited one verse all night 97
- recited Qur'an weeping 94
- staying awake 32
Thaʿlabī, al- 94
Thawbān 52
Thawr ibn Yazīd
- doubted pilgrimage 90
theodicy 121
throne of God 104
Thursday
- fast day 87–8
Tirmidhī, al- viii, 131
tomb visitation 179n.
trade 143, 147, 148–9
transliteration vii
Transoxania 10
travel to holy sites 124
tribes 10
tubbān 37, 39
turban 39n.
Tus 23
Tustar 184

ʿUbādah ibn al-Ṣāmit 3
ʿUbayd Allāh ibn Mūsa al-ʿAbsī
- would not raise head or laugh 62
ʿUbayd ibn ʿUmayr
- for avoiding rulers 136
- on mark of prostration 74
Uḥud 3
ulema 123, 159, 182
ʿUmar ibn ʿAbd al-ʿAzīz 5, 120, 144, 146
- celibacy 35
- for recollection, contemplation 104
- for recollection of death 106
- patched clothing 38
- power of predicting future 120

ʿUmar ibn al-Khaṭṭāb 11, 92, 120, 166, 169
– accepting alms 154
– against eating meat 27
– against gnawing 24
– against group supplication 84
– against loud speech in mosque 55
– against poetry 57
– for poetry 58
– his poverty 21
– led group supplication 102
– rough clothing 38, 130
– rough diet 28, 130
– sex only for procreation 34
– weeping at qur'anic recitation 94
ʿUmar ibn Dharr al-Hamdānī 126
ʿUmayr ibn Hāniʾ
– supererogatory prayers 73
Umayyads 114, 124, 125, 134
Umm al-Aswad bint Zayd al-ʿAdawīyah
– forgetting from sin 27
Umm al-Dardā' 102, 105
Umm Jaʿfar 29
ʿUqbah ibn ʿAbd al-Ghāfir
– doubted pilgrimage 90
ʿUqbah ibn ʿĀmir al-Juhanī 166n.
ʿUrwah ibn Ruwaym al-Lakhmī 8
ʿUrwah ibn al-Zubayr
– fasted 30 or 40 years 86
usury 149
ʿUtbah al-Ghulām 87, 151
– against living by religion 153
– contemplation and weeping 104
– lived by plaiting palm fronds 147
ʿUthmān ibn Abī al-ʿĀṣ
– withdrawal 50
ʿUthmān ibn ʿAffān 34, 125, 134
– against poetry 57n.
– recited Qur'an in a night 97
ʿUthmān ibn Maẓʿūn
– celibacy 33
ʿUthmān ibn Zāidah
– rulers' fire 41
Uways al-Qaranī
– almsgiving 67
ʿuzlah 49

vegetarianism 26–8, 34
visionary experience 14
Vööbus, Arthur 14

Waardenburg, Jacques 14n.
Wahb ibn Munabbih 35
– against withdrawal 53
– beaten to death 109
– not sleeping by night 32
– recollection of death 105–6
Wāʾil ibn Shaqīq ibn Salamah 136
wājib al-ḥuqūq 191
Wakīʿ ibn Jarrāḥ 8, 23
– among *abdāl* 117
– fasted perpetually 87
– impossibility of living only on the licit 29
Walīd ibn ʿAbd al-Malik, al- 37
waqf 140, 157–8, 173
waraʿ 24, 39–41, 79, 151
Wasit 187
watad 76
Weber, Max 179, 194
weeping 30, 35, 43–8, 62, 78, 128
– at hearing poetry 58
– over activity in market 150
– preferred to almsgiving 67–8
– secret 63
– while contemplating 104, 106
– while hearing, reciting Qur'an 78–9, 92–5, 160
– while supplicating 81
wells 137
Wensinck, A. J. viii, 133
wiping face 82, 168
wird 97
withdrawal 49v53, 122
witr 72, 93
women and renunciant movement 17
wool 37–9, 62, 162, 178, 184
– under other clothes 64
wuḍūʾ 69, 70
Wuhayb ibn al-Ward 21
– against laughter 61
– against supererogatory works in public 64–5
– dream interpretation 119–20

Yaḥyá ibn Abī Kathīr
- hid poverty 22
Yaḥyá ibn al-Mutawakkil 23
Yaḥyá ibn Ja'dah
- explanation of ritual prayer 80
Yaḥyá ibn Sa'īd al-Qaṭṭān 126
- against laughter 61
Yaḥyá ibn Waththāb
- wretchedess after praying 43
Yaḥyá ibn Yaḥyá al-Nāysābūrī 116
Yanagihashi, Hiroyuki 2n.
Yassá 70
Yathrib 3, 108
Yazīd ibn Abān al-Raqāshī
- cold water 25
- eating little 25
- incompetent traditionist 175
Yazīd ibn 'Abd Allāh ibn al-Shikhkhīr
- recited Qur'an till overcome 92
Yazīd ibn al-Walīd 146n.
Yazīd ibn Hārūn 164
Yazīd ibn Marthad
- barefoot, wearing wool 39
- weeping 47
Yazīd ibn Maysarah
- refused stipend 147
Yazīd ibn Mu'āwiyah 125
Yazīd ibn Sharīk al-Taymī
- limited his profit 149
- recollection of death 106
Yücesoy, Hayrettin 156n.
Yūnus ibn 'Ubayd 151, 153
Yūsuf ibn Asbāṭ 17, 52
- against food from illicit sources 29
- against laughing, joking 61
- for inward, outward renunciation 165–6

Zādhān
- miraculous bread 124–5
- stillness in ritual prayer 76
- weeping 48
- would display worse side of cloth 151
Zaehner, R. C. 15n.
zāhid 10–12, 137, 148, 166
zakāh 13, 73, 85, 140–1, 144, 145, 155, 157
zakat al-fiṭr 146
zandaqah 185
Zanj rebellion 41
Zaydīyah 185
Zayn al-'Ābidīn see 'Alī Zayn al-'Ābidīn
Zayn al-Dīn al-'Irāqī 169
Zecharia 162
Zeus 114
Ziyād al-Numayrī
- fear 45
Ziyād ibn Abī Ziyād
- vegetarianism 27
- withdrawal 49
- wool 39
Ziyād ibn Ḥudayr
- for withdrawal 49
- wept over Prophet's suffering 48
Zoroastrianism 71–2
Zubayd al-Yāmī
- dirhams like dung 150
Zufar 170
Zuhayr al-Azdī 138
zuhd 10, 12, 130, 165–6, 175, 182
zuhdīyāt 107
Zuhrī, al- 39
- alms to whom 144–5, 146
- fasted perpetually 86
- minimal definition of *nāsik* 165
- recited Qur'an daily in Ramaḍān 98
zūr
- identified with chess 66
Zurārah ibn 'Awfá
- wept over qur'anic verse 94

www.ingramcontent.com/pod-product-compliance
Lightning Source LLC
Chambersburg PA
CBHW031808220426
43662CB00007B/572
* 9 7 8 3 1 1 0 9 9 1 6 0 4 *